A Sequence for Academic Writing

SIXTH EDITION

Laurence Behrens
University of California, Santa Barbara

Leonard J. Rosen
Bentley University

PEARSON

Boston   Columbus   Indianapolis   New York   San Francisco   Upper Saddle River
Amsterdam   Cape Town   Dubai   London   Madrid   Milan   Munich   Paris
Montréal   Toronto   Delhi   Mexico City   São Paulo   Sydney   Hong Kong
Seoul   Singapore   Taipei   Tokyo

Senior Acquisitions Editor: Brad Potthoff
Vice President, Marketing: Roxanne McCarley
Senior Supplements Editor: Donna Campion
Executive Digital Producer: Stefanie A. Snajder
Digital Media Editor: Sara Gordus
Content Specialist: Erin Jenkins
Project Manager: Savoula Amanatidis
Project Coordination and Text Design: Integra-Chicago
Electronic Page Makeup: Integra
Cover Design Manager: Barbara Atkinson
Cover Designer: Wendy Ann Fredericks
Cover Art: © Ingram Publishing/SuperStock
Photo Researcher: The Bill Smith Group
Senior Manufacturing Buyer: Dennis J. Para
Printer and Binder: RR DONNELLEY
Cover Printer: Lehigh-Phoenix Color Corporation–Hagerstown

For permission to use copyrighted material, grateful acknowledgment is made to the copyright holders on pp. 319–324, which are hereby made part of this copyright page.

Library of Congress Cataloging-in-Publication Data
Behrens, Laurence.
   A sequence for academic writing/Laurence Behrens, University of California, Santa Barbara; Leonard J. Rosen, Bentley University.—Sixth Edition.
      pages cm.
   Rev. ed. of: A sequence for academic writing/Bonnie Beedles, Laurence Behrens, Leonard J. Rosen, 5th ed.
   Includes bibliographical references and indexes.
   ISBN 13: 978-0-321-90681-6
   ISBN 10: 0-321-90681-0
   1. English language—Rhetoric.   2. Academic writing.   I. Rosen, Leonard J.   II. Title.
   PE1408.B46926 2015
   808'.042—dc23

                                                                    2014005415

6 16

Student Edition
ISBN-10:   0-321-90681-0
ISBN-13: 978-0-321-90681-6

À La Carte Edition
ISBN-10:   0-321-99658-5
ISBN-13: 978-0-321-99658-9

PEARSON   www.pearsonhighered.com

To the memory of Philip Rodkin (1968–2014)

PART TWO: STRATEGIES
Chapter 6—Writing as a Process

A Sequence for Academic Writing evolved out of another of our texts, *Writing and Reading Across the Curriculum (WRAC)*. Through twelve editions over the past thirty years, *WRAC* has helped more than a million students prepare for the writing to be done well beyond the freshman composition course. *WRAC* features a rhetoric in which students are introduced to the core skills of summary, critique, synthesis, and analysis and a reader that presents readings in the disciplines to which students can apply the skills learned in the earlier chapters.

Because the skills of summary, critique, synthesis, and analysis are so central to academic thinking and writing, many instructors—both those teaching writing across the curriculum and those using other approaches to composition instruction—have found *WRAC* a highly useful introduction to college-level writing. We therefore adapted the rhetoric portion of *WRAC*, creating a separate book that instructors can use apart from any additional reading content they choose to incorporate into their writing courses. *A Sequence for Academic Writing* is both an adaptation of *WRAC* and an expansion: It includes chapters, sections, and additional writing assignments not found in the parent text.

WHAT'S NEW IN THIS EDITION?

The sixth edition of *A Sequence for Academic Writing* represents a significant revision of the previous edition.

- The model student summary and argument in Chapters 1 and 4, respectively, have been replaced with papers on new subjects. The new example summary is based on Paul Bloom's provocative essay "The Baby in the Well: The Case Against Empathy," an argument against using our tendency to identify with the suffering of others to guide both our personal responses and our public policy. The new model argument synthesis in Chapter 4 examines the problem of bullying in America and argues for a response that mixes state mandates with local initiatives. The synthesis builds on articles on the subject in the chapter itself (and on other sources) to explore the characteristics of bullying, its extent and (often tragic) effects, state anti-bullying mandates, less-than-successful national programs, and local, on-the-ground solutions.

- Chapter 8, on "Practicing Academic Writing," offers an entirely new focus on the "Ethical Dilemmas in Everyday Life." Students will choose from more than a dozen scenarios (what philosophers call "ethical thought experiments") and apply classic principles of ethics—like utilitarianism—to argue for one or another course of action. The scenarios themselves are fascinating (e.g., which six out of ten people would you allow onto a lifeboat?) More instructive, still, is the process of applying one or another ethical theory in the process of developing student arguments.

- Two research librarians have helped update Chapter 7 ("Locating, Mining, and Citing Sources") to incorporate current practices and techniques on conducting research, using the latest digital tools and methods. The chapter includes coverage of the 2010 APA guidelines for citation format, along with the 2009 Modern Language Association guidelines—changes that reflect the latest editions of the MLA and APA manuals.
- New introductions and conclusions in Chapter 6 and new example graphs, charts, and tables (on the topic of immigration) in Chapter 1 contribute to the new edition's current feel.

The sixth edition of *A Sequence for Academic Writing* offers a major revision of a familiar text that freshens examples, clarifies and expands instruction, and generally makes more accessible a book that has helped introduce numerous students to source-based writing in a variety of academic settings. As ever, we rely on the criticism of colleagues to improve our work, and we invite you to contact the publisher with suggested revisions.

ORGANIZATION AND KEY FEATURES

We proceed through a sequence from "Summary, Paraphrase, and Quotation" to "Critical Reading and Critique," to "Explanatory Synthesis" and "Argument Synthesis," to "Analysis." Students will find in Chapter 6 a discussion of the writing process that is reinforced throughout the text. Chapter 7, "Locating, Mining, and Citing Sources," introduces students to the tools and techniques they will need in order to apply the skills learned earlier to sources they gather themselves when conducting research.

The book ends with a controlled research assignment in Chapter 8, "Practicing Academic Writing." We make a special effort in all chapters to address the issue of plagiarism and have added a new section on the topic in Chapter 7. Both there and in Chapter 1, we offer techniques for steering well clear of plagiarism, at the same time encouraging students to live up to the highest ethical standards.

Key features in *A Sequence for Academic Writing* include *boxes*, which sum up important concepts in each chapter; brief writing *exercises*, which prompt individual and group activities; *writing assignments*, which encourage students to practice the skills they learn in each chapter; and *model papers*, which provide example responses to writing assignments discussed in the text.

While we are keenly aware of the overlapping nature of the skills on which we focus and while we could endlessly debate an appropriate order in which to cover these skills, a book is necessarily linear. We have chosen the sequence that makes the most sense to us. Teachers should feel free to use these chapters in whatever order they decide is most useful to their individual aims and philosophies. Understanding the material in a later chapter does not, in most cases, depend on students' having read material in the earlier chapters.

SUPPLEMENTS

Instructor's Manual

The *Instructor's Manual (IM)* provides sample syllabi and assignment ideas for traditional and Web-based courses. Each IM chapter opens with a summary of the chapter in the student text, followed by specific instruction on that chapter's focus. Writing/Critical Thinking Activities offer additional exercises that make use of Internet sources, and Revision Activities are also provided for Chapters 1 to 8. In addition, each IM chapter provides extensive lists of Web source material for both students and instructors. Contact your Pearson representative for access.

MyWritingLab: Now Available for Composition

MyWritingLab   MyWritingLab is an online homework, tutorial, and assessment program that provides engaging experiences to today's instructors and students. By incorporating rubrics into the writing assignments, faculty can create meaningful assignments, grade them based on their desired criteria, and analyze class performance through advanced reporting. For students who enter the course underprepared, MyWritingLab offers a diagnostic test and personalized remediation so that students see improved results and instructors spend less time in class reviewing the basics. Rich multimedia resources, including a text-specific ebook in many courses, are built in to engage students and support faculty throughout the course. Visit www.mywritinglab.com for more information.

ACKNOWLEDGMENTS

We would like to thank the following reviewers for their help in the preparation of this text: John M. Brentar, Cleveland State University; Debra J. Brown, Crowder College; Matthew Hodgson, Eastern Washington University; Dr. Barbara Rowland, Spoon River College; William Water, University of Houston–Downtown; and Jessica Wilkie, Monroe Community College.

We would also like to thank reviewers of previous editions of this text: Cora Agatucci, Central Oregon Community College; Elizabeth Baines, Truckee Meadows Community College; Patricia Baldwin, Pitt Community College; Sherri Brouillette, Millersville University; Bryce Campbell, Victor Valley College; Margaret L. Clark, Florida Community College at Jacksonville; Bruce Closser, Andrews University; Diane Z. De Bella, University of Colorado; Clinton R. Gardner, Salt Lake Community College; Grey Glau, Arizona State University; Margaret Graham, Iowa State University; Susanmarie Harrington, Indiana University and Purdue University Indianapolis; Pat Hartman, Cleveland State University; Wendy Hayden, University of Maryland; Georgina Hill, Western Michigan University; Jane M. Kinney, Valdosta State University; Susan E.

Knutson, University of Minnesota–Twin Cities; Cathy Leaker, North Carolina State University; Randall McClure, Minnesota State University–Mankato; Kate Miller, Central Michigan University; Lyle W. Morgan, Pittsburg State University; Jamil Mustafa, Lewis University; Joan Perkins, University of Hawaii; Catherine Quick, Stephen F. Austin State University; Deborah Richey, Owens Community College; Emily Rogers, University of Illinois–Urbana Champaign; Amanda McGuire Rzicznek, Bowling Green State University; William Scott Simkins, University of Southern Mississippi; Doug Swartz, Indiana University Northwest; Marcy Taylor, Central Michigan University; Zach Waggoner, Western Illinois University; Heidemarie Z. Weidner, Tennessee Technological University; Betty R. Youngkin, The University of Dayton; and Terry Meyers Zawacki, George Mason University. We are also grateful to UCSB librarian Lucia Snowhill for helping us update the reference sources in Chapter 7.

The authors wish to thank Barbara Magalnick for her valuable contributions to the summary and practice chapters. For their numerous comments and suggestions on improving and updating the research chapter, "Locating, Mining, and Citing Sources," we thank Ayanna Gaines, associate librarian at Ventura College, and Richard Caldwell, head of library instruction at the University of California, Santa Barbara Library. And for his consultation on the model synthesis "Responding to Bullies" in Chapter 4, we gratefully acknowledge the assistance of Philip Rodkin, Professor of Psychology at the University of Illinois at Urbana-Champaign.

Finally, special thanks to our senior editor, Brad Potthoff, and to our project manager, Savoula Amanatidis for helping shepherd the manuscript through the editorial and production process. And our continued gratitude to Joe Opiela, longtime friend, supporter, and publisher.

LAURENCE BEHRENS
LEONARD J. ROSEN

In your sociology class, you are assigned to write a paper on the role of peer groups in influencing attitudes toward smoking. Your professor expects you to read some of the literature on the subject as well as to conduct interviews with members of such groups. For an environmental studies course, you must write a paper on how one or more industrial plants in a particular area have been affecting the local ecosystem. In your film studies class, you must select a contemporary filmmaker—you are trying to decide between Quentin Tarantino and Sofia Coppola—and examine how at least three of his or her films demonstrate a distinctive point of view.

These writing assignments are typical of those you will undertake during your college years. In fact, such assignments are also common in professional life: for instance, scientists writing environmental impact statements, social scientists writing accounts of their research for professional journals, and film critics showing how the latest effort by a filmmaker fits into the general body of his or her work.

CORE SKILLS

To succeed in such assignments, you will need to develop and hone particular skills in critical reading, thinking, and writing. You must develop—not necessarily in this order—the abilities to

- read and accurately *summarize* a selection of material on your subject;
- determine the quality and relevance of your sources through a process of *critical reading* and assessment;
- *synthesize* different sources by discovering the relationships among them and showing how these relationships produce insights about the subject under discussion;
- *analyze* objects or phenomena by applying particular perspectives and theories;
- develop effective techniques for (1) discovering and using pertinent, authoritative information and ideas and (2) presenting the results of your work in generally accepted disciplinary formats.

A Sequence for Academic Writing will help you to meet these goals. In conversations with faculty across the curriculum, time and again we have been struck by the shared desire to see students thinking and writing in subject-appropriate ways. Psychology, biology, and engineering teachers want their students to think, talk, and write like psychologists, biologists, and engineers. We set out, therefore, to learn the strategies writers use to enter conversations in their respective disciplines, and we discovered that four readily learned strategies—summary, critique, synthesis, and analysis—provide the basis for the great majority of writing in freshman- through senior-level courses and in courses across disciplines. We therefore made these skills the centerpiece of instruction in this book.

APPLICATIONS BEYOND COLLEGE

While summary, critique, synthesis, and analysis are primary critical thinking and writing skills practiced throughout the university, these skills are also crucial to the work you will do in your life beyond the university. You will write e-mails, letters, and reports that will explain and persuade; you will evaluate the work of others; you will be expected to gather multiple viewpoints on a topic and to digest these viewpoints (that is, to summarize each and to synthesize all into a coherent whole); you will be called on to conduct close analyses in order to learn how things work or what their constituent parts may be. In sum, the skills you gain in learning how to summarize, evaluate, synthesize, and analyze will serve you well both in college and beyond.

Part One ▪ *Structures*

1 ▪ Summary, Paraphrase, and Quotation

▪ WHAT IS A SUMMARY?

The best way to demonstrate that you understand the information and the ideas in any piece of writing is to compose an accurate and clearly written summary of that piece. By a summary we mean a brief restatement, in your own words, of the content of a passage (a group of paragraphs, a chapter, an article, a book). This restatement should focus on the central idea of the passage. The briefest of summaries (one or two sentences) will do no more than this. A longer, more complete summary will indicate, in condensed form, the main points in the passage that support or explain the central idea. It will reflect the order in which these points are presented and the emphasis given to them. It may even include some important examples from the passage. But it will not include minor details. It will not repeat points simply for the purpose of emphasis. And it will not contain any of your own opinions or conclusions. A good summary, therefore, has three central qualities: brevity, completeness, and objectivity.

▪ CAN A SUMMARY BE OBJECTIVE?

Of course, the last quality mentioned above, objectivity, might be difficult to achieve in a summary. By definition, writing a summary requires you to select some aspects of the original and leave out others. Since deciding what to select and what to leave out calls for your personal judgment, your summary really is a work of interpretation. And, certainly, your interpretation of a passage may differ from another person's.

One factor affecting the nature and quality of your interpretation is your prior knowledge of the subject. For example, if you're attempting to summarize an anthropological article and you're a novice in that field, then your summary of the article will likely differ from that of your professor, who has spent 20 years studying this particular area and whose judgment about what is more or less significant is undoubtedly more reliable than your own. By the same token, your personal or professional frame of reference may also affect your interpretation. A union representative and a management representative attempting to summarize the latest management offer would probably come up with two very different accounts. Still, we believe that in most cases it's possible to produce a reasonably objective summary of a passage if you make a conscious, good-faith effort to be unbiased and to prevent your own feelings on the subject from distorting your account of the text.

Where Do We Find Written Summaries?

Here are just a few of the types of writing that involve summary:

ACADEMIC WRITING

- **Critique papers.** Summarize material in order to critique it.
- **Synthesis papers.** Summarize to show relationships between sources.
- **Analysis papers.** Summarize theoretical perspectives before applying them.
- **Research papers.** Note-taking and reporting research require summary.
- **Literature reviews.** Overviews of work presented in brief summaries.
- **Argument papers.** Summarize evidence and opposing arguments.
- **Essay exams.** Demonstrate understanding of course materials through summary.

WORKPLACE WRITING

- **Policy briefs.** Condense complex public policy.
- **Business plans.** Summarize costs, relevant environmental impacts, and other important matters.
- **Memos, letters, and reports.** Summarize procedures, meetings, product assessments, expenditures, and more.
- **Medical charts.** Record patient data in summarized form.
- **Legal briefs.** Summarize relevant facts of cases.

■ USING THE SUMMARY

In some quarters, the summary has a bad reputation—and with reason. Summaries often are provided by writers as substitutes for analyses. As students, many of us have summarized books that we were supposed to review critically. All the same, the summary does have a place in respectable college work. First, writing a summary is an excellent way to understand what you read. This in itself is an important goal of academic study. If you don't understand your source material, chances are you won't be able to refer to it usefully in an essay or research paper. Summaries help you understand what you read because they force you to put the text into your own words. Practice with writing summaries also develops your general writing habits because a good summary, like any other piece of good writing, is clear, coherent, and accurate.

Second, summaries are useful to your readers. Let's say you're writing a paper about the McCarthy era in the United States, and in part of that paper you want to discuss Arthur Miller's *Crucible* as a dramatic treatment of the subject. A summary of the plot would be helpful to a reader who hasn't seen or read—or who doesn't remember—the play. Or perhaps you're writing a paper about the politics of recent American military interventions. If your reader isn't likely to be familiar with American actions in Kosovo and Afghanistan, it would be a good idea to summarize these events at some early point in the paper. In many cases (an exam, for instance), you can use a summary to demonstrate your knowledge of what your professor already knows; when writing a paper, you can use a summary to inform your professor about some relatively unfamiliar source.

Third, summaries are required frequently in college-level writing. For example, on a psychology midterm, you may be asked to explain Carl Jung's theory of the collective unconscious and to show how it differs from Sigmund Freud's theory of the personal unconscious. You may have read about this theory in your textbook or in a supplementary article, or your instructor may have outlined it in his or her lecture. You can best demonstrate your understanding of Jung's theory by summarizing it. Then you'll proceed to contrast it with Freud's theory—which, of course, you must also summarize.

■ THE READING PROCESS

It may seem to you that being able to tell (or retell) in summary form exactly what a passage says is a skill that ought to be taken for granted in anyone who can read at high school level. Unfortunately, this is not so: For all kinds of reasons, people don't always read carefully. In fact, it's probably safe to say that usually they don't. Either they read so inattentively that they skip over words, phrases, or even whole sentences, or, if they do see the words in front of them, they see them without registering their significance.

When a reader fails to pick up the meaning and implications of a sentence or two, usually there's no real harm done. (An exception: You could lose credit on an exam or paper because you failed to read or to realize the significance of a crucial direction by your instructor.) But over longer stretches—the paragraph, the section, the article, or the chapter— inattentive or haphazard reading interferes with your goals as a reader: to perceive the shape of the argument, to grasp the central idea, to determine the main points that compose it, to relate the parts of the whole, and to note key examples. This kind of reading takes a lot more energy and determination than casual reading. But, in the long run, it's an energy-saving method because it enables you to retain the content of the material and to use that content as a basis for your own responses. In other words, it allows you to develop an accurate and coherent written discussion that goes beyond summary.

Critical Reading for Summary

- *Examine the context.* Note the credentials, occupation, and publications of the author. Identify the source in which the piece originally appeared. This information helps illuminate the author's perspective on the topic he or she is addressing.
- *Note the title and subtitle.* Some titles are straightforward, whereas the meanings of others become clearer as you read. In either case, titles typically identify the topic being addressed and often reveal the author's attitude toward that topic.
- *Identify the main point.* Whether a piece of writing contains a thesis statement in the first few paragraphs or builds its main point without stating it up front, look at the entire piece to arrive at an understanding of the overall point being made.
- *Identify the subordinate points.* Notice the smaller subpoints that make up the main point, and make sure you understand how they relate to the main point. If a particular subpoint doesn't clearly relate to the main point you've identified, you may need to modify your understanding of the main point.
- *Break the reading into sections.* Notice which paragraph(s) make up a piece's introduction, body, and conclusion. Break up the body paragraphs into sections that address the writer's various subpoints.
- *Distinguish between points, examples, counterarguments.* Critical reading requires careful attention to what a writer is doing as well as what he or she is saying. When a writer quotes someone else or relays an example of something, ask yourself why this is being done. What point is the example supporting? Is another source being quoted as support for a point or as a counterargument that the writer sets out to address?
- *Watch for transitions within and between paragraphs.* In order to follow the logic of a piece of writing, as well as to distinguish between points, examples, and counterarguments, pay attention to the transitional words and phrases writers use. Transitions function like road signs, preparing the reader for what's next.

(continues)

> • *Read actively and recursively.* Don't treat reading as a passive, linear progression through a text. Instead, read as though you are engaged in a dialogue with the writer: Ask questions of the text as you read, make notes in the margin, underline key ideas in pencil, put question or exclamation marks next to passages that confuse or excite you. Go back to earlier points once you finish a reading, stop during your reading to recap what's come so far, and move back and forth through a text.

■ HOW TO WRITE SUMMARIES

Every article you read will present a unique challenge as you work to summarize it. As you'll discover, saying in a few words what has taken someone else a great many can be difficult. But like any other skill, the ability to summarize improves with practice. Here are a few pointers to get you started. They represent possible stages, or steps, in the process of writing a summary. These pointers are not meant to be ironclad rules; rather, they are designed to encourage habits of thinking that will allow you to vary your technique as the situation demands.

Guidelines for Writing Summaries

- *Read the passage carefully.* Determine its structure. Identify the author's purpose in writing. (This will help you distinguish between more important and less important information.) Make a note in the margin when you get confused or when you think something is important; highlight or underline points sparingly, if at all.

- *Reread.* This time divide the passage into sections or stages of thought. The author's use of paragraphing will often be a useful guide. Label, on the passage itself, each section or stage of thought. Underline key ideas and terms. Write notes in the margin.

- *Write one-sentence summaries,* on a separate sheet of paper, of each stage of thought.

- *Write a thesis—a one- or two-sentence summary of the entire passage.* The thesis should express the central idea of the passage, as you have determined it from the preceding steps. You may find it useful to follow the approach of most newspaper stories—naming the what, who, why, where, when, and how of the matter. For persuasive passages, summarize in a sentence the author's conclusion. For descriptive passages, indicate the subject of the description and

(continues)

its key feature(s). Note: In some cases, a suitable thesis may already be in the original passage. If so, you may want to quote it directly in your summary.

- *Write the first draft of your summary* by (1) combining the thesis with your list of one-sentence summaries or (2) combining the thesis with one-sentence summaries plus significant details from the passage. In either case, eliminate repetition and less important information. Disregard minor details or generalize them (e.g., George H. W. Bush and Bill Clinton might be generalized as "recent presidents"). Use as few words as possible to convey the main ideas.

- *Check your summary against the original passage* and make whatever adjustments are necessary for accuracy and completeness.

- *Revise your summary,* inserting transitional words and phrases where necessary to ensure coherence. Check for style. Avoid a series of short, choppy sentences. Combine sentences for a smooth, logical flow of ideas. Check for grammatical correctness, punctuation, and spelling.

■ DEMONSTRATION: SUMMARY

To demonstrate these points at work, let's go through the process of summarizing a passage of expository material—that is, writing that is meant to inform and/or persuade. The following essay, "The Baby in the Well," concerns the topic of empathy, that aspect of our human nature that permits us to identify with others, "to feel their pain," so to speak, and then to offer our help. The question of "Who deserves our help—and why?" is an interesting and difficult one. The personal empathy we feel for someone who has suffered a terrible loss or simply for someone in difficult circumstances (like the homeless person we pass on the street) will likely prompt strong feelings in us. Such feelings do us credit as individuals. But should our empathic impulses always serve as a guide for our personal actions? More broadly, should they serve as a guide for elected officials charged with designing and implementing public policies—for the homeless, for instance, or the chronically underemployed?

In "The Baby in the Well," Paul Bloom makes a provocative and counterintuitive argument about empathy. You may agree or disagree with his thesis. But before you take a position, you'll have to understand the point he's making and the support he offers for that point. "The Baby in the Well" is a challenging essay. Some of Bloom's terminology may be unfamiliar (for instance, "cognitive neuroscience"—the study of the brain and how we think; or "neural systems"—the physical pathways our minds take in forming a thought or feeling). So keep a dictionary nearby. (Or, if you're online, type "define [the unfamiliar term]" into the Google or Bing search box.)

More challenging than the vocabulary may be ideas that test the limits of your understanding. But dealing with difficult ideas will be a common experience in your college-level classes. Indeed, it's the whole point of studying topics you don't know. What is important is that you use a systematic approach to understanding challenging reading material. We offer one such approach here. You may be pleasantly surprised: With a systematic approach and some perseverance, you will grasp the challenging material—and you will feel good about that.

First, read Bloom's essay with care. Try to identify its component parts and understand how they work together to create a coherent argument.

THE BABY IN THE WELL: THE CASE AGAINST EMPATHY*
Paul Bloom

Paul Bloom, professor of psychology and cognitive science at Yale University, is also co-editor-in-chief of the scientific journal Behavioral and Brain Sciences. *He is the author of numerous articles and books, including* How Children Learn the Meaning of Words *(2000) and* How Pleasure Works: The New Science of How We Like What We Like *(2010). This article appeared in* The New Yorker *on May 20, 2013.*

In 2008, Karina Encarnacion, an eight-year-old girl from Missouri, wrote to President-elect Barack Obama with some advice about what kind of dog he should get for his daughters. She also suggested that he enforce recycling and ban unnecessary wars. Obama wrote to thank her, and offered some advice of his own: "If you don't already know what it means, I want you to look up the word 'empathy' in the dictionary. I believe we don't have enough empathy in our world today, and it is up to your generation to change that."

This wasn't the first time Obama had spoken up for empathy. Two years earlier, in a commencement address at Xavier University, he discussed the importance of being able "to see the world through the eyes of those who are different from us—the child who's hungry, the steelworker who's been laid off, the family who lost the entire life they built together when the storm came to town." He went on, "When you think like this—when you choose to broaden your ambit of concern and empathize with the plight of others, whether they are close friends or distant strangers—it becomes harder not to act, harder not to help."

The word "empathy"—a rendering of the German *Einfühlung*, "feeling into"—is only a century old, but people have been interested for a long time in the moral implications of feeling our way into the lives of others. In "The Theory of Moral Sentiments" (1759), Adam Smith observed that sensory experience alone could not spur us toward sympathetic engagement with others: "Though our brother is upon the rack, as long as we ourselves are at our ease, our senses will never inform us of what he suffers." For Smith, what made us moral beings was the

---

imaginative capacity to "place ourselves in his situation...and become in some measure the same person with him, and thence form some idea of his sensations, and even feel something which, though weaker in degree, is not altogether unlike them."

In this sense, empathy is an instinctive mirroring of others' experience— James Bond gets his testicles mashed in "Casino Royale," and male moviegoers grimace and cross their legs. Smith talks of how "persons of delicate fibres" who notice a beggar's sores and ulcers "are apt to feel an itching or uneasy sensation in the correspondent part of their own bodies." There is now widespread support, in the social sciences, for what the psychologist C. Daniel Batson calls "the empathy-altruism hypothesis." Batson has found that simply instructing his subjects to take another's perspective made them more caring and more likely to help.

5   Empathy research is thriving these days, as cognitive neuroscience undergoes what some call an "affective revolution." There is increasing focus on the emotions, especially those involved in moral thought and action. We've learned, for instance, that some of the same neural systems that are active when we are in pain become engaged when we observe the suffering of others. Other researchers are exploring how empathy emerges in chimpanzee and other primates, how it flowers in young children, and the sort of circumstances that trigger it.

This interest isn't just theoretical. If we can figure out how empathy works, we might be able to produce more of it. Some individuals stanch their empathy through the deliberate endorsement of political or religious ideologies that promote cruelty toward their adversaries, while others are deficient because of bad genes, abusive parenting, brutal experience, or the usual unhappy goulash of all of the above. At an extreme lie the 1 percent or so of people who are clinically described as psychopaths. A standard checklist for the condition includes "callousness; lack of empathy"; many other distinguishing psychopathic traits, like lack of guilt and pathological lying, surely stem from this fundamental deficit. Some blame the empathy-deficient for much of the suffering in the world. In *The Science of Evil: On Empathy and the Origins of Cruelty* (Basic Books), Simon Baron-Cohen goes so far as to equate evil with "empathy erosion."

In a thoughtful new book on bullying, *Sticks and Stones* (Random House), Emily Bazelon writes, "The scariest aspect of bullying is the utter lack of empathy"—a diagnosis that she applies not only to the bullies but also to those who do nothing to help the victims. Few of those involved in bullying, she cautions, will turn into full-blown psychopaths. Rather, the empathy gap is situational: bullies have come to see their victims as worthless; they have chosen to shut down their empathetic responses. But most will outgrow—and perhaps regret— their terrible behavior. "The key is to remember that almost everyone has the capacity for empathy and decency—and to tend that seed as best as we possibly can," she maintains.

Two other recent books, *The Empathic Civilization* (Penguin), by Jeremy Rifkin, and *Humanity on a Tightrope* (Rowman & Littlefield), by Paul R. Ehrlich and Robert E. Ornstein, make the powerful argument that empathy has been the main driver of human progress, and that we need more of it if our species is to survive. Ehrlich and Ornstein want us "to emotionally join a global family." Rifkin calls for us to make the leap to "global empathic consciousness." He sees this as the last best hope for saving the world from environmental destruction, and concludes with the plaintive question "Can we reach biosphere consciousness and global empathy in time to avoid planetary collapse?" These are sophisticated books, which provide extensive and accessible reviews of the scholarly literature on empathy. And, as befits the spirit of the times, they enthusiastically champion an increase in empathy as a cure for humanity's ills.

This enthusiasm may be misplaced, however. Empathy has some unfortunate features—it is parochial, narrow-minded, and innumerate.[1] We're often at our best when we're smart enough not to rely on it.

10   In 1949, Kathy Fiscus, a three-year-old girl, fell into a well in San Marino, California, and the entire nation was captivated by concern. Four decades later, America was transfixed by the plight of Jessica McClure—Baby Jessica—the eighteen-month-old who fell into a narrow well in Texas, in October 1987, triggering a fifty-eight-hour rescue operation. "Everybody in America became godmothers and godfathers of Jessica while this was going on," President Reagan remarked.

The immense power of empathy has been demonstrated again and again. It is why Americans were riveted by the fate of Natalee Holloway, the teen-ager who went missing in Aruba, in 2005. It's why, in the wake of widely reported tragedies and disasters—the tsunami of 2004, Hurricane Katrina the year after, or Sandy last year—people gave time, money, and even blood. It's why, last December [2012], when twenty children were murdered at Sandy Hook Elementary School, in Newtown, Connecticut, there was a widespread sense of grief, and an intense desire to help. Last month [April, 2013], of course, saw a similar outpouring of support for the victims of the Boston Marathon bombing.

Why do people respond to these misfortunes and not to others? The psychologist Paul Slovic points out that, when Holloway disappeared, the story of her plight took up far more television time than the concurrent genocide in Darfur. Each day, more than ten times the number of people who died in Hurricane Katrina die because of preventable diseases, and more than thirteen times as many perish from malnutrition.

There is, of course, the attention-getting power of new events. Just as we can come to ignore the hum of traffic, we become oblivious of problems that seem unrelenting, like the starvation of children in Africa—or homicide in the United States. In the past three decades, there were some sixty mass shootings, causing about five hundred deaths; that is, about one-tenth of 1 percent of the homicides in America. But mass murders get splashed onto television screens, newspaper headlines, and the Web; the biggest ones settle into our collective memory—Columbine, Virginia Tech, Aurora, Sandy Hook. The 99.9 percent of

[1] By *innumerate* Bloom means unable to think quantitatively, especially in terms of conceiving or appreciating large numbers. Used in this context, *innumerate* means unable to conceive of the great numbers of people who are or will become victims of natural or man-made disasters.

other homicides are, unless the victim is someone you've heard of, mere background noise.

The key to engaging empathy is what has been called "the identifiable victim effect." As the economist Thomas Schelling, writing forty-five years ago, mordantly observed, "Let a six-year-old girl with brown hair need thousands of dollars for an operation that will prolong her life until Christmas, and the post office will be swamped with nickels and dimes to save her. But let it be reported that without a sales tax the hospital facilities of Massachusetts will deteriorate and cause a barely perceptible increase in preventable deaths—not many will drop a tear or reach for their checkbooks."

15   You can see the effect in the lab. The psychologists Tehila Kogut and Ilana Ritov asked some subjects how much money they would give to help develop a drug that would save the life of one child, and asked others how much they would give to save eight children. The answers were about the same. But when Kogut and Ritov told a third group a child's name and age, and showed her picture, the donations shot up—now there were far more to the one than to the eight.

The number of victims hardly matters—there is little psychological difference between hearing about the suffering of five thousand and that of five hundred thousand. Imagine reading that two thousand people just died in an earthquake in a remote country, and then discovering that the actual number of deaths was twenty thousand. Do you now feel ten times worse? To the extent that we can recognize the numbers as significant, it's because of reason, not empathy.

In the broader context of humanitarianism, as critics like Linda Polman have pointed out, the empathetic reflex can lead us astray. When the perpetrators of violence profit from aid—as in the "taxes" that warlords often demand from international relief agencies—they are actually given an incentive to commit further atrocities. It is similar to the practice of some parents in India who mutilate their children at birth in order to make them more effective beggars. The children's debilities tug at our hearts, but a more dispassionate analysis of the situation is necessary if we are going to do anything meaningful to prevent them.

A "politics of empathy" doesn't provide much clarity in the public sphere, either. Typically, political disputes involve a disagreement over whom we should empathize *with*. Liberals argue for gun control, for example, by focusing on the victims of gun violence; conservatives point to the unarmed victims of crime, defenseless against the savagery of others. Liberals in favor of tightening federally enforced safety regulations invoke the employee struggling with work-related injuries; their conservative counterparts talk about the small businessman bankrupted by onerous requirements. So don't suppose that if your ideological opponents could only ramp up their empathy they would think just like you.

On many issues, empathy can pull us in the wrong direction. The outrage that comes from adopting the perspective of a victim can drive an appetite for retribution. (Think of those statutes named for dead children: Megan's Law, Jessica's Law, Caylee's Law.) But the appetite for retribution is typically indifferent to long-term consequences. In one study, conducted by Jonathan Baron and Ilana Ritov, people were asked how best to punish a company for producing a vaccine that caused the death of a child. Some were told that a higher fine would make the company work harder to manufacture a safer product; others were told that a higher fine would discourage the company from making the vaccine, and since there were no acceptable alternatives on the market the punishment would lead to more deaths. Most people didn't care; they wanted the company fined heavily, whatever the consequence.

20   This dynamic regularly plays out in the realm of criminal justice. In 1987, Willie Horton, a convicted murderer who had been released on furlough from the Northeastern Correctional Center, in Massachusetts, raped a woman after beating and tying up her fiancé. The furlough program came to be seen as a humiliating mistake on the part of Governor Michael Dukakis, and was used against him by his opponents during his run for President, the following year. Yet the program may have *reduced* the likelihood of such incidents. In fact, a 1987 report found that the recidivism rate in Massachusetts dropped in the eleven years after the program was introduced, and that convicts who were furloughed before being released were less likely to go on to commit a crime than those who were not. The trouble is that you can't point to individuals who *weren't* raped, assaulted, or killed as a result of the program, just as you can't point to a specific person whose life was spared because of vaccination.

        There's a larger pattern here. Sensible policies often have benefits that are merely statistical, but victims have names and stories. Consider global warming—what Rifkin calls the "escalating entropy bill that now threatens catastrophic climate change and our very existence." As it happens, the limits of empathy are especially stark here. Opponents of restrictions on CO_2 emissions are flush with identifiable victims—all those who will be harmed by increased costs, by business closures. The millions of people who at some unspecified future date will suffer the consequences of our current inaction are, by contrast, pale statistical abstractions.

        The government's failure to enact prudent long-term policies is often attributed to the incentive system of democratic politics (which favors short-term fixes), and to the powerful influence of money. But the politics of empathy is also to blame. Too often, our concern for specific individuals today means neglecting crises that will harm countless people in the future.

        Moral judgment entails more than putting oneself in another's shoes. As the philosopher Jesse Prinz points out, some acts that we easily recognize as wrong, such as shoplifting or tax evasion, have no identifiable victim. And plenty of good deeds—disciplining a child for dangerous behavior, enforcing a fair and impartial procedure for determining who should get an organ transplant, despite the suffering of those low on the list—require us to put our empathy to one side. Eight deaths are worse than one, even if you know the name of the one; humanitarian aid can, if poorly targeted, be counterproductive; the threat posed by climate change warrants the sacrifices entailed by efforts to ameliorate it. "The decline of violence may owe something to an expansion of empathy," the psychologist Steven Pinker has written, "but it also owes much to harder-boiled faculties like prudence, reason, fairness, self-control, norms and taboos, and conceptions of human rights." A reasoned, even counter-empathetic analysis of moral obligation and likely consequences is a better guide to planning for the future than the gut wrench of empathy.

Rifkin and others have argued, plausibly, that moral progress involves expanding our concern from the family and the tribe to humanity as a whole. Yet it is impossible to empathize with seven billion strangers, or to feel toward someone you've never met the degree of concern you feel for a child, a friend, or a lover. Our best hope for the future is not to get people to think of all humanity as family—that's impossible. It lies, instead, in an appreciation of the fact that, even if we don't empathize with distant strangers, their lives have the same value as the lives of those we love.

25   That's not a call for a world without empathy. A race of psychopaths might well be smart enough to invent the principles of solidarity and fairness. (Research suggests that criminal psychopaths are adept at making moral judgments.) The problem with those who are devoid of empathy is that, although they may recognize what's right, they have no motivation to act upon it. Some spark of fellow feeling is needed to convert intelligence into action.

But a spark may be all that's needed. Putting aside the extremes of psychopathy, there is no evidence to suggest that the less empathetic are morally worse than the rest of us. Simon Baron-Cohen observes that some people with autism and Asperger's syndrome, though typically empathy-deficient, are highly moral, owing to a strong desire to follow rules and insure that they are applied fairly.

Where empathy really does matter is in our personal relationships. Nobody wants to live like Thomas Gradgrind—Charles Dickens's caricature utilitarian, who treats all interactions, including those with his children, in explicitly economic terms. Empathy is what makes us human; it's what makes us both subjects and objects of moral concern. Empathy betrays us only when we take it as a moral guide.

Newtown, in the wake of the Sandy Hook massacre, was inundated with so much charity that it became a burden. More than eight hundred volunteers were recruited to deal with the gifts that were sent to the city—all of which kept arriving despite earnest pleas from Newtown officials that charity be directed elsewhere. A vast warehouse was crammed with plush toys the townspeople had no use for; millions of dollars rolled in to this relatively affluent community. We felt their pain; we wanted to help. Meanwhile—just to begin a very long list—almost twenty million American children go to bed hungry each night, and the federal food-stamp program is facing budget cuts of almost 20 percent. Many of the same kindly strangers who paid for Baby Jessica's medical needs support cuts to state Medicaid programs—cuts that will affect millions. Perhaps fifty million Americans will be stricken next year by food-borne illness, yet budget reductions mean that the FDA will be conducting two thousand fewer safety inspections. Even more invisibly, next year the average American will release about twenty metric tons of carbon dioxide into the atmosphere, and many in Congress seek to loosen restrictions on greenhouse gases even further.

Such are the paradoxes of empathy. The power of this faculty has something to do with its ability to bring our moral concern into a laser pointer of focused attention. If a planet of billions is to survive, however, we'll need to take into consideration the welfare of people not yet harmed—and, even more, of people not yet born. They have no names, faces, or stories to grip our conscience or stir our fellow feeling. Their prospects call, rather, for deliberation and calculation. Our hearts will always go out to the baby in the well; it's a measure of our humanity. But empathy will have to yield to reason if humanity is to have a future.

Read, Reread, Highlight

Let's consider our recommended pointers for writing a summary.

As you reread the passage, note in the margins of the article important points, transitions, and questions you may have. Consider the essay's significance as a whole and its stages of thought. What does it say? How is it organized? How does each part of the passage fit into the whole? What do all these points add up to? Here is how a few paragraphs (5–9) of Bloom's article might look after you mark the main ideas by highlighting and by marginal notations.

Empathy research has increasing focus on moral thought, emotion, and action.

Empathy research is thriving these days, as cognitive neuroscience undergoes what some call an "affective revolution." There is increasing focus on the emotions, especially those involved in moral thought and action. We've learned, for instance, that some of the same neural systems that are active when we are in pain become engaged when we observe the suffering of others. Other researchers are exploring how empathy emerges in chimpanzee and other primates, how it flowers in young children, and the sort of circumstances that trigger it.

Psychopaths lack empathy—a cause of much suffering in the world.

This interest isn't just theoretical. If we can figure out how empathy works, we might be able to produce more of it. Some individuals stanch their empathy through the deliberate endorsement of political or religious ideologies that promote cruelty toward their adversaries, while others are deficient because of bad genes, abusive parenting, brutal experience, or the usual unhappy goulash of all of the above. At an extreme lie the one percent or so of people who are clinically described as psychopaths. A standard checklist for the condition includes "callousness; lack of empathy"; many other distinguishing psychopathic traits, like lack of guilt and pathological lying, surely stem from this fundamental deficit. Some blame the empathy-deficient for much of the suffering in the world. In

Evil as "empathy erosion"

The Science of Evil: On Empathy and the Origins of Cruelty (Basic), Simon Baron-Cohen goes so far as to equate evil with "empathy erosion."

Empathy absent in bullies—and those who witness bullying and stand by.

In a thoughtful new book on bullying, *Sticks and Stones* (Random House), Emily Bazelon writes, "The scariest aspect of bullying is the utter lack of empathy"—a diagnosis that she applies not only to the bullies but also to those who do nothing to help the victims. Few of those involved in bullying, she cautions, will turn into full-blown psychopaths. Rather, the empathy gap is situational: bullies have come to see their victims as worthless; they have chosen to shut down their empathetic responses. But most will outgrow—and perhaps regret—their terrible behavior. "The key is to remember that almost everyone has the capacity for empathy and decency—and to tend that seed as best as we possibly can," she maintains.

Recent authors argue that empathy is a force for progress and even necessary for human survival.

Two other recent books, *The Empathic Civilization* (Penguin), by Jeremy Rifkin, and *Humanity on a Tightrope* (Rowman & Littlefield), by Paul R. Ehrlich and Robert E. Ornstein, make the powerful argument that empathy has been the main driver of human progress, and that we need more of it if our species is to survive. Ehrlich and Ornstein want us "to emotionally join a global family." Rifkin calls for us to make the leap to "global empathic consciousness." He sees this as the last best hope for saving the world from environmental destruction, and concludes with the plaintive question "Can we reach biosphere consciousness and global empathy in time to avoid planetary collapse?" These are sophisticated books, which provide extensive and accessible reviews of the scholarly literature on empathy. And, as befits the spirit of the times, they enthusiastically champion an increase in empathy as a cure for humanity's ills.

Pivot point: Shifts focus from the benefits to the problems of empathy.

This enthusiasm may be misplaced, however. Empathy has some unfortunate features—it is parochial, narrow-minded, and innumerate. We're often at our best when we're smart enough not to rely on it.

Divide into Stages of Thought

When a selection doesn't contain section headings, as is the case with "The Baby in the Well," how do you determine where one section—stage of thought—ends and the next one begins? Assuming that what you have read is coherent and unified, this should not be difficult. (When a selection is unified, all of its parts pertain to the main subject; when a selection is coherent, the parts follow one another in logical order.) Look, particularly, for transitional sentences at the beginning of paragraphs. Such sentences generally work in one or both of the following ways: (1) they summarize what has come before; (2) they set the stage for what is to follow.

Look at the sentence that opens paragraph 9: "This enthusiasm may be misplaced, however." Notice how this sentence signals a sudden shift in focus. Bloom began by discussing the prevailing view of empathy and offered examples to demonstrate this discussion. He also pointed to recent books supporting this view. But now he tells us that empathy may be overrated and goes on to explain why. The second sentence of paragraph 9 amplifies the first: "Empathy has some unfortunate features—it is parochial, narrow-minded, and innumerate." He offers reasons for his initial statement, announcing in the process the focus of his remaining essay. Bloom is in total control of his subject, setting up his thesis mid-essay in a way that would be totally surprising if not for the subtitle of his article ("The Case Against Empathy"). Now he has our attention. We want to know more about what he means by "This enthusiasm may be misplaced." In the third and final sentence of that paragraph, he writes: "We're often at our best when we're smart enough not to rely on [empathy]." The setup is now ready to take us in another direction from the beginning of the article.

Each section of an article generally takes several paragraphs to develop. Between paragraphs, and almost certainly between sections of an article, you will usually find transitions that help you understand what you have just read and what you are about to read. For articles like Bloom's that have no sub- (that is, section) headings, try writing your own section headings in the margins as you take notes. Articles with such headings make your job easier. But note that *if* a selection is well written, you'll be able to identify how the writer develops an argument or explanation over distinct sections of thought.

Here we divide Bloom's article into eight sections. This division is not absolute. Some readers might identify seven sections, others six. The number is less important than the clarity with which you understand, and can reproduce in your summary, the author's step-by-step logic.

> **Section 1:** *Definition and importance of empathy* (paragraphs 1–4).
>
> **Section 2:** *Empathy necessary to human survival?* (paragraphs 5–8).
>
> **Section 3:** *The problem with empathy: Its focus on "babies in wells"* (paragraphs 9–11).
>
> **Section 4:** *How empathy operates* (paragraphs 12–16).
>
> **Section 5:** *How empathy leads us astray* (paragraphs 17–22).
>
> **Section 6:** *Empathy isn't enough* (paragraphs 23–24).
>
> **Section 7:** *Concession: Where empathy does matter* (paragraphs 25–27).
>
> **Section 8:** *Conclusion: Empathy should yield to reason* (paragraphs 28–29).

Write a Brief Summary of Each Stage of Thought

The purpose of this step is to wean you from the language of the original passage so that you are not tied to it when writing the summary. Here are brief summaries for each stage of thought in the sections of "The Baby in the Well."

Section 1: *Definition and importance of empathy* (paragraphs 1–4).

> Many believe that what makes us moral beings is empathy, the ability to see the world from others' points of view, to feel their pain and distress, and to feel the impulse to help them.

Section 2: *Empathy necessary to human survival?* (paragraphs 5–8).

> Empathy research focuses on how our moral impulses are affected when we see or sense others who are in pain. Some people feel no

distress at the pain of others, but most are capable of empathy, a quality Bloom believes is necessary not only for human progress but also for the survival of our species.

Section 3: *The problem with empathy: its focus on "babies in wells"* (paragraphs 9–11).

Empathy is "parochial, narrow-minded, and innumerate."[2] It tends to focus on individuals or relatively small groups of individuals who are in well-publicized distress.

Section 4: *How empathy operates* (paragraphs 12–16).

Because of the "identifiable victim effect," people care about the effects of highly publicized tragedies on people whose faces they can see. But at the same time, they seem oblivious to large-scale catastrophes such as genocide, mass starvation, and deaths due to preventable illnesses as well as to routine homicides that occur in the thousands every year.

Section 5: *How empathy leads us astray* (paragraphs 17–22).

So empathy "can lead us astray." Our empathetic impulses may over-power our "dispassionate analysis of a situation." Acting on impulses of empathy may help a relatively small number of identifiable indi-viduals, but it may also hurt many other individuals of whom we are less aware, who don't have "names or stories," or with whose values we don't politically sympathize.

Section 6: *Empathy isn't enough* (paragraphs 23–24).

Moral judgment often requires us to put empathy aside, to assume that all lives have the same value, and to use qualities like "pru-dence, reason, fairness [and] self-control" to plan for the well-being of humanity as a whole.

Section 7: *Concession: Where empathy does matter* (paragraphs 25–27).

No one wants to live in a world without empathy, a quality that is so vital in maintaining our human relationships.

Section 8: *Conclusion: Empathy should yield to reason* (paragraphs 28–29).

But as a moral guide, empathy should "yield to reason." Assistance to the few is often wasted because it is too much or it is unneeded. But "guided by deliberation and calculation," assistance to the many is essential for the future well-being of the billions of people who constitute humankind.

---

[2] See definition of *innumerate*, p. 10.

Write a Thesis: A Brief Summary of the Entire Passage

The thesis is the most general statement of a summary (or any other type of academic writing). It is the statement that announces the paper's subject and the claim that you or—in the case of a summary—another author will be making about that subject. Every paragraph of a paper illuminates the thesis by providing supporting detail or explanation. The relationship of these paragraphs to the thesis is analogous to the relationship of the sentences within a paragraph to the topic sentence. Both the thesis and the topic sentences are general statements (the thesis being the more general) that are followed by systematically arranged details.

To ensure clarity for the reader, *the first sentence of your summary should begin with the author's thesis, regardless of where it appears in the article itself.* An author may locate her thesis at the beginning of her work, in which case the thesis operates as a general principle from which details of the presentation follow. This is called a *deductive* organization: thesis first, supporting details second. Alternatively, an author may locate his thesis at the end of the work, in which case the author begins with specific details and builds toward a more general conclusion, or thesis. This is called an *inductive* organization. And, as you might expect, an author might locate the thesis anywhere between beginning and end, at whatever point it seems best positioned—which is what Bloom chooses to do.

A thesis consists of a subject and an assertion about that subject. How can we go about fashioning an adequate thesis for a summary of Bloom's article? Probably no two versions of Bloom's thesis statement would be worded identically. But it is fair to say that any reasonable thesis will indicate that Bloom's subject is the inadequacy of empathy for dealing with large-scale human suffering, an inadequacy resulting from what he calls the "identifiable victim effect"—our tendency to respond favorably more to individuals whose names and faces we know than to large numbers of present or future victims who remain anonymous to us.

Does Bloom make a statement anywhere in this passage that pulls all this together? Examine paragraph 9 and you will find his thesis—two sentences that sum up the problems with empathy: "Empathy has some unfortunate features—it is parochial, narrow-minded, and innumerate. We're often at our best when we're smart enough not to rely on it." You may have learned that a thesis statement must be expressed in a single sentence. We would offer a slight rewording of this generally sound advice and say that a thesis statement must be *expressible* in a single sentence. For reasons of emphasis or style, a writer might choose to distribute a thesis across two or more sentences. Certainly, the sense of Bloom's thesis can take the form of a single statement, one that explains why it's a good idea not to rely on empathy. For reasons largely of emphasis, he divides his thesis into two sentences.

Here is a one-sentence version of Bloom's two-sentence thesis, using his language: It's best not to rely on empathy because this emotion can be "parochial, narrow-minded, and innumerate." Notice that such a statement anticipates a summary of the *entire* article: both the discussion leading up to Bloom's thesis and his discussion after. To put this thesis in our own words and alert readers that the idea is Bloom's, not ours, we might recast it as follows:

> In "The Baby in the Well: The Case Against Empathy," Paul Bloom argues that while empathy is important in fostering positive human relationships, we should prefer reason as a guide to social policy because empathy's focus on the distress of one individual may blind us to the suffering of thousands whose names and faces we do not know.

The first sentence of a summary is crucially important, for it orients readers by letting them know what to expect in the coming paragraphs. In the example above, the sentence refers directly to an article, its author, and the thesis for the upcoming summary. The author and title reference could also be indicated in the summary's title (if this were a freestanding summary), in which case their mention could be dropped from the thesis statement. And lest you become frustrated too quickly with how much effort it takes to come up with this crucial sentence, keep in mind that writing an acceptable thesis for a summary takes time. In this case, it took three drafts, roughly ten minutes, to compose a thesis and another few minutes of fine-tuning after a draft of the entire summary was completed. The thesis needed revision because the first draft was vague; the second draft was improved but too specific on a secondary point; the third draft was more complete but too general on a key point:

> **Draft 1:** In "The Baby in the Well: The Case Against Empathy," Paul Bloom argues that we should not rely on empathy.
>
> (Vague. It's not clear from this statement why Bloom thinks we should not rely on empathy.)
>
> **Draft 2:** In "The Baby in the Well: The Case Against Empathy," Paul Bloom argues against empathy because of its focus on the distress of the individual rather than on the suffering of large numbers of people.
>
> (Better, but the thesis should note that Bloom acknowledges the value of empathy and indicate what he sees as a preferable alternative to empathy.)
>
> **Draft 3:** In "The Baby in the Well: The Case Against Empathy," Paul Bloom argues that while empathy has its place, we should prefer reason because empathy's focus on the distress of one individual may blind us to the suffering among thousands of individuals.
>
> (Close—but a better thesis would formulate a more precise phrase than "has its place" and would introduce the crucial idea of the "identifiable victim affect"—one indicated in the final thesis in the phrase "whose names and faces we do not know.")
>
> **Final Draft:** In "The Baby in the Well: The Case Against Empathy," Paul Bloom argues that while empathy is important in fostering positive human relationships, we should prefer reason as a guide to social policy because empathy's focus on the distress of one individual may blind us to the suffering of thousands whose names and faces we do not know.

Write the First Draft of the Summary

Let's consider two possible summaries of Bloom's article: (1) a short summary, combining a thesis with brief section summaries, and (2) a longer summary, combining thesis, brief section summaries, and some carefully chosen details. Again, keep in mind that you are reading final versions; each of the following summaries is the result of at least two full drafts. Highlighting indicates transitions added to smooth the flow of the summary. The thesis sentence is also highlighted.

Summary 1: Combine Thesis Sentence with Brief Section Summaries

In "The Baby in the Well: The Case Against Empathy," Paul Bloom argues that while empathy is important in fostering positive human relationships, we should prefer reason as a guide to social policy because empathy's focus on the distress of one individual may blind us to the suffering of thousands whose names and faces we do not know. Bloom begins with an uncontroversial point: Many believe that what makes us moral beings is empathy, the ability to see the world from others' points of view, to feel their pain and distress, and to feel the impulse to help them. Most people are capable of empathy, a quality Bloom believes is necessary not only for human progress but also for the survival of our species.

There is a downside to empathy, however: It is "parochial, narrow-minded, and innumerate." Empathy tends to focus on the distress of individuals or relatively small groups of individuals whose names and faces we know, a phenomenon known as the "identifiable victim effect." But the same people who feel empathetic toward individuals can be oblivious to large-scale catastrophes such as genocide, mass starvation, and deaths due to preventable illnesses as well as to routine homicides that occur in the thousands every year. Because our empathetic impulses may overpower our "dispassionate analysis of a situation," empathy can "lead us astray." When we act only on impulses of empathy, we may help a relatively small number of identifiable individuals, but we often ignore many other individuals who don't have "names or stories" or with whose political values we don't sympathize.

For this reason, good moral judgment often requires us to put empathy aside, to assume that all lives have the same value, and to use qualities like "prudence, reason, fairness [and] self-control" to plan for the well-being of humanity as a whole. Of course, no one wants to live in a world without empathy. As a moral guide, however, empathy should "yield to reason." Our generous assistance to the few is often wasted. But assistance to the many, "guided by deliberation and calculation," is essential for the future well-being of the billions of people who constitute humankind.

The Strategy of the Shorter Summary

This short summary consists essentially of a restatement of Bloom's thesis plus the section summaries, modified, expanded a little, and even slightly rearranged for stylistic purposes. You'll recall that Bloom locates his thesis midway through the article, in paragraph 9. But note that this model summary *begins* with a restatement of his thesis. Notice also the relative weight given to the section summaries within the model. Bloom's main argument, that empathy is "parochial, narrow-minded, and innumerate," is summarized in paragraph 2 of the model. The other paragraphs combine summaries of material leading up to the main argument and material explaining the implications of the argument—primarily, that reason is a better guide to both moral judgment and social policy than empathy. Paragraph 1 of the short summary combines material from the article's Sections 1 and 2 (paragraphs 1–8 of the article); paragraph 2 combines material from the article's Sections 3–5 (paragraphs 9–22); and paragraph 3 combines summaries of Sections 6, 7, and 8 (paragraphs 23–29).

Notice the insertion of several (highlighted) transitional phrases. The first, "Bloom begins with an uncontroversial assertion," bridges the thesis and the first section of the article itself in which Bloom focuses on the benefits and even the study of empathy. The second, "There is a downside, however," sets up the sentence that represents the main idea of the article focusing on problems associated with empathy. The third and fourth highlights, "For this reason" and "of course" in paragraph 3, serve respectively as a transition between paragraphs and as an introduction to a brief concession sentence. The concession, which Bloom makes in paragraphs 25–27, acknowledges the fact that no one wants to live in a world without empathy; it then reaffirms the main idea of the thesis: that the welfare of humankind's billions is better left to "deliberation and calculation" than to empathy.

Summary 2: Combine Thesis Sentence, Section Summaries, and Carefully Chosen Details

The thesis and brief section summaries could also be used as the outline for a more detailed summary. However, most of the details in the passage won't be necessary in a summary. It isn't necessary even in a longer summary of this passage to discuss all of Bloom's examples of the kind of situations that evoke (or fail to evoke) empathy. It would be appropriate, though, to mention *some* examples of such situations or to describe the lab experiment that demonstrates how the "identifiable victim effect" works.

Such details don't appear in the first summary, but in a longer summary, a few carefully selected examples might be desirable for clarity. How do you decide which examples to include? One hint may be their degree of prominence: The fact that Bloom opens with Barack Obama's comments on empathy and devotes the first four paragraphs of his article to detailing the comments of important individuals like Obama and Adam Smith is an indication that such references may be worth mentioning in a longer summary. And the fact that Bloom titles the article "The Baby in the Well" suggests the importance of explaining the significance of this striking image in illustrating Bloom's overall thesis. Otherwise, it may not make much difference which examples you cite. In the following longer summary, the writer discusses the case of Willie Horton, the convicted murderer who was furloughed and, while on release, subsequently committed a horrific crime. Other examples cited by Bloom, however, might work just as well in illustrating his point that reason is better than empathy as a guide to enlightened social policy.

You won't always know which details to include and which to exclude. Developing good judgment in comprehending and summarizing texts is largely a matter of reading skill and prior knowledge (see p. 2). Consider the analogy of the seasoned mechanic who can pinpoint an engine problem by simply listening to a characteristic sound that to a less-experienced person is just noise. Or consider the chess player who can plot three separate winning strategies from a board position that to a novice looks like a hopeless jumble. In the same way, the more practiced a reader you are, the more knowledgeable you will become about the subject and the better able you will be to make critical distinctions between elements of greater and lesser importance. In the meantime, read as carefully as you can and use your own best judgment as to how to present your material.

Here's one version of a completed summary with carefully chosen details. Note that we have highlighted phrases and sentences added to the original, briefer summary.

> In "The Baby in the Well: The Case Against Empathy" Paul Bloom argues that while empathy is important in fostering positive human relationships, we should prefer reason as a guide to social policy because empathy's focus on the distress of one individual may blind us to the suffering of thousands whose names and faces we do not know. Bloom begins by citing assertions of the importance of empathy from well-known figures like Barack Obama and Adam Smith. He points out that many believe that what makes us moral beings is empathy, the ability to see the world from others' points of view, to feel their pain and distress, and to feel the impulse to help them. Some people, either because of their own belief systems or because of abuse they have suffered at the hands of others, lack this essential human capacity. Bullies, for example, according to Emily Bazelon, show "an utter lack of empathy." Fortunately, most people are capable of this quality that Bloom believes is necessary not only for human progress but also for the survival of our species.
>
> There is a downside to empathy, however: It is "parochial, narrow-minded, and innumerate." Empathy tends to focus on the distress of individuals or relatively small groups of individuals whose names and faces we know, a phenomenon known as the "identifiable victim effect." Bloom explains how America becomes transfixed by the plight of young children who fall into

wells: In 1949 it was three-year-old Kathy Ficus; in 1987 it was 18-month-old Jessica McClure (Baby Jessica). Americans also poured out their empathy to Natalee Holloway, who disappeared in Aruba in 2005, as well as to the victims of both natural disasters, like tsunamis and hurricanes, and mass killings like the Sandy Hook school shooting and the Boston Marathon bombing. But the same people who feel empathetic toward individuals and relatively small groups of individuals can be oblivious to large-scale catastrophes such as genocide, mass starvation, and deaths due to preventable illnesses as well as to routine homicides that occur in the thousands every year. A lab experiment has shown that people tend to be more generous in donating money for the development of a life-saving drug when they know the name and age—and can see the photo—of a particular child who needs the drug.

Because our empathetic impulses may overpower our "dispassionate analysis of a situation," empathy can "lead us astray." When we act only on impulses of empathy, we may help a relatively small number of identifiable individuals, but we often ignore many other individuals who don't have "names or stories" or with whose political values we don't sympathize. The non-identifiable individuals include those who would be helped if we acted on the basis of reason rather than empathy. Bloom cites the case of those Massachusetts citizens who are safer as the result of a prison furlough program that was successful in reducing crime; however, the program was discredited because of a single notorious case in which a prisoner out on furlough committed a horrendous act that created understandable empathy toward the victim.

For this reason, good moral judgment often requires us to put empathy aside, to assume that all lives have the same value, and to use qualities like "prudence, reason, fairness [and] self-control" to plan for the well-being of humanity as a whole. Of course, no one wants to live in a world without empathy. Empathy is particularly important in our personal relationships, in ensuring that we treat one another with care. As a moral guide, however, empathy should "yield to reason." Our generous assistance to the few is often wasted. But assistance to the many, "guided by deliberation and calculation," is essential for the future well-being of the billions of people who constitute humankind.

The Strategy of the Longer Summary

Compared with the first, briefer summary, this effort (75 percent longer than the first) includes several specific examples that illustrate Bloom's thesis about the "parochial, narrow-minded, and innumerate" features of empathy. It begins by emphasizing the great value that we place on empathy; it more fully develops the way that empathetic thinking embodies the "identifiable victim effect," and it expands upon the reasons, in terms of social policy, for preferring reason to empathy as a moral guide.

The final two of our suggested steps for writing summaries are (1) to check your summary against the original passage, making sure that you have included all the important ideas, and (2) to revise so that the summary reads smoothly and coherently. The structure of this summary generally reflects the structure of the original article—with one significant departure, as noted earlier. Bloom uses a modified inductive approach, stating his thesis midway through the article. The summary, however, states the thesis immediately, then proceeds deductively to develop that thesis.

■ HOW LONG SHOULD A SUMMARY BE?

The length of a summary depends both on the length of the original passage and on the use to which the summary will be put. If you are summarizing an entire article, a good rule of thumb is that your summary should be no longer than one-fourth the length of the original passage. Of course, if you were summarizing an entire chapter or even an entire book, it would have to be much shorter than that. The longer summary above is one-fifth the length of Paul Bloom's original. Although it shouldn't be very much longer, you have seen (p. 20) that it could be quite a bit shorter.

The length as well as the content of the summary also depends on the *purpose* to which it will be put. Let's suppose you decided to use Bloom's piece in a paper about bullying (such as the model argument synthesis on pp. 140–151). In this case, you would pay particular attention to what Bloom writes in paragraphs 6 and 7 about people characterized by a partial or total lack of empathy and whose behavior exhibits itself as bullying. You would probably also draw upon Emily Bazelon's comment about "the scariest aspect of bullying [being] a lack of empathy." On the other hand, in a paper dealing with some aspect of social policy (for example, parole reform or reducing the urban homicide rate), you might draw upon Bloom's larger point that "reasoned...analysis of moral obligation and likely consequences is a better guide to planning for the future than the gut wrench of empathy." So, depending on your purpose, you would summarize one particular section of the article or another. We will see this process more fully demonstrated in the upcoming chapters on syntheses.

Exercise 1.1

Individual and Collaborative Summary Practice

Turn to the end of Chapter 2 and read Ethan Gilsdorf's radio talk, "Why We Need Violent Video Games" (pp. 81–83). Follow the steps for writing summaries outlined above—read, underline, and divide into stages of thought. Write a one- or two-sentence summary of each stage of thought in Gilsdorf's presentation. Then gather in groups of three or four classmates and compare your summary sentences. Discuss the differences in your sentences, and come to some consensus about the divisions in Gilsdorf's stages of thought—and the ways in which to best sum them up.

As a group, write a one- or two-sentence thesis statement summing up the entire passage. You could go even further and, using your individual summary sentences—or the versions of them your group revised—put together a brief summary of Gilsdorf's presentation. Model your work on the brief summary of Bloom's article on page 20.

■ SUMMARIZING GRAPHS, CHARTS, AND TABLES

In your reading in the sciences and social sciences, you will often find data and concepts presented in nontext forms—as figures and tables. Such visual devices offer a snapshot, a pictorial overview of material that is more quickly and clearly communicated in graphic form than as a series of (often complicated) sentences. Note that in essence, graphs, charts, and tables are themselves summaries. The writer uses a graph, which in an article or book is often labeled as a numbered "figure," and presents the quantitative results of research as points on a line or a bar or as sections ("slices") of a pie. Pie charts show relative proportions, or percentages. Graphs, especially effective in showing patterns, relate one variable to another: for instance, income to years of education or sales figures of a product over a period of three years.

Writers regularly draw on graphs, charts, and tables to provide information or to offer evidence for points they are arguing. Consider the following passage from the prefatory "Discussion" to the study done for the Center for Immigration Studies (CIS), *Immigrants in the United States: A Profile of America's Foreign-Born Population*, by Steven A. Camarota:

> There are many reasons to examine the nation's immigrant population. First, immigrants and their minor children now represent one-sixth of the U.S. population. Moreover, understanding how immigrants are doing is the best way to evaluate the effects of immigration policy. Absent a change in policy, between 12 and 15 million new immigrants (legal and illegal) will likely settle in the United States in the next decade. And perhaps 30 million new immigrants will arrive in the next 20 years. Immigration policy determines the number allowed in, the selection criteria used, and the level of resources devoted to controlling illegal immigration. The future, of course, is not set and when formulating immigration policy, it is critically important to know the impact of recent immigration.
>
> It is difficult to understate the impact of immigration on the socio-demographics of the United States. New immigration plus births to immigrants added more than 22 million people to the U.S. population in the last decade, equal to 80 percent of total population growth. Immigrants and their young children (under 18) now account for more than one in five public school students, one-fourth of those in poverty, and nearly one-third of those without health insurance, creating very real challenges for the nation's schools, health care systems, and physical infrastructure. The large share of immigrants who arrive as adults with relatively few years of schooling is the primary reason so many live in poverty, use welfare programs, or lack health insurance, not their legal status or an unwillingness to work.

Despite the fact that a large share of immigrants have few years of schooling, most immigrants do work. In fact, the share of immigrant men holding a job is higher than native-born men. Moreover, immigrants make significant progress the longer they reside in the United States. This is also true for the least educated. While many immigrants do very well in the United States, on average immigrants who have been in the country for 20 years lag well behind natives in most measure of economic well-being.

Camarota, who is the director of research at CIS, uses a good deal of data that likely came from graphs, charts, and tables. In the following pages, we present graphs, charts, and tables from a variety of sources, all focused on the subject of U.S. immigration.

Bar Graphs

Figure 1.1 is a *bar graph* indicating the countries that have sent the highest number of immigrants to the United States in the decades from 1901–1910 through 2001–2010. The horizontal—or x—axis indicates the decades

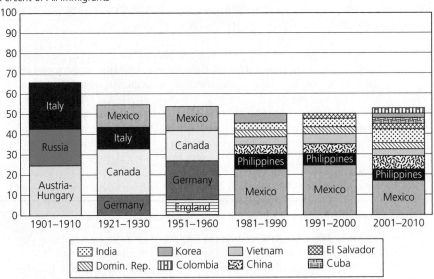

■ Figure 1.1   Top Sending Countries: Selected Periods[3]

---

[3]"Figure 2. Top Sending Countries "Comprising at Least Half of All L[egal] P[ermanent] R[esidents]. Selected Periods." Ruth Ellen Wasem [Specialist in Immigration Policy], "U.S. Immigration Policy: Chart Book of Key Trends, C[ongressional] R[esearch] S[ervice]: Report for Congress." p. 3. Source: CRS Analysis of Table 2, Statistical Yearbook of Immigration, U.S. Department of Homeland Security, Office of Immigration Statistics, FY2010. www.crs.gov, http://www.fas.org/sgp/crs/homesec/R42988.pdf.

from 1901 through 2010. The vertical—or y—axis on the left indicates the percent of immigrants represented by each country. Each vertical bar for each decade is subdivided into sections representing the countries that sent the most immigrants in that decade. Note that in the decade 1901 to 1910, the three top sending countries were Italy, Russia, and Austria-Hungary. A hundred years later, in the decade 2001 through 2010, the top sending countries were led by Mexico, the Philippines, and China. (Note that the decades from 1931 through 1950 and from 1961 through 1980 are not represented in the graph.)

Here is a summary of the information presented in Figure 1.1:

> Between 1900 and 2010, the flow of immigration to the United States has dramatically shifted from Europe to Asia and the Americas. In the decade from 1901 to 1910, three European countries—Italy, Russia, and Austria-Hungary—accounted for most of the immigrant flow to this country. Starting in the next decade, however, two countries in the Americas—Mexico and Canada—became the top sources of immigrants to the United States. Mexico has remained a top sending country for most of the twentieth century and into the present century, currently accounting for more immigrants than any other nation. At the same time, immigration from Mexico dropped off slightly in the decade from 2001 to 2010. All of other top sending countries during this decade are in Asia and South and Central America. The top sending Asian countries are Korea, India, Vietnam, China, and the Philippines; those from the Americas include—in addition to Mexico—Colombia, Cuba, El Salvador, and the Dominican Republic. Collectively, immigrants from the Asian and American countries represented on the chart in the 2001–2010 decade account for slightly more than 50 percent of all immigrants admitted.

Figure 1.2 is a horizontal bar graph summarizing the results of an opinion survey concerning the requirements that should be levied on illegal immigrants. The Pew survey shows that 76 percent of respondents believe that such immigrants should have to show that they can speak and understand English (23 percent oppose such a requirement). A slight majority of 56 percent believes that illegal immigrants should be required to pay fines, and a similar percentage believes that illegal immigrants should have to wait ten years before their applications for citizenship can be accepted. In this type of graph, an imaginary line runs vertically through each bar. The shaded portion of the bar on each side of the line represents a particular value (in this case, the percentages having a particular opinion), and the length of each portion of the bar is proportional to the percentage.

Exercise 1.2

Summarizing Graphs

Write a brief summary of the data in Figure 1.2. Use our summary of Figure 1.1 as a general model.

Most Favor Requiring Those in U.S. Illegally to Learn English

Legislation allowing undocumented immigrants to stay legally should require them to ...

■ Oppose   ☐ Favor

Showing they can speak and understand English	23	76
Paying fines	41	56
A ten-year waiting period for most	43	55

Pew Research Center/USA Today June 12–16, 2013. Q47.

■ Figure 1.2   Survey on Favored Requirements for Illegal Immigrants[4]

Line Graphs

Line graphs are useful for showing trends over a period of time. Usually, the horizontal axis indicates years, months, or shorter periods, and the vertical

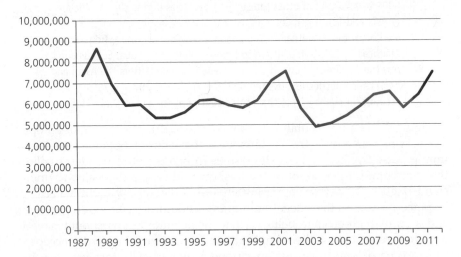

■ Figure 1.3   Nonimmigrant Visas Issued by the U.S. Department of State[5]

---

[4] Pew Research Center. "Immigration: Key Data Points from Pew Research." 26 June 2013. 3rd chart. http://www.pewresearch.org/key-data-points/immigration-tip-sheet-on-u-s-public-opinion/.

[5] "Figure 6. Nonimmigrant Visas Issued by the U.S. Department of State." Source: CRS presentation of data from Table XVIII of the annual reports of the U.S. Department of State Office of Visa Statistics. Ruth Ellen Wasem [Specialist in Immigration Policy], "U.S. Immigration Policy: Chart Book of Key Trends, C[ongressional] R[esearch] S[ervice]: Report for Congress. p. 7. www.crs.gov http://www.fas.org/sgp/crs/homesec/R42988.pdf.

axis indicates a quantity: dollars, barrels, personnel, sales, anything that can be counted. The line running from left to right indicates the changing values, over a given period, of the object of measurement. Frequently, a line graph will feature multiple lines (perhaps in different colors, perhaps some solid, others dotted, etc.), each indicating a separate variable to be measured. Thus, a line graph could show the changing approval ratings of several presidential candidates over the course of a campaign season. Or it could indicate the number of iPads versus Android tablets sold in a given year.

Figure 1.3 is a line graph indicating the fluctuations in the number of non-immigrant ("legal temporary") visas issued by the U.S. State Department from 1987 through 2011. The number of such visas reached its highest level—nearly nine million—in 1988–1989. The lowest number of visas—fewer than five million—was issued in 2004. Following the line allows us to discern the pattern of nonimmigrant migration. By combining the information gleaned from this figure with other information gathered from other sources, you may be able to make certain conjectures or draw certain conclusions about the patterns of immigration.

In Figure 1.4, we have a double line graph, which allows us to view at the same time the changes in authorized immigration and the changes in unauthorized immigration. The horizontal axis lists only three years, and to the right of the vertical axis we see two types of immigrants categorized. With only three years being considered and with the key numbers printed right

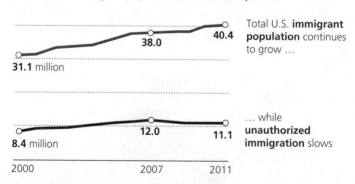

Since 2000, the immigrant population has increased by **30%.**

Total U.S. **immigrant population** continues to grow ...

38.0   **40.4**

31.1 million

... while **unauthorized immigration** slows

12.0   **11.1**

8.4 million

2000   2007   2011

Immigrant population and unauthorized immigrant population estimates based on separate data sets. See Pew Research Hispanic Center, "A Nation of Immigrants," Jan. 29, 2013.

Figure 1.4   Growth of Total U.S. Immigrant Population Compared to Decline in Unauthorized Immigration[6]

[6]"Growth of Total U.S. Immigrant Population Compared to Decline in Unauthorized Immigration." Pew Research Hispanic Center tabulations of 2011 American Community Survey (1% IPUMS) Chart 5. http://www.pewhispanic.org/2013/02/15/u-s-immigration-trends/ph_13-01-23_ss_immigration_01_title/.

below each line, the reader can easily absorb a great deal of information in an efficient way. The two simple lines are dramatic evidence of the increase of the immigrant population in the years from 2000 to 2011.

Exercise 1.3

Summarizing Line Graphs

Write a brief summary of the key data in Figure 1.4. Use our summary of Figure 1.1 (or your summary of Figure 1.2) as a model.

Pie Charts

Bar and line graphs are useful for visually comparing numerical quantities. *Pie charts*, on the other hand, are useful for visually comparing percentages of a whole. The pie represents the whole; the individual slices represent the relative sizes of the parts.

Figure 1.5 is an exploded pie chart, created by pulling out at least one individual slice of the pie to emphasize the data represented. The chart shows that among foreign-born adults ages 25 or older, more than twice as many of that group have a high school diploma or equivalent than those who don't. This simple chart, produced by the Pew Research Hispanic Center and based on the U.S. Census Bureau's 2011 American Community Survey, provides only one key fact about immigrants. There is no break-down of sending countries or any other pertinent data.

Most *immigrant adults are high school graduates...*

Percent of foreign-born adults ages 25 and older...

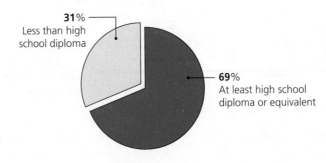

31%
Less than high school diploma

69%
At least high school diploma or equivalent

Pew Research Hispanic Center tabulations of 2011 American Community Survey (1% IPUMS)

▮ Figure 1.5   Percentages of Immigrants with and Without High School Diplomas[7]

[7] "Percentages of Immigrant Adults with and Without High School Diplomas." Pew Research Hispanic Center tabulations of 2011 American Community Survey (1% IPUMS). http://www .pewhispanic.org/2013/02/15/u-s-immigration-trends/ph_13-01-23_ss_immigration_01_ title/. Chart 14.

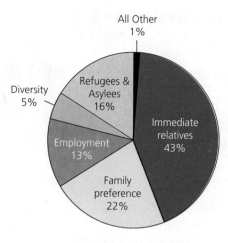

1.1 Million LPRs in FY2011

| Figure 1.6   Breakdown of Legal Permanent Residents (LPRs) in Fiscal Year 2011.[8]

Figure 1.6 is a more complex pie chart indicating the major categories of immigrants who were classified as legal permanent residents (LPRs) in fiscal year 2011. This chart shows that almost 65 percent of such immigrants entered the United States because of family ties to immigrants already in the country.

Exercise 1.4

Summarizing Pie Charts

Write a brief summary of the data in Figure 1.6. Use our summary of Figure 1.1 (or your summary of Figure 1.2) as a model.

Other Charts: Bubble Maps, Pictograms, and Interactive Charts

A *bubble map* is a type of chart characterized by discs of various sizes placed on a map of the world, a country, or a smaller region. The relative sizes of the discs represent various percentages or absolute numbers, making it easy to see at a glance which countries or regions have larger or smaller numbers of whatever variable is represented by the disc.

---

[8] Ruth Ellen Wasem [Specialist in Immigration Policy], "U.S. Immigration Policy: Chart Book of Key Trends, C[ongressional] R[esearch] S[ervice]: Report for Congress. www.crs.gov, http://www.fas.org/sgp/crs/homesec/R42988.pdf, p. 5 (second chart—pie).

The United States is the **world's leader** *as a destination for immigrants.*

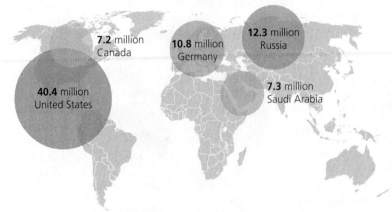

2011 American Community Survey (1% IPUMS) for U.S. and 2010 World Bank estimates for all others.

Figure 1.7   The United States Is World's Leader as Destination for Immigrants[9]

Figure 1.7 depicts a bubble map in which variously sized bubbles, placed over particular countries or regions, represent the total number of immigrants in a particular country. A quick look at the map reveals that the United States has by far the greatest number of immigrants (40.4 million), followed by Russia—far behind with only 12.3 million immigrants.

Pictograms are charts that use drawings or icons to represent persons or objects. For example, a pictogram depicting the resources available to a particular nation engaged in a war might use icons of soldiers, tanks, planes, artillery, and so on, with each icon representing a given number of units.

Figure 1.8 is a pictogram depicting three categories of immigrant visas issued in 2012: temporary worker visas (including those "H" visa workers who have high-level or other specialized skills), permanent immigrant visas, and a third (miscellaneous) category, consisting of intra-company transferees and their families, along with other temporary workers and their families.

In this particular figure, each icon of an individual represents approximately 10,000 immigrants. Each of the three major classes of immigrant visas is subdivided into several categories. So, for example, the temporary worker visa category is subdivided into those who have specialty occupations, those who are agricultural workers, those who are seasonal workers, and those who are family members of the workers. The other two main categories of visas are subdivided in other ways, based upon the makeup of those categories.

---

[9]Pew Research Hispanic Center. "The U.S. is the World's Leader as a Destination for Immigrants." Tabulations of 2011 American Community Survey (1% IPUMS), Chart 3. http://www.pewhispanic .org/2013/02/15/u-s-immigration-trends/ph_13-01-23_ss_immigration_01_title/.

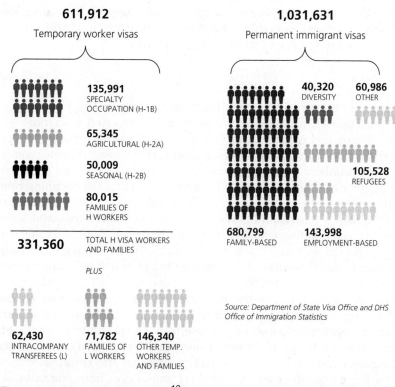

Visas Issued in 2012   = 10,000 *visas*

611,912
Temporary worker visas

135,991
SPECIALTY
OCCUPATION (H-1B)

65,345
AGRICULTURAL (H-2A)

50,009
SEASONAL (H-2B)

80,015
FAMILIES OF
H WORKERS

331,360   TOTAL H VISA WORKERS
AND FAMILIES

PLUS

62,430
INTRACOMPANY
TRANSFEREES (L)

71,782
FAMILIES OF
L WORKERS

146,340
OTHER TEMP.
WORKERS
AND FAMILIES

1,031,631
Permanent immigrant visas

40,320
DIVERSITY

60,986
OTHER

105,528
REFUGEES

680,799
FAMILY-BASED

143,998
EMPLOYMENT-BASED

*Source: Department of State Visa Office and DHS
Office of Immigration Statistics*

Figure 1.8   Visas Issued in 2012[10]

Interactive charts, found online, allow you to bring up concealed data by moving your cursor over particular areas. (If all the data were actually shown on the chart, it would overwhelm the graphic.) For example, locate the following two interactive maps from the *New York Times*.

Go to: Google or Bing

Search terms: "snapshot global migration new york times"

"immigration explorer new york times"

The global migration graphic is a bubble map. Moving your cursor over any particular bubble will bring up a box showing the increase or decrease in immigrants for that particular country. The size of the bubble is proportional to the size of the increase or decrease in immigration.

---

[10] "Visas Issued in 2012." Jill H. Wilson, Brookings Institute, "Immigration Facts: Temporary Foreign Workers" 18 June 2013. Pictogram under paragraph 2. http://www.brookings.edu/research/reports/2013/06/18-temporary-workers-wilson.

The immigration explorer map depicts the immigrant component of every county in the United States. Moving your cursor over any particular county will reveal the number of foreign-born residents of that county, along with its total population in the year 2000. A simple calculation will reveal the percentage of foreign-born residents in each county.

Tables

A table presents numerical data in rows and columns for quick reference. If the writer chooses, tabular information can be converted to graphic information. Charts and graphs are preferable when the writer wants to emphasize a pattern or relationship; tables are preferable when the writer wants to emphasize numbers. While the previous charts are focused on a relatively small number of countries and other variables (such as the declining rate of unauthorized immigration and the educational levels of legal immigrants), this table breaks down immigration into numerous countries and several regions.[11] Note that this table is divided into two sets of data: immigration by world region and immigration by country. While the regional component of the table allows us to focus on the "big picture," in terms of sources of immigrants to the United States, the longer country component allows us to draw finer distinctions among the countries that make up these regions.

A table may contain so much data that you would not want to summarize *all* of it for a particular paper. In this case, you would summarize the *part* of a table that you find useful. Here is a summary drawn from the information from Figure 1.9 focusing primarily on those regions and countries that provide the largest numbers and the smallest numbers of immigrants, but also pointing out other interesting data points. Notice that the summary requires the writer to read closely and discern which information is significant. The table reports raw data and does not speak for itself. Toward the end of the summary the writer, who draws upon data from other sources (such as the bar graph in Figure 1.1) and who also calculates percentages, speculates on the reason for the changing numbers of immigrants from Pakistan and then sums up her overall impression of the data in the table:

> During the years 2010 to 2012, by far the largest number of legal immigrants to the United States came from Asian countries, primarily The People's Republic of China, India, and the Philippines. After Asia, North America—chiefly Mexico, the Caribbean countries, and Central America—provided the greatest number of immigrants. Together, these two regions accounted for more than 73 percent of the more than 1,031,000 immigrants who entered the United States legally in 2012. By contrast, the region of Oceania—made up of Melanesia,

[11] Randall Monger and James Yankay, Table 3: "Legal Permanent Resident Flow by Region and Country of Birth: Fiscal Years 2010 to 2012." *U.S. Legal Permanent Residents 2012*, March 2013, p. 4. Department of Homeland Security, Office of Immigration Statistics Policy Directorate. http://www.dhs.gov/sites/default/files/publications/ois_lpr_fr_2012_2.pdf.

Region and Country of Birth	2012		2011		2010	
	Number	Percent	Number	Percent	Number	Percent
REGION						
Total	**1,031,631**	**100.0**	**1,062,040**	**100.0**	**1,042,625**	**100.0**
Africa	107,241	10.4	100,374	9.5	101,355	9.7
Asia	429,599	41.6	451,593	42.5	422,063	40.5
Europe	81,671	7.9	83,850	7.9	88,801	8.5
North America	327,771	31.8	333,902	31.4	336,553	32.3
Caribbean	127,477	12.4	133,680	12.6	139,951	13.4
Central America	40,675	3.9	43,707	4.1	43,951	4.2
Other North America	159,619	15.5	156,515	14.7	152,651	14.6
Oceania	4,742	0.5	4,980	0.5	5,345	0.5
South America	79,401	7.7	86,096	8.1	87,178	8.4
Unknown	1,206	0.1	1,245	0.1	1,330	0.1
COUNTRY						
Total	**1,031,631**	**100.0**	**1,062,040**	**100.0**	**1,042,625**	**100.0**
Mexico	146,406	14.2	143,446	13.5	139,120	13.3
China, People's Republic	81,784	7.9	87,016	8.2	70,863	6.8
India	66,434	6.4	69,013	6.5	69,162	6.6
Philippines	57,327	5.6	57,011	5.4	58,173	5.6
Dominican Republic	41,566	4.0	46,109	4.3	53,870	5.2
Cuba	32,820	3.2	36,452	3.4	33,573	3.2
Vietnam	28,304	2.7	34,157	3.2	30,632	2.9
Haiti	22,818	2.2	22,111	2.1	22,582	2.2
Colombia	20,931	2.0	22,635	2.1	22,406	2.1

Figure 1.9   Legal Permanent Resident Flow by Region and Country of Birth, Fiscal Years 2010 to 2012[12]

[12] "Legal Permanent Resident Flow by Region and Country of Birth, Fiscal Years 2010 to 2012." Source: U.S. Department of Homeland Security, Computer Linked Application Information Management System (CLAIMS), Legal Immigrant Data, Fiscal Years 2010 to 2012. Dept. of Homeland Security, "U.S. Legal Permanent Residents 2012." p. 4. http://www.dhs.gov/sites/default/files/publications/ois_lpr_fr_2012_2.pdf.

Region and Country of Birth	2012		2011		2010	
	Number	Percent	Number	Percent	Number	Percent
Korea South	20,846	2.0	22,824	2.1	22,227	2.1
Jamaica	20,705	2.0	19,662	1.9	19,825	1.9
Iraq	20,369	2.0	21,133	2.0	19,855	1.9
Burma	17,383	1.7	16,518	1.6	12,925	1.2
El Salvador	16,256	1.6	18,667	1.8	18,806	1.8
Pakistan	14,740	1.4	15,546	1.5	18,258	1.8
Bangladesh	14,705	1.4	16,707	1.6	14,819	1.4
Ethiopia	14,544	1.4	13,793	1.3	14,266	1.4
Nigeria	13,575	1.3	11,824	1.1	13,376	1.3
Canada	12,932	1.3	12,800	1.2	13,328	1.3
Iran	12,916	1.3	14,822	1.4	14,182	1.4
All other countries	354,270	34.3	359,794	33.9	360,377	34.6

(Countries ranked by 2012 LPR flow)

Source: U.S. Department of Homeland Security, Computer Linked Application Information Management System (CLAIMS), Legal Immigrant Data, Fiscal Years 2010 to 2012.

Figure 1.9   Continued

Micronesia, and Polynesia, islands in the tropical Pacific—accounted during the same year for only half of 1 percent of total U.S. legal immigration. Europe in 2012 provided about 8 percent of the total— a far cry from a century ago when this region provided more than 60 percent of total U.S. immigrants.

In terms of individual countries during the period 2010–2012, Mexico, by a huge margin, provided more immigrants to the United States than any other country, with the number rising at a small but steady rate in all three years. As indicated above, China was second after Mexico as the source country of the highest numbers of immigrants, though the pattern in these three years does not indicate a trend: There were 17,000 more Chinese immigrants in 2011 than there were in 2010, but in 2012 the number dropped by more than 5,000. On the other hand, immigration from the Dominican Republic shows a steady drop: from 53,780 in 2010 to 46,109 in 2011 to 42,566 in 2012. Pakistan also provided 20 percent fewer immigrants in 2012 than it did in 2010, a significant decline possibly related to the war against the Taliban and to American military strikes in that country. On the whole, however, during this three-year period, there were no major shifts in total numbers of immigrants, with increases or decreases no greater than 3 percent.

Exercise 1.5

Summarizing Tables

Focus on other data in Figure 1.9 and write a brief summary of your own. Or use a search engine to locate another table on the general topic of immigration and summarize its data.

■ PARAPHRASE

In certain cases, you may want to *paraphrase* rather than summarize material. Writing a paraphrase is similar to writing a summary: It involves recasting a passage into your own words, so it requires your complete understanding of the material. The difference is that while a summary is a shortened version of the original, the paraphrase is approximately the same length as the original.

Why write a paraphrase when you can quote the original? You may decide to offer a paraphrase of material written in language that is dense, abstract, archaic, or possibly confusing.

Let's consider some examples. If you were investigating the ethical concerns relating to the practice of in vitro fertilization, you might conclude that you should read some medical literature. You might reasonably want to hear from the doctors who are themselves developing, performing, and questioning the procedures that you are researching. In professional journals and bulletins, physicians write to one another, not to the general public. They use specialized language. If you wanted to refer to the following technically complex selection, you might need to write a paraphrase.

> [I]t is not only an improvement in the success-rate that participating research scientists hope for but, rather, developments in new fields of research in in-vitro gene diagnosis and in certain circumstances gene therapy. In view of this, the French expert J. F. Mattei has asked the following question: "Are we forced to accept that in vitro fertilization will become one of the most compelling methods of genetic diagnosis?" Evidently, by the introduction of a new law in France and Sweden (1994), this acceptance (albeit with certain restrictions) has already occurred prior to the application of in vitro fertilization reaching a technically mature and clinically applicable phase. This may seem astonishing in view of the question placed by the above-quoted French expert: the idea of embryo production so as to withhold one or two embryos before implantation presupposes a definite "attitude towards eugenics." And to destroy an embryo merely because of its genetic characteristics could signify the reduction of a human life to the sum of its genes. Mattei asks: "In face of a molecular judgment on our lives, is there no possibility for appeal? Will the diagnosis of inherited monogenetic illnesses soon be extended to genetic predisposition for multi-factorial illnesses?"[13]

Like most literature intended for physicians, the language of this selection is somewhat forbidding to nonspecialists, who will have trouble with phrases such as "predisposition for multi-factorial illnesses." As a courtesy to your readers and in an effort to maintain a consistent tone and level in your essay, you could paraphrase this paragraph from a medical newsletter. First, of course, you must understand the meaning of the passage, perhaps no small task. But, having read the material carefully (and consulted a dictionary), you might prepare a paraphrase like this one:

> Writing in *Biomedical Ethics*, Dietmar Mieth reports that fertility specialists today want not only to improve the success rates of their procedures but also to diagnose and repair genetic problems before they implant fertilized eggs. Because the result of the in vitro process is often more fertilized eggs than can be used in a procedure, doctors may examine test-tube embryos for genetic defects and "withhold one or two" before implanting them. The practice of selectively implanting embryos raises concerns about eugenics and the rights of rejected embryos. On what genetic grounds will specialists distinguish flawed from healthy embryos and make a decision whether or not to implant? The appearance of single genes linked directly to

---

[13] Dietmar Mieth, "In Vitro Fertilization: From Medical Reproduction to Genetic Diagnosis," *Biomedical Ethics: Newsletter of the European Network for Biomedical Ethics* 1.1 (1996): 45.

specific, or "monogenetic," illnesses could be grounds for destroying an embryo. More complicated would be genes that predispose people to an illness but in no way guarantee the onset of that illness. Would these genes, which are only one factor in "multi-factorial illnesses," also be labeled undesirable and lead to embryo destruction? Advances in fertility science raise difficult questions. Already, even before techniques of genetic diagnosis are fully developed, legislatures are writing laws governing the practices of fertility clinics.

We begin our paraphrase with the same "not only/but also" logic of the original's first sentence, introducing the concepts of genetic diagnosis and therapy. The next four sentences in the original introduce concerns of a "French expert." Rather than quote Mieth quoting the expert and immediately mentioning new laws in France and Sweden, we decided (first) to explain that in vitro fertilization procedures can give rise to more embryos than needed. We reasoned that nonmedical readers would appreciate our making explicit the background knowledge that the author assumes other physicians possess. Then we quote Mieth briefly ("withhold one or two" embryos) to provide some flavor of the original. We maintain focus on the ethical questions and wait until the end of the paraphrase before mentioning the laws to which Mieth refers. Our paraphrase is roughly the same length as the original, and it conveys the author's concerns about eugenics. As you can see, the paraphrase requires a writer to make decisions about the presentation of material. In many, if not most, cases, you will need to do more than simply "translate" from the original, sentence by sentence, to write your paraphrase.

When you come across a passage that you don't understand, the temptation is to skip over it. Resist this temptation! Use a paraphrase as a tool for explaining to yourself the main ideas of a difficult passage. By translating another writer's language into your own, you clarify what you understand and pinpoint what you don't. The paraphrase therefore becomes a tool for learning the subject.

The following pointers will help you write paraphrases.

How to Write Paraphrases

- Make sure that you understand the source passage.
- Substitute your own words for those of the source passage; look for synonyms that carry the same meaning as the original words.
- Rearrange your own sentences so that they read smoothly. Sentence structure, even sentence order, in the paraphrase need not be based on that of the original. A good paraphrase, like a good summary, should stand by itself.

Paraphrases are generally about the same length as (and sometimes shorter than) the passages on which they are based. But sometimes clarity requires that a paraphrase be longer than a tightly compacted source passage. For example, suppose you wanted to paraphrase this statement by Sigmund Freud:

> We have found out that the distortion in dreams which hinders our understanding of them is due to the activities of a censorship, directed against the unacceptable, unconscious wish-impulses.

If you were to paraphrase this statement (the first sentence in the Tenth Lecture of his *General Introduction to Psychoanalysis*), you might come up with something like this:

> It is difficult to understand dreams because they contain distortions. Freud believed that these distortions arise from our internal censor, which attempts to suppress unconscious and forbidden desires.

Essentially, this paraphrase does little more than break up one sentence into two and somewhat rearrange the sentence structure for clarity.

Like summaries, then, paraphrases are useful devices, both in helping you to understand source material and in enabling you to convey the essence of this source material to your readers. When would you choose to write a summary instead of a paraphrase (or vice versa)? The answer depends on your purpose in presenting the source material. As we've said, summaries are generally based on articles (or sections of articles) or books. Paraphrases are generally based on particularly difficult (or important) paragraphs or sentences. You would seldom paraphrase a long passage, or summarize a short one, unless there were particularly good reasons for doing so. (A lawyer might want to paraphrase several pages of legal language so that his or her client, who is not a lawyer, could understand it.) The purpose of a summary is generally to save your reader time by presenting him or her with a brief version of a lengthy source. The purpose of a paraphrase is generally to clarify a short passage that might otherwise be unclear. Whether you summarize or paraphrase may also depend on the importance of your source. A particularly important source—if it is not too long—may rate a paraphrase. If it is less important or peripheral to your central argument, you may write a summary instead. And, of course, you may choose to summarize only part of your source—the part that is most relevant to the point you are making.

Exercise 1.6

Paraphrasing

Locate and photocopy three relatively complex, but brief, passages from readings currently assigned in your other courses. Paraphrase these passages, making the language more readable and understandable. Attach the photocopies to the paraphrases.

■ QUOTATIONS

A *quotation* records the exact language used by someone in speech or writing. A *summary*, in contrast, is a brief restatement in your own words of what someone else has said or written. And a *paraphrase* is also a restatement, although one that is often as long as the original source. Any paper in which you draw upon sources will rely heavily on quotation, summary, and paraphrase. How do you choose among the three?

Remember that the papers you write should be your own—for the most part: your own language and certainly your own thesis, your own inferences, and your own conclusion. It follows that references to your source materials should be written primarily as summaries and paraphrases, both of which are built on restatement, not quotation. You will use summaries when you need a *brief* restatement and paraphrases, which provide more explicit detail than summaries, when you need to follow the development of a source closely. When you quote too much, you risk losing ownership of your work: More easily than you might think, your voice can be drowned out by the voices of those you've quoted. So *use quotation sparingly,* as you would a pungent spice.

Nevertheless, quoting just the right source at the right time can significantly improve your papers. The trick is to know when and how to use quotations.

Quotations can be direct or indirect. A *direct* quotation is one in which you record precisely the language of another. An *indirect* quotation is one in which you report what someone has said without repeating the words exactly as spoken (or written):

Direct quotation: Franklin D. Roosevelt said, "The only thing we have to fear is fear itself."

Indirect quotation: Franklin D. Roosevelt said that we have nothing to fear but fear itself.

The language in a direct quotation, which is indicated by a pair of quotation marks (" "), must be faithful to the wording of the original passage. When using an indirect quotation, you have the liberty of changing words (although not changing meaning). For both direct and indirect quotations, *you must credit your sources,* naming them either in (or close to) the sentence that includes the quotation or in a parenthetical citation. (See Chapter 7, pp. 274–280, for specific rules on citing sources properly.)

Choosing Quotations

You'll find that using quotations can be particularly helpful in several situations.

Quoting Memorable Language

You should quote when the source material is worded so eloquently or powerfully that to summarize or paraphrase it would be to sacrifice much of the impact and significance of the meaning. Here, for example, is the historian

John Keegan describing how France, Germany, Austria, and Russia slid inexorably in 1914 into the cataclysm of World War I:

> In the event, the states of Europe proceeded, as if in a dead march and a dialogue of the deaf, to the destruction of their continent and its civilization.

No paraphrase could do justice to the power of Keegan's words as they appear in his book *The First World War* (1998). You would certainly want to quote them in any paper dealing with the origins of this conflict.

When to Quote

- Use quotations when another writer's language is particularly memorable and will add interest and liveliness to your paper.
- Use quotations when another writer's language is so clear and economical that to make the same point in your own words would, by comparison, be ineffective.
- Use quotations when you want the solid reputation of a source to lend authority and credibility to your own writing.

Quoting Clear and Concise Language

You should quote a source when its language is particularly clear and economical—when your language, by contrast, would be wordy. Read this passage from a biology text by Patricia Curtis:

> The honeybee colony, which usually has a population of 30,000 to 40,000 workers, differs from that of the bumblebee and many other social bees or wasps in that it survives the winter. This means that the bees must stay warm despite the cold. Like other bees, the isolated honeybee cannot fly if the temperature falls below 10°C (50°F) and cannot walk if the temperature is below 7°C (45°F). Within the wintering hive, bees maintain their temperature by clustering together in a dense ball; the lower the temperature, the denser the cluster. The clustered bees produce heat by constant muscular movements of their wings, legs, and abdomens. In very cold weather, the bees on the outside of the cluster keep moving toward the center, while those in the core of the cluster move to the colder outside periphery. The entire cluster moves slowly about on the combs, eating the stored honey from the combs as it moves.[14]

A summary of this paragraph might read:

> Honeybees, unlike many other varieties of bee, are able to live through the winter by "clustering together in a dense ball" for body warmth.

---

[14] Patricia Curtis, "Winter Organization," *Biology*, 2nd ed. (New York: Worth, 1976): 822–23.

A paraphrase of the same passage would be considerably more detailed:

> Honeybees, unlike many other varieties of bee (such as bumblebees), are able to live through the winter. The 30,000 to 40,000 bees within a honeybee hive could not, individually, move about in cold winter temperatures. But when "clustering together in a dense ball," the bees generate heat by constantly moving their body parts. The cluster also moves slowly about the hive, those on the periphery of the cluster moving into the center, those in the center moving to the periphery, and all eating honey stored in the combs. This nutrition, in addition to the heat generated by the cluster, enables the honeybee to survive the cold winter months.

In both the summary and the paraphrase we've quoted Curtis's "clustering together in a dense ball," a phrase that lies at the heart of her description of wintering honeybees. For us to describe this clustering in any language other than Curtis's would be pointless when her description is admirably brief and precise.

Quoting Authoritative Language

You should use quotations that lend authority to your work. When quoting an expert or a prominent political, artistic, or historical figure, you elevate your own work by placing it in esteemed company. Quote respected figures to establish background information in a paper, and your readers will tend to perceive that information as reliable. Quote the opinions of respected figures to endorse a statement that you've made, and your statement becomes more credible to your readers. Here, in a discussion of space flight, the writer David Chandler refers to a physicist and a physicist-astronaut:

> A few scientists—notably James Van Allen, discoverer of the Earth's radiation belts—have decried the expense of the manned space program and called for an almost exclusive concentration on unmanned scientific exploration instead, saying this would be far more cost-effective.
>
> Other space scientists dispute that idea. Joseph Allen, physicist and former shuttle astronaut, says, "It seems to be argued that one takes away from the other. But before there was a manned space program, the funding on space science was zero. Now it's about $500 million a year."

In the first paragraph Chandler has either summarized or used an indirect quotation to incorporate remarks made by James Van Allen into the discussion on space flight. In the second paragraph, Chandler directly quotes Joseph Allen. Both quotations, indirect and direct, lend authority and legitimacy to the article, for both James Van Allen and Joseph Allen are experts on the subject of space flight. Note that Chandler provides brief but effective biographies of his sources, identifying each one, so that their qualifications to speak on the subject are known to all:

James Van Allen, *discoverer of the Earth's radiation belts* ...
Joseph Allen, *physicist and former shuttle astronaut* ...

The phrases in italics are *appositives*. Their function is to rename the nouns they follow by providing explicit, identifying detail. Any information about a person that can be expressed in the following sentence pattern can be made into an appositive phrase:

James Van Allen is the *discoverer of the Earth's radiation belts*.
He has decried the expense of the manned space program.

Sentence with an appositive:

James Van Allen, *discoverer of the Earth's radiation belts,* has decried the expense of the manned space program.

Appositives (in the example above, "discoverer of the Earth's radiation belts") efficiently incorporate identifying information about the authors you quote, while adding variety to the structure of your sentences.

Incorporating Quotations into Your Sentences

Quoting Only the Part of a Sentence or Paragraph That You Need

We've said that a writer selects passages for quotation that are especially vivid, memorable, concise, or authoritative. Now put these principles into practice. Suppose that while conducting research on college sports, you've come across the following, written by Robert Hutchins, former president of the University of Chicago:

> If athleticism is bad for students, players, alumni, and the public, it is even worse for the colleges and universities themselves. They want to be educational institutions, but they can't. The story of the famous halfback whose only regret, when he bade his coach farewell, was that he hadn't learned to read and write is probably exaggerated. But we must admit that pressure from trustees, graduates, "friends," presidents, and even professors has tended to relax academic standards. These gentry often overlook the fact that a college should not be interested in a fullback who is a half-wit. Recruiting, subsidizing and the double educational standard cannot exist without the knowledge and the tacit approval, at least, of the colleges and universities themselves. Certain institutions encourage susceptible professors to be nice to athletes now admitted by paying them for serving as "faculty representatives" on the college athletic board.[15]

---

[15] Robert Hutchins, "Gate Receipts and Glory," *Saturday Evening Post* 3 Dec. 1983: 38.

Suppose that in this paragraph you find a gem, a sentence with striking language that will enliven your discussion:

> These gentry often overlook the fact that a college should not be interested in a fullback who is a half-wit.

Incorporating the Quotation into the Flow of Your Own Sentence

Once you've selected the passage you want to quote, you need to work the material into your paper in as natural and fluid a manner as possible. Here's how we would quote Hutchins:

> Robert Hutchins, former president of the University of Chicago, asserts that "a college should not be interested in a fullback who is a half-wit."

Note that we've used an appositive to identify Hutchins. And we've used only the part of the paragraph—a single clause—that we thought memorable enough to quote directly.

Avoiding Freestanding Quotations

A quoted sentence should never stand by itself, as in the following example:

> Various people associated with the university admit that the pressures of athleticism have caused a relaxation of standards. "These gentry often overlook the fact that a college should not be interested in a fullback who is a half-wit." But this kind of thinking is bad for the university and even worse for the athletes.

Even if it were followed by a parenthetical citation, a freestanding quotation would be jarring to the reader. You need to introduce the quotation with a *signal phrase* that attributes the source, not in a parenthetical citation but in some other part of the sentence—beginning, middle, or end. Thus, you could write:

> As Robert Hutchins notes, "These gentry often overlook the fact that a college should not be interested in a fullback who is a half-wit."

Here's a variation with the signal phrase in the middle:

> "These gentry," asserts Robert Hutchins, "often overlook the fact that a college should not be interested in a fullback who is a half-wit."

Another alternative is to introduce a sentence-long quotation with a colon:

> But Robert Hutchins disagrees: "These gentry often overlook the fact that a college should not be interested in a fullback who is a half-wit."

Use colons also to introduce indented quotations (as when we introduce long quotations in this chapter).

When attributing sources in signal phrases, try to vary the standard *states, writes, says,* and so on. Stronger verbs you might consider are: *asserts, argues, maintains, insists, asks,* and even *wonders.*

Exercise 1.7

Incorporating Quotations

Return to the article "The Baby in the Well" by Paul Bloom (pp. 8–14). Find sentences that you think make interesting points. Imagine you want to use these points in a paper you're writing on empathy. Write five different sentences that use a variety of the techniques discussed thus far to incorporate whole sentences as well as phrases from Bloom's article.

Using Ellipses

Using quotations becomes somewhat complicated when you want to quote the beginning and end of a passage but not its middle. Here's part of a paragraph from Thoreau's *Walden:*

> To read well, that is to read true books in a true spirit, is a noble exercise, and one that will task the reader more than any exercise which the customs of the day esteem. It requires a training such as the athletes underwent, the steady intention almost of the whole life to this object. Books must be read as deliberately and reservedly as they were written.[16]

And here is how we can use this material in a quotation:

> Reading well is hard work, writes Henry David Thoreau in *Walden,* "that will task the reader more than any exercise which the customs of the day esteem.... Books must be read as deliberately and reservedly as they were written."

Whenever you quote a sentence but delete words from it, as we have done above, indicate this deletion to the reader with three spaced periods—called an "ellipsis"— in the sentence at the point of deletion. The rationale for using an ellipsis mark is that a direct quotation must be reproduced *exactly* as it was written or spoken. When writers delete or change any part of the quoted material, readers must be alerted so they don't think the changes were part of the original. When deleting an entire sentence or sentences from a quoted paragraph, as in the example above, end the sentence you have quoted with a period, place the ellipsis, and continue the quotation.

---

[16] Henry David Thoreau, *Walden* (New York: Signet Classic, 1960): 72.

If you are deleting the middle of a single sentence, use an ellipsis in place of the deleted words:

> "To read well...is a noble exercise, and one that will task the reader more than any exercise which the customs of the day esteem."

If you are deleting material from the end of one sentence through to the beginning of another sentence, add a sentence period before the ellipsis:

> "It requires a training such as the athletes underwent....Books must be read as deliberately and reservedly as they were written."

If you begin your quotation of an author in the middle of his or her sentence, you need not indicate deleted words with an ellipsis. Be sure, however, that the syntax of the quotation fits smoothly with the syntax of your sentence:

> Reading "is a noble exercise," writes Henry David Thoreau.

Using Brackets to Add or Substitute Words

Use brackets whenever you need to add or substitute words in a quoted sentence. The brackets indicate to the reader a word or phrase that does not appear in the original passage but that you have inserted to prevent confusion. For example, when a pronoun's antecedent would be unclear to readers, delete the pronoun from the sentence and substitute an identifying word or phrase in brackets. When you make such a substitution, no ellipsis mark is needed. Assume that you wish to quote either of the underlined sentences in the following passage by Jane Yolen:

> Golden Press's *Walt Disney's Cinderella* set the new pattern for America's Cinderella. This book's text is coy and condescending. (Sample: "And her best friends of all were—guess who—the mice!") The illustrations are poor cartoons. And Cinderella herself is a disaster. She cowers as her sisters rip her homemade ball gown to shreds. (Not even homemade by Cinderella, but by the mice and birds.) She answers her stepmother with whines and pleadings. She is a sorry excuse for a heroine, pitiable and useless. She cannot perform even a simple action to save herself, though she is warned by her friends, the mice. She does not hear them because she is "off in a world of dreams." Cinderella begs, she whimpers, and at last has to be rescued by—guess who—the mice![17]

In quoting one of these sentences, you would need to identify to whom the pronoun *she* refers. You can do this inside the quotation by using brackets:

> Jane Yolen believes that "[Cinderella] is a sorry excuse for a heroine, pitiable and useless."

---

[17] Jane Yolen, "America's 'Cinderella,'" *Children's Literature in Education* 8 (1977): 22.

When the pronoun begins the sentence to be quoted, you can identify the pronoun outside the quotation and begin quoting your source one word later:

> Jane Yolen believes that in the Golden Press version, Cinderella "is a sorry excuse for a heroine, pitiable and useless."

When to Summarize, Paraphrase, and Quote

SUMMARIZE:

- To present main points of a lengthy passage (article or book)
- To condense peripheral points necessary to discussion

PARAPHRASE:

- To clarify a short passage
- To emphasize main points

QUOTE:

- To capture another writer's particularly memorable language
- To capture another writer's clearly and economically stated language
- To lend authority and credibility to your own writing

Here's another example of a case where the pronoun needing identification occurs in the middle of the sentence to be quoted. Newspaper reporters must use brackets when quoting a source, who in an interview might say this:

> After the fire they did not return to the station house for three hours.

If the reporter wants to use this sentence in an article, he or she needs to identify the pronoun:

> An official from City Hall, speaking on the condition that he not be identified, said, "After the fire [the officers] did not return to the station house for three hours."

You will also need to add bracketed information to a quoted sentence when a reference essential to the sentence's meaning is implied but not stated directly. Read the following paragraph from Walter Isaacson's biography of Albert Einstein, *Einstein: His Life and Universe*:

> Newton had bequeathed to Einstein a universe in which time had an absolute existence that tick-tocked along independent of objects

and observers, and in which space likewise had an absolute existence. Gravity was thought to be a force that masses exerted on one another rather mysteriously across empty space. <u>Within this framework, objects obeyed mechanical laws that had proved remarkably accurate—almost perfect—in explaining everything from the orbits of the planets, to the diffusion of gases, to the jiggling of molecules, to the propagation of sound (though not light) waves.</u>

If you wanted to quote only the underlined sentence above, you would need to provide readers with a bracketed explanation; otherwise, the phrase "this framework" would be unclear. Here is how you would manage the quotation:

> According to Walter Isaacson, Newton's universe was extremely regular and predictable:
>> Within this framework [that time and space exist independently of their observation and that gravity results from masses exerting a remote attraction on one another], objects obeyed mechanical laws that had proved remarkably accurate—almost perfect—in explaining everything from the orbits of the planets, to the diffusion of gases, to the jiggling of molecules, to the propagation of sound (though not light) waves. (223)

Incorporating Quotations into Your Sentences

- **Quote only the part of a sentence or paragraph that you need.** Use no more of the writer's language than necessary to make or reinforce your point.
- **Incorporate the quotation into the flow of your own sentence.** The quotation must fit, both syntactically and stylistically, into your surrounding language.
- **Avoid freestanding quotations.** A quoted sentence should never stand by itself. Use a *signal phrase*—at the beginning, the middle, or the end of the sentence—to attribute the source of the quotation.
- **Use ellipsis marks.** Indicate deleted language in the middle of a quoted sentence with ellipsis marks. Deleted language at the beginning or end of a sentence generally does not require ellipsis marks.
- **Use brackets to add or substitute words.** Use brackets to add or substitute words in a quoted sentence when the meaning of the quotation would otherwise be unclear—for example, when the antecedent of a quoted pronoun is ambiguous.

Exercise 1.8

Using Brackets

Write your own sentences incorporating the following quotations. Use brackets to clarify information that isn't clear outside its original context—and refer to the original sources to remind yourself of this context.

From the David Chandler paragraph on James Van Allen (p. 43):

a.   Other space scientists *dispute that idea.*

b.   Now *it's about $500 million a year.*

From the Jane Yolen excerpt on Cinderella (p. 47):

a.   *This book's* text is coy and condescending.

b.   *She* cannot perform even a simple action to save herself, though she is warned by her friends, the mice.

c.   She does not hear *them* because she is "off in a world of dreams."

Remember that when you quote the work of another, you are obligated to credit—or cite—the author's work properly; otherwise, you may be guilty of plagiarism. See pages 274–280 for guidance on citing sources.

■ AVOIDING PLAGIARISM

Plagiarism is generally defined as the attempt to pass off the work of another as one's own. Whether born out of calculation or desperation, plagiarism is the least tolerated offense in the academic world. The fact that most plagiarism is unintentional—arising from an ignorance of the conventions rather than deceitfulness—makes no difference to many professors.

The ease of cutting and pasting whole blocks of text from Web sources into one's own paper makes it tempting for some to take the easy way out and avoid doing their own research and writing. But, apart from the serious ethical issues involved, the same technology that makes such acts possible also makes it possible for instructors to detect them. Software marketed to instructors allows them to conduct Web searches, using suspicious phrases as keywords. The results often provide irrefutable evidence of plagiarism.

Of course, plagiarism is not confined to students. Recent years have seen a number of high-profile cases—some of them reaching the front pages of newspapers—of well-known scholars who were shown to have copied passages from sources into their own book manuscripts without proper attribution. In some cases, the scholars maintained that these appropriations were simply a matter of carelessness, that in the press and volume of work, they had lost track of which words were theirs and which were the words of their sources. But such excuses sounded hollow: These careless acts inevitably embarrassed the scholars professionally, tarnished their otherwise fine work and reputations, and disappointed their many admirers.

You can avoid plagiarism and charges of plagiarism by following the basic rules provided on page 52.

Following is a passage from an article by Richard Rovere on Senator Joseph P. McCarthy, along with several student versions of the ideas represented.

> McCarthy never seemed to believe in himself or in anything he had said. He knew that Communists were not in charge of American foreign policy. He knew that they weren't running the United States Army. He knew that he had spent five years looking for Communists in the government and that—although some must certainly have been there, since Communists had turned up in practically every other major government in the world—he hadn't come up with even one.[18]

One student version of this passage reads:

> McCarthy never believed in himself or in anything he had said. He knew that Communists were not in charge of American foreign policy and weren't running the United States Army. He knew that he had spent five years looking for Communists in the government, and although there must certainly have been some there, since Communists were in practically every other major government in the world, he hadn't come up with even one.

Clearly, this is intentional plagiarism. The student has copied the original passage almost word for word.

Here is another version of the same passage:

> McCarthy knew that Communists were not running foreign policy or the Army. He also knew that although there must have been some Communists in the government, he hadn't found a single one, even though he had spent five years looking.

This student has attempted to put the ideas into her own words, but both the wording and the sentence structure are so heavily dependent on the original passage that even if it *were* cited, most professors would consider it plagiarism.

In the following version, the student has sufficiently changed the wording and sentence structure, and she uses a *signal phrase* (a phrase used to introduce a quotation or paraphrase, signaling to the reader that the words to follow come from someone else) to properly credit the information to Rovere so that there is no question of plagiarism:

> According to Richard Rovere, McCarthy was fully aware that Communists were running neither the government nor the Army. He also knew that he hadn't found a single Communist in government, even after a lengthy search (192).

---

[18] Richard Rovere, "The Most Gifted and Successful Demagogue This Country Has Ever Known," *New York Times Magazine*, 30 Apr. 1967.

And although this is not a matter of plagiarism, as noted above, it's essential to quote accurately. You are not permitted to change any part of a quotation or to omit any part of it without using brackets or ellipses.

Rules for Avoiding Plagiarism

- Cite *all* quoted material and *all* summarized and paraphrased material, unless the information is common knowledge (e.g., the Civil War was fought from 1861 to 1865).
- Make sure that both the *wording* and the *sentence structure* of your summaries and paraphrases are substantially your own.

WRITING ASSIGNMENT: SUMMARY

Read the following article by Marcia Wood, which originally appeared in the government periodical *Agricultural Research*. Write a summary of the article, following the directions in this chapter for dividing the article into sections, for writing a one-sentence summary of each section, and then for joining section summaries with a thesis. Prepare for the summary by making notes in the margins. You may find it useful to recall that well-written pieces often telegraph clues to their own structure as a device for assisting readers. Such clues can be helpful when preparing a summary. Your finished product should be the result of two or more drafts.

Note: Additional summary assignments will be found in Chapter 8, "Practicing Academic Writing," focusing on ethical dilemmas.

BREAKFAST HELPS KIDS HANDLE BASIC MATH, STUDY SUGGESTS

Marcia Wood

Even people who know a lot about the human brain may be impressed by the extent to which eating a single breakfast—or skipping it—can influence a child's ability to solve math problems.

Just ask scientist Terry Pivik, whose research with 81 children has shown that those who ate breakfast were better able to tackle dozens of math problems in rapid-fire succession than peers who didn't have a morning meal.

As a psychophysiologist, Pivik studies how our brains influence our behavior. Based in Little Rock, Arkansas, he directs the Brain Function Laboratory at the Agricultural Research Service-funded Arkansas Children's Nutrition Center and is a research professor in pediatrics at the University of Arkansas for Medical Sciences.

In his study of healthy 8- to 11-year-old volunteers, Pivik used EEG (electroencephalographic) sensors to harmlessly record electrical activity generated in regions of children's brains involved in solving math problems. The sensors were fitted into a soft cap that the youngsters wore as they viewed simple math problems presented to them on a computer monitor, calculated the answer in their heads, and then quickly selected one answer from among three onscreen choices.

In all, the kids had a little more than 1 second to process each problem.

Each child took two math tests in the morning. Half of the children ate breakfast during a break in the testing; the others did not.

5   Factors that could skew results were carefully controlled. For example, to prevent sleepiness, a watchful nurse and a wristband-mounted monitor that the volunteers wore ensured that each child had a full 8 hours of rest the night before the tests.

EEG data showed that "children who skipped breakfast had to exert more effort to perform the mental math that the tests required and to stay focused on the task at hand," says Pivik. "In contrast, those who ate the breakfast that we provided used less mental effort to solve the problems, stayed more focused on the tests, and improved their scores in the post-breakfast test."

Previous studies by researchers elsewhere have shown an association between nutrition and academic performance. However, the design of the Arkansas study had some important differences. "We carefully controlled when the kids either had breakfast or skipped it, and what they ate," Pivik explains. "To the best of our knowledge, this is the first published study, with kids of this age group, that both controlled the morning meal and used EEG technology to monitor brain activity while the children were processing mathematical information."

Pivik and nutrition center colleagues Yuyuan Gu and Kevin B. Tennal, along with Stephen D. Chapman—formerly at the center—published their findings in a peer-reviewed article in *Physiology & Behavior* in 2012.

The research is part of ongoing investigations in Pivik's lab to discover more about how to nourish the brain and enhance children's ability to learn. "There's much more to uncover about the role that nutrition plays in influencing the neural networks that kids engage when they're doing mental arithmetic," Pivik says. "We're addressing this knowledge gap because math skills are so critical in today's world."

2 ■ Critical Reading and Critique

■ CRITICAL READING

When writing papers in college, you are often called on to respond critically to source materials. Critical reading requires the abilities to both summarize and evaluate a presentation. As you have seen in Chapter 1, a *summary* is a brief restatement in your own words of the content of a passage. An *evaluation* is a more ambitious undertaking. In your college work, you read to gain and *use* new information. But because sources are not equally valid or equally useful, you must learn to distinguish critically among them by evaluating them.

There is no ready-made formula for determining validity. Critical reading and its written equivalent—the *critique*—require discernment, sensitivity, imagination, knowledge of the subject, and, above all, willingness to become involved in what you read. These skills are developed only through repeated practice. But you must begin somewhere, and so we recommend you start by posing two broad questions about passages, articles, and books that you read: (1) To what extent does the author succeed in his or her purpose? (2) To what extent do you agree with the author?

Question 1: To What Extent Does the Author Succeed in His or Her Purpose?

All critical reading *begins with an accurate summary*. Before attempting an evaluation, you must be able to locate an author's thesis and identify the selection's content and structure. You must understand the author's *purpose*. Authors write to inform, to persuade, and to entertain. A given piece may be primarily *informative* (a summary of the research on cloning), primarily *persuasive* (an argument on what the government should do to alleviate homelessness), or primarily *entertaining* (a play about the frustrations of young lovers). Or it may be all three (as in John Steinbeck's novel *The Grapes of Wrath*, about migrant workers during the Great Depression). Sometimes authors are not fully conscious of their purpose. Sometimes their purpose changes as they write. Also, multiple purposes can overlap: A piece of writing may need to inform the reader about an issue in order to make a persuasive point. But if the finished piece is coherent, it will have a primary reason for having been written, and it should be apparent that the author is attempting primarily to inform, persuade, or entertain a particular audience.

To identify this primary reason—this purpose—is your first job as a critical reader. Your next job is to determine how successful the author has been in achieving this objective.

Where Do We Find Written Critiques?

Here are just a few of the types of writing that involve critique:

ACADEMIC WRITING

- **Research papers** critique sources in order to establish their usefulness.
- **Position papers** stake out a position by critiquing other positions.
- **Book reviews** combine summary with critique.
- **Essay exams** demonstrate understanding of course material by critiquing it.

WORKPLACE WRITING

- **Legal briefs and legal arguments** critique previous arguments made or anticipated by opposing counsel.
- **Business plans and proposals** critique other less cost-effective, efficient, or reasonable approaches.
- **Policy briefs** communicate strengths and weaknesses of policies and legislation through critique.

As a critical reader, you bring various criteria, or standards of judgment, to bear when you read pieces intended to inform, persuade, or entertain.

Writing to Inform

A piece intended to inform will provide definitions, describe or report on a process, recount a story, give historical background, and/or provide facts and figures. An informational piece responds to questions such as:

What (or who) is _____?

How does _____ work?

What is the controversy or problem about?

What happened?

How and why did it happen?

What were the results?

What are the arguments for and against _____?

To the extent that an author answers these and related questions and that the answers are a matter of verifiable record (you could check for accuracy if you had the time and inclination), the selection is intended to inform. Having identified such an intention, you can organize your response by considering three other criteria: accuracy, significance, and fair interpretation of information.

Evaluating Informative Writing

Accuracy of Information   If you are going to use any of the information presented, you must be satisfied that it is trustworthy. One of your responsibilities as a critical reader, then, is to find out if the information is accurate. This means you should check facts against other sources. Government publications are often good resources for verifying facts about political legislation, population data, crime statistics, and the like. You can also search key terms in library databases and on the Web. Since material on the Web is essentially self-published, however, you must be especially vigilant in assessing its legitimacy. A wealth of useful information is now available on the Internet—as are distorted "facts," unsupported opinion, and hidden agendas.

Significance of Information   One useful question that you can put to a reading is "So what?" In the case of selections that attempt to inform, you may reasonably wonder whether the information makes a difference. What can the reader gain from this information? How is knowledge advanced by the publication of this material? Is the information of importance to you or to others in a particular audience? Why or why not?

Fair Interpretation of Information   At times you will read reports whose sole purpose is to relate raw data or information. In these cases, you will build your response on Question 1, introduced on page 54: To what extent does the author succeed in his or her purpose? More frequently, once an author has presented information, he or she will attempt to evaluate or interpret it—which is only reasonable, since information that has not been evaluated or interpreted is of little use. One of your tasks as a critical reader is to make a distinction between the author's presentation of facts and figures and his or her attempts to evaluate them. Watch for shifts from straightforward descriptions of factual information ("20 percent of the population") to assertions about what this information means ("a *mere* 20 percent of the population"), what its implications are, and so on. Pay attention to whether the logic with which the author connects interpretation with facts is sound. You may find that the information is valuable but the interpretation is not. Perhaps the author's conclusions are not justified. Could you offer a contrary explanation for the same facts? Does more information need to be gathered before firm conclusions can be drawn? Why?

Writing to Persuade

Writing is frequently intended to persuade—that is, to influence the reader's thinking. To make a persuasive case, the writer must begin with an assertion that is arguable, some statement about which reasonable people could disagree. Such an assertion, when it serves as the essential organizing principle of the article or book, is called a *thesis*. Here are two examples:

> Because they do not speak English, many children in this affluent land are being denied their fundamental right to equal educational opportunity.

> Bilingual education, which has been stridently promoted by a small group of activists with their own agenda, is detrimental to the very students it is supposed to serve.

Thesis statements such as these—and the subsequent assertions used to help support them—represent conclusions that authors have drawn as a result of researching and thinking about an issue. You go through the same process yourself when you write persuasive papers or critiques. And just as you are entitled to evaluate critically the assertions of authors you read, so your professors—and other students—are entitled to evaluate *your* assertions, whether they be written arguments or comments made in class discussion.

Keep in mind that writers organize arguments by arranging evidence to support one conclusion and to oppose (or dismiss) another. You can assess the validity of an argument and its conclusion by determining whether the author has (1) clearly defined key terms, (2) used information fairly, and (3) argued logically and not fallaciously (see pp. 61–65).

Exercise 2.1

Informative and Persuasive Thesis Statements

With a partner from your class, identify at least one informative and one persuasive thesis statement from two passages of your own choosing. Photocopy these passages and highlight the statements you have selected.

As an alternative, and also working with a partner, write one informative and one persuasive thesis statement for *three* of the topics listed at the end of this exercise. For example, for the topic of prayer in schools, your informative thesis statement could read:

> Both advocates and opponents of school prayer frame their position as a matter of freedom.

Your persuasive thesis statement might be worded:

> As long as schools don't dictate what kinds of prayers students should say, then school prayer should be allowed and even encouraged.

Don't worry about taking a position that you agree with or feel you could support; this exercise doesn't require that you write an essay. The topics:

school prayer

gun control

immigration

stem cell research

grammar instruction in English class

violent lyrics in music

teaching computer skills in primary schools

curfews in college dormitories

course registration procedures

Evaluating Persuasive Writing

Read the argument that follows on the cancellation of the National Aeronautics and Space Administration's lunar program. We will illustrate our discussion on defining terms, using information fairly, and arguing logically by referring to Charles Krauthammer's argument, which appeared as an op-ed in the *Washington Post* on July 17, 2009. The model critique that follows these illustrations will be based on this same argument.

THE MOON WE LEFT BEHIND *

Charles Krauthammer

Michael Crichton once wrote that if you told a physicist in 1899 that within a hundred years humankind would, among other wonders (nukes, commercial airlines), "travel to the moon, and then lose interest...the physicist would almost certainly pronounce you mad." In 2000, I quoted these lines expressing Crichton's incredulity at America's abandonment of the moon. It is now 2009 and the moon recedes ever further.

Next week marks the 40th anniversary of the first moon landing. We say we will return in 2020. But that promise was made by a previous president, and this president [Obama] has defined himself as the antimatter to George Bush. Moreover, for all of Barack Obama's Kennedyesque qualities, he has expressed none of Kennedy's enthusiasm for human space exploration.

So with the Apollo moon program long gone, and with Constellation,[1] its supposed successor, still little more than a hope, we remain in retreat from space. Astonishing. After countless millennia of gazing and dreaming, we finally got off the ground at Kitty Hawk in 1903. Within 66 years, a nanosecond in human history, we'd landed on the moon. Then five more landings, 10 more moonwalkers and, in the decades since, nothing.

To be more precise: almost 40 years spent in low Earth orbit studying, well, zero-G nausea and sundry cosmic mysteries. We've done it with the most beautiful, intricate, complicated—and ultimately, hopelessly impractical—machine ever built by man: the space shuttle. We turned this magnificent bird into a truck for hauling goods and people to a tinkertoy we call the international space station, itself created in a fit of post-Cold War internationalist absentmindedness as a place where people of differing nationality can sing "Kumbaya" while weightless.

[1]Constellation was a NASA human spaceflight program designed to develop post–space shuttle vehicles capable of traveling to the moon and perhaps to Mars. Authorized in 2005, the program was canceled by President Obama in 2010.

5   The shuttle is now too dangerous, too fragile and too expensive. Seven more flights and then it is retired, going—like the Spruce Goose[2] and the Concorde[3]— into the Museum of Things Too Beautiful and Complicated to Survive.

America's manned space program is in shambles. Fourteen months from today, for the first time since 1962, the United States will be incapable not just of sending a man to the moon but of sending anyone into Earth orbit. We'll be totally grounded. We'll have to beg a ride from the Russians or perhaps even the Chinese.

So what, you say? Don't we have problems here on Earth? Oh, please. Poverty and disease and social ills will always be with us. If we'd waited for them to be rectified before venturing out, we'd still be living in caves.

Yes, we have a financial crisis. No one's asking for a crash Manhattan Project. All we need is sufficient funding from the hundreds of billions being showered from Washington—"stimulus" monies that, unlike Eisenhower's interstate highway system or Kennedy's Apollo program, will leave behind not a trace on our country or our consciousness—to build Constellation and get us back to Earth orbit and the moon a half-century after the original landing.

Why do it? It's not for practicality. We didn't go to the moon to spin off cooling suits and freeze-dried fruit. Any technological return is a bonus, not a reason. We go for the wonder and glory of it. Or, to put it less grandly, for its immense possibilities. We choose to do such things, said JFK, "not because they are easy, but because they are hard." And when you do such magnificently hard things—send sailing a Ferdinand Magellan or a Neil Armstrong—you open new human possibility in ways utterly unpredictable.

10   The greatest example? Who could have predicted that the moon voyages would create the most potent impetus to—and symbol of—environmental consciousness here on Earth: Earthrise, the now iconic Blue Planet photograph brought back by Apollo 8?

Ironically, that new consciousness about the uniqueness and fragility of Earth focused contemporary imagination away from space and back to Earth. We are now deep into that hyper-terrestrial phase, the age of iPod and Facebook, of social networking and eco-consciousness.

But look up from your BlackBerry one night. That is the moon. On it are exactly 12 sets of human footprints—untouched, unchanged, abandoned. For the first time in history, the moon is not just a mystery and a muse, but a nightly rebuke. A vigorous young president once summoned us to this new frontier, calling the voyage "the most hazardous and dangerous and greatest adventure on which man has ever embarked." And so we did it. We came. We saw. Then we retreated.

How could we?

---

[2] Spruce Goose was the informal name bestowed by critics on the H4 Hercules, a heavy transport aircraft designed and built during World War II by the Hughes Aircraft Company. Built almost entirely of birch (not spruce) because of wartime restrictions on war materials, the aircraft boasted the largest height and wingspan of any aircraft in history. Only one prototype was built, and the aircraft made only one flight, on November 2, 1947. It is currently housed at the Evergreen Aviation Museum in McMinnville, Oregon.

[3] Admired for its elegant design as well as its speed, the Concorde was a supersonic passenger airliner built by a British-French consortium. It was first flown in 1969, entered service in 1976 (with regular flights to and from London, Paris, Washington, and New York), and was retired in 2003, a casualty of economic pressures. Only twenty Concordes were built.

Critical Reading Practice

Look back at the Critical Reading for Summary box on pages 5–6 of Chapter 1. Use each of the guidelines listed there to examine the essay by Charles Krauthammer. Note in the margins of the selection, or on a separate sheet of paper, the essay's main point, subpoints, and use of examples.

Persuasive Strategies

Clearly Defined Terms   The validity of an argument depends to some degree on how carefully an author has defined key terms. Take the assertion, for example, that American society must be grounded in "family values." Just what do people who use this phrase mean by it? The validity of their argument depends on whether they and their readers agree on a definition of "family values"—as well as what it means to be "grounded in" family values. If an author writes that in the recent past, "America's elites accepted as a matter of course that a free society can sustain itself only through virtue and temperance in the people,"[4] readers need to know what exactly the author means by "elites" and by "virtue and temperance" before they can assess the validity of the argument. In such cases, the success of the argument—its ability to persuade—hinges on the definition of a term. So, in responding to an argument, be sure you (and the author) are clear on what exactly is being argued. Unless you are, no informed response is possible.

Note that in addition to their *denotative* meaning (their specific or literal meaning), many words carry a *connotative* meaning (their suggestive, associative, or emotional meaning). For example, the denotative meaning of "home" is simply the house or apartment where one lives. But the connotative meaning—with its associations of family, belongingness, refuge, safety, and familiarity—adds a significant emotional component to this literal meaning. (See more on connotation in "Emotionally Loaded Terms," pp. 61–62.)

In the course of his argument, Krauthammer writes of "America's abandonment of the moon" and of the fact that we have "retreated" from lunar exploration. Consider the words "abandon" and "retreat." What do these words mean to you? Look them up in a dictionary for precise definitions (note all possible meanings provided). In what contexts are we most likely to see these words used? What emotional meaning and significance do they generally carry? For example, what do we usually think of people who abandon a marriage or military units that retreat? To what extent does it appear to you that Krauthammer is using these words in accordance with one or more of their dictionary definitions, their denotations? To what extent does the force of his argument also depend upon the power of these words' connotative meanings?

---

[4] Charles Murray, "The Coming White Underclass," *Wall Street Journal*, October 20, 1993.

When writing a paper, you will need to decide, like Krauthammer, which terms to define and which you can assume the reader will define in the same way you do. As the writer of a critique, you should identify and discuss any undefined or ambiguous term that might give rise to confusion.

Fair Use of Information   Information is used as evidence in support of arguments. When you encounter such evidence, ask yourself two questions: (1) "Is the information accurate and up to date?" At least a portion of an argument becomes invalid when the information used to support it is wrong or stale. (2) "Has the author cited *representative* information?" The evidence used in an argument must be presented in a spirit of fair play. An author is less than ethical when he presents only the evidence favoring his own views even though he is well aware that contrary evidence exists. For instance, it would be dishonest to argue that an economic recession is imminent and to cite only indicators of economic downturn while ignoring and failing to cite contrary (positive) evidence.

"The Moon We Left Behind" is not an information-heavy essay. The success of the piece turns on the author's powers of persuasion, not on his use of facts and figures. Krauthammer does, however, offer some key facts relating to Project Apollo and the fact that President Obama was not inclined to back a NASA-operated lunar-landing program. And, in fact, Krauthammer's fears were confirmed in February 2010, about six months after he wrote "The Moon We Left Behind," when the president canceled NASA's plans for further manned space exploration flights in favor of government support for commercial space operations.

Logical Argumentation: Avoiding Logical Fallacies

At some point, you'll need to respond to the logic of the argument itself. To be convincing, an argument should be governed by principles of *logic*— clear and orderly thinking. This does *not* mean that an argument cannot be biased. A biased argument—that is, an argument weighted toward one point of view and against others, which is in fact the nature of argument— may be valid as long as it is logically sound.

Let's examine several types of faulty thinking and logical fallacies you will need to watch for.

Emotionally Loaded Terms   Writers sometimes attempt to sway readers by using emotionally charged words. Words with positive connotations (e.g., "family values") are intended to sway readers to the author's point of view; words with negative connotations (e.g., "paying the price") try to sway readers away from an opposing point of view. The fact that an author uses emotionally loaded terms does not necessarily invalidate an argument. Emotional appeals are perfectly legitimate and time-honored modes of persuasion. But in academic writing, which is grounded in logical argumentation, they should not be the *only* means of persuasion. You should be sensitive to *how* emotionally loaded terms are being used. In particular, are they being used deceptively or to hide the essential facts?

We've already noted Krauthammer's use of the emotionally loaded terms "abandonment" and "retreat" when referring to the end of the manned space program. Notice also his use of the term "Kumbaya" in the sentence declaring that the international space station was "created in a fit of post-Cold War internationalist absentmindedness as a place where people of differing nationality can sing 'Kumbaya' while weightless." "Kumbaya" is an African-American spiritual dating from the 1930s, often sung by scouts around campfires. The song uses the word "Kumbaya" to connote spiritual unity among peoples, but in more recent times, the term has been used sarcastically to poke fun at what is viewed as a rose-colored optimism about human nature. Is Krauthammer drawing upon the emotional power of the original meaning or upon the more recent significance of this term? How does his particular use of "Kumbaya" strengthen (or weaken) his argument? What appears to be the difference in his mind between the value of the international space station and the value of returning to the moon? As someone evaluating the essay, you should be alert to this appeal to your emotions and then judge whether the appeal is fair and convincing. Above all, you should not let an emotional appeal blind you to shortcomings of logic, ambiguously defined terms, or a misuse of facts.

Ad Hominem Argument   In an *ad hominem* argument, the writer rejects opposing views by attacking the person who holds them. By calling opponents names, an author avoids the issue. Consider this excerpt from a political speech:

> I could more easily accept my opponent's plan to increase revenues by collecting on delinquent tax bills if he had paid more than a hundred dollars in state taxes in each of the past three years. But the fact is, he's a millionaire with a millionaire's tax shelters. This man hasn't paid a wooden nickel for the state services he and his family depend on. So I ask you: Is *he* the one to be talking about taxes to *us?*

It could well be that the opponent has paid virtually no state taxes for three years, but this fact has nothing to do with, and is used as a ploy to divert attention from, the merits of a specific proposal for increasing revenues. The proposal is lost in the attack against the man himself, an attack that violates principles of logic. Writers (and speakers) should make their points by citing evidence in support of their views and by challenging contrary evidence.

In "The Moon We Left Behind," Krauthammer's only individual target is President Obama. While he does, at several points, unfavorably compare Obama to Kennedy, he does not do so in an *ad hominem* way. That is, he attacks Obama less for his personal qualities than for his policy decision to close down NASA's manned space program. At most, he laments that Obama "has expressed none of Kennedy's enthusiasm for human space exploration."

Faulty Cause and Effect The fact that one event precedes another in time does not mean that the first event has caused the second. An example: Fish begin dying by the thousands in a lake near your hometown. An environmental group immediately cites chemical dumping by several manufacturing plants as the cause. But other causes are possible: A disease might have affected the fish; the growth of algae might have contributed to the deaths; or acid rain might be a factor. The origins of an event are usually complex and are not always traceable to a single cause. So you must carefully examine cause-and-effect reasoning when you find a writer using it. In Latin, this fallacy is known as *post hoc, ergo propter hoc* ("after this, therefore because of this").

Toward the end of "The Moon We Left Behind," Krauthammer declares that having turned our "imagination away from space and back to Earth...[w]e are now deep into that hyper-terrestrial phase, the age of iPod and Facebook, of social networking and eco-consciousness." He appears here to be suggesting a pattern of cause and effect: that as a people, we are no longer looking outward but, rather, turning inward; and this shift in our attention and focus has resulted in—or at least is a significant cause of—the death of the manned space program. Questions for a critique might include the following: (1) To what extent do you agree with Krauthammer's premise that we live in an inward-looking, rather than an outward-looking, age and that it is fair to call our present historical period "the age of iPod and Facebook"? (2) To what extent do you agree that because we may live in such an age, the space program no longer enjoys broad public or political support?

Either/Or Reasoning Either/or reasoning also results from an unwillingness to recognize complexity. If in analyzing a problem an author artificially restricts the range of possible solutions by offering only two courses of action and then rejects the one that he opposes, he cannot logically argue that the remaining course of action, which he favors, is therefore the only one that makes sense. Usually, several other options (at least) are possible. For whatever reason, the author has chosen to overlook them. As an

Tone

Tone refers to the overall emotional effect produced by a writer's choice of language. Writers might use especially emphatic words to create a tone: A film reviewer might refer to a "magnificent performance," or a columnist might criticize "sleazeball politics."

These are extreme examples of tone; tone can also be more subtle, particularly if the writer makes a special effort *not* to inject emotion into

(continues)

> the writing. As we indicated in the section on emotionally loaded terms, the fact that a writer's tone is highly emotional does not necessarily mean that the writer's argument is invalid. Conversely, a neutral tone does not ensure an argument's validity.
>
> Many instructors discourage student writing that projects a highly emotional tone, considering it inappropriate for academic or preprofessional work. (One sure sign of emotion: the exclamation mark, which should be used sparingly.)

example, suppose you are reading a selection on genetic engineering in which the author builds an argument on the basis of the following:

> Research in gene splicing is at a crossroads: Either scientists will be carefully monitored by civil authorities and their efforts limited to acceptable applications, such as disease control; or, lacking regulatory guidelines, scientists will set their own ethical standards and begin programs in embryonic manipulation that, however well intended, exceed the proper limits of human knowledge.

Certainly, other possibilities for genetic engineering exist beyond the two mentioned here. But the author limits debate by establishing an either/or choice. Such a limitation is artificial and does not allow for complexity. As a critical reader, you need to be on the alert for reasoning based on restrictive, either/or alternatives.

Hasty Generalization   Writers are guilty of hasty generalization when they draw their conclusions from too little evidence or from unrepresentative evidence. To argue that scientists should not proceed with the Human Genome Project because a recent editorial urged that the project be abandoned is to make a hasty generalization. That lone editorial may be unrepresentative of the views of most individuals—both scientists and laypeople—who have studied and written about the matter. To argue that one should never obey authority because Stanley Milgram's Yale University experiments in the 1960s showed the dangers of obedience is to ignore the fact that Milgram's experiments were concerned primarily with obedience to *immoral* authority. The experimental situation was unrepresentative of most routine demands for obedience—for example, to obey a parental rule or to comply with a summons for jury duty—and a conclusion about the malevolence of all authority would be a hasty generalization.

False Analogy   Comparing one person, event, or issue to another may be illuminating, but it can also be confusing or misleading. Differences between the two may be more significant than their similarities, and conclusions drawn from one may not necessarily apply to the other. A candidate for governor or president who argues that her experience as CEO of a major business would make her effective in governing a state or the country is assuming an analogy between the business and the political/civic worlds that does not hold up to examination. Most businesses are hierarchical, or top down: when a CEO issues an order, he or she can expect it to be carried out without argument. But governors and presidents command only their own executive branches. They cannot issue orders to independent legislatures or courts (much less private citizens); they can only attempt to persuade. In this case the implied analogy fails to convince the thoughtful reader or listener.

Begging the Question   To beg the question is to assume as proven fact the very thesis being argued. To assert, for example, that America does not need a new health care delivery system because America currently has the best health care in the world does not prove anything: It merely repeats the claim in different—and equally unproven—words. This fallacy is also known as *circular reasoning*.

Non Sequitur *Non sequitur*   is Latin for "it does not follow"; the term is used to describe a conclusion that does not logically follow from the premise. "Since minorities have made such great strides in the past few decades," a writer may argue, "we no longer need affirmative action programs." Aside from the fact that the premise itself is arguable (*have* minorities made such great strides?), it does not follow that because minorities *may* have made great strides, there is no further need for affirmative action programs.

Oversimplification   Be alert for writers who offer easy solutions to complicated problems. "America's economy will be strong again if we all 'buy American,'" a politician may argue. But the problems of America's economy are complex and cannot be solved by a slogan or a simple change in buying habits. Likewise, a writer who argues that we should ban genetic engineering assumes that simple solutions ("just say no") will be sufficient to deal with the complex moral dilemmas raised by this new technology.

Exercise 2.3

Understanding Logical Fallacies

Make a list of the nine logical fallacies discussed in the preceding section. Briefly define each one in your own words. Then, in a group of three or four classmates, review your definitions and the examples we've provided for each logical fallacy. Collaborate with your group to find or invent additional examples for each of the fallacies. Compare your examples with those generated by the other groups in your class.

Writing to Entertain

Authors write not only to inform and persuade but also to entertain. One response to entertainment is a hearty laugh, but it is possible to entertain without encouraging laughter: A good book or play or poem may prompt you to reflect, grow wistful, become elated, get angry. Laughter is only one of many possible reactions. Like a response to an informative piece or an argument, your response to an essay, poem, story, play, novel, or film should be precisely stated and carefully developed. Ask yourself some of the following questions (you won't have space to explore all of them, but try to consider the most important ones):

- Did I care for the portrayal of a certain character?
- Did that character (or a group of characters united by occupation, age, ethnicity, etc.) seem overly sentimental, for example, or heroic?
- Did his adversaries seem too villainous or stupid?
- Were the situations believable?
- Was the action interesting or merely formulaic?
- Was the theme developed subtly or powerfully, or did the work come across as preachy or unconvincing?
- Did the action at the end of the work follow plausibly from what had come before? Was the language fresh and incisive or stale and predictable?

Explain as specifically as possible what elements of the work seemed effective or ineffective and why. Offer an overall assessment, elaborating on your views.

Question 2: To What Extent Do You Agree with the Author?

A critical evaluation consists of two parts. The first part, just discussed, assesses the accuracy and effectiveness of an argument in terms of the author's logic and use of evidence. The second part, discussed here, responds to the argument—that is, agrees or disagrees with it.

Identify Points of Agreement and Disagreement

Be precise in identifying where you agree and disagree with an author. State as clearly as possible what *you* believe, in relation to what the author believes, as presented in the piece. Whether you agree enthusiastically, agree with reservations, or disagree, you can organize your reactions in two parts:

- Summarize the author's position.
- State your own position and explain why you believe as you do. The elaboration, in effect, becomes an argument itself, and this is true regardless of the position you take.

Any opinion that you express is effective to the extent you support it by supplying evidence from your reading (which should be properly cited), your observation, or your personal experience. Without such evidence, opinions cannot be authoritative. "I thought the article on inflation was lousy." Or: "It was terrific." Why? "I just thought so, that's all." Such opinions have no value because the criticism is imprecise: The critic has taken neither the time to read the article carefully nor the time to carefully explore his or her own reactions.

Exercise 2.4

Exploring Your Viewpoints—in Three Paragraphs

Go to a Web site that presents short persuasive essays on current social issues, such as reason.com, opinion-pages.org, drudgereport.com, or Speakout.com. Or go to an Internet search engine like Google or Bing and type in a social issue together with the word "articles," "editorials," or "opinion," and see what you find. Locate a selection on a topic of interest that takes a clear, argumentative position. Print out the selection on which you choose to focus.

- Write one paragraph summarizing the author's key argument.
- Write two paragraphs articulating your agreement or disagreement with the author. (Devote each paragraph to a *single* point of agreement or disagreement.)

Be sure to explain why you think or feel the way you do and, wherever possible, cite relevant evidence—from your reading, experience, or observation.

Explore the Reasons for Agreement and Disagreement: Evaluate Assumptions

One way of elaborating your reactions to a reading is to explore the underlying *reasons* for agreement and disagreement. Your reactions are based largely on assumptions that you hold and how those assumptions compare with the author's. An *assumption* is a fundamental statement about the world and its operations that you take to be true. Often, a writer will express an assumption directly, as in this example:

> #1 One of government's most important functions is to raise and spend tax revenues on projects that improve the housing, medical, and nutritional needs of its citizens.

In this instance, the writer's claim is a direct expression of a fundamental belief about how the world, or some part of it, should work. The argumentative claim *is* the assumption. Just as often, an argument and its underlying assumption are not identical. In these cases, the assumption is some other statement that is implied by the argumentative claim—as in this example:

> #2 Human spaceflight is a waste of public money.

The logic of this second statement rests on an unstated assumption relating to the word *waste*. What, in this writer's view, is a *waste* of money? What is an effective or justified use? In order to agree or not with statement #2, a critical reader must know what assumption(s) it rests on. A good candidate for such an assumption would be statement #1. That is, a person who believes statement #1 about how governments ought to raise and spend money could well make statement #2. This may not be the only assumption underlying statement #2, but it could well be one of them.

Inferring and Implying Assumptions

Infer and *imply* are keywords relating to hidden, or unstated, assumptions; you should be clear on their meanings. A critical reader *infers* what is hidden in a statement and, through that inference, brings what is hidden into the open for examination. Thus, the critical reader infers from statement #2 on human spaceflight the writer's assumption (statement #1) on how governments should spend money. At the same time, the writer of statement #2 *implies* (hints at but does not state directly) an assumption about how governments should spend money. There will be times when writers make statements and are unaware of their own assumptions.

Assumptions provide the foundation on which entire presentations are built. You may find an author's assumptions invalid—that is, not supported by factual evidence. You may disagree with value-based assumptions underlying an author's position—for instance, what constitutes "good" or "correct" behavior. In both cases, you may well disagree with the conclusions that follow from these assumptions. Alternatively, when you find that your own assumptions are contradicted by actual experience, you may be forced to conclude that certain of your fundamental beliefs about the world and how it works were mistaken.

An Example of Hidden Assumptions from the World of Finance

An interesting example of an assumption fatally colliding with reality was revealed during a recent congressional investigation into the financial meltdown of late 2008 precipitated by the collapse of the home mortgage market—itself precipitated, many believed, by an insufficiently regulated banking and financial system run amuck. During his testimony before the House Oversight Committee in October of that year, former Federal Reserve chairman Alan Greenspan was grilled by committee chairman Henry Waxman (D-CA) about his "ideology"—essentially an assumption or set of assumptions that become a governing principle. (In the following transcript, you can substitute the word "assumption" for "ideology.")

Greenspan responded, "I do have an ideology. My judgment is that free, competitive markets are by far the unrivaled way to organize economies. We have tried regulation; none meaningfully worked." Greenspan defined an ideology as "a conceptual framework [for] the way people deal with reality. Everyone has one. You have to. To exist, you need an ideology." And he pointed out that the assumptions on which he and the Federal Reserve operated were supported by "the best banking lawyers in the business...and an outside counsel of expert professionals to advise on regulatory matters."

Greenspan then admitted that in light of the economic disaster engulfing the nation, he had found a "flaw" in his ideology—that actual experience had violated some of his fundamental beliefs. The testimony continues:

> Chairman Waxman: You found a flaw?
>
> Mr. Greenspan: I found a flaw in the model that I perceived is the critical functioning structure that defines how the world works, so to speak.
>
> Chairman Waxman: In other words, you found that your view of the world, your ideology, was not right, it was not working.
>
> Mr. Greenspan: Precisely. That's precisely the reason I was shocked, because I had been going for 40 years or more with very considerable evidence that it was working exceptionally well.[5]

The lesson? All the research, expertise, and logical argumentation in the world will fail if the premise (assumption, ideology) on which it is based turns out to be "flawed."

How do you determine the validity of assumptions once you have identified them? In the absence of more scientific criteria, you start by considering how well the author's assumptions stack up against your own experience, observations, reading, and values—while remaining honestly aware of the limits of your own personal knowledge.

Readers will want to examine the assumption at the heart of Krauthammer's essay: that continuing NASA's manned space program and, in particular, the program to return human beings to the moon is a worthwhile enterprise. The writer of the critique that follows questions this assumption. But you may not: You may instead fully support such a program. That's your decision, perhaps made even *before* you read Krauthammer's essay, perhaps as a *result* of having read it. What you must do as a critical reader is to recognize assumptions, whether they are stated or not. You should spell them out and then accept or reject them. Ultimately, your agreement or disagreement with an author will rest on your agreement or disagreement with that author's assumptions.

---

[5]United States. Cong. House Committee on Oversight and Government Reform. *The Financial Crisis and the Role of Federal Regulators.* 110th Cong., 2nd sess. Washington: GPO, 2008.

■ CRITIQUE

In Chapter 1 we focused on summary—the condensed presentation of ideas from another source. Summary is fundamental to much of academic writing because such writing relies so heavily on the works of others for the support of its claims. It's not going too far to say that summarizing is the critical thinking skill from which a majority of academic writing builds. However, most academic thinking and writing goes beyond summary. Generally, we use summary to restate our understanding of things we see or read. We then put that summary to use. In academic writing, one typical use of summary is as a prelude to critique.

A *critique* is a *formalized, critical reading of a passage.* It is also a personal response, but writing a critique is considerably more rigorous than saying that a movie is "great" or a book is "fascinating" or "I didn't like it." These are all responses, and, as such, they're a valid, even essential, part of your understanding of what you see and read. But such responses don't illuminate the subject—even for you—if you haven't explained how you arrived at your conclusions.

Your task in writing a critique is to turn your critical reading of a passage into a systematic evaluation in order to deepen your reader's (and your own) understanding of that passage. When you read a selection to critique, determine the following:

- What an author says
- How well the points are made
- What assumptions underlie the argument
- What issues are overlooked
- What implications can be drawn from such an analysis

When you write a critique, positive or negative, include the following:

- A fair and accurate summary of the passage
- Information and ideas from other sources (your reading or your personal experience and observations) if you think these are pertinent
- A statement of your agreement or disagreement with the author, backed by specific examples and clear logic
- A clear statement of your own assumptions

Remember that you bring to bear on any subject an entire set of assumptions about the world. Stated or not, these assumptions underlie every evaluative comment you make. You therefore have an obligation, both to the reader and to yourself, to clarify your standards by making your assumptions explicit. Not only do your readers stand to gain by your forthrightness, but you do as well. The process of writing a critical assessment forces you to examine your own knowledge, beliefs, and assumptions. Ultimately, the critique is a way of learning about yourself—yet another example of the ways in which writing is useful as a tool for critical thinking.

How to Write Critiques

You may find it useful to organize a critique into five sections: introduction, summary, assessment of the presentation (on its own terms), your response to the presentation, and conclusion.

The box on pages 71–72 offers guidelines for writing critiques. These guidelines do not constitute a rigid formula. Most professional authors write critiques that do not follow the structure outlined here. Until you are more confident and practiced in writing critiques, however, we suggest you follow these guidelines. They are meant not to restrict you, but rather to provide a workable sequence for writing critiques until a more fully developed set of experiences and authorial instincts are available to guide you.

Guidelines for Writing Critiques

- *Introduce.* Introduce both the passage under analysis and the author. State the author's main argument and the point(s) you intend to make about it.

    Provide background material to help your readers understand the relevance or appeal of the passage. This background material might include one or more of the following: an explanation of why the subject is of current interest; a reference to a possible controversy surrounding the subject of the passage or the passage itself; biographical information about the author; an account of the circumstances under which the passage was written; a reference to the intended audience of the passage.

- *Summarize.* Summarize the author's main points, making sure to state the author's purpose for writing.

- *Assess the presentation.* Evaluate the validity of the author's presentation, distinct from your points of agreement or disagreement. Comment on the author's success in achieving his or her purpose by reviewing three or four specific points. You might base your review on one or more of the following criteria:

    Is the information accurate?

    Is the information significant?

    Has the author defined terms clearly?

    Has the author used and interpreted information fairly?

    Has the author argued logically?

(continues)

- *Respond to the presentation.* Now it is your turn to respond to the author's views. With which views do you agree? With which do you disagree? Discuss your reasons for agreement and disagreement, when possible tying these reasons to assumptions—both the author's and your own. Where necessary, draw on outside sources to support your ideas.

- *Conclude.* State your conclusions about the overall validity of the piece—your assessment of the author's success at achieving his or her aims and your reactions to the author's views. Remind the reader of the weaknesses and strengths of the passage.

■ DEMONSTRATION: CRITIQUE

The critique that follows is based on Charles Krauthammer's op-ed piece "The Moon We Left Behind" (pp. 58–60), which we have already begun to examine. In this formal critique, you will see that it is possible to agree with an author's main point, at least provisionally, yet disagree with other elements of the argument. Critiquing a different selection, you could just as easily accept the author's facts and figures but reject the conclusion he draws from them. As long as you carefully articulate the author's assumptions and your own, explaining in some detail your agreement and disagreement, the critique is yours to take in whatever direction you see fit.

Let's summarize the preceding sections by returning to the core questions that guide critical reading. You will see how, when applied to Krauthammer's argument, they help to set up a critique.

To What Extent Does the Author Succeed in His or Her Purpose?

To answer this question, you will need to know the author's purpose. Krauthammer wrote "The Moon We Left Behind" to persuade his audience that manned space flight must be supported. He makes his case in three ways: (1) he attacks the Obama administration's decision to "retreat" from the moon—i.e., to end NASA's manned space program; (2) he argues for the continuation of this program; and (3) he rebuts criticisms of the program. He aims to achieve this purpose by unfavorably comparing President Obama to President Kennedy, who challenged the nation to put a man on the moon within a decade; by arguing that we should return to the moon for "the wonder and glory of it"; and by challenging the claims that (a) we need first to fix the problems on earth and that (b) we can't afford such a program. One of the main tasks of the writer of a critique of Krauthammer is to explain the extent to which Krauthammer has achieved his purpose.

To What Extent Do You Agree with the Author? Evaluate Assumptions

Krauthammer's argument rests upon two assumptions: (1) it is an essential characteristic of humankind to explore—and going to the moon was a great and worthwhile example of exploration; and (2) inspiring deeds are worth our expense and sacrifice—and thus continuing NASA's manned program and returning to the moon is worth our time, effort, and money. One who critiques Krauthammer must determine the extent to which she or he shares these assumptions. The writer of the model critique does, in fact, share Krauthammer's first assumption while expressing doubt about the second.

One must also determine the persuasiveness of Krauthammer's arguments for returning to the moon, as well as the persuasiveness of his counterarguments to those who claim this program is too impractical and too expensive. The writer of the model critique believes that Krauthammer's arguments are generally persuasive, even (in the conclusion) judging them "compelling." On the other hand, the critique ends on a neutral note—taking into account the problems with Krauthammer's arguments.

Remember that you don't need to agree with an author to believe that he or she has succeeded in his or her purpose. You may well admire how cogently and forcefully an author has argued without necessarily accepting her position. Conversely, you may agree with a particular author while acknowledging that he has not made a very strong case—and perhaps has even made a flawed one—for his point of view. For example, you may heartily approve of the point Krauthammer is making—that the United States should return to the moon. At the same time, you may find problematic the substance of his arguments and/or his strategy for arguing, particularly the dismissive manner in which he refers to the U.S. efforts in space over the past forty years:

> To be more precise: almost 40 years spent in low Earth orbit studying, well, zero-G nausea and sundry cosmic mysteries. We've done it with the most beautiful, intricate, complicated—and ultimately, hopelessly impractical—machine ever built by man: the space shuttle. We turned this magnificent bird into a truck for hauling goods and people to a tinkertoy we call the international space station....

Perhaps you support Krauthammer's position but find his sarcasm distasteful. That said, these two major questions for critical analysis (whether the author has been successful in his purpose and the extent to which you agree with the author's assumptions and arguments) are related. You will typically conclude that an author whose arguments have failed to persuade you has not succeeded in her purpose.

The selections you are likely to critique will be those, like Krauthammer's, that argue a specific position. Indeed, every argument you read is an invitation to agree or disagree. It remains only for you to speak up and justify your own position.

MODEL CRITIQUE

Andrew Harlan

Professor Rose Humphreys

Writing 2

11 January 2014

A Critique of Charles Krauthammer's

"The Moon We Left Behind"

(1)   In his 1961 State of the Union address, President John F. Kennedy issued a stirring challenge: "that this nation should commit itself to achieving the goal, before this decade is out, of landing a man on the Moon and returning him safely to the Earth." At the time, Kennedy's proposal seemed like science fiction. Even the scientists and engineers of the National Aeronautics and Space Administration (NASA) who were tasked with the job didn't know how to meet Kennedy's goal. Spurred, however, partly by a unified national purpose and partly by competition with the Soviet Union, which had beaten the United States into space with the first artificial satellite in 1957, the Apollo program to land men on the moon was launched. On July 20, 1969, Kennedy's challenge was met when Apollo 11 astronauts Neil Armstrong and Buzz Aldrin landed their lunar module on the Sea of Tranquility.

(2)   During the next few years, five more Apollo flights landed on the moon. In all, twelve Americans walked on the lunar surface; some even rode on a 4-wheeled "Rover," a kind of lunar dune buggy. But in December 1972 the Apollo program was cancelled. Since that time, some 40 years ago, humans have frequently returned to space, but none have returned to the moon. In February 2010 President Obama ended NASA's moon program, transferring responsibility for manned space exploration to private industry and re-focusing the government's resources on technological development and innovation. The administration had signaled its intentions earlier, in 2009. In July of that year, in an apparent attempt to rouse public opinion against the President's revised priorities for space exploration, Charles Krauthammer wrote "The Moon We Left Behind." It is these revised priorities that are the focus of

Harlan 2

his op-ed piece, a lament for the end of lunar exploration and a powerful, if flawed, critique of the administration's decision.

3 Trained as a doctor and a psychiatrist, Charles Krauthammer is a prominent conservative columnist who has won the Pulitzer Prize for his political commentary. Krauthammer begins and ends his op-ed with expressions of dismay and anger at "America's abandonment of the moon." He unfavorably compares the current president, Barack Obama, with the "vigorous young" John F. Kennedy, in terms of their support for manned space exploration. It is inconceivable to Krauthammer that a program that achieved such technical glories and fired the imaginations of millions in so short a span of time has fallen into such decline.

4 Krauthammer anticipates the objections to his plea to keep America competitive in manned space exploration and to return to the moon. We have problems enough on earth, critics will argue. His answer: "If we waited to solve these perennial problems before continuing human progress, we'd still be living in caves." Concerning the expense of continuing the space program, Krauthammer argues that a fraction of the funds being "showered" on the government's stimulus programs (some $1 trillion) would be sufficient to support a viable space program. And as for practicality, he dismisses the idea that we need a practical reason to return to the moon. "We go," he argues, "for the wonder and glory of it. Or, to put it less grandly, for its immense possibilities." Ultimately, Krauthammer urges us to turn away from our mundane preoccupations and look up at the moon where humans once walked. How could Americans have gone so far, he asks, only to retreat?

5 In this opinion piece, Charles Krauthammer offers a powerful, inspiring defense of the American manned space program; and it's hard not to agree with him that our voyages to the moon captured the imagination and admiration of the world and set a new standard for scientific and technical achievement. Ever since that historic day in July 1969, people have been asking, "If we can land a man on the moon, why can't we [fill in your favorite social or political challenge]?" In a way, the fact that going to the moon was not especially practical

Harlan 3

made the achievement even more admirable: we went not for gain but rather to explore the unknown, to show what human beings, working cooperatively and exercising their powers of reason and their genius in design and engineering, can accomplish when sufficiently challenged. "We go," Krauthammer reminds us, "for the wonder and glory of it...for its immense possibilities."

(6)   And what's wrong with that? For a relatively brief historical moment, Americans, and indeed the peoples of the world, came together in pride and anticipation as Apollo 11 sped toward the moon and, days later, as the lunar module descended to the surface. People collectively held their breaths after an oxygen tank explosion disabled Apollo 13 on the way to the moon and as the astronauts and Mission Control guided the spacecraft to a safe return. A renewed moon program might similarly help to reduce divisions among people—or at least among Americans—and highlight the reality that we are all residents of the same planet, with more common interests (such as protecting the environment) than is often apparent from our perennial conflicts. Krauthammer's praise of lunar exploration and its benefits is so stirring that many who do not accept his conclusions may share his disappointment and indignation at its demise.

(7)   "The Moon We Left Behind" may actually underestimate the practical aspects of moon travel. "Any technological return," Krauthammer writes, "is a bonus, not a reason." But so many valuable bonuses have emerged from space flight and space exploration that the practical offshoots of lunar exploration may in fact be a valid reason to return to the moon. For instance, the technology developed from the special requirements of space travel has found application in health and medicine (breast cancer detection, laser angioplasty), industrial productivity and manufacturing technology, public safety (radiation hazard detectors, emergency rescue cutters), and transportation (studless winter tires, advanced lubricants, aids to school bus design) ("NASA Spinoffs"). A renewed moon program would also be practical in providing a huge employment stimulus to the economy. According to the NASA Langley Research Center, "At its peak, the Apollo program employed 400,000 people and

Harlan 4

required the support of over 20,000 industrial firms and universities" ("Apollo Program"). Returning to the moon would create comparable numbers of jobs in aerospace engineering, computer engineering, biology, general engineering, and meteorology, along with hosts of support jobs, from accounting to food service to office automation specialists ("NASA Occupations").

(8)   Krauthammer's emotional call may be stirring, but he dismisses too quickly some of the practical arguments against a renewed moon program. He appears to assume a degree of political will and public support for further lunar exploration that simply does not exist today. First, public support may be lacking—for legitimate reasons. It is not as if with a renewed lunar program we would be pushing boundaries and exploring the unknown: we would not be *going* to the moon; we would be *returning* to the moon. A significant percentage of the public, after considering the matter, may reasonably conclude: "Been there, done that." They may think, correctly or not, that we should set our sights elsewhere rather than collecting more moon rocks or taking additional stunning photographs from the lunar surface. Whatever practical benefits can be derived from going to the moon, many (if not all) have already been achieved. It would not be at all unreasonable for the public, even a public that supports NASA funding, to say, "Let's move on to other goals."

(9)   Second, Krauthammer's argument that poverty and disease and social ills will always be with us is politically flawed. This country faces financial pressures more serious than those at any other time since the Great Depression; and real, painful choices are being made by federal, state, and local officials about how to spend diminished tax dollars. The "vigorous young" JFK, launching the moon program during a time of expansion and prosperity, faced no such restrictions. Krauthammer's dismissal of ongoing poverty and other social ills is not likely to persuade elected representatives who are shuttering libraries, closing fire stations, ending unemployment benefits, and curtailing medical services. Nor will a public that is enduring these cuts be impressed by Krauthammer's call to "wonder and glory." Accurately or not, the public is likely to see the matter in terms of choices between a re-funded lunar program

Harlan 5

(nice, but optional) and renewed jobless benefits (essential). Not many politicians, in such distressed times, would be willing to go on record by voting for "nice" over "essential"—not if they wanted to keep their jobs.

⑩   Finally, it's surprising—and philosophically inconsistent—for a conservative like Krauthammer, who believes in a smaller, less free-spending government, to be complaining about the withdrawal of massive government support for a renewed moon program. After all, the government hasn't banned moon travel; it has simply turned over such projects to private industry. If lunar exploration and other space flights appear commercially viable, there's nothing to prevent private companies and corporations from pursuing their own programs.

⑪   In "The Moon We Left Behind," Charles Krauthammer stirs the emotions with his call for the United States to return to the moon; and, in terms of practical spinoffs, such a return could benefit this country in many ways. Krauthammer's argument is compelling, even if he too easily discounts the financial and political problems that will pose real obstacles to a renewed lunar program. Ultimately, what one thinks of Krauthammer's call to renew moon exploration depends on how one defines the human enterprise and the purpose of collective agreement and collective effort—what we call "government." To what extent should this purpose be to solve problems in the here and now? To what extent should it be to inquire and to push against the boundaries for the sake of discovery and exploration, to learn more about who we are and about the nature of our universe? There have always been competing demands on national budgets and more than enough problems to justify spending every tax dollar on problems of poverty, social justice, crime, education, national security, and the like. Krauthammer argues that if we are to remain true to our spirit of inquiry, we cannot ignore the investigation of space because scientific and technological progress is also a human responsibility. He argues that we can—indeed, we must—do both: look to our needs here at home and also dream and explore. But the public may not find his argument convincing.

Harlan 6

Works Cited

"Apollo Program." *Apollo Program HSF*. National Aeronautics and Space
Administration, 2 July 2009. Web. 16 Sept. 2010.

Harwood, William. "Obama Kills Moon Program, Endorses Commercial Space."
Spaceflight Now. Spaceflight Now, 1 Feb. 2010. Web. 13 Sept. 2010.

Kennedy, John F. "Rice University Speech." 12 Sept. 1962. *Public Papers of
the Presidents of the United States*. Vol. 1., 1962. 669–70. Print.

---. "Special Message to the Congress on Urgent National Needs." *John
F. Kennedy Presidential Library and Museum*. John F. Kennedy
Presidential Library and Museum, 25 May 1961. Web. 14 Sept. 2010.

Krauthammer, Charles. "The Moon We Left Behind." *Washington Post* 17
July 2009: A17. Print.

"NASA Occupations." *Nasajobsoccupations*. National Aeronautics and Space
Administration, 28 July 2009. Web. 12 Sept. 2010.

"NASA Spinoffs: Bringing Space Down to Earth." *The Ultimate Space Place*.
National Aeronautics and Space Administration, 2 Feb. 2004. Web.
18 Sept. 2010.

Exercise 2.5

Informal Critique of the Model Critique

Before reading our analysis of this model critique, write your own informal response to it. What are its strengths and weaknesses? To what extent does the critique follow the general Guidelines for Writing Critiques that we outlined on pages 71–72? To the extent that it varies from the guidelines, speculate on why. Jot down ideas for a critique that takes a different approach to Krauthammer's op-ed.

Critical Reading for Critique

• *Use the tips from Critical Reading for Summary on page 5.* Remember to examine the context; note the title and subtitle; identify the main point; identify the subpoints; break the reading into sections;

(continues)

distinguish between points, examples, and counterarguments; watch for transitions within and between paragraphs; and read actively.

- *Establish the writer's primary purpose in writing.* Is the piece meant primarily to inform, persuade, or entertain?
- *Evaluate informative writing. Use these criteria (among others):*
    Accuracy of information
    Significance of information
    Fair interpretation of information
- *Evaluate persuasive writing. Use these criteria (among others):*
    Clear definition of terms
    Fair use and interpretation of information
    Logical reasoning
- *Evaluate writing that entertains. Use these criteria (among others):*
    Interesting characters
    Believable action, plot, and situations
    Communication of theme
    Use of language
- *Decide whether you agree or disagree with the writer's ideas, position, or message.* Once you have determined the extent to which an author has achieved his or her purpose, clarify your position in relation to the writer's.

The Strategy of the Critique

- Paragraphs 1 and 2 of the model critique introduce the topic. They provide a context by way of a historical review of America's lunar-exploration program from 1962 to 1972, leading up to the president's decision to scrub plans for a return to the moon. The two-paragraph introduction also provides a context for Krauthammer's—and the world's—admiration for the stunning achievement of the Apollo program. The second paragraph ends with the thesis of the critique, the writer's overall assessment of Krauthammer's essay.
- Paragraphs 3–4 introduce Krauthammer and summarize his arguments.
    - Paragraph 3 provides biographical information about Krauthammer and describes his disappointment and indignation at "America's abandonment of the moon."
    - Paragraph 4 treats Krauthammer's anticipated objections to the continuation of the manned space program and rebuttals to these objections.

- Paragraphs 5, 6, and 7 support Krauthammer's argument.
  - Paragraphs 5 and 6 begin the writer's evaluation, focusing on the reasons that Krauthammer finds so much to admire in the lunar-exploration program. Most notably: it was a stunning technological achievement that brought the people of the world together (if only briefly). The writer shares this admiration.
  - Paragraph 7 indirectly supports Krauthammer by pointing out that even though he downplays the practical benefits of lunar exploration, the space program has yielded numerous practical technological spinoffs.
- Paragraphs 8–10 focus on the problems with Krauthammer's argument.
  - In paragraph 8, the writer points out that there is little public support for returning to the moon, a goal that many people will see as already accomplished and impractical for the immediate future.
  - Paragraph 9 argues that Krauthammer underestimates the degree to which an electorate worried about skyrocketing deficits and high unemployment would object to taxpayer dollars being used to finance huge government spending on a renewed lunar program.
  - Paragraph 10 points out how surprising it is that a conservative like Krauthammer would advocate a government-financed manned space program when the same goal could be accomplished by private enterprise.
- Paragraph 11 concludes the critique, summing up the chief strengths and weaknesses of Krauthammer's argument and pointing out that readers' positions will be determined by their views on the "human enterprise" and the purpose of government. How do we balance our "human responsibility" for the expansion of knowledge and technology with the competing claims of education, poverty, crime, and national security?

WRITING ASSIGNMENT: CRITIQUE

Read and then write a critique of "Why We Need Violent Video Games" by Ethan Gilsdorf, which was originally presented as a talk on WBUR 90.9, Boston's National Public Radio (NPR) station, on January 13, 2013.

Before reading, review the tips presented in the Critical Reading for Critique box (pp. 79–80). When you're ready to write your critique, start by jotting down notes in response to the tips for critical reading and the earlier discussions of evaluating writing in this chapter. What assumptions does Gilsdorf make? Review the logical fallacies on pages 61–65, and identify any that appear in the essay. Work out your ideas on paper, perhaps producing an outline. Then write a rough draft of your critique. Review the reading and revise your rough draft at least once before considering it finished. You may want to look ahead to Chapter 6, "Writing as a Process," to help guide you through writing your critique.

For an additional exercise in writing critiques, see Chapter 8, a practice chapter that assembles readings on ethical dilemmas. You will have the opportunity to write a critique that you then place into a larger argument.

WHY WE NEED VIOLENT VIDEO GAMES

Ethan Gilsdorf[6]

In the wake of the Sandy Hook Elementary School killings, pundits, parents and media have jumped on video game violence as a possible scapegoat.

Right after his tête-à-tête with gun rights advocates, Vice President Biden convened meetings with video game industry leaders. Then there was a "Videogames Return Program" run by a group called SouthingtonSOS, based in a community neighboring Newtown. The notion: On a designated day, anyone could redeem their old copies of "Thrill Kill," "Postal 2" and "Call of Duty" for gift vouchers for more family-oriented, non-lethal entertainment. (In the end, that program was cancelled, likely due to fears of negative publicity.)

Now, even as President Obama announced Wednesday four major legislative proposals and 23 executive actions to curb gun violence, suspicion still clouds the gaming industry. Even the National Rifle Association blames violent video games for this nation's blood lust.

Remember rock 'n' roll? Comic books? Heavy metal and rap music? Dungeons & Dragons? We've all been down this clichéd road before. For now, anyway, we will not see the repeat of what often happens when our well-meaning citizenry seeks to demonize the latest scourge on America's youth. So erase the image of mountains of XBox and PS3 cartridges and discs set afire by angry mothers.

5   Still, the search for cause and effect remains a noble pursuit. If only we could stop our troubled young men (and so often they are troubled, young and men) from being exposed to X, then we wouldn't be asking ourselves, again and again, "Why?"

In the case of Newtown, gunman Adam Lanza was a gamer. But he didn't fit the profile of the typical first-person shooter fan. He liked non-violent games such as Dance Dance Revolution. Yes, a game that teaches you how to dance, not how to blow apart the chest cavities of other dancers.

Amidst all the soul-searching and finger-pointing, video game industry spokespeople are quick to note that no credible study shows a direct relationship between TV, movie or video game violence, and aggression. And, as those

[6]Ethan Gilsdorf, "Why We Need Violent Video Games." WBUR 90.9, Boston's NPR News Station. 13 Jan. 2013. Radio.

opposed to restrictions or bans on video games frequently cite, the youth violent crime rate is at an all-time low.

Paradoxically, could it be that violent video games are an important outlet for aggression? That, on the whole, these games and "play violence" let us express anger and aggression in a safe way? Perhaps violent video games aren't only "not so bad," but actually help keep the real-world killings where they belong—in our imaginations, as harmless fantasies.

It may seem counter-intuitive to suggest this. But in my experience, gaming—be it video games, or live-action role-playing, or D&D, or the greatest war game of all, American football—offer relatively safe, participatory narratives where we get to play good or evil, the aggressor or the defender, the killer or the killed. We engage in the fight. Our hearts race and our blood pumps. We have an emotional stake in the action, even if that action is largely make-believe. There are bangs and bruises from foam-rubber swords, and yes, concussions from errant tackles. But for men (and some women) who need to run and hunt and hit, I'll take a broken rib or swollen ego over actual carnage on the battlefield or playground. The vast, vast majority of players don't let their violent fantasies get the better of them, or others.

10 We have perhaps civilized ourselves more quickly than our psyches know what to do with. Not long ago in our nation's Tame-the-Wild-West mythology, any trouble with the neighboring tribe was settled with tomahawks and shotguns. Centuries prior, in other eras, we settled scores with battle axes. Our species still craves action.

Our most violent video games are another expression, another evolution of this same phenomenon. They're simply another way to feel the fear, scare away the zombies and save the day. They offer a hunt/shoot/kill scenario as a way to solve problems because, well, our psyches seem to need these visceral, adrenaline-rich experiences. That's why they sell so well.

Vision quests, ropes courses, and roller coasters offer similar thrills. But we can't very well go deer hunting or jump out of airplanes every weekend, can we?

In response to the Newtown deaths, a better question to ask might be this: Why does our culture continue to fail young, vulnerable men like Lanza—men often described as "intelligent but withdrawn," who disengage from society so completely as to become mass killers?

In Lanza's case, he was described as "smart but shy," a "genius" and a "Goth." A skinny kid estranged from his father. A nerd.

15 If some of these men are hopelessly mentally ill, then we need to do all we can to prevent their access to real guns. But sane or depressed, many men feel powerless. Many feel angry. Many feel disengaged. They just want a stake in the action.

Video games might be the best outlet they've got.

3 ■ Explanatory Synthesis

■ WHAT IS A SYNTHESIS?

A *synthesis* is a written discussion that draws on two or more sources. It follows that your ability to write syntheses depends on your ability to infer relationships among sources like these:

- Essays
- Fiction
- Interviews
- Articles
- Lectures
- Visual media

This process is nothing new for you because you infer relationships all the time—say, between something you've read in the newspaper and something you've seen for yourself, or between the teaching styles of your favorite and least favorite instructors. In fact, if you've written research papers, you've already written syntheses.

In a *synthesis*, you make explicit the relationships that you have inferred among separate sources.

Summary and Critique as a Basis for Synthesis

The skills you've already learned and practiced in the previous two chapters will be vital in writing syntheses. Before you're in a position to draw relationships between two or more sources, you must understand what those sources say; you must be able to *summarize* those sources. Readers will frequently benefit from at least partial summaries of sources in your synthesis essays. At the same time, you must go beyond summary to make judgments—judgments based on your *critical reading* of your sources: what conclusions you've drawn about the quality and validity of these sources, whether you agree or disagree with the points made in your sources, and why you agree or disagree.

Inference as a Basis for Synthesis: Moving Beyond Summary and Critique

In a synthesis, you go beyond the critique of individual sources to determine the relationships among them. Is the information in source B, for example, an extended illustration of the generalizations in source A? Would it be useful to compare and contrast source C with source B? Having read and considered sources A, B, and C, can you infer something else—in other words, D (not a source, but your own idea)?

Because a synthesis is based on two or more sources, you will need to be selective when choosing information from each. It would be neither possible nor desirable, for instance, to discuss in a ten-page paper on the American Civil War every point that the authors of two books make about their subject. What you as a writer must do is select from each source the ideas and information that best allow you to achieve your purpose.

■ PURPOSE

Your purpose in reading source materials and then drawing on them to write your own material is often reflected in the wording of an assignment. For instance, consider the following assignments on the Civil War:

American History: Evaluate the author's treatment of the origins of the Civil War.

Economics: Argue the following proposition, in light of your readings: "The Civil War was fought not for reasons of moral principle but for reasons of economic necessity."

Government: Prepare a report on the effects of the Civil War on Southern politics at the state level between 1870 and 1917. Focus on one state.

Mass Communications: Discuss how the use of photography during the Civil War may have affected the perceptions of the war by Northerners living in industrial cities.

Literature: Select two Southern writers of the twentieth century whose work you believe was influenced by the divisive effects of the Civil War. Discuss the ways this influence is apparent in a novel or a group of short stories written by each author. The works should not be *about* the Civil War.

Applied Technology: Compare and contrast the technology of warfare available in the 1860s with the technology available a century earlier.

Each of these assignments creates a particular purpose for writing. Having located sources relevant to your topic, you would select for possible use in a paper only the parts of those sources that helped you in fulfilling this purpose. And how you used those parts—how you related them to other material from other sources—would also depend on your purpose.

Example: Same Sources, Different Uses

If you were working on the government assignment, you might draw on the same source as a student working on the literature assignment by referring to Robert Penn Warren's novel *All the King's Men*, about Louisiana politics in the early part of the twentieth century. But because the purposes of the two

Where Do We Find Written Syntheses?

Here are just a few of the types of writing that involve synthesis:

ACADEMIC WRITING

- **Analysis papers** synthesize and apply several related theoretical approaches.
- **Research papers** synthesize multiple sources.
- **Argument papers** synthesize different points into a coherent claim or position.
- **Essay exams** demonstrate understanding of course material through comparing and contrasting theories, viewpoints, or approaches in a particular field.

WORKPLACE WRITING

- **Newspaper and magazine articles** synthesize primary and secondary sources.
- **Position papers and policy briefs** compare and contrast solutions for solving problems.
- **Business plans** synthesize ideas and proposals into one coherent plan.
- **Memos and letters** synthesize multiple ideas, events, and proposals into concise form.
- **Web sites** synthesize information from various sources to present in Web pages and related links.

assignments are different, you and the other student would make different uses of this source. The parts or aspects of the novel that you find worthy of detailed analysis might be mentioned only in passing—or not at all—by the other student.

■ USING YOUR SOURCES

Your purpose determines not only what parts of your sources you will use but also how you will relate those parts to one another. Since the very essence of synthesis is the combining of information and ideas, you must have some basis on which to combine them. *Some relationships among the material in your sources must make them worth synthesizing.* It follows that the better able you are to discover such relationships, the better able you will be to use your sources in writing syntheses. Notice that the mass communications assignment requires you to draw a *cause-and-effect* relationship between photographs of the war and Northerners' perceptions of the war. The applied technology assignment requires you to *compare and contrast* state-of-the-art weapons technology in the eighteenth and nineteenth centuries. The economics assignment requires you to *argue* a proposition. In each case, *your purpose will determine how you relate your source materials to one another.*

Consider some other examples. You may be asked on an exam question or in the instructions for a paper to *describe* two or three approaches to prison reform during the past decade. You may be asked to *compare and contrast* one country's approach to imprisonment with another's. You may be asked to *develop an argument* of your own on this subject, based on your reading. Sometimes (when you are not given a specific assignment) you determine your own purpose: You are interested in exploring a particular subject; you are interested in making a case for one approach or another. In any event, your purpose shapes your essay. Your purpose determines which sources you research, which ones you use, which parts of them you use, at which points in your paper you use them, and in what manner you relate them to one another.

■ TYPES OF SYNTHESES: EXPLANATORY AND ARGUMENT

In this and the next chapter we categorize syntheses into two main types: *explanatory* and *argument.* The easiest way to recognize the difference between the two types may be to consider the difference between a news article and an editorial on the same subject. For the most part, we'd say that the main purpose of the news article is to convey *information* and that the main purpose of the editorial is to convey *opinion* or *interpretation.* Of course, this distinction is much too simplified: News articles often convey opinion or bias, sometimes subtly, sometimes openly; and editorials often convey unbiased information along with opinion. But as a practical matter we can generally agree on the distinction between a news article that primarily conveys information and an editorial that primarily conveys opinion. Consider the balance of explanation and argumentation in the following two selections.

What Are Genetically Modified (GM) Foods?

GENETICALLY MODIFIED FOODS AND ORGANISMS

The United States Department of Energy

November 5, 2008

Combining genes from different organisms is known as recombinant DNA technology, and the resulting organism is said to be "genetically modified," "genetically engineered," or "transgenic." GM products (current or those in development) include medicines and vaccines, foods and food ingredients, feeds, and fibers.

Locating genes for important traits—such as those conferring insect resistance or desired nutrients—is one of the most limiting steps in the process.
However, genome sequencing and discovery programs for hundreds of organisms are generating detailed maps along with data-analyzing technologies to
understand and use them.

In 2006, 252 million acres of transgenic crops were planted in 22 countries
by 10.3 million farmers. The majority of these crops were herbicide- and insect-
resistant soybeans, corn, cotton, canola, and alfalfa. Other crops grown commercially or field-tested are a sweet potato resistant to a virus that could decimate
most of the African harvest, rice with increased iron and vitamins that may alleviate chronic malnutrition in Asian countries, and a variety of plants able to survive
weather extremes.

On the horizon are bananas that produce human vaccines against infec-
tious diseases such as hepatitis B; fish that mature more quickly; cows that are
resistant to bovine spongiform encephalopathy (mad cow disease); fruit and nut
trees that yield years earlier, and plants that produce new plastics with unique
properties.

WHY A GM FREEZE?

The GM Freeze Campaign

November 11, 2010

Genetic modification in food and farming raises many fundamental environmental, social, health and ethical concerns. There is increasing evidence of
contamination of conventional crops and wild plants, and potential damage to
wildlife. The effects on human health of eating these foods remain uncertain and
some scientists are calling for much more rigorous safety testing. It is clear that
further research into all these issues is vital. Furthermore the public has not been
properly involved in decision making processes, despite strong public support
for the precautionary approach to GM in the [United Kingdom] and the [European
Union].

Much more time is needed to assess the need for and implications of using
genetic modification in food and farming, in particular the increasing control of corporations who rely on patents to secure their future markets.

Both of these passages deal with the topic of genetically modified (GM)
foods. The first is excerpted from a largely informational Web site published
by the U.S. Department of Energy, which oversees the Human Genome
Project, the government's ongoing effort to map gene sequences and
apply that knowledge. We say the DOE account is "largely informational"

because readers can find a great deal of information here about genetically modified foods. At the same time, however, the DOE explanation is subtly biased in favor of genetic modification: note the absence of any language raising questions about the ethics or safety of GM foods; note also the use of terms like "desired nutrients" and "insect resistance"—with their positive connotations. The DOE examples show GM foods in a favorable light, and the passage as a whole assumes the value and importance of genetic manipulation.

As we see in the second passage, however, that assumption is not shared by all. Excerpted from a Web site advocating a freeze on genetically modified crops, the second passage primarily argues against the ethics and safety of such manipulation, calling for more study before modified crops are released widely into the environment. At the same time, the selection provides potentially important explanatory materials: (1) the claim that there is "increasing evidence of contamination of conventional crops and wild plants, and potential damage to wildlife"; (2) the claim that corporations control GM crops, and potentially the food supply, through patents. We can easily and quickly confirm these claims through research; if confirmed, the information—which is nested in a primarily argumentative piece—could prove useful in a paper on GM foods.

So while it is fair to say that most writing can be broadly categorized as explanatory or argumentative, understand that in practice, many of the materials you read will be a mix: *primarily* one or the other but not altogether one or the other. It will be your job as an alert, critical reader to determine when authors are explaining or arguing—sometimes in the same sentence.

For instance, you might read the following in a magazine article: "The use of goats to manufacture anti-clotting proteins for humans in their milk sets a dangerous precedent." Perhaps you did not know that scientists have genetically manipulated goats (by inserting human genes) to create medicines. That much of the statement is factual. It is explanatory. Whether or not this fact "sets a dangerous precedent" is an argument. You could agree or not with the argument, but your views would not change the fact about the genetic manipulation of farm animals. Even within a single sentence, then, you must be alert to distinguishing between explanation and argument.

■ HOW TO WRITE SYNTHESES

Although writing syntheses can't be reduced to a lockstep method, it should help you to follow the guidelines listed in the box below.

In this chapter, we'll focus on explanatory syntheses. In the next chapter, we'll discuss the argument synthesis.

Guidelines for Writing Syntheses

- *Consider your purpose in writing.* What are you trying to accomplish in your paper? How will this purpose shape the way you approach your sources?

- *Select and carefully read your sources* according to your purpose. Then reread the passages, mentally summarizing each. Identify those aspects or parts of your sources that will help you fulfill your purpose. When rereading, *label* or *underline* the sources' main ideas, key terms, and any details you want to use in the synthesis.

- *Take notes on your reading.* In addition to labeling or underlining key points in the readings, you might write brief one- or two-sentence summaries of each source. This will help you in formulating your thesis statement and in choosing and organizing your sources later.

- *Formulate a thesis.* Your thesis is the main idea that you want to present in your synthesis. It should be expressed as a complete sentence. You might do some predrafting about the ideas discussed in the readings in order to help you work out a thesis. If you've written one-sentence summaries of the readings, looking over the summaries will help you to brainstorm connections between readings and to devise a thesis.

  When you write your synthesis drafts, you will need to consider where your thesis fits in your paper. Sometimes the thesis is the first sentence, but more often it is *the final sentence of the first paragraph.* If you are writing an *inductively arranged* synthesis (see p. 137), the thesis sentence may not appear until the final paragraphs.

- *Decide how you will use your source material.* How will the information and the ideas in the passages help you fulfill your purpose?

- *Develop an organizational plan,* according to your thesis. How will you arrange your material? It is not necessary to prepare a formal outline. But you should have some plan that will indicate the order in which you will present your material and the relationships among your sources.

- *Draft the topic sentences for the main sections.* This is an optional step, but you may find it a helpful transition from organizational plan to first draft.

- *Write the first draft* of your synthesis, following your organizational plan. Be flexible with your plan, however. Frequently, you will use an outline to get started. As you write, you may discover new ideas and make room for them by adjusting the outline. When this

(continues)

happens, reread your work frequently, making sure that your thesis still accounts for what follows and that what follows still logically supports your thesis.

- *Document your sources.* You must do this by crediting sources within the body of the synthesis—citing the author's last name and the page number from which the point was taken—and then providing full citation information in a list of "Works Cited" at the end. Don't open yourself to charges of plagiarism! (See pp. 50–52.)

- *Revise your synthesis,* inserting transitional words and phrases where necessary. Make sure that the synthesis reads smoothly, logically, and clearly from beginning to end. Check for grammatical correctness, punctuation, and spelling.

Note: The writing of syntheses is a recursive process, and you should accept a certain amount of backtracking and reformulating as inevitable. For instance, in developing an organizational plan (Step 6 of the procedure), you may discover a gap in your presentation that will send you scrambling for another source—back to Step 2. You may find that formulating a thesis and making inferences among sources occur simultaneously; indeed, inferences are often made before a thesis is formulated. Our recommendations for writing syntheses will give you a structure that will get you started. But be flexible in your approach; expect discontinuity and, if possible, be assured that through backtracking and reformulating, you will produce a coherent, well-crafted paper.

■ THE EXPLANATORY SYNTHESIS

Many of the papers you write in college will be more or less explanatory in nature. An explanation helps readers understand a topic. Writers explain when they divide a subject into its component parts and present them to the reader in a clear and orderly fashion. Explanations may entail descriptions that re-create in words some object, place, emotion, event, sequence of events, or state of affairs.

- As a student reporter, you may need to explain an event—to relate when, where, and how it took place.

- In a science lab, you would observe the conditions and results of an experiment and record them for review by others.

- In a political science course, you might review research on a particular subject—say, the complexities underlying the debate over gay marriage—and then present the results of your research to your professor and the members of your class.

Your job in writing an explanatory paper—or in writing the explanatory portion of an argumentative paper—is not to argue a particular point, but rather *to present the facts in a reasonably objective manner.* Of course, explanatory papers, like other academic papers, should be based on a thesis (see pp. 99–100). But the purpose of a thesis in an explanatory paper is less to advance a particular opinion than to focus the various facts contained in the paper.

■ DEMONSTRATION: EXPLANATORY SYNTHESIS—GOING UP? AN ELEVATOR RIDE TO SPACE

To illustrate how the process of synthesis works, we'll begin with a number of short extracts from several articles on the same subject.

Suppose you were writing a paper on an intriguing idea you came across in a magazine: a space elevator—a machine that would lift objects into earth orbit, and beyond, not by blasting them free of earth's gravity using rockets but by lifting them in ways similar to (but also different from) the way elevators on earth lift people and material in tall buildings. Once considered a fancy of science fiction, the idea has received serious attention among scientists and even NASA. In fact, an elevator to space could be built relatively soon.

Fascinated by the possibility of an elevator to space being built in your lifetime, you decide to conduct some research with the goal of *explaining* what you discover to interested classmates.

Exercise 3.1

Exploring the Topic

Read the selections that follow on the subject of space elevators. Before continuing with the discussion after the selections, write a page or two of responses. You might imagine the ways an elevator to space might change you and, more broadly, the economy, the military, and international relations. What do you imagine will concern some people about a space elevator? What do you think might be of interest to journalists, the military, politicians, businesspeople, entertainers, artists?

In the following pages we present excerpts from the kinds of source materials you might locate during the research process.

Note: To save space and for the purpose of demonstration, we offer excerpts from three sources only; a full list of sources appears in the "Works Cited" of the model synthesis on pages 119–120. In preparing your paper, of course, you would draw on the entire articles from which these extracts were taken. (The discussion of how these passages can form the basis of an explanatory synthesis resumes on p. 91.)

THE HISTORY OF THE SPACE ELEVATOR

P.K. Aravind

P. K. Aravind teaches in the Department of Physics at the Worcester Polytechnic Institute, Worcester, Massachusetts. The following is excerpted from "The Physics of the Space Elevator" in The American Journal of Physics *(May 2007).*

I. Introduction

A space elevator is a tall tower rising from a point on the Earth's equator to a height well above a geostationary orbit,* where it terminates in a counterweight (see Fig. 1a). Although the idea of such a structure is quite old, it is only within the last decade or so that it has attracted serious scientific attention. NASA commissioned some studies of the elevator in the 1990s that concluded that it would be feasible to build one and use it to transport payload cheaply into space and also to launch spacecraft on voyages to other planets.[1] Partly as a result of this study, a private organization called Liftport[2] was formed in 2003 with the goal of constructing a space elevator and enlisting the support of universities, research labs, and businesses that might have an interest in this venture. Liftport's website features a timer that counts down the seconds to the opening of its elevator on 12 April 2018. Whether that happens or not, the space elevator represents an application of classical mechanics to an engineering project on a gargantuan scale that would have an enormous impact on humanity if it is realized. As such, it is well worth studying and thinking about for all the possibilities it has to offer.

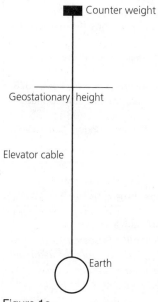

Figure 1a

This article explains the basic mechanical principles underlying the construction of the space elevator and discusses some of its principal applications. It should be accessible to anyone who has had a course in undergraduate mechanics and could help give students in such a course a feeling for some of the contemporary applications of mechanics. Before discussing the physics of the space elevator, we recall some of the more interesting facts of its history. The earliest mention of anything like the elevator seems to have been in the book of Genesis, which talks of an attempt by an ancient civilization to build a tower to heaven—the "Tower of Babel"—that came to naught because of a breakdown of

*Geostationary orbit, also referred to as geostationary earth orbit (or GEO), marks the altitude above the earth's equator (22,236 miles) at which a satellite will rotate at the same speed as the earth itself and, thus, appear to remain motionless in the sky.

communication between the participants. In more recent times the concept of the space elevator was first proposed by the Russian physicist Konstantin Tsiolkovsky in 1895 and then again by the Leningrad engineer, Yuri Artsutanov, in 1960.[3] The concept was rediscovered by the American engineer, Jerome Pearson,[4] in 1975. In 1978 Arthur Clarke brought the idea to the attention of the general public through his novel *Fountains of Paradise*[5] and at about the same time Charles Sheffield, a physicist, wrote a novel[6] centered on the same concept. Despite this publicity, the idea of the elevator did not really catch on among scientists because an analysis of its structure showed that no known material was strong enough to build it.

This pessimism was largely neutralized by the discovery of carbon nanotubes in 1991.[7] Carbon nanotubes, which are essentially rolled up sheets of graphite, have a tensile strength greatly exceeding that of any other known material. Their high tensile strength, combined with their relatively low density, makes nanotubes an excellent construction material for a space elevator and led to a resurgence of interest in the concept.

Notes

1. See the story "Audacious and outrageous: Space elevators" at http://science.nasa.gov/headlines/y2000/ast07sep_1.htm.
2. Liftport, http://www.liftport.com/.
3. K. E. Tsiolkowskii, *Dreams of Earth and Sky* 1895, reissue, Athena Books, Barcelona-Singapore, 2004. Y. Artsutanov, "V Kosmos na Elektrovoze" "To the cosmos by electric train" Komsomolskaya Pravda, 31 July 1960.
4. J. Pearson, "The orbital tower: A spacecraft launcher using the Earth's rotational energy," Acta Astronaut. 2, 785–799 1975.
5. Arthur C. Clarke, *Fountains of Paradise* Harcourt Bruce Jovanovich, New York, 1978.
6. Charles Sheffield, *The Web Between the Worlds* Baen, Simon and Schuster, Riverdale, NY, 2001.
7. S. Iijima, "Helical microtubules of graphitic carbon," Nature London 354, 56–58 1991.

APPLICATIONS OF THE SPACE ELEVATOR

Bradley C. Edwards

Bradley Edwards, director of research for the Institute for Scientific Research (ISR), is the best-known advocate of the space elevator. Rejected as a young man from the astronaut corps due to health concerns, he earned an advanced degree in physics and worked at the Los Alamos National Laboratory on projects related to space technologies. The selection that follows is excerpted from a 2003 report (The Space Elevator: National Institute for Advanced Concepts Phase II Report) *prepared on the completion of a grant from NASA.*

Every development must have some value to be worth doing. In the case of the space elevator there are both short and long-term applications.... The immediate first use of the space elevator is deployment of Earth-orbiting satellites for telecommunications, military, Earth monitoring, etc....

The traditional markets the space elevator will address include:

- Telecommunications
- Remote sensing
- Department of Defense

The U.S. satellite launch market is expected to be at 110 launches per year when we enter the market.[1]

However, we plan to extend this traditional base and target smaller institutions who are interested in space activities—clients who, until now, have been unable to afford it. The new markets we will encourage and target include:

- Solar Energy Satellites (clean, limitless power from space)
- Space-System Test-Bed (universities, aerospace)
- Environmental Assessment (pollution, global change)
- Agricultural Assessment (crop analysis, forestry)
- Private Communications Systems (corporate)
- National Systems (developing countries)
- Medical Therapy (aging, physical handicaps, chronic pain)
- Entertainment/Advertising (sponsorships, remote video adventures)
- Space Manufacturing (biomedical, crystal, electronics)
- Asteroid Detection (global security)
- Basic Research (biomedical, commercial production, university programs)
- Private Tracking Systems (Earth transportation inventory, surveillance)
- Space Debris Removal (International environmental)
- Exploratory Mining Claims (robotic extraction)
- Tourism/Communities (hotels, vacations, medical convalescence)

We expect solar power satellites to be one of the major markets to develop when we become operational and have begun dialogs with [British Petroleum] Solar about launch requirements and interest. Solar power satellites consist of square miles of solar arrays that collect solar power and then beam the power back to Earth for terrestrial consumption. Megawatt systems will have masses of several thousand tons[2] and will provide power at competitive rates to fossil fuels, without pollution, if launch costs get below $500/lb. . . .

5   Another market we expect to emerge is solar system exploration and development. Initially this would be unmanned but a manned segment, based on the Mars Direct (Zubrin) scenario, could emerge early after elevator operations begin. The exploration market would include:

- Exploratory and mining claims missions to asteroids, Mars, Moon, and Venus
- Science-based, university and private sponsored missions
- In-situ resource production on Mars and Moon

- Large mapping probes for Mars and the asteroids
- Near-Earth object catastrophic impact studies from space

The exploration market would be expected to consist of only a few lifts a year within two years of operations but each mission would be a larger one and produce substantial media attention. In the long-term, such practices will increase our revenue as manned activities in space grow.

Another market to consider in the coming decades is space tourism. We may encourage tourism early on with day-long joyrides to space and later possibly lease a ribbon for long-term, hotels in space. Such activities will produce positive public perception and broaden the long-term market. In a recent survey by Zogby International it was found that "7% of affluent (people) would pay $20 million for 2-week orbital flight; 19% would pay $100,000 for 15-minute sub-orbital flight." These numbers indicate a possible future market that could be tapped as well.

Notes
1. Zogby International
2. NASA and ESA studies

GOING UP*

Brad Lemley

The following excerpt appeared in the July 2004 issue of Discover magazine.

Ocean-based platform for a space elevator

The key to conquering the solar system is inside a black plastic briefcase on Brad Edwards's desk. Without ceremony, he pops open the case to reveal it: a piece of black ribbon about a foot long and a half-inch wide, stretched across a steel frame.

Huh? No glowing infinite-energy orb, no antigravity disk, just a hunk of tape with black fibers. "This came off a five-kilometer-long spool," says Edwards, tapping it with his index finger. "The technology is moving along quickly."

The ribbon is a piece of carbon-nanotube composite. In as little as 15 years, Edwards says, a version that's three feet wide and thinner than the page you are reading could be anchored to a platform 1,200 miles off the coast of Ecuador and stretch upward 62,000 miles into deep space, kept taut by the centripetal force provided by Earth's rotation. The expensive, dangerous business of rocketing people and cargo into space would become obsolete as elevators climb the ribbon and hoist occupants to any height they fancy: low, for space tourism; geosynchronous, for communications satellites; or high, where Earth's rotation would help fling spacecraft to the moon, Mars, or beyond. Edwards contends that a space elevator could drop payload costs to $100 a pound versus the space shuttle's $10,000. And it would cost as little as $6 billion to build—less than half what Boston spent on the Big Dig highway project.

Science fiction writers, beginning with Arthur C. Clarke in his 1979 novel, *The Fountains of Paradise,* and a few engineers have kicked around fantastic notions of a space elevator for years. But Edwards's proposal—laid out in a two-year $500,000 study funded by the NASA Institute for Advanced Concepts— strikes those familiar with it as surprisingly practical. "Brad really put the pieces together," says Patricia Russell, associate director of the institute. "Everyone is intrigued. He brought it into the realm of reality."

5   "It's the most detailed proposal I have seen so far. I was delighted with the simplicity of it," says David Smitherman, technical manager of the advanced projects office at NASA's Marshall Space Flight Center. "A lot of us feel that it's worth pursuing."

Still, there's many a slip between speculative space proposals and the messy real world. The space shuttle, to name one example, was originally projected to cost $5.5 million per launch; the actual cost is more than 70 times as much. The International Space Station's cost may turn out to be 10 times its original $8 billion estimate. While NASA takes the space elevator seriously, the idea is officially just one of dozens of advanced concepts jostling for tight funding, and it was conspicuously absent from President Bush's January 14 [2004] address, in which he laid out plans for returning to the moon by 2020, followed by a manned mission to Mars.

So the United States does not appear to be in a mad rush to build an elevator to heaven anytime soon. On the other hand, for reasons Edwards makes abundantly clear, the United States cannot afford to dither around for decades with his proposal. "The first entity to build a space elevator will own space," he says. And after several hours spent listening to Edwards explain just how and why that is so, one comes away persuaded that he is probably right.

Climber

Ascent vehicles will vary in size, configuration, and power, depending on function. All will climb via tractorlike treads that pinch the ribbon like the wringers of an old-fashioned washing machine. Power for the motors will come from photovoltaic cells on the climbers' undersides that are energized by a laser beamed up from the anchor station. At least two additional lasers will be located elsewhere in case clouds block the anchor station's beam.

Counterweight

A deployment booster, carried aloft in pieces by a vehicle such as the space shuttle and assembled in low Earth orbit, will unfurl two thin strips of ribbon stretching from Earth to deep space. Once the strips are anchored to a site on Earth,

Space elevator in earth orbit showing tether and laser
power beam

230 unmanned climbers will "zip" together and widen the strips. Those climbers
will then remain permanently at the far end of the ribbon, just below the deployment booster, to serve as a counterweight.

Consider Your Purpose

We asked a student, Sheldon Kearney, to read these three selections and
to use them (and others) as sources in an explanatory paper on the space
elevator. (We also asked him to write additional comments describing
the process of developing his ideas into a draft.) His paper (the final
version begins on p. 112) drew on eighteen selections on space elevator
technology. How did he—how would you—go about synthesizing the
sources?

First, remember that before considering the *how,* you must consider the
why. In other words, what is your *purpose* in synthesizing these sources?
You might use them for a paper dealing with a broader issue: the commer-
cialization of space, for instance. If this were your purpose, any sources on
the space elevator would likely be used in only one section devoted to cost-
effective options for lifting materials from earth into zero gravity. Because
such a broader paper would consider topics other than the space elevator
(for instance, a discussion of business opportunities in earth orbit or of
possible legal problems among companies operating in space), it would
need to draw on sources unrelated to space elevators.

For a business or finance course, you might search for sources that
would help you present options for private and government funding of
space elevators. The sources gathered by Sheldon Kearney could help
explain the technology, but, again, you would need to find other sources
to investigate the advantages and disadvantages of public versus private
funding or types of private funding. Your overall intention would still be
explanatory, yet your focus and your selection of sources would need to

broaden from what a space elevator is (the focus of his present paper) to a consideration of the ways in which different classes of investors could pay for actual construction. *Your purpose in writing, then, governs your choice of sources.*

Assume that your goal is to write an explanation of space elevators: a *synthesis* that will explain what the elevator is, how it works, its pros and cons, and why advocates believe it should be built. As part of a larger paper, this explanation would be relatively brief. But if your intention is to explain in greater detail, for an audience of nonspecialists, the basics of space elevator technology and the challenges we can expect with its development, then you will write a paper much like the one Kearney has, the development of which you'll follow in the coming pages. The goal: to present information but not advance a particular opinion or slant on the subject.

Exercise 3.2

Critical Reading for Synthesis

Review the three readings on space elevators and list the ways they explain the technology, address potential advantages and disadvantages, and identify obstacles to construction. Make your list as specific and detailed as you can. Assign a source to each item on the list.

Formulate a Thesis

The difference between a purpose and a thesis is primarily a difference of focus. Your purpose provides direction to your research and gives a focus to your paper. Your thesis sharpens this focus by narrowing it and formulating it in the words of a single declarative statement. (Chapter 6 has more on formulating thesis statements.)

Since Kearney's purpose in this case was to synthesize source material with little or no comment, his thesis would be the most obvious statement he could make about the relationship among the source readings. By "obvious" we mean a statement that is broad enough to encompass the main points of all the readings. Taken as a whole, what do they *mean?* Here Kearney describes the process he followed in coming up with a thesis for his explanatory synthesis:

> I began my writing process by looking over all the readings and noting the main point of each reading in a sentence on a piece of paper.
>
> Then I reviewed all of these points and identified the patterns in the readings. These I recorded underneath my list of main points: All the readings focus on the space elevator: definition, construction, technical obstacles, uses, potential problems. The readings explain a technology that has significant business, military, and environmental implications.

Looking over these points, I drafted what I thought was a preliminary thesis. This thesis summed up for me the information I found in my sources:

> Building a space elevator has garnered the attention of NASA, the U.S. Air Force, foreign nations, private industry, and scientists alike as a feasible and cost effective means of reaching into space.

This was a true statement, the basis of my first draft. What ended up happening, though (I realized this even before my instructor read the draft and commented), was that my supposed thesis wasn't a thesis at all. Instead, I had written a statement that allowed me to write a series of summaries and bullet points and call that a paper. So this first effort was not successful, although one good thing happened: in my conclusion, when I forced myself to sum up, I wrote a sentence that looked more like an organizing thesis statement:

> The development of the space elevator will undoubtedly become a microcosm of the human spirit, for better and for worse.

This statement seemed more promising, and my instructor suggested I use this as my thesis. But the more I thought about "microcosm of the human spirit," the more nervous I got about explaining what the "human spirit" is. That seemed to me too large a project. I figured that might be a trap, so I used a different thesis for my second draft:

> Building the space elevator could lead to innovation and exploration; but there could be problems—caused both by technology and by people—that could derail the project.

This version of the thesis allowed me to write more of a synthesis, to get a conversation going with the sources. After I wrote a second draft, I revised the thesis again. This time, I wanted to hint more directly at the types of problems we could expect. I introduced "earth-bound conflicts" to suggest that the familiar battles we fight down here could easily follow us into space:

> If built, the space elevator would likely promote a new era of innovation and exploration. But one can just as easily imagine progress being compromised by familiar, earth-bound conflicts.

I added "if built" to plant a question that would prepare readers for a discussion of obstacles to constructing the elevator. Originally this thesis was one sentence, but it was long and I split it into two.

Decide How You Will Use Your Source Material

To begin, you will need to summarize your sources—or, at least, be *able* to summarize them. That is, the first step to any synthesis is understanding what your sources say. But because you are synthesizing *ideas* rather than sources, you will have to be more selective than if you were writing a simple summary. In your synthesis, you will not use *all* the ideas and information in every source, only the ones related to your thesis. Some sources might be summarized in their entirety; others, only in part. Look over your earlier notes or sentences discussing the topics covered in the readings, and refer back to the readings themselves. Focusing on the more subtle elements of the issues addressed by the authors, expand your earlier summary sentences. Write brief phrases in the margin of the sources, underline key phrases or sentences, or take notes on a separate sheet of paper or in a word processing file or electronic data-filing program. Decide how your sources can help you achieve your purpose and support your thesis.

For example, how might you use a diagram to explain the basic physics of the space elevator? How would you present a discussion of possible obstacles to the elevator's construction or likely advantages to the country, or business, that builds the first elevators? How much would you discuss political or military challenges?

Develop an Organizational Plan

An organizational plan is your map for presenting material to the reader. What material will you present? To find out, examine your thesis. Do the content and structure of the thesis (that is, the number and order of assertions) suggest an organizational plan for the paper? For example, consider Kearney's revised thesis:

> If built, the space elevator would likely promote a new era of innovation and exploration. But one can just as easily imagine progress being compromised by familiar, earth-bound conflicts.

Without knowing anything about space elevators, a reader of this thesis could reasonably expect the following:

- Definition of the space elevator: What is it? How does it work?
- "If built"—what are the obstacles to building a space elevator?
- What innovations?
- What explorations?
- What problems ("conflicts") on earth would jeopardize construction and use of a space elevator?

Study your thesis, and let it help suggest an organization. Expect to devote at least one paragraph of your paper to developing each section that your thesis promises. Having examined the thesis closely and identified likely sections, think through the possibilities of arrangement. Ask yourself: What information does the reader need to understand first? How do I build on this first section—what block of information will follow? Think of each section in relation to others until you have placed them all and have worked your way through to a plan for the whole paper.

Bear in mind that any one paper can be written—successfully—according to a variety of plans. Your job before beginning your first draft is to explore possibilities. Sketch a series of rough outlines:

- Arrange and rearrange your paper's likely sections until you develop a plan that both enhances the reader's understanding and achieves your objectives as a writer.
- Think carefully about the logical order of your points: Does one idea or point lead to the next?
- If not, can you find a more logical place for the point, or are you just not clearly articulating the connections between the ideas?

Your final paper may well deviate from your final sketch; in the act of writing you may discover the need to explore new material, to omit planned material, to refocus or to reorder your entire presentation. Just the same, a well-conceived organizational plan will encourage you to begin writing a draft.

Summary Statements

In notes describing the process of organizing his material, Kearney refers to all the sources he used, including the three excerpted in this chapter.

> In reviewing my sources and writing summary statements, I detected four main groupings of information:
>
> - The technology for building a space elevator is almost here. Only one major obstacle remains: building a strong enough tether.
> - Several sources explained what the space elevator is and how it could change our world.
> - Another grouping of articles discussed the advantages of the elevator and why we need it.
> - A slightly different combination of articles presented technical challenges and also problems that might arise among nations, such as competition.

I tried to group some of these topics into categories that would have a logical order. What I first wanted to communicate was the sense that the technical obstacles to building a space elevator have been (or soon will be) solved or, in theory, at least, are solvable.

Early in the paper, likely in the paragraph after the introduction, I figured I should explain exactly what a space elevator is.

I would then need to explain the technical challenges—mainly centered on the tether and, possibly, power issues. After covering the technical challenges, I could follow with the challenges that people could pose (based largely on competition and security needs).

I also wanted to give a sense that there's considerable reason for optimism about the space elevator. It's a great idea, but, typically, people could get in the way of their own best interests and defeat the project before it ever got off the ground.

I returned to my thesis and began to think about a structure for the paper.

> Building the space elevator could lead to innovation and exploration, but there could be problems—caused both by technology and by people—that could derail the project.

Based on his thesis, Kearney developed an outline for an eight-paragraph paper, including introduction and conclusion:

1. Introduction: The space elevator <u>can</u> be built a lot sooner than we think.
2. The basic physics of a space elevator is not that difficult to understand.
3. The key to the elevator's success is making a strong tether. Scientists believe they have found a suitable material in carbon nanotubes.
4. Weather and space junk pose threats to the elevator, but these potential problems are solvable with strategic placement of the elevator and sophisticated monitoring systems.
5. Powering the elevator will be a challenge, but one likely source is electricity collected by solar panels and beamed to the climber.
6. Space elevators promise important potential benefits: cost of transporting materials to space will be drastically reduced; industries, including tourism, would take advantage of a zero-gravity environment; and more.
7. Among the potential human-based (as opposed to technology-based) problems to building a space elevator: a new space race; wars to prevent one country from gaining strategic advantage over others, ownership, and access.
8. A space elevator could be inspiring and could usher in a new era of exploration.

Write the Topic Sentences

Writing draft versions of topic sentences (an optional step) will get you started on each main idea of your synthesis and will help give you the sense of direction you need to proceed. Here are Kearney's draft topic sentences for sections, based on the thesis and organizational plan he developed. Note that when read in sequence following the thesis, these sentences give an idea of the logical progression of the essay as a whole.

- A space elevator is exactly what it sounds like.
- A space elevator is not a standard elevator, but a rope—or tether—with a counterweight at the far end kept in place by centrifugal force extending 60,000 miles into space.
- There already exists a single material strong enough to act as a tether for the space elevator, carbon nanotubes.
- Because the space elevator would reach from earth through our atmosphere and into space, it would face a variety of threats to the integrity of its tether.
- Delivering power to the climbers is also a major point of consideration.
- The ability of a space elevator to lift extremely heavy loads from earth into space is beneficial for a number of reasons.
- Ownership, as any homeowner can tell you, comes with immense responsibly; and ownership of a technology that could change the world economy would almost certainly create huge challenges.
- The ambition to build a tower so high it would scrape the heavens is an idea stretching back as far as the story of the Tower of Babel.

Organize a Synthesis by Idea, Not by Source

A synthesis is a blending of sources organized by *ideas*. The following rough sketches suggest how to organize and how *not* to organize a synthesis. The sketches assume you have read seven sources on a topic, sources A–G.

INCORRECT: ORGANIZING BY SOURCE + SUMMARY

Thesis

Summary of source A in support of the thesis.

Summary of source B in support of the thesis.

(continues)

Summary of source C in support of the thesis.

(etc.)

Conclusion

This is *not* a synthesis because it does not blend sources. Each source stands alone as an independent summary. No dialogue among sources is possible.

Correct: Organizing by Idea

Thesis

First idea: Refer to and discuss *parts* of sources (perhaps A, C, F) in support of the thesis.

Second idea: Refer to and discuss *parts* of sources (perhaps B, D) in support of the thesis.

Third idea: Refer to and discuss *parts* of sources (perhaps A, E, G) in support of the thesis.

(etc.)

Conclusion

This *is* a synthesis because the writer blends and creates a dialogue among sources in support of an idea. Each organizing idea, which can be a paragraph or group of related paragraphs, in turn supports the thesis.

Write Your Synthesis

Here is the first draft of Kearney's explanatory synthesis. Thesis and topic sentences are highlighted. Modern Language Association (MLA) documentation style, explained in Chapter 7, is followed throughout.

Alongside this first draft we have included comments and suggestions for revision from Kearney's instructor. For purposes of demonstration, these comments are likely to be more comprehensive than the selective comments provided by most instructors.

■ EXPLANATORY SYNTHESIS: FIRST DRAFT

Kearney 1

Sheldon Kearney

Professor Leslie Davis

Technology and Culture

October 1, 2014

The Space Elevator

(1) A space elevator is exactly what it sounds like: an elevator reaching into space. And though some thirty years ago the notion of a such an elevator was little more than science fiction, today, building a space elevator has garnered the attention of NASA, the U.S. Air Force, foreign nations, private industry, and scientists alike as a feasible and cost-effective means of reaching into space.

(2) A space elevator is not a standard elevator, but a rope—or tether—with a counterweight at the far end kept in place by centrifugal force extending 60,000 miles into space (citation needed). The rotation of the earth combined with the weight and size of the tether would keep the line taught. As __ notes, imagine a rope hanging down from the earth rather than extending up (citation needed). Rather than having a counterweight moving cargo up and down the tether, as in a conventional elevator, a space elevator would make use of mechanical climbers to move cargo into and down from space. (Image needed for this?)

(3) There already is a material strong enough to act as a tether for the space elevator, carbon nanotubes.

Title and Paragraph 1

Your title could be more interesting and imaginative. Your first paragraph has no organizing statement, no thesis. Devise a statement—or find one in the draft (see your last paragraph—"microcosm of the human spirit")—that can create a map for your readers. Finally, expand the first paragraph and make it an interesting (fascinating?) transition into the world of space elevators.

Paragraph 2

Consider using an image to help readers understand what a space elevator is and how it works. Also consider using an analogy—what is the space elevator like that readers would understand?

Kearney 2

Discovered in 1991 by Sumio Iijima, carbon nanotubes have been tested in labs to be X times stronger and X times lighter than steel (get stats). In theory the production of a carbon nanotube ribbon only a meter wide and millimeters thick would be strong enough to act as the space elevator's tether. "Small quantities of some nanotubes have been made that are sufficiently strong enough to be used in a space elevator," though the scale of production would need to be drastically increased to build the tether needed for the space elevator (Olson interview).

Paragraph 3
The tether is a crucial component of the space elevator. Any obstacles to building? Expand this part of the explanation.

(4) Threats. Because the space elevator would reach from Earth through our atmosphere and into space, there are threats it will face to the integrity of its tether. Weather conditions such as hurricanes and lightning pose a threat to the space elevator, as do impacts from Earth-bound objects, i.e. planes, as well as low earth orbit objects such as satellites and meteors and orbital debris. These types of threats have possible solutions. Locating the space elevator off of the Galapagos Islands in open water, if possible, minimizes the likelihood of lightning, wind, and hurricanes damaging the elevator. In this sight, the occurrence of such events are extremely rare (footnote needed, as well as image provided by Edwards). Furthermore, by attaching the space elevator to a large ocean vessel, such as a deep water oil platform, it would be possible to move the tether in the case of severe weather conditions. The ability to move the space elevator

Paragraphs 4 and 5
Reverse the order of paragraphs 4 and 5. "Power" is a core element of the elevator's success. A discussion of "threats" assumes the space elevator is already functional. Logically, "power" should come first.

Kearney 3

is important: NASA estimates that there are some 500,000 objects within the Earth's orbit that could catastrophically damage the space elevator (NASA sight and Edwards).

⑤   Delivering power to the climbers is also a major point of consideration. Bringing along the fuel would be prohibitively heavy due to the length of the trip, as would dragging a long power cord. Powering the elevator with laser beams of electricity generated by solar cells on the ground has been proposed by advocates of the space elevator. Lasers powerful enough to be used to fuel the climbers are already commercially available (Olsen interview).

⑥   The ability of a space elevator to lift extremely heavy loads from Earth into space is beneficial for a number of reasons. Chemical rockets are only able to carry approximately 6% of their total weight into space as cargo, with the remaining 94% used for fuel to escape the Earth's gravity and launch vehicles (Swan, 2006 2.2). For a space elevator, however, the immense strength of the tether would allow for mechanical climbers to lift extremely heavy loads. There are several obvious advantages to a space elevator:

Paragraph 6

This paragraph, currently in both sentence and bullet format, needs to be split up and expanded. The cost analysis is an important piece of justifying the space elevator. Expand this discussion and explain the expected savings. Also, as part of justifying a new thesis re: "the human spirit," expand your bulleted list of benefits. Possibly develop a full paragraph for each bullet.

- As the tether's strength builds over time, there is virtually no limit to the strength and payload capacity of the elevator.

- Inexpensive access to space would quickly permit the development of entirely new space-based industries like tourism and manufacturing.

- The increased ability to place satellites into space would increase the security

Kearney 4

and amount of digital information needed in the global economy.

- The development of a space elevator could also further act as a launching point for future interplanetary exploration.

(7) Dr. Edwards notes that "the first entity to build a space elevator will own space" (Edwards 2000 needed). In this he is certainly correct. But ownership, as any homeowner can tell you, comes with immense responsibility; and ownership of a technology that could change the world economy would almost certainly create huge challenges (Eric Westling Interview). Key questions to consider:

- Will the creation of one space elevator create a new space race between nations?
- Will one nation's desire to prevent its construction lead to war?
- Who will own the elevator?
- Who will have access to space via the elevator?

(8) The ambition to build a tower so high it would scrape the heavens is an idea stretching back as far as the story of the Tower of Babel. For these ancient builders their ambition was too great and they were punished. The development of the space elevator will undoubtedly become a microcosm of the human spirit, for better and for worse. A space elevator will inspire untold technological developments and usher in a yet unknown expansion of the human condition as we begin in earnest to explore beyond the confines and limitations of the Earth. Yet, the development of a space elevator will almost certainly act as a lightning rod for international conflict.

Paragraph 7

Similar to the comment re: paragraph 6: split the current paragraph and expand bulleted points. If your paper is to account "for better and for worse" elements of the human spirit (see par. 8), then you need a full discussion of problems associated with the elevator. Presently, only these abbreviated bullets suggest possible problems. Expand—possibly a paragraph for each bullet.

Paragraph 8

You have found your thesis in this paragraph: "The developments...for better and for worse." Consider moving this sentence to the head of the paper and building out the conclusion to discuss the space elevator and "the human spirit."

Revise Your Synthesis: Global, Local, and Surface Revisions

Many writers find it helpful to plan for three types of revision: global, local, and surface.

Global revisions affect the entire paper: the thesis, the type and pattern of evidence employed, and the overall organization. A global revision may also emerge from a change in purpose—say, when a writer realizes that a paper works better as an argument than as an explanation. In this case, Kearney decided to revise globally based on his instructor's suggestion to use a statement from the conclusion as a thesis in the second draft. The immediate consequence of this decision: Kearney realized he needed to expand substantially the discussion of the benefits of the space elevator and also its potential problems. Such an expansion would make good on the promise of his new thesis for the second draft (a reformulation of his "human spirit" statement at the end of the first draft): "Building the space elevator could lead to innovation and exploration, but there could be problems—caused both by technology and by people—that could derail the project."

Local revisions affect paragraphs: topic and transitional sentences; the type of evidence presented within a paragraph; evidence added, modified, or dropped within a paragraph; logical connections from one sentence or set of sentences within a paragraph to another.

Surface revisions deal with sentence style and construction, word choice, and errors of grammar, mechanics, spelling, and citation form.

Revising the First Draft: Highlights

Global

- At present, the paper has no organizing thesis. Consider moving the sentence underlined in the final paragraph to the first paragraph and letting it serve as your thesis for the revision. "Microcosm of the human spirit" is promising because our reach into space does speak to the human spirit.

- Be careful in your conclusion not to move your explanatory synthesis into the territory of argument. The paragraph as written shifts away from your sources to your personal point of view concerning what might happen post-development of a space elevator.

- Expand the bullet points on the benefits and key challenges facing development of the space elevator (paragraphs 6–7). Expanded, each bullet point could become a paragraph. Considered together, these discussions of benefits and challenges could justify your explanatory claim about "microcosm."

- In paragraph 6, explain in more detail the cost advantages of the space elevator. Relatively inexpensive access to space is one of the key benefits.

Local

- Your introduction needs work. Create more of a context for your topic that moves readers to your (new) thesis. The topic is fascinating. Show your fascination to readers! Work as well on your concluding paragraph; assuming you move the underlined statement in that paragraph to your introduction (where it would serve as a thesis), the remaining conclusion will be weak.

- Expand your discussion of power requirements for the elevator (paragraph 5) and move that before your discussion of threats (currently paragraph 4). Logic: a discussion of threats assumes an operational space elevator, one of the requirements of which is a dependable power supply.

- Expand your discussion of the tether in paragraph 3—a key component of the elevator. We need to know more, including obstacles to making the tether.

- Graphic images could be very helpful to your explanation of the space elevator. You consider using them in paragraphs 2 and 4.

- Assuming you expand the paper and justify your explanatory claim about the development of the elevator providing a "microcosm of the human spirit," you could expand your conclusion. What do you mean, exactly, by "human spirit"—and, also, by "for better and for worse"?

Surface

- Avoid weak verbs (see the first sentence of paragraph 5). Revise passive constructions such as "has been proposed by" in paragraph 5 and "were punished" in paragraph 8.

- Avoid constructions like "there is" and "there are" in paragraphs 3 and 4.

- Watch for errors like "taught" vs. "taut" in paragraph 2 and "sight" vs. "site" in paragraph 4.

- Fix grammatical errors—for instance, subject-verb agreement in paragraph 4: "the occurrence of such events "are" or "is"?

Exercise 3.3

Revising the Explanatory Synthesis

Try your hand at creating a final draft of the paper on pages 112–120 by following the revision suggestions above and using your own best judgment about how to improve the first draft. Make global, local, and surface changes. After writing your own version of the paper, compare it with the revised version of our student paper below.

MODEL EXPLANATORY SYNTHESIS

Sheldon Kearney

Professor Leslie Davis

Technology and Culture

October 12, 2014

Going Up? An Elevator Ride to Space

(1)   In his 1979 science fiction novel *The Fountains of Paradise,* Arthur C. Clarke introduced his readers to space elevators. While Clarke's idea of a platform that would ride a tether into space (eliminating the need for rockets) was not new, his novel helped focus scientific imaginations on the possibilities. A space elevator is exactly what it sounds like: a platform rising from the ground, not to the top floor of a building but into the weightlessness of earth orbit. It's a real-life Tower of Babel, built to "reach unto heaven" (Gen. 11.4). For thirty years, the elevator has been little more than science fiction hinting at future space tourism, manufacturing in zero gravity, mining of asteroids, abundant solar power beamed to anywhere on earth, and dramatically less expensive inter-planetary travel. Today, however, NASA, the U.S. Air Force, and private industry regard the technology as both feasible and cost-effective. If built, the space elevator would likely promote a new era of innovation and exploration. But one can just as easily imagine progress being compromised by familiar, earth-bound conflicts.

(2)   The physics of a space elevator should be familiar to any child who has spun a rope with a rock attached to one end: as the arm spins, the rope remains extended to its full length in the air, apparently defying gravity. The rope and the rock stay up because centrifugal force acts to push the weight outward, while the rope keeps the rock from flying off. In the case of a space elevator, instead of the child spinning the weight, it is the earth that's spinning. And instead of a rope perhaps three feet in length extending taut from the child's hand out to the rock, the far end of a space tether would be attached to a weight extending 62,000 miles from earth (Aravind 125–26; Kent 3). Movement up and down the tether would not involve the

Kearney 2

use of a counterweight and pulley system, as with terrestrial elevators, but rather a mechanical climber to ferry cargo to and from space.

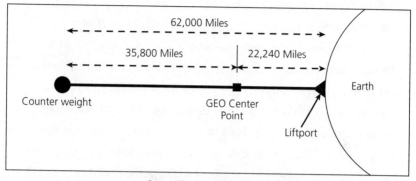

Space Elevator Basic Layout

Figure 1 "The space elevator...is a 1-meter wide tether stretching from the surface of the earth out to a point some 62,000 miles in orbit. The base of the ribbon is attached to a platform on the surface (floating at sea) while the space end of the tether extends past geosynchronous orbit to a counter weight. Lifters...would clamp onto the tether and, using a series of rollers powered by lasers, ascend and descend in order to carry people, material, and cargo to and from orbit." (Kent 3)

When the space elevator was first envisioned, no known material was strong enough to serve as a tether. Then in 1991, Sumio Iijima, a Japanese physicist and materials scientist at Meijo University in Nagoya, discovered the carbon nanotube: "a material that is theoretically one hundred or more times stronger and ten times lighter than steel" (Kent iii). In principle, the production of a carbon nanotube ribbon only a meter wide and millimeters thick would be strong enough to act as the tether for a space elevator. According to Brad Edwards, a former NASA scientist and leading proponent of space elevators, a nanotube strong enough to serve as a tether will soon be available (Interview, NOVA), though the scale of production would have to increase dramatically to achieve the required 62,000 mile length. Because scaling to that extent could create an "unavoidable presence of defects" (Pugno), materials investigation continues. But Edwards is confident enough to predict an operational space elevator by 2031 (Liftport). Production of nanotubes aside, the major obstacles to construction are not

Kearney 3

technical but rather financial (funds must be found to build the elevator); legal (the 62,000 mile tether cannot interfere with existing satellites); and political (interests representing the chemical rocket industry will object to and likely attempt to thwart the elevator) (Edwards, *Phase II* 40).

NASA has been sufficiently intrigued by the concept to join with the Spaceward Foundation in creating "The Space Elevator Games," which awards cash prizes to promising elevator technologies (Shelef). Key modifications to terrestrial elevators have already been designed. For instance, because carrying the fuel necessary to power the elevator platform would render the project as expensive as chemical rockets (which also carry their own fuel), engineers believe that ground-based lasers, powered by the sun, could aim energy beams that would power the mechanical climber. Such lasers are already produced in the United States (LaserMotive).

Figure 2   Ocean-based platform for a
space elevator

Figure 3   Space elevator in earth orbit showing tether and laser power beam
Source: Images created by Brad Edwards with permission.

(5) Because the space elevator would reach from Earth through our atmo-sphere and into space, the tether would be vulnerable to damage or cata-strophic failure from airplanes, space debris, meteors, and violent storms. Impact threats like these also have likely solutions, one being to locate the space elevator in a weather-stable climate—for example, off the Galapagos Islands—in open water, which would minimize the likelihood of damage from lightning or wind (SpaceRef). Attaching the earth-end of the elevator to a large ocean vessel, such as a deep water oil platform, would permit moving a tether threatened by impending collisions with space debris or meteors, which would be tracked by an array of telescopes (Edwards, *Phase I* 5.8; *Phase II* 23).

(6) At present, NASA and other space agencies around the globe are limited to ferrying relatively small quantities of cargo into space, with dozens of launches needed to build (for example) the international space station. Today, at a per-kilogram cost of $11,000, chemical rockets are able to carry only 6% of their total weight into space as cargo, with the remain-ing 94% used for fuel to escape the Earth's gravity and to launch vehicles (Swan 2.2). For a space elevator, however, the immense strength of the tether would allow mechanical climbers to lift extremely heavy loads for roughly $100 per kilogram. Edwards estimates that within as few as two

years of operation, the elevator could be "capable of supporting a 22 ton
(20,000 kg) climber with a 14 ton (13,000 kg) payload" (*Phase I* 1.4).
He and others estimate the cost of building a space elevator within the
next ten to twenty years to be a tiny fraction of the cost of a trip to Mars
(*Phase 1* 1.8; Lemley).

⑦   The construction of a space elevator could usher in a new era of exploration and development akin to the reach of the railroad across the continental
United States. In this case, however, not only would the economy of a nation
be transformed but also, possibly, the global economy. With the low-cost lifting
of materials into orbit commonplace, the dreams of science fiction writers could
come true, including "mining the asteroid belt, building zero-G hotels, sailing
the solar winds to the moon or Mars, [and] disposing of our radioactive waste
by shooting it into the sun" (Taylor). Inexpensive access to space would quickly
permit the development of entirely new space-based industries. Proposals
already exist to use a space elevator to develop orbiting solar arrays capable of
providing cheap, abundant, and clean electrical power to almost anywhere in
the world (Edwards, *Phase I* 1.7). Such a clean and economically viable energy
source made available to much of the world could decrease dependence on fossil fuels and the nations that export them (Swan 2.3.1.), which in turn could
potentially transform the political and economic landscape here on earth.

⑧   The comparatively inexpensive satellite launches made possible by
a space elevator would secure global data transfer, including communications. A recent study conducted by the University of California, San Diego,
concluded that "the average American consumes about 34 gigabytes of data
and information each day" (Bilton). The invention of the iPhone and other
Web- and video-capable mobile devices as well as the global proliferation
of high-speed Internet in recent years have only increased the need for
secure, fast data transfer. Satellites, along with cell towers and fiber-optic
cables, form the pillars of this transfer. With regular, relatively inexpensive
access to earth orbit provided by a space elevator, military and commercial
interests could have replacement satellites ready for deployment in the

Kearney 6

event of malfunctions (or attack). Sufficient redundancy could be built into these systems to secure the communications and data exchange on which the global economy will increasingly depend.

(9)   A space elevator could also prove crucial to the success of future interplanetary exploration, since cheap access to space would make manned missions economically feasible. In January 2010 President Obama's proposed federal budget eliminated NASA's Constellation program, which planned for manned missions to the moon within ten years. A working space elevator would significantly reduce the cost of such programs and could make them more attractive in the future. Space agencies would be able to build vehicles on earth, where they are more easily and cheaply assembled, and lift large pieces into space for final assembly.

(10)   But no one should imagine that the construction of a space elevator will bring only good news or that every predicted benefit will be achieved. The prospect of building a space elevator (like the prospect of building an antiballistic missile system) carries with it the potential for fatal misunderstandings and conflicts. For example, a platform in space could provide the builder with enormous military and economic advantages that other nations might find intolerable. We don't need to look much further than the last century to know that nations will launch wars to block rivals from seizing territory that would confer real or perceived advantages. It is not difficult to imagine a scenario in which Russia or China would vigorously protest America's building an elevator capable of creating a military advantage. Even if the United States explained its peaceful intentions, other nations might remain skeptical and, acting out of self-preservation, rush to build their own elevators.

(11)   And just as nations with nuclear bomb-making capacity strongly discourage other nations from joining that club, one can easily imagine the United States discouraging Iran, for instance, from building a space elevator. Already doubtful of that country's claims for peaceful nuclear development, the United States might also doubt Iran's stated peaceful intentions for a space elevator and move to block its development. The resulting political struggle might look

very much like the current effort to keep Iran from becoming a nuclear state. An alternate scenario: other nations, incapable of building the elevator but not willing to see the United States have one, could launch attacks to disable it. Edwards has already considered the implications of a bomb exploding a mechanical climber and severing the nanotube tether (*Phase II* 38).

(12)   Economic gains, real or perceived, of the nation that builds an elevator could also create problems. Not every nation could afford to build its own elevator. Who, then, would control access? Would poor(er) nations be welcomed to share in the expected bounty? Would the elevator become one more resource that separates nations into haves and have-nots? One can imagine the country that builds and operates the elevator saying to others: "You don't cooperate with us here on earth, so we won't grant you cheap access to space." In this scenario, the elevator could become a political and economic weapon.

(13)   Ninety-eight countries, including the United States and Russia, have signed the Outer Space Treaty, which prohibits the placing of nuclear weapons and other weapons of mass destruction into space and establishes the principle that no country can claim sovereignty of space or celestial bodies beyond earth. The spirit of the agreement is hopeful in being "[i]nspired by the great prospects opening up before mankind as a result of man's entry into outer space" (3); but the agreement is somber as well in recognizing implicitly that nations act in their own interests: "The exploration and use of outer space, including the Moon and other celestial bodies, shall be carried out for the benefit and in the interests of all countries, irrespective of their degree of economic or scientific development, and shall be the province of all mankind" (4). Proponents hope that the nations that build space elevators will adhere to these principles and not seek to make earth orbit the ultimate high ground for economic and military advantage.

(14)   The construction of an elevator to space should excite our collective imaginations; but, human nature being what it is, no one should be surprised if conflicts, along with our hopes, follow the platform into orbit. This is no reason not to pursue research and construction: the elevator and what it makes

Kearney 8

possible could bring great benefits, including pharmaceuticals and exotic materials manufactured in zero gravity, space tourism, endless supplies of renewable energy, secure communications, and a cost-effective platform from which to explore the solar system and beyond. But the space elevator will likely also act as a lightning rod for international competition. In this way, it could well become just another stage on which to play out our quarrels on earth.

Kearney 9

Works Cited

Aravind, P. K. "The Physics of the Space Elevator." *American Journal of Physics* 75.2 (2007): 125–30. PDF file.

The Bible. Introd. and notes by Robert Carroll and Stephen Prickett. Oxford: Oxford UP, 1998. Print. Oxford World's Classics. Authorized King James Vers.

Bilton, Nick. "Part of the Daily American Diet, 34 Gigabytes of Data." *New York Times*. New York Times, 3 Dec. 2009. Web. 14 Sept. 2014.

Clarke, Arthur C. *Fountains of Paradise*. London: V. Gollancz, 1979. Print.

Edwards, Bradley C. Interview. *NOVA: Science Now, Ask the Expert*. PBS, 16 Jan. 2007. Web. 16 Sept. 2014.

---. Interview by Sander Olson. *Nextbigfuture.com*. Lifeboat Foundation, 1 Dec. 2009. Web. 25 Sept. 2014.

---. *The Space Elevator: National Institute for Advanced Concepts Phase I Report*. N.p.: 2000. PDF file.

---. *The Space Elevator: National Institute for Advanced Concepts Phase II Report*. N.p.: 2003. PDF file.

Kent, Jason R. *Getting into Space on a Thread: Space Elevator as Alternative Access to Space*. Maxwell AFB: Air War College, 2007. PDF file.

LaserMotive. Home page. *Lasermotive.com*. LaserMotive, n.d. Web. 14 Sept. 2014.

Kearney 10

Lemley, Brad. "Going Up." *Discovermagazine.com*. Discover Magazine,
      25 July 2004. Web. 12 Sept. 2014.

Liftport. Home page. *Liftport.com*. Liftport, 2003. Web. 20 Sept. 2010.
      Kearney 10

Pugno, Nicola M. "On the Strength of the Carbon Nanotube-based Space
      Elevator Cable: From Nanomechanics to Megamechanics." *Journal of
      Physics: Condensed Matter* 18 (2006): 1971–90. PDF file.

Shelef, Ben. "Did You Just Say 'a Space Elevator'?!" *Spaceward.org*.
      Spaceward Foundation, 2008. Web. 18 Sept. 2014.

SpaceRef Interactive. "LiftPort Announces Support of the Space Elevator
      Concept by the National Space Society." *SpaceRef.com*. SpaceRef
      Interactive, 25 June 2003. Web. 12 Sept. 2014.

Swan, Cathy W., and Peter A. Swan. "Why We Need a Space Elevator."
      Space Policy 22.2 (2006): 86–91. *Science Direct*. Web. 12 Sept. 2014.

Taylor, Chris. "Space Elevator Entrepreneurs Shoot for the Starts." *CNN
      .com*. Cable News Network, 8 Dec. 2009. Web. 14 Sept. 2014.

United Nations. "Treaty on Principles Governing the Activities of States
      in the Exploration and Use of Outer Space, Including the Moon and
      Other Celestial Bodies." *Treaties and Principles on Outer Space*. New
      York: United Nations, 2002: 3–8. PDF file.

Critical Reading for Synthesis

- *Use the tips from Critical Reading for Summary on page 5.*
  Remember to examine the context; note the title and subtitle; identify
  the main point; identify the subpoints; break the reading into sections; distinguish between points, examples, and counterarguments;
  watch for transitions within and between paragraphs; and read
  actively and recursively.

- *Establish the writer's primary purpose.* Use some of the guidelines
  discussed in Chapter 2. Is the piece primarily informative, persuasive, or entertaining? Assess whether the piece achieves its purpose.

(continues)

- *Read to identify a key idea.* If you begin reading your source materials with a key idea or topic already in mind, read to identify what your sources have to say about the idea.

- *Read to discover a key idea.* If you begin the reading process without a key idea in mind, read to discover a key idea that your sources address.

- *Read for relationships.* Regardless of whether you already have a key idea or you are attempting to discover one, your emphasis in reading should be on noting the ways in which the readings relate to each other, to a key idea, and to your purpose in writing the synthesis.

WRITING ASSIGNMENT: ETHICAL DILEMMAS IN EVERYDAY LIFE

Now we'll give you an opportunity to practice your skills in planning and writing an explanatory synthesis. See Chapter 8, pages 281–318, where we provide a variety of sources on the ways "thought experiments" in ethics—scenarios that ask you to decide on courses of right action (and to justify your decisions)—can serve as a guide for facing everyday ethical dilemmas. When there is no clear right and wrong choice, how do you decide? To what principles can you turn for guidance? Your task in the synthesis will be to understand the *process* of ethical decision making and to explain that process to readers less knowledgeable than you on the topic.

Note that your instructor may want you to complete related assignments in Chapter 8, which ask you to write summaries in preparation for writing a larger explanatory synthesis.

Exercise 3.4

Exploring Online Sources

The online databases available through your school's library, as well as Internet search engines such as Google and Bing, will yield many sources beyond the ones gathered for you on the topic of "Ethical Dilemmas in Everyday Life" in Chapter 8. Read the articles on pages 285–312. Then use one or more of your library's databases or conduct an Internet search to locate additional sources on this topic. You are likely to find more recent sources than those reprinted here. If you end up using any Internet sources for the explanatory synthesis assignment, review our cautionary discussion about using Web-based sources (p. 257).

---

4. Argument Synthesis

■ WHAT IS AN ARGUMENT SYNTHESIS?

An argument is an attempt to persuade a reader or listener that a particular and debatable claim is true. Writers argue in order to establish facts, to make statements of value, and to recommend policies. For instance, answering the question *Why do soldiers sometimes commit atrocities in wartime?* would involve making an argument. To develop this argument, researchers might conduct experiments, interview experts, collect historical evidence, and examine and interpret data. The researchers might then present their findings at professional conferences and in journals and books. The extent to which readers (or listeners) accept these findings will depend on the quality of the supporting evidence and the care with which the researchers have argued their case. What we are calling an argument *synthesis* draws upon evidence from a variety of sources in an attempt to persuade others of the truth or validity of a debatable claim.

By contrast, the explanatory synthesis, as we have seen, is fairly modest in purpose. It emphasizes the sources themselves, not the writer's use of sources to persuade others. The writer of an explanatory synthesis aims to inform, not persuade. Here, for example, is a thesis devised for an explanatory synthesis on the ubiquity of cell phones in contemporary life:

> Cell phones make it possible for us to be always within reach, though many people would prefer *not* to be always within reach.

This thesis summarizes two viewpoints about the impact of cell phones on contemporary life, arguing neither for nor against either viewpoint.

An argument thesis, however, is *persuasive* in purpose. A writer working with the same source material might conceive and support an opposing thesis:

> Cell phones have ruined our ability to be isolated, to be willfully *out of touch* with the rest of the world.

So the thesis for an argument synthesis is a claim about which reasonable people could disagree. It is a claim with which—given the right arguments— your audience might be persuaded to agree. The strategy of your argument synthesis is therefore to find and use convincing *support* for your *claim*.

The Elements of Argument: Claim, Support, and Assumption

One way of looking at an argument is to see it as an interplay of three essential elements: claim, support, and assumption. A *claim* is a proposition or conclusion that you are trying to prove. You prove this claim by using *support* in the form of fact, statistics, or expert opinion. Linking your supporting evidence to your claim is your *assumption* about the subject. This assumption, also called a *warrant*, is an underlying belief or principle about some aspect of the world and how it operates (see our discussion of assumptions in Chapter 2, pp. 67–69). By their nature, assumptions (which are often unstated) tend to be more general than either claims or supporting evidence.

Here are the essential elements of an argument advocating parental restriction of television viewing for high school students:

Claim

> High school students should be restricted to no more than two hours of TV viewing per day.

Support

> An important new study and the testimony of educational specialists reveal that students who watch more than two hours of TV a night have, on average, lower grades than those who watch less TV.

Assumption

> Excessive TV viewing adversely affects academic performance.

As another example, here's an argumentative claim on the topic of computer-mediated communication (CMC)—a term sociologists use to describe online contacts among friends and family:

> CMC threatens to undermine human intimacy, connection, and ultimately community.

Here are the other elements of this argument:

Support

- People are spending increasing amounts of time in cyberspace: In 1998, the average Internet user spent more than four hours per week online, a figure that has quadrupled in the past fifteen years.
- College health officials report that excessive Internet use threatens many college students' academic and psychological well-being.
- New kinds of relationships fostered on the Internet often pose challenges to preexisting relationships.

Assumptions

- The communication skills used and the connections formed during Internet contact fundamentally differ from those used and formed during face-to-face contact.
- "Real" connection and a sense of community are sustained by face-to-face contact, not by Internet interactions.

For the most part, arguments should be constructed logically so that assumptions link evidence (supporting facts, statistics, and expert opinions) to claims. As we'll see, however, logic is only one component of effective arguments.

Exercise 4.1

Practicing Claim, Support, and Assumption

Devise two sets of claims, support, and assumptions. First, in response to the example above on computer-mediated communication and relationships, write a one-sentence claim addressing the positive impact (or potentially positive impact) of CMC on relationships—whether you personally agree with the claim or not. Then list the supporting statements on which such a claim might rest and the assumption that underlies them. Second, write a claim that states your own position on any debatable topic you choose. Again, devise statements of support and relevant assumptions.

The Three Appeals of Argument: *Logos, Ethos, Pathos*

Speakers and writers have never relied on logic alone in advancing and supporting their claims. More than 2000 years ago, the Athenian philosopher and rhetorician Aristotle explained how speakers attempting to persuade others to their point of view could achieve their purpose by relying on one or more *appeals,* which he called *logos, ethos,* and *pathos.*

Since we frequently find these three appeals employed in political argument, we'll use political examples in the following discussion. All three appeals are also used extensively in advertising, legal cases, business documents, and many other types of argument. Bear in mind that in academic writing, the appeal to logic (*logos*) is by far the most commonly used appeal.

Logos

Logos is the rational appeal, the appeal to reason. Academic presentations, including the papers you will write across the curriculum, build almost exclusively on appeals to logic and evidence. If writers and speakers expect to persuade their audiences, they must argue logically and must supply appropriate evidence to support their case. Logical arguments are commonly of two types (often combined): deductive and inductive.

Deductive Reasoning   The *deductive* argument begins with a generalization, then cites a specific case related to that generalization from which follows a conclusion. An example of a deductive argument may be seen in President John F. Kennedy's address to the nation in June 1963 on the need for sweeping civil rights legislation. Kennedy begins with the generalizations that it "ought to be possible...for American students of any color to attend any public institution they select without having to be backed up by troops" and that "it ought to be possible for American citizens of any color to register and vote in a free election without interference or fear of reprisal." Kennedy then provides several specific examples (primarily recent events in Birmingham, Alabama) and statistics to show that this was not the case. He concludes:

> We face, therefore, a moral crisis as a country and a people. It cannot be met by repressive police action. It cannot be left to increased demonstrations in the streets. It cannot be quieted by token moves or talk. It is time to act in the Congress, in your state and local legislative body, and, above all, in all of our daily lives.

Underlying Kennedy's argument is this reasoning:

All Americans should enjoy certain rights. (*assumption*)

Some Americans do not enjoy these rights. (*support*)

We must take action to ensure that all Americans enjoy these rights. (*claim*)

Inductive Reasoning   Another form of logical argumentation is *inductive* reasoning. A speaker or writer who argues inductively begins not with a generalization, but with several pieces of specific evidence. The speaker then draws a conclusion from this evidence. For example, in a debate on gun control, former Senator Robert C. Byrd cited specific examples of rampant crime involving guns: "I read of young men being viciously murdered for a pair of sneakers, a leather jacket, or $20." He also offered statistical evidence of the increasing crime rate: "in 1951, there were 3.2 policemen for every felony committed in the United States; this year nearly 3.2 felonies will be committed per every police officer." He concluded, "Something has to change. We have to stop the crimes that are distorting and disrupting the way of life for so many innocent, law-respecting Americans. The bill that we are debating today attempts to do just that."

Former Senator Edward M. Kennedy also used statistical evidence in arguing for passage of the Racial Justice Act of 1990, which was designed to ensure that minorities are not disproportionately singled out for the death penalty. Kennedy pointed out that between 1973 and 1980, seventeen defendants in Fulton County, Georgia, were charged with killing police officers, but that the only defendant who received the death sentence was a black man. Kennedy also cited statistics to show that "those who killed whites were 4.3 times more likely to receive the death penalty than were killers of blacks" and that "in Georgia, blacks who killed whites received the death penalty 16.7 percent of the time, while whites who killed received the death penalty only 4.2 percent of the time."

Maintaining a Critical Perspective   Of course, the mere piling up of evidence does not in itself make the speaker's case. As Donna Cross explains in "Politics: The Art of Bamboozling,"[1] politicians are very adept at "card-stacking"—lining up evidence in favor of a conclusion without bothering to mention (or barely mentioning) contrary evidence. And statistics can be selected and manipulated to prove anything, as demonstrated in Darrell Huff's landmark book *How to Lie with Statistics* (1954). Moreover, what appears to be a logical argument may in fact be fundamentally flawed. (See Chapter 2 for a discussion of logical fallacies and faulty reasoning strategies.)

On the other hand, the fact that evidence can be distorted, statistics misused, and logic fractured does not mean that these tools of reason should be dismissed. It means only that audiences have to listen and read critically and to question the use of statistics and other evidence.

Exercise 4.2

Using Deductive and Inductive Logic

Choose an issue currently being debated at your school or a college-related issue about which you are concerned. Write a claim about this issue. Then write two paragraphs addressing your claim—one in which you organize your points deductively (beginning with your claim and following with support) and one in which you organize them inductively (presenting supporting evidence and following with a claim). Possible issues might include college admissions policies, classroom crowding, or grade inflation. Alternatively, you could base your paragraphs on a claim generated in Exercise 4.1.

Ethos

Ethos, or the ethical appeal, is based not on the ethics relating to the subject under discussion, but rather on the ethical status of the person making the argument. A person making an argument must have a certain degree of credibility: That person must be of good character, have sound sense, and be qualified to argue based either on expert experience with the subject matter or on carefully conducted research. Students writing in academic settings establish their appeal to *ethos* by developing presentations that are well organized, carefully reasoned, and thoroughly referenced with source citations. These are the hallmarks of writers and speakers who care deeply about their work. If you care, your audience will care and consider your argument seriously.

Appeals to *ethos* are usually most explicit in political contests. For example, Elizabeth Cervantes Barrón, running for senator as the Peace and Freedom candidate, establishes her credibility this way: "I was born

---

[1] Donna Cross, *Word Abuse: How the Words We Use Use Us* (New York: Coward, 1979).

and raised in central Los Angeles. I grew up in a multiethnic, multicultural environment where I learned to respect those who were different from me....I am a teacher and am aware of how cutbacks in education have affected our children and our communities." On the other end of the political spectrum, the American Independent gubernatorial candidate Jerry McCready also begins with an ethical appeal: "As a self-employed businessman, I have learned firsthand what it is like to try to make ends meet in an unstable economy being manipulated by out-of-touch politicians." Both candidates are making an appeal to *ethos,* an appeal based on the strength of their personal qualities for the office they seek. Both argue, in effect, "Trust me. My experience makes me a credible, knowledgeable candidate."

L. A. Kauffman is not running for office but writing an article arguing against socialism as an ideology around which to build societies.[2] To establish his credibility as someone who understands socialism well enough to criticize it meaningfully, Kauffman begins with an appeal to *ethos:* "Until recently, I was executive editor of the journal *Socialist Review.* Before that I worked for the Marxist magazine, *Monthly Review.* My bookshelves are filled with books of Marxist theory, and I even have a picture of Karl Marx up on my wall." Thus, Kauffman establishes his credentials to argue knowledgeably about Marxism.

Exercise 4.3

Using Ethos

Return to the claim you used for Exercise 4.2, and write a paragraph in which you use an appeal to *ethos* to make a case for that claim.

Pathos

Finally, speakers and writers appeal to their audiences by using *pathos,* an appeal to the emotions. Writers in academic settings rely heavily on the force of logic and evidence and rarely make appeals to *pathos.* Beyond academic settings, however, appeals to the emotions are commonplace. Nothing is inherently wrong with using an emotional appeal. Indeed, because emotions often move people far more successfully than reason alone, speakers and writers would be foolish not to use emotion. And it would be a drab, humorless world if human beings were not subject to the sway of feeling as well as reason. The emotional appeal becomes problematic only when it is the *sole* or *primary* basis of the argument.

President Ronald Reagan was a master of emotional appeal. He closed his first Inaugural Address with a reference to the view from the Capitol to the Arlington National Cemetery, where lie thousands of markers of "heroes":

> Under one such marker lies a young man, Martin Treptow, who
> left his job in a small-town barbershop in 1917 to go to France with

---

[2] L. A. Kauffman, "Socialism: No," *Progressive,* 1 Apr. 1993.

the famed Rainbow Division. There, on the western front, he was killed trying to carry a message between battalions under heavy artillery fire. We're told that on his body was found a diary. On the flyleaf under the heading, "My Pledge," he had written these words: "America must win this war. Therefore, I will work, I will save, I will sacrifice, I will endure, I will fight cheerfully and do my utmost, as if the issue of the whole struggle depended on me alone." The crisis we are facing today does not require of us the kind of sacrifice that Martin Treptow and so many thousands of others were called upon to make. It does require, however, our best effort and our willingness to believe in ourselves and to believe in our capacity to perform great deeds, to believe that together with God's help we can and will resolve the problems which now confront us.

Surely, Reagan implies, if Martin Treptow can act so courageously and so selflessly, we can do the same. His logic is somewhat unclear because the connection between Martin Treptow and ordinary Americans of 1981 is rather tenuous (as Reagan concedes), but the emotional power of the heroism of Martin Treptow, whom reporters were sent scurrying to research, carries the argument.

A more recent president, Bill Clinton, also used *pathos*. Addressing an audience of the nation's governors about his welfare plan, Clinton closed his remarks by referring to a conversation he had had with a welfare mother who had gone through the kind of training program Clinton was advocating. Asked by Clinton whether she thought that such training programs should be mandatory, the mother said, "I sure do." Clinton in his remarks explained what she said when he asked her why:

> "Well, because if it wasn't, there would be a lot of people like me home watching the soaps because we don't believe we can make anything of ourselves anymore. So you've got to make it mandatory." And I said, "What's the best thing about having a job?" She said, "When my boy goes to school, and they say, 'What does your mama do for a living?' he can give an answer."

Clinton counts on the emotional power in that anecdote to set up his conclusion: "We must end poverty for Americans who want to work. And we must do it on terms that dignify all of the rest of us, as well as help our country to work better. I need your help, and I think we can do it."

Exercise 4.4

Using Pathos

Return to the claim you used for Exercises 4.2 and 4.3, and write a paragraph in which you use an appeal to *pathos* to argue for that claim.

The Limits of Argument

Our discussion of *ethos* and *pathos* indicates a potentially troubling but undeniable reality: Arguments are not won on the basis of logic and evidence alone. In the real world, arguments don't operate like academic debates. If the purpose of argument is to get people to change their minds or to agree that the writer's or speaker's position on a particular topic is the best available, then the person making the argument must be aware that factors other than evidence and good reasoning come into play when readers or listeners are considering the matter.

These factors involve deep-seated cultural, religious, ethnic, racial, and gender identities, moral preferences, and the effects of personal experiences (either pleasant or unpleasant) that are generally resistant to logic and evidence, however well framed. You could try—using the best available arguments—to convince someone who is pro-life to agree with the pro-choice position (or vice versa). Or you could try to persuade someone who opposes capital punishment to believe that state-endorsed executions are necessary for deterrence (or for any other reason). You might even marshal your evidence and logic to try to persuade someone whose family members have had run-ins with the law that police efforts are directed at protecting the law-abiding.

However, on such emotionally loaded topics, it is extremely difficult, if not impossible, to get people to change their minds because they are so personally invested in their beliefs. As Susan Jacoby, author of *The Age of American Unreason*, notes, "Whether watching television news, consulting political blogs, or (more rarely) reading books, Americans today have become a people in search of validation for opinions that they already hold."[3] Put Jacoby's claim to the test: On any given evening, watch a half-hour of Fox News and MSNBC News. The news coverage of at least a few stories will likely overlap. Can you detect a slant, or bias, in this coverage? Which program would a political conservative be inclined to watch? A liberal? Why?

Fruitful Topics for Argument

The tenacity with which people hold onto longtime beliefs does not mean, however, that they cannot change their minds or that subjects like abortion, capital punishment, and gun control should be off-limits to reasoned debate. The past twenty years has seen some contentious issues, like gay marriage, resolved both in the courts and through elections; and reasoned argument—as well as appeals to *pathos* and *ethos*—has played a significant role. Still, you should be aware of the limits of argument. The most fruitful

---

[3]Susan Jacoby, "Talking to Ourselves: Americans Are Increasingly Close-Minded and Unwilling to Listen to Opposing Views," *Los Angeles Times* 20 Apr. 2008: M10.

topics for argument in a freshman composition setting tend to be those on which most people are persuadable, either because they know relatively little about the topic or because deep-rooted cultural, religious, or moral beliefs are not involved. At least initially in your career as a writer of academic papers, it's probably best to avoid "hot-button" topics that are the focus of broader cultural debates and to focus instead on topics in which *pathos* plays less of a part.

For example, most people are not emotionally invested in plug-in hybrid or hydrogen-powered vehicles, so an argument on behalf of the more promising technology for the coming decades will not be complicated by deep-seated beliefs. Similarly, most people don't know enough about the mechanics of sleep to have strong opinions on how to deal with sleep deprivation. Your arguments on such topics, therefore, will provide opportunities both to inform your readers or listeners and to persuade them that your arguments, if well reasoned and supported by sound evidence, are at least plausible, if not entirely convincing.

■ DEMONSTRATION: DEVELOPING AN ARGUMENT SYNTHESIS—RESPONDING TO BULLIES

To demonstrate how to plan and draft an argument synthesis, let's suppose that your composition instructor has assigned a research paper and that in pondering possible topics you find yourself considering what can be done to discourage widespread bullying in American schools. Perhaps you have a personal motivation to write on this topic: You were bullied as a child or recall watching others being bullied but did nothing to intervene. So you do some preliminary reading and discover that the problem of bullying is widespread and that forty-nine states have adopted anti-bullying legislation. Still, however, the problem persists. What can be done to solve it?

You have a topic, and you have a guiding question for a paper.

Suppose, in preparing to write a paper in which you will argue for a workable solution to the problem of bullying, you locate (among others) the following sources:

- "Bullying Statistics" (a Web site)
- *The 2011 National School Climate Survey: The Experiences of Lesbian, Gay, Bisexual and Transgender Youth in Our Nation's Schools* (a report)
- *Olweus Bullying Prevention Program: Scope and Sequence* (a publisher's catalogue description of a widely adopted anti-bullying program)
- "Bullying—And the Power of Peers" (a scholarly article also delivered as a paper at a White House conference on bullying)

Carefully read these sources (which follow), noting the kinds of evidence—facts, expert opinions, and statistics—you could draw on to develop an *argument synthesis*. These passages are excerpts only; in preparing your paper, you would draw on the entire articles, reports, and Web sites from which these passages were taken. And you would draw on more sources than these in your search for supporting materials (as the writer of the model synthesis has done; see pp. 148–151). But these four sources provide a good introduction to the subject. Our discussion of how these passages can form the basis of an argument synthesis resumes on page 136.

BULLYING STATISTICS
Pacer.org

- **Nearly one-third of all school-aged children are bullied each year—upwards of 13 million students.**
  - Nationwide, 20 percent of students in grades 9–12 experienced bullying. Source: The 2011 Youth Risk Behavior Surveillance System (Centers for Disease Control and Prevention).
  - Nationwide, 28 percent of students in grades 6–12 experienced bullying. Source: The 2008–2009 School Crime Supplement (National Center for Education Statistics and Bureau of Justice Statistics).

- **64 percent of children who were bullied did not report it; only 36 percent reported the bullying**. (Petrosino 2010) Petrosino, Anthony J. *What Characteristics of Bullying, Bullying Victims, and Schools Are Associated with Increased Reporting of Bullying to School Officials?* Washington, DC: National Center for Education Evaluation and Regional Assistance, 2010.

- More than half of bullying situations (57 percent) stop when a peer intervenes on behalf of the student being bullied. Wendy M.Craig, Lynn D. Hawkins, Debra J. Pepler. *Naturalistic Observations of Peer Interventions in Bullying.* Social Development, Volume 10, Issue 4, pages 512–527, November 2001.

Statistics about bullying of students with disabilities

- Only 10 U.S. studies have been conducted on the connection between bullying and developmental disabilities, but all of these studies found that **children with disabilities were two to three times more likely** to be bullied than their nondisabled peers. ("Disabilities: Insights from Across Fields and Around the World," 2009).

- Researchers discovered that students with disabilities were more worried about school safety and being injured or harassed by other peers compared to students without a disability (Saylor & Leach, 2009).

- The National Autistic Society reports that 40 percent of children with autism and 60 percent of children with Asperger's syndrome have experienced bullying.

THE 2011 NATIONAL SCHOOL CLIMATE SURVEY: THE EXPERIENCES OF LESBIAN, GAY, BISEXUAL AND TRANSGENDER YOUTH IN OUR NATION'S SCHOOLS

Joseph Kosciw,
Emily Greytak,
Mark Bartkiewicz,
Madelyn Boesen, and
Neal Palmer

In 1999, the Gay, Lesbian and Straight Education Network (GLSEN) identified the need for national data on the experiences of lesbian, gay, bisexual, and transgender (LGBT) students and launched the first National School Climate Survey (NSCS). At the time, the school experiences of LGBT youth were under-documented and nearly absent from national studies of adolescents. For more than a decade, the biennial NSCS has documented the unique challenges LGBT students face and identified interventions that can improve school climate. The survey explores the prevalence of anti-LGBT language and victimization, the effect that these experiences have on LGBT students' achievement and well-being, and the utility of interventions in lessening the negative effects of a hostile school climate and promoting a positive educational experience. The survey also examines demographic and community-level differences in LGBT students' experiences. The NSCS remains one of the few studies to examine the school experiences of LGBT students nationally, and its results have been vital to GLSEN's understanding of the issues that LGBT students face, thereby informing the authors' ongoing work to ensure safe and affirming schools for all.

In their 2011 survey, the authors examine the experiences of LGBT students with regard to indicators of negative school climate:

1. hearing biased remarks, including homophobic remarks, in school;
2. feeling unsafe in school because of personal characteristics, such as sexual orientation, gender expression, or race/ethnicity;
3. missing classes or days of school because of safety reasons; and
4. experiencing harassment and assault in school.

They also examine:

1. the possible negative effects of a hostile school climate on LGBT students' academic achievement, educational aspirations, and psychological well-being;
2. whether or not students report experiences of victimization to school officials or to family members and how these adults address the problem; and
3. how the school experiences of LGBT students differ by personal and community characteristics.

In addition, they demonstrate the degree to which LGBT students have access to supportive resources in school, and they explore the possible benefits of these resources, including:

1. Gay-Straight Alliances (GSAs) or similar clubs;
2. anti-bullying/harassment school policies and laws;
3. supportive school staff; and
4. curricula that are inclusive of LGBT-related topics.

OLWEUS BULLYING PREVENTION PROGRAM: SCOPE AND SEQUENCE

Publisher Catalogue Description

What Is the Olweus Bullying Prevention Program?

The Olweus Bullying Prevention Program (OBPP) is the most researched and best-known bullying prevention program available today. With over thirty-five years of research and successful implementation all over the world, OBPP is a whole-school program that has been proven to prevent or reduce bullying throughout a school setting.

OBPP is used at the school, classroom, and individual levels and includes methods to reach out to parents and the community for involvement and support. School administrators, teachers, and other staff are primarily responsible for introducing and implementing the program. These efforts are designed to improve peer relations and make the school a safer and more positive place for students to learn and develop.

What Are the Goals of OBPP?

The goals of the program are

- to reduce existing bullying problems among students
- to prevent the development of new bullying problems
- to achieve better peer relations at school

For Whom Is OBPP Designed?

OBPP is designed for students in elementary, middle, and junior high schools (students ages five to fifteen years old). All students participate in most aspects of the program, while students identified as bullying others, or as targets of bullying, receive additional individualized interventions.

With some adaptation, the program can also be used in high schools, although research has not measured the program's effectiveness beyond tenth grade. In addition, classroom support materials are not currently available for high school students. Chapter 17 of the program's Schoolwide Guide talks about adapting the program for use in a high school setting.

WHITE HOUSE REPORT/BULLYING—AND THE POWER
OF PEERS

Promoting Respectful Schools
Philip Rodkin

Using Peers to Intervene

In a review of bullying-reduction programs, Farrington and Ttofi (2009) found that interventions that involve peers, such as using students as peer mediators or engaging bystanders to disapprove of bullying and support victims of harassment, were associated with *increases* in victimization! In fact, of 20 program elements included in 44 school-based programs, work with peers was the *only* program element associated with significantly *more* bullying and victimization. (In contrast, there were significant and positive effects for parent training and school meetings in reducing bullying.) Still other reviews of bullying intervention programs have found generally weak effects (Merrell, Gueldner, Ross, & Isava, 2008).

These disheartening results speak to the fact that peer influences can be a constructive or destructive force on bullying and need to be handled with knowledge, skill, and care. Antisocial peer groups can undermine behavioral interventions. For peer mediation to be effective, students who are chosen to be peer mediators should probably be popular and prosocial (Pellegrini et al., 2010; Pepler et al., 2010; Vaillancourt et al., 2010).

Some of the most innovative, intensive, grassroots uses of peer relationships to reduce bullying, such as the You Have the Power! program in Montgomery County, Maryland, have not been scientifically evaluated. The final verdict awaits on some promising programs that take advantage of peer relationships to combat bullying, such as the Finnish program KiVa (Salmivalli et al., 2010), which has a strong emphasis on influencing onlookers to support the victim rather than encourage the bully, and the Steps to Respect program (Frey et al., 2010), which works at the elementary school level.

Teachers can ask what *kind* of bully they face when dealing with a victimization problem. Is the bully a member of a group, or is he or she a group leader? How are bullies and victims situated in the peer ecology? Educators who exclusively target peripheral, antisocial cliques as the engine of school violence problems may leave intact other groups that are more responsible for mainstream peer support of bullying. A strong step educators could take would be to periodically ask students about bullying and their social relationships. (See "What Teachers Can Do.")

• • •

5   The task ahead is to better integrate bullies and the children they harass into the social fabric of the school and better inform educators of how to recognize, understand, and help guide children's relationships. With guidance from caring, engaged adults, youth can organize themselves as a force that makes bullying less effective as a means of social connection or as an outlet for alienation.

What Teachers Can Do

- **Ask students about bullying.** Survey students regularly on whether they are being harassed or have witnessed harassment. Make it easier for students to come to an adult in the school to talk about harassment by building staff-student relationships, having suggestion boxes where students can provide input anonymously, or administering schoolwide surveys in which students can report confidentially on peers who bully and on the children whom they harass. Consider what bullying accomplishes for a bully. Does the bully want to gain status? Does the bully use aggression to control others?

- **Ask students about their relationships.** Bullying is a destructive, asymmetric relationship. Know whom students hang out with, who their friends are, and whom they dislike. Know whom students perceive to be popular and unpopular. Connect with students who have no friends. School staff members vary widely in their knowledge of students' relationships and tend to underestimate the level of aggression among peers.

- **Build democratic classroom and school climates.** Identify student leaders who can encourage peers to stand against bullying. Assess whether student social norms are *really* against bullying. Train teachers to better understand and manage student social dynamics and handle aggression with clear, consistent consequences. Master teachers not only promote academic success, but also build relationships, trust, and a sense of community.

- **Be an informed consumer of antibullying curriculums.** Antibullying interventions can be successful, but there are significant caveats. Some bullies would benefit from services that go beyond bullying-reduction programs. Some programs work well in Europe, but not as well in the United States. Most antibullying programs have not been rigorously evaluated, so be an informed consumer when investigating claims of success. Even with a well-developed antibullying curriculum, understanding students' relationships at your school is crucial.

- **Remember that bullying is also a problem of values.** Implement an intellectually challenging character education or socioemotional learning curriculum. Teach students how to achieve their goals by being assertive rather than aggressive. Always resolve conflicts with civility among and between staff and students. Involve families.

Exercise 4.5

Critical Reading for Synthesis

Having read the selections related to bullying, pages 131–135, write a one-sentence summary of each. On the same page, list two or three topics that you think are common to several of the selections. Beneath each topic, list the authors who have something to say on that topic and briefly note what they have to say. Finally, for each topic, jot down what *you* have to say. Now regard your effort: With each topic you have created a discussion point suitable for inclusion in a paper. (Of course, until you determine the claim of such a paper, you won't know to what end you might put the discussion.) Write a paragraph or two in which you introduce the topic and then conduct a brief conversation among the interested parties (including yourself).

Consider Your Purpose

Your specific purpose in writing an argument synthesis is crucial. What exactly you want to do will affect your claim and how you organize the evidence. Your purpose may be clear to you before you begin research, or it may not emerge until after you have completed your research. Of course, the sooner your purpose is clear to you, the fewer wasted motions you will make. On the other hand, the more you approach research as an exploratory process, the likelier that your conclusions will emerge from the sources themselves rather than from preconceived ideas. Each new writing project will have its own rhythm in this regard. Be flexible in your approach: Through some combination of preconceived structures and invigorating discoveries, you will find your way to the source materials that will yield a promising paper.

Let's say that while reading these four (and additional) sources related to bullying, you share the concern of many who believe that bullies traumatize too many vulnerable children and prevent them from feeling safe at school. Perhaps you believe that bullying is fundamental to human nature, or at least to some people's human nature, and that laws will do little to change the behavior. Perhaps you believe that laws shape, or at least constrain, human behavior all the time: the laws against murder or theft, for instance, or, more mundanely, speeding. You may believe that laws *do* have a role to play in lessening if not preventing bullying and that we should be willing to sacrifice some freedom of speech to prevent bullies from menacing their victims through text messages and online postings.

Most people will bring at least some personal history to this topic, and personal history is often a good place to begin. Mine that history for insights, and use them if you're able to guide you in posing questions and in developing arguments. Your purpose in writing, then, emerges from these kinds of responses to the source materials you find.

Making a Claim: Formulate a Thesis

As we indicated in the introduction to this chapter, one useful way of approaching an argument is to see it as making a *claim*. A claim is a proposition, a conclusion you have made, that you are trying to prove or demonstrate. If your purpose is to argue that bullies can learn to moderate their behavior if they are integrated into a healthy peer group, then that claim (generally expressed in one-sentence form as a *thesis*) is at the heart of your argument. You will draw support from your sources as you argue logically for your claim.

Not every piece of information in a source is useful for supporting a claim. You must read with care and select the opinions, facts, and statistics that best advance your position. You may even find yourself drawing support from sources that make claims entirely different from your own. For example, in researching the subject of bullying prevention, you may come across an anti-bullying program that you know has been proven ineffective by researchers; yet that source's presentation of statistics concerning the prevalence of bullying may be sound, and you may end up using those statistics in your argument. Perhaps you will find information in these sources to help support your own contrary arguments.

You might use one source as part of a *counterargument*—an argument opposing your own—so that you can demonstrate its weaknesses and, in the process, strengthen your own claim. On the other hand, the author of one of your sources may be so convincing in supporting a claim that you adopt it yourself, either partially or entirely. The point is that *the argument is in your hands.* You must devise it yourself and use your sources in ways that will support the claim you present in your thesis.

You may not want to divulge your thesis until the end of the paper, thereby drawing the reader along toward your conclusion, allowing the thesis to flow naturally out of the argument and the evidence on which it is based. If you do this, you are working *inductively.* Or you may wish to be more direct and (after an introduction) *begin* with your thesis, following the thesis statement with evidence and reasoning to support it. If you do this, you are working *deductively.* In academic papers, deductive arguments are far more common than inductive ones.

Based on your reactions to reading sources—and perhaps also on your own inclinations as a student—you may find yourself essentially in sympathy with a view of anti-bullying programs shared by several of your sources: that despite being required by the states' anti-bullying legislation, these programs do not work because they prescribe a one-size-fits-all approach to a complex problem. At the same time, you may feel that the suffering bullies cause is too great to do nothing. Most important, you conclude that a local approach to bullying makes sense, one that builds on the wisdom of parents, teachers, and community leaders who know the children involved and who know the local culture in which bullying occurs. You review your sources and begin working on a thesis. After a few tries, you develop this thesis:

> A blend of local, ground-up strategies and state-mandated programs and laws promises to be the best approach to dealing with bullying in American schools.

Decide How You Will Use Your Source Material

Your claim commits you to introducing the problem of bullying, explaining top-down anti-bullying legislation and its limitations, explaining ground-up strategies and their limitations, and arguing for a combined approach to changing the behavior of bullies. The sources (some provided here, some located elsewhere) offer information and ideas—evidence—that will allow you to support your claim. For instance, the catalogue description of the *Olweus Bullying Prevention Program* (OBPP) establishes the principles of a widely adopted one-size-fits-all approach to bullying prevention. Yet the "White house Report" by Rodkin cautions that "some programs [like Olweus] work well in Europe, but not as well in the United States." (These and several other sources not included in this chapter will be cited in the model argument paper.)

Develop an Organizational Plan

Having established your overall purpose and your claim, having developed a thesis (which may change as you write and revise the paper), and having decided how to draw upon your source materials, how do you logically organize your paper? In many cases, a well-written thesis will suggest an organization. In the case of the bullying project, the first part of your paper would define the problem of bullying and discuss the legislative response. The second part would argue that there are problems associated with anti-bullying legislation. The third part would introduce a solution to these problems. Sorting through your material and categorizing it by topic and subtopic, you might compose the following outline:

I. Introduction
   A. Graphic example of bullying
   B. Background: Who is bullied
   C. Cyberbullying
      1. Definition
      2. Suicides
   D. Anti-bullying laws
      1. Laws criminalize bullying
      2. Laws mandate education to reduce bullying

Thesis

II. Problems with anti-bullying laws
   A. Laws implemented in a rush (after Columbine)
   B. Elements of some laws unconstitutional
   C. Laws don't follow standard definitions
   D. Effectiveness of anti-bullying programs uneven

III. An alternate solution to the problem of bullying
   A. Rationale and blueprint for alternate approach
   B. A local "ground-up" solution
      1. Emily Bazelon
      2. Lee Hirsch and Cynthia Lowen
      3. Philip Rodkin

   C. Concession
       1. Local solutions possibly flawed
       2. Local solutions should be evaluated
   IV. Conclusion: Blended approach needed

Formulate an Argument Strategy

The argument that emerges through this outline will build not only on evidence drawn from sources but also on the writer's assumption that a top-down legislative approach can be combined with a bottom-up grass-roots approach to achieve a meaningful reduction in bullying behaviors. Some readers may disagree.

Those who believe that local solutions to complex problems are preferable to broad, one-size-fits-all solutions would likely want to emphasize school-specific initiatives for combating the problem of bullying. They would place more confidence in parents and educators on the ground to devise effective solutions than they would in state-wide laws designed to combat bullying.

By contrast, those who believe that laws are the proper vehicle to address deep-rooted social problems (for instance, racism) would likely have more confidence in the legislative process—that is, in broad, system-wide fixes. On learning that laws intending to address bullying aren't working, they would be more inclined to fix the one-size-fits-all laws rather than risk implementing hundreds of local solutions that could not be readily evaluated for effectiveness. So people on both sides of the argument might not only reject an approach that runs counter to their own position on the top-down/ground-up spectrum, but might also be wary of a recommendation to blend approaches. It will be the writer's job to convince skeptics that a combined approach is workable. Everyone wants to prevent bullying, but different views on one key assumption will determine which solutions are pursued.

Writers can accept or partially accept an opposing assumption by making a *concession*, in the process establishing themselves as reasonable and willing to compromise (see p. 158). The *claim* of the argument about the best way to combat bullying is primarily a claim about *policy*, about actions that should (or should not) be taken. An argument can also concern a claim about *facts* (Does X exist? How can we define X? Does X lead to Y?), a claim about *value* (What is X worth?), or a claim about *cause and effect* (Why did X happen?).

The present argument rests to some degree on a dispute about cause and effect. No one disputes that bullying remains an intractable problem, but many have disputed how and why bullying occurs and how it is best handled. After the events at Columbine in 1999 and following the suicides of teenagers who suffered the torments of bullies, states rushed to enact tough anti-bullying legislation. But research has shown that the link between suicide and being bullied is not at all clear and that suicide, very likely, is influenced by other factors. Still, legislators were quick to enact laws assuming that the cause-and-effect relationship was clear. Lawmakers also assumed that anti-bullying education would reduce bullying behavior, but research shows that this is not happening in any substantial way. So there is plenty of room for argument on this topic. Essentially, the argument reduces to this question: Which causes (which anti-bullying programs) will lead to the most desirable effects (a reduction in bullying)?

Draft and Revise Your Synthesis

The final draft of an argument synthesis, based on the outline above, follows. Thesis and topic sentences are highlighted. A note on documentation: While the topic leans more toward the social sciences than it does the humanities, the writer—completing a research assignment for a freshman composition class—has used Modern Language Association (MLA) documentation style as his instructor requested. MLA style is used most often in the humanities.

A *cautionary note:* When writing syntheses, it is all too easy to become careless in properly crediting your sources. Before drafting your paper, review the section on Avoiding Plagiarism (pp. 50–52).

MODEL ARGUMENT SYNTHESIS

Simmons 1

Peter Simmons

Professor Lettelier

Composition 201

8 November 2014

Responding to Bullies

(1)   On the school bus the nerdy kid with glasses tries to keep his head down. A group of older, bigger kids gets on. One of the older kids sits next to the nerdy kid, who asks, hopefully, "You're my buddy, right?" The other kid turns to him and says, "I'm not your buddy. I will f—g end you. I will shove a broomstick up your a—. You're going to die in so much pain." Another day, the nerdy kid is repeatedly punched by a kid across the aisle, who then jabs him in the arm with the point of a pencil. These scenes from the recent documentary film *Bully* are repeated in some form or other thousands of times every day.

(2)   According to some estimates, more than thirteen million school-aged children, one in five students, are bullied each year in the United States. Nearly two-thirds of bullying behavior goes unreported, and of those who suffer,

Simmons 2

a disproportionate number are the most vulnerable of children, those with learning disabilities or those who dare to break social norms, such as LGBT [lesbian, gay, bisexual, and transgender] youth (Pacer's; Kosciw et al.). At one time, victims could find some relief at home or in the summer—away from school busses, corridors, and playgrounds where bullies lurk. The Internet has taken even that refuge away. Bullies now follow their victims online with hateful instant messages and postings on Facebook. Tyler Clementi, a Rutgers freshman, jumped off the George Washington Bridge after his roommate remotely recorded and posted online a private, consensual, same-sex encounter. In another horrifying case, a twelve-year-old girl jumped from an abandoned silo to her death after two classmates, twelve and fourteen, urged her to "drink bleach and die." Subsequently, one of the harassers posted a message on Facebook admitting, "Yes, I bullied Rebecca and she killed herself but IDGAF [I don't give a ----]." Bullying is a harsh and routine fact of life for school-age kids all over the country. What do we, as a society, propose to do about this? Are tough anti-bullying laws the answer?

③   Over the last fifteen years, responding to bully-related suicides and the horrors of Columbine, state governments have passed two-part anti-bullying laws. The first part of the law makes it a crime to commit especially vicious behaviors associated with bullying; the second, educational part requires school districts to implement anti-bullying programs. On its face, a two-part program that punishes bullies and teaches behaviors designed to reduce bullying seems sensible. But is it effective? The answer, unfortunately, is "no"—at least for the moment. Laws that punish the worst offenders with prison time or juvenile detention may make parents and legislators feel as if they're getting tough. But, in fact, bullying remains widespread, and relatively few cases rise to the level of criminal behavior. At the same time, several key initiatives introduced in local school districts seems to be showing some promise in addressing this difficult problem. In the end, a blend of local, ground-up strategies and state-mandated programs and laws promises to be the best approach to dealing with bullying in American schools.

(4)   The first state to adopt anti-bullying legislation was Georgia, in 1999, in response to the Columbine tragedy earlier that year when Dylan Klebold and Eric Harris killed a teacher and twelve classmates and left twenty-one wounded. The assault triggered a national outcry and a demand to understand what happened. Eva Porter, author of *Bully Nation*, argues that the media too-quickly (and incorrectly) pegged the shooters as young men who'd been bullied and retaliated with lethal force. "The nation," she writes, "fearing a repeat of the tragedy—adopted a zero-tolerance attitude toward many normal, albeit painful, aspects of childhood behavior and development, and defined them as bullying."

(5)   Understandably, legislators wanted to prevent bullied kids from becoming Klebold- and Harris-like killers. In the eleven years following the attack, a span that included several highly publicized teen suicides associated with bullying, forty-nine state legislatures adopted 120 anti-bullying bills ("School"). This rush to action was so hasty that experts began wondering about the extent to which these legislative measures were "informed by research, not singular high profile incidents" like Columbine (Patchin) or prompted by "the perceived urgent need to intervene" (Smith et al.).

(6)   No one can doubt the good intentions of legislators who want to reduce bullying. Yet the laws they enacted may be too blunt an instrument to deal with the most common forms of bullying. Civil rights activists are concerned that anti-cyberbullying laws, in particular, could curtail freedom of speech (Bazelon, "Anti"). In 2011, responding to the bully-related suicide of fourteen-year-old Jamey Rodemeyer, the Make It Better Project argued that "[c]riminalizing bullying is not the answer" (Gay-Straight Alliance). Writing about the case, Daniel Villarreal explains why: "While some... bullying could even rise to the level of criminal harassment, criminalizing bullying overall could result in over-reaching laws that punish any student who 'causes emotional harm' or 'creates a hostile environment'—two vague, subjective criteria that could well qualify any online insult or cafeteria put down as a criminal offense." Villarreal could have been predicting the future. In 2012,

Simmons 4

the Missouri Supreme Court struck down part of an anti-bullying law (enacted after a bullying-related suicide) that violated free speech ("Mo. High Court"). LGBT youth are easy targets for bullies. When a national organization that supports LGBT youth opposes anti-bullying laws intended to help them, the wisdom of such laws is put into serious question.

(7)   The second problem with anti-bullying legislation is that states do not generally follow "research-based definitions of bullying" (Sacco 3–8), even though most researchers have adopted a definition crafted by Dan Olweus, the Norwegian psychologist credited with conducting the first large-scale, controlled study of bullying in 1978. According to Olweus, a "person is bullied when he or she is exposed, repeatedly and over time, to negative actions on the part of one or more other persons, and he or she has difficulty defending himself or herself." Olweus introduced the element of an "imbalance of power" that results from bullies using their physical strength or social position to inflict emotional or physical harm ("Bullying").

(8)   "[A]t least ten different definitions" are being used in state laws, according to Emily Bazelon, author of *Sticks and Stones: Defeating the Culture of Bullying*—and, for her, that's a problem. A frequent commentator on the subject, Bazelon argues that "'bullying' isn't the same as garden-variety teasing or a two-way conflict. The word is being overused," she writes, "expanding, accordionlike, to encompass both appalling violence or harassment and a few mean words" ("Defining"). Anti-bullying researchers at Harvard and New York University note that teens take care to distinguish "drama"—the more typical verbal and emotional jousting among teenagers—from bullying. Drama can be more easily shrugged off as "so high school" and helps teens avoid thinking of themselves as hapless victims (Boyd and Marwick). When school-based programs fail to realize that what some students dismiss as "drama" is really "bullying," the effectiveness of anti-bullying programs is in doubt as schools may miss a lot of hurtful behaviors. "To me this is an issue about reporting, underreporting specifically," says educational psychologist Philip Rodkin. "It's also about

teenagers wanting to diminish the importance of some negative interaction, which sometimes is exactly the right thing to do, sometimes not at all the right thing" (Personal). At the same time, there is also the danger that too many harmless behaviors can be labeled as bullying. As one superintendent who is implementing the tough, new anti-bullying law in New Jersey says: "students, or their parents, will find it easier to label minor squabbles bullying than to find ways to work out their differences" (Dolan, qtd. in Hu).

(9)   A third problem with anti-bullying laws—and perhaps the most serious—is that they require school districts to adopt anti-bullying programs of unproven value. Educators are rushing to comply with these laws, and they are adopting pre-made, one-size-fits-all programs that have not been shown to work. In an analysis of forty-two studies, researchers at Texas A&M International University evaluated the effectiveness of school-based anti-bullying efforts. The combined studies involved 34,713 elementary, middle, and high school students and "measure[d] some element of bullying behavior or aggression toward peers" (Ferguson et al. 407). The researchers concluded that "school-based anti-bullying programs are not practically effective in reducing bullying or violent behaviors in the schools" (410). Another review of sixteen anti-bullying studies involving 15,386 K–12 students concluded "that school bullying interventions may produce modest positive outcomes... [but] are more likely to influence knowledge, attitudes, and self-perceptions rather than actual bullying behaviors" (Merrell et al.). These are "disheartening" results (Swearer et al. 42; Rodkin).

(10)   The world's most well-known anti-bullying program, the Olweus Bullying Prevention Program (OBPP), is a "whole-school" approach that "is used at the school, classroom, and individual levels and includes methods to reach out to parents and the community for involvement and support" (Hazelden). Backed by thirty-five years of research, Olweus has demonstrated the effectiveness of his approach in Norwegian schools. Schools worldwide, including many in the United States, have used OBPP. But researchers have been unable to show that the Olweus program is

consistently effective outside of Norway. A University of Washington study found that in American schools OBPP had "no overall effect" in preventing bullying (Bauer, Lozano, and Rivera). With their larger class sizes and racial, ethnic, and economic diversity, American schools may differ too greatly from Norwegian schools for OBPP to succeed. Or the Olweus program may need to be adapted in ways that have not yet been developed.

(11)   To sum up, definitions in anti-bullying laws are inconsistent; the effectiveness of anti-bullying programs is unproven; and cyberbullying laws may threaten free speech. Still, bullying persists and we must respond. Each day, 160,000 children skip school because they don't want to confront their tormentors (National). Even bullies are at risk: "Nearly 60 percent of boys whom researchers classified as bullies in grades six through nine were convicted of at least one crime by the age of 24. Even more dramatic, 40 percent of them had three or more convictions by age 24" (Fox et al. 2). While bullying in childhood may not be the sole or even main *cause* of later criminal behavior (another possibility: there may be abuse in the home), these statistics provide all the more reason to intervene in the bully/victim relationship. Both victims and bullies require our help.

(12)   Fresh approaches to the problem of bullying are needed, and Rodkin suggests a sensible, potentially fruitful direction: "The task ahead," he writes in a report presented at a 2011 White House Conference on Bullying Prevention, "is to better integrate bullies and the children they harass into the social fabric of the school and better inform educators of how to recognize, understand, and help guide children's relationships." Rodkin's recommendations favor an on-the-ground, local approach with individual students rather than a broad, mandated program. Mary Flannery of the National Education Association agrees that, ultimately, bullies and their victims must be engaged one on one:

> Many bullying programs apply a one-size-fits-all approach to problems on campus. They train teachers and support professionals to be watchful and consistent (often at a high price). But while it's critically important for every adult on

campus to recognize and stop bullying, Colby College professor Lyn Mikel Brown, co-director of the nonprofit Hardy
Girls, Healthy Women, believes most of these "top-down"
programs look promising, but don't go far enough.

"You really have to do this work with students,"
Brown says. "Those programs don't allow for the messy,
on-the-ground work of educating kids. That's what has
to happen and it looks different in different schools and
communities."

(13)   When legislators criminalize bullying and require schools to implement anti-bullying programs, they take the kind of top-down approach
that Mikel Brown believes doesn't go far enough. The researchers who conducted the comprehensive "Overview of State Anti-Bullying Legislation"
agree: "legal responses and mandates can at their best only facilitate the
harder non-legal work that schools must undertake to create a kinder,
braver world" (Sacco 22).

(14)   What might this "harder non-legal" work look like?

(15)   In *Sticks and Stones,* Bazelon advises an approach that involves
children, parents, and educators working in local school- and child-specific
settings. She advises bullied kids to confide in a sympathetic adult or a
trusted group. Those being harassed online should contact Web sites to
remove offensive content. To those who witness bullying, she suggests that
dramatic action (stepping in to break up a fight) isn't necessary—though
private, low-key action, like sending a supportive note, may be. Bazelon
advises educators to conduct surveys to clearly define the problem of bullying at their school (309–19) and make "an ongoing annual, monthly, weekly,
even daily commitment" to reducing bullying (317).

(16)   In their companion book to the widely praised documentary film *Bully*
(2011), Lee Hirsch and Cynthia Lowen offer an action plan for fostering
an inclusive and safe school environment. Their guidelines help parents to
distinguish between appropriate and inappropriate use of the Internet and

Simmons 8

urge parents to discuss bullying openly, along with strategies for reporting bullying to school authorities and promoting responsible behavior. Hirsch and Lowen provide educators with checklists to help determine whether or not effective anti-cyberbullying policies are in place. They also encourage explicit conversations among teachers about the nature and extent of the bullying problem in their school, and they suggest specific prevention and intervention strategies (159–70).

(17)   Like Bazelon, Rodkin recommends surveying students about bullying to gain a clear sense of the problem. He also recommends identifying students with no friends and finding ways to involve them in student life; encouraging peer groups to reject bullying; evaluating anti-bullying programs; and promoting character education that teaches students to be "assertive rather than aggressive" (White House).

(18)   All of these approaches involve "messy, on-the-ground work" that employs local experts to respond to local problems. Until researchers determine that one or another top-down approach to the problem of bullying will succeed in a wide variety of school environments, it seems best to develop a school-by-school, ground-up approach. This kind of grass-roots strategy could help integrate both bullied children and bullies into the broader school culture. Of course, there's no guarantee that the ground-up approach to combating bullying will work any better than top-down, comprehensive programs like OBPP. Leaving large social problems like bullying for locals to resolve may result in uneven and unacceptable solutions. A parallel case: Challenged by President Kennedy to rid this country of racist Jim Crow laws, many advocates of local "solutions" who had no interest in changing the status quo argued that people on the ground, in the local communities, know best. "Leave the problem to us," they said. "We'll fix it." They didn't, of course, and it took courageous action by people like Martin Luther King, Jr., and President Lyndon Johnson to force a comprehensive solution.

(19)   Racism may still be with us, but not to the extent it was in the 1960s, and we have (at least in part) a top-down, national approach to thank for

that. It's clear that local approaches to bullying can be inept. To take one example from the movie *Bully*, a principal tries making a victim shake hands with his tormentor as if that, alone, would end the problem. It didn't. So researchers must evaluate the effectiveness of local solutions as rigorously as they do top-down solutions. If evaluations show that local solutions aren't effective, we should expect that community leaders, parents, and teachers will search for solutions that work. To the extent that they don't and bullying persists, state and federal authorities should step in with their own solutions, but only after their top-down, one-size-fits-all programs can be shown to work.

20   We should be pushing for anti-bullying programs that blend the top-down approach of state-mandated programs and the ground-up approach that tailors programs to the needs of specific communities. The state has the right to insist that every child be safe in a school environment and be free from the threat of bullying. At the same time, local teachers, parents, and administrators are often in the best position to know what approaches will show the greatest benefits in their own communities. Such a blended approach could well yield the best set of solutions to the complex and pervasive problem of bullying. And then, perhaps, the nerdy kid could ride the school bus in peace—or even in friendly conversation with his former tormentors.

Works Cited

Bauer, N. S., P. Lozano, and F. P. Rivara. "The Effectiveness of the Olweus Bullying Prevention Program In Public Middle Schools: A Controlled Trial." *Journal of Adolescent Health* 40.3 (2007): 266–74. *PubMed.* Web. 15 Oct. 2014.

Bazelon, Emily. "Anti-Bully Laws Get Tough with Schools." Interview by Scott Simon. *NPR.org.* National Public Radio, 17 Sept. 2011. Web. 14 Oct. 2014.

Simmons 11

---. "Defining Bullying Down." *New York Times*. New York Times, 11 Mar. 2013. Web. 16 Oct. 2014.

---. *Sticks and Stones: Defeating the Culture of Bullying and Rediscovering the Power of Character and Empathy*. New York: Random, 2013. Print.

Boyd, Danah, and Alice Marwick. "Bullying as True Drama." *New York Times*. New York Times, 22 Sept. 2011. Web. 15 Oct. 2014.

Bully. Dir. Lee Hirsch. The Weinstein Company, 2011. *Netflix*. Web. 17 Oct. 2014.

"Bullying Definition." *Stopbully.gov*. U.S. Department of Health & Human Services, n.d. Web. 15 Oct. 2014.

Copeland, William E., Dieter Wolke, Adrian Angold, and E. Jane Costello. "Adult Psychiatric Outcomes of Bullying and Being Bullied by Peers in Childhood and Adolescence." *JAMA Psychiatry* 70.4 (2013): 419–26. *PubMed*. Web. 15 Oct. 2014.

Ferguson, Christopher J., Claudia San Miguel, John C. Kilburn, Jr., and Patricia Sanchez. "The Effectiveness of School-Based Anti-Bullying Programs: A Meta-Analytic Review." *Criminal Justice Review* 32.4 (2007): 401–14. *Sage Publications*. Web. 15 Oct. 2014.

Flannery, Mary Ellen. "Bullying: Does It Get Better?" *National Education Association*. National Education Association, Jan./Feb. 2011. Web. 16 Oct. 2014.

Fox, James Alan, Delbert S. Elliott, R. Gil Kerlikowske, Sanford A. Newman, and William Christenson. *Bullying Prevention Is Crime Prevention*. *Fightcrime.org*. Fight Crime/Invest in Kids, 2003. PDF file.

Gay-Straight Alliance Project. "Make It Better." *Gay-Straight Alliance Project*. GSANetwork, 26 Sept. 2011. Web. 15 Oct. 2014.

Hazelden Foundation. "Olweus Bullying Prevention Program: Scope and Sequence." *Hazelden.org*. Hazelden, 2007. PDF file.

Hirsch, Lee, Cynthia Lowen, and Dina Santorelli, eds. *Bully: An Action Plan for Teachers and Parents to Combat the Bullying Crisis*. New York: Weinstein Books, 2012. Print.

Simmons 12

Hu, Winnie. "Bullying Law Puts New Jersey Schools on Spot." *New York Times*. New York Times, 20 Aug. 2011. Web. 12 Oct. 2014.

Kosciw, Joseph G., Emily A. Greytak, Mark J. Bartkiewicz, Madelyn J. Boesen, and Neal A. Palmer. *The 2011 National School Climate Survey: The Experiences of Lesbian, Gay, Bisexual and Transgender Youth in Our Nation's Schools*. New York: Gay, Lesbian and Straight Education Network, 2012.

Merrell, Kenneth W, Barbara A. Gueldner, Scott W. Ross, and Duane M. Isava. "How Effective are School Bullying Intervention Programs? A Meta-analysis of Intervention Research." *School Psychology Quarterly* 23.1 (2008): 26–42. PDF file.

"Mo. High Court Strikes Down Part of Harassment Law." *Associated Press Wire Report*. Associated Press, 30 May 2012. Web. 15 Oct. 2014.

National Education Association. "Nation's Educators Continue Push for Safe, Bully-free Environments." *National Education Association*. National Education Association, 8 Oct. 2012. Web. 18 Oct. 2014.

Olweus, Dan. *Bullying at School: What We Know and What We Can Do*. Oxford, England: Blackwell, 1993. Print.

Pacer's National Bullying Prevention Center. "Bullying Statistics." *Pacer. org*. Pacer Center, Inc., 2012. Web. 16 Oct. 2014.

Patchin, Justin W. "Most Cases Aren't Criminal/Room For Debate: Cyberbullying and a Student's Suicide." *New York Times*. New York Times, 30 Sept. 2010. Web. 16 Oct. 2014.

Porter, Susan Eva. "Overusing the Bully Label: Unfriendliness, Exclusion, and Unkind Remarks Aren't Necessarily Bullying." *Los Angeles Times*. Tribune Company, 15 Mar. 2013. Web. 15 Oct. 2014.

Rodkin, Philip C. Personal Interview. 15 Oct. 2014.

---. "White House Report/Bullying—And the Power of Peers." *Educational Leadership: Promoting Respectful Schools* 69.1 (2011): 10–16. *ASCD*. Web. 16 Oct. 2014.

Sacco, Dena, Katharine Silbaugh, Felipe Corredor, June Casey, and Davis Doherty. *An Overview of State Anti-Bullying Legislation and Other*

Simmons 13

Related Laws. Cambridge: Berkman Center for Internet and Society,
2012. PDF file.

"School Bullying Laws Exist in Most States, U.S. Department of Education
Reports Analysis of Policies." *TheHuffingtonPost.com*. HPMG News,
10 Aug. 2012. Web. 13 Oct. 2014.

Smith, J., David, Barry H. Schneider, Peter K. Smith, and Katerina
Ananiadou. "The Effectiveness of Whole-School Antibullying
Programs: A Synthesis of Evaluation Research." *School Psychology
Review* 33.4 (2004): 547–60. PDF file.

Swearer, Susan M., Dorothy L. Espelage, Tracy Vaillancourt, and Shelly
Hymel. "What Can Be Done About School Bullying? Linking Research
to Educational Practice." *Educational Researcher* 39.1 (2010): 38–47.
AERA. Web. 14 Oct. 2014.

Villarreal, Daniel. "Jamey Rodemeyer's Bullies Are Happy He's Dead, but Is
It a Bad Idea to Prosecute Them?" *Queerty*. Queerty, Inc., 27 Sept.
2011. Web. 16 Oct. 2014.

The Strategy of the Argument Synthesis

In his argument synthesis, Peter Simmons attempts to support a *claim*—one
that favors blending local and statewide solutions to combat the problem of
bullying—by offering *support* in the form of facts: statistics establishing bullying as an ongoing problem despite anti-bullying laws, news of a court's re-
jecting elements of an anti-bullying law, and studies concluding that anti-bullying programs are largely ineffective. Simmons also supports his claim with
expert opinions like those of Bazelon, Rodkin, and the authors of a Harvard
study who state that anti-bullying laws can "only facilitate the harder non-
legal work" of reducing bullying. However, recall that Simmons's claim rests
on an *assumption* about the value of local solutions to broad problems when
system-wide solutions (that is, laws) aren't working. His ability to change
our minds about bullying depends partially on the extent to which we, as
readers, share his assumption. Readers who distrust local solutions may not
be swayed. (See our discussion of assumptions in Chapter 2, pp. 67–69.)

Recall that an assumption, sometimes called a warrant, is a generalization or principle about how the world works or should work—a

fundamental statement of belief about facts or values. Assumptions are often deeply rooted in people's psyches, sometimes derived from lifelong experiences and observations and, yes, prejudices. Assumptions are not easily changed, even by the most logical of arguments. Simmons makes explicit his assumption about the limitations of laws and the usefulness of local solutions. Though you are under no obligation to do so, stating assumptions explicitly will clarify your arguments to readers.

A discussion of the model argument's paragraphs, along with the argument strategy for each, follows. Note that the paper devotes one or more paragraphs to developing each section of the outline on pages 138–139. Note also that Simmons avoids plagiarism by the careful attribution and quotation of sources.

- **Paragraph 1:** Simmons opens with a heart-wrenching example of bullying from the documentary film *Bully* and states that the example is, unfortunately, repeated throughout the United States on a daily basis.

  Argument strategy: Opening with an anecdote can engage the emotions of readers. In a paper treating a problem as emotionally sensitive as bullying, this is an effective strategy.

- **Paragraph 2:** Simmons then uses statistics to establish that bullying is a pervasive problem that afflicts our most vulnerable children, and he introduces the digital age's contribution to such aggression: cyberbullying. He relates the tragic end of a college freshman who took his life in response to being bullied. Simmons poses questions to the reader: How should we respond? Are tough laws the answer?

  Argument strategy: Simmons prepares the ground of his argument with statistics and by extending bullying to the Internet. The tragic story of Clementi further engages readers emotionally. He then moves to include readers among the "we": what are *we*, readers included, going to do about the problem of bullying?

- **Paragraph 3:** Simmons answers the question raised by the Clementi suicide. What we, as a society, have done about bullying is to adopt two-part anti-bullying legislation that makes especially vicious behaviors unlawful and obligates schools to adopt anti-bullying programs. Simmons states, directly, that the laws are ineffective. At the same time, he points to local, ground-up initiatives that have shown promise in combating bullying. The critique of top-down laws, on the one hand, and the suggested promise of local initiatives, on the other, sets up his thesis advocating a *blended* solution to the problem.

  Argument strategy: This is the first instance of Simmons declaring his position on the problem of bullying. In the first two paragraphs, he establishes the groundwork that prepares him to take a stand here. His thesis is clear, assertive, and arguable and suggests that two broad sections will follow: a review of problems associated with broad anti-bullying laws and suggested local solutions that will come "from the ground up."

- **Paragraphs 4–5:** These paragraphs explain how anti-bullying laws came into being after the events of Columbine. Simmons quotes a school administrator's critique of what she thought was hasty and flawed thinking that prompted the laws (that Klebold and Harris were bullied kids out for revenge). Well-intentioned legislators, enacting laws to prevent other such atrocities, criminalized ordinary, if painful, behaviors associated with bullying. This was a "rush to action," writes Simmons, based more on high-profile media accounts than on research.

  Argument strategy: Simmons understands the need to take preventative action in response to the Columbine shootings. However, that action may have been based on an incomplete or faulty understanding of what actually happened at Columbine. If legislators didn't fully understand the problem facing them, then it's little surprise the laws they drafted are proving ineffective. Simmons supports this powerful critique with the opinions of three experts.

- **Paragraphs 6–10:** These paragraphs constitute the section of the paper detailing three major problems with anti-bullying laws. Paragraph 6 addresses the first problem: Tough cyberbullying laws have in at least one case been shown to violate freedom of speech. The rush to keep bullies from traumatizing victims online may have ineffectively balanced the right to protect victims and the right of everyone, bullies included, to say what they want online. Paragraphs 7 and 8 address what Simmons identifies as the second problem associated with anti-bullying laws, that they misunderstand the definition of bullying. Here Simmons introduces the distinction between bullying and drama. Simmons devotes Paragraphs 9 and 10 to what in his view is the most serious problem concerning anti-bullying legislation: that in their rush to comply with the educational mandates of the legislation, school districts and teachers are reaching for broad, one-size-fits-all solutions like the Olweus Bullying Prevention Program. The problem, writes Simmons, is that anti-bullying programs don't work—a claim he supports with several scholarly studies.

  Argument strategy: Simmons devotes these paragraphs to arguments against current anti-bullying laws. He is persuasive in using a gay advocacy organization, which might be expected to support anti-bullying laws on hateful speech, to argue that such laws may jeopardize civil liberties. By focusing on inconsistent definitions of bullying, Simmons shrewdly questions how legislators can solve a problem they can't define. And by using research to cast doubt on the effectiveness of one-size-fits-all anti-bullying programs, he strikes at the heart of anti-bullying legislation that seeks both to punish and to educate. Simmons must do an effective job in these paragraphs, for readers who aren't convinced that anti-bullying laws are sufficiently flawed won't agree that we need to search for new solutions. By the time readers finish Paragraph 10, Simmons has prepared them for the turn in the argument to his proposed local solutions.

- **Paragraph 11:** In this transitional paragraph, Simmons reviews the ways in which anti-bullying laws don't work. He summarizes the three main problems with these laws, and he restates how damaging bullying can be both for victims and bullies.

   Argument strategy: This paragraph marks the pivot point in the argument and provides a rationale for considering another approach to the problem of bullying.

- **Paragraphs 12–14:** Simmons explicitly states the need for a new approach to the problem of bullying and introduces two key sources (Rodkin and Flannery) to provide expert support for the position that an on-the-ground, local solution is needed. Paragraph 12 opens with a quotation from Philip Rodkin, whose approach relies not on broad, system-wide actions but on integrating particular bullies into the "social fabric of the school." In the same paragraph, Mary Flannery quotes a Colby College professor who introduces a key distinction: "top-down" and "on-the-ground." Simmons emphasizes this distinction in Paragraph 13 by quoting Harvard researchers who claim that anti-bullying laws can "only facilitate" a solution and are not themselves the answer. Paragraph 14 poses a brief, crucial question that Simmons devotes the rest of the argument to answering.

   Argument strategy: These three paragraphs turn the paper toward local solutions to the problem of bullying. To help make this turn, Simmons introduces perhaps his most important source, the Colby College professor quoted by Flannery. Simmons adopts Mikel Brown's language—"one-size-fits-all," "top-down," and "on-the-ground"— as his own. These terms help focus his argument: The legislative approach to bullying is a top-down, one-size-fits-all solution; what's needed are on-the-ground (local) solutions.

- **Paragraphs 15–19:** In these paragraphs, Simmons makes his argument for a local, ground-up response to bullying. His research has directed him to the work of four writers—Bazelon, Hirsch and Lowen, and Rodkin—whose policy recommendations favor addressing problems through direct interaction with victims and with bullies. These experts focus on the local approach and offer a clear alternative to the system-wide, top-down approach that Simmons has argued against in the first half of the paper. Simmons gives a paragraph each to Bazelon (#15), Hirsch and Lowen (#16), and Rodkin (#17). Then, in Paragraphs 18 and 19, he raises an argument against his own position and concedes that researchers should assess local, ground-up solutions for effectiveness just as they do one-size-fits-all solutions like the Olweus program.

   Argument strategy: In these paragraphs, Simmons argues in favor of his solution, relying on expert opinion to do so. It's a wise choice, for he's had no direct experience working with victims of bullying or with bullies themselves. In these paragraphs, he makes an important concession to would-be critics by insisting that researchers evaluate local solutions for effectiveness just as they do broad, system-wide solutions. He appreciates that there's nothing inherently superior about "local wisdom" and provides an example of a flawed local solution from the documentary film *Bully*. He also concedes there will be an important role for system-wide solutions once they are proven to be effective.

- **Paragraph 20:** In his conclusion, Simmons leaves room for a blended approach to the problem of bullying: guidance from the top informed by the on-the-ground perspective of local experts. He appreciates the role the state has to play in keeping students safe. Ultimately he is migrating to a position of compromise. He ends with an echo of his lead-in example, suggesting that one day the bullied might be able to coexist peaceably with the bully.

  Argument strategy: Simmons has given his readers a clear argument, one with a debatable thesis. He has supported his thesis with carefully researched facts and expert opinions. His tone throughout is reasonable, and he makes the effort to understand the motives of those who might disagree with him. His conclusion reinforces this conciliatory spirit by suggesting that one day, when there are more successful top-down approaches, a "blended" solution may emerge. There is wisdom to be gained from all sides in the debate.

Another approach to an argument synthesis based on the same and additional sources could argue that anti-bullying laws are not yet working in the intended manner and should be changed. Such a position could draw on exactly the same support, both facts and expert opinion, that Simmons uses to demonstrate the inadequacies of current laws. But instead of making a move to local solutions, the writer could assert that a problem as widespread and significant as bullying must be addressed at the state and federal levels. Whatever your approach to a subject, in first *critically examining* the various sources and then *synthesizing* them to support a position about which you feel strongly, you are engaging in the kind of critical thinking that is essential to success in a good deal of academic and professional work.

■ DEVELOPING AND ORGANIZING THE SUPPORT FOR YOUR ARGUMENTS

Experienced writers seem to have an intuitive sense of how to develop and present supporting evidence for their claims; this sense is developed through much hard work and practice. Less experienced writers wonder what to say first and, having decided on that, wonder what to say next. There is no single method of presentation, but the techniques of even the most experienced writers often boil down to a few tried and tested arrangements.

As we've seen in the model synthesis in this chapter, the key to devising effective arguments is to find and use those kinds of support that most persuasively strengthen your claim. Some writers categorize support into two broad types: *evidence* and *motivational appeals*. Evidence, in the form of facts, statistics, and expert testimony, helps make the appeal to reason. Motivational appeals—appeals grounded in emotion and upon the authority of the speaker—are employed to get people to change their minds, to agree with the writer or speaker, or to decide upon a plan of activity.

Following are the most common strategies for using and organizing support for your claims.

Summarize, Paraphrase, and Quote Supporting Evidence

In most of the papers and reports you will write in college and in the professional world, evidence and motivational appeals derive from your summarizing, paraphrasing, and quoting of material in sources that either have been provided to you or that you have independently researched. For example, in Paragraph 12 of the model argument synthesis, Simmons uses a long quotation from a writer at the National Education Association to introduce three key terms into the synthesis: "one-size-fits-all," "top-down," and "on-the-ground." You will find a number of brief quotations woven into sentences throughout. In addition, you will find summaries and paraphrases. In each case, Simmons is careful to cite the source.

Provide Various Types of Evidence and Motivational Appeals

Keep in mind that you can use appeals to both reason and emotion. The appeal to reason is based on evidence that consists of a combination of *facts* and *expert testimony*. For example, the sources by the Pacer organization and Kosciw (in Paragraph 1) and by Fox and the National Education Association (in Paragraph 11) factually establish the extent of bullying in America. Simmons draws on expert testimony by incorporating the opinions of Bazelon and others who argue that current anti-bullying programs are not working as intended.

Use Climactic Order

Climactic order is the arrangement of examples or evidence in order of anticipated impact on the reader, least to greatest. Organize by climactic order when you plan to offer a number of categories or elements of support for your claim. Recognize that some elements will be more important—and likely more persuasive—than others. The basic principle here is that you should *save the most important evidence for the end* because whatever you say last is what readers are likely to remember best. A secondary principle is that whatever you say first is what they are *next* most likely to remember. Therefore, when you have several reasons to offer in support of your claim, an effective argument strategy is to present the second most important, then one or more additional reasons, and finally the most important reason. Paragraphs 7–11 of the model synthesis do exactly this.

Use Logical or Conventional Order

Using a logical or conventional order involves using as a template a pre-established pattern or plan for arguing your case.

- One common pattern is describing or arguing a *problem/solution*. The model synthesis uses this pattern: You begin with an introduction in which you typically define the problem (perhaps explaining its origins), offer one or more solutions, then conclude. In the case of the model synthesis, Paragraphs 1–3 introduce the problem, Paragraphs 4–10 establish shortcomings of current solutions, and (after a transition) Paragraphs 12–19 suggest solutions.

- Another common pattern presents *two sides of a controversy*. Using this pattern, you introduce the controversy and (in an argument synthesis) your own point of view or claim; then you explain the other side's arguments, providing reasons why your point of view should prevail.

- A third common pattern is *comparison-and-contrast*. This pattern is so important that we will discuss it separately in the next section.

The order in which you present elements of an argument is sometimes dictated by the conventions of the discipline in which you are writing. For example, lab reports and experiments in the sciences and social sciences often follow this pattern: *Opening* or *Introduction, Methods and Materials* (of the experiment or study), *Results, Discussion*. Legal arguments often follow the so-called IRAC format: *Issue, Rule, Application, Conclusion*.

Present and Respond to Counterarguments

When developing arguments on a controversial topic, you can effectively use *counterargument* to help support your claims. When you use counterargument, you present an argument *against* your claim and then show that this argument is weak or flawed. The advantage of this technique is that you demonstrate that you are aware of the other side of the argument and that you are prepared to answer it.

Here is how a counterargument is typically developed:

I. Introduction and claim
II. Main opposing argument
III. Refutation of opposing argument
IV. Main positive argument

Use Concession

Concession is a variation of counterargument. As in counterargument, you present an opposing viewpoint, but instead of dismissing that position, you *concede* that it has some validity and even some appeal, although your own position is the more reasonable one. This concession bolsters your standing as a fair-minded person who is not blind to the virtues of the other side. In the model synthesis, Simmons acknowledges that local solutions to the problem of bullying may rely too heavily on folk wisdom that may be inept or just plain wrong. Bullies and victims, for instance, cannot just shake hands and make the problem go away. Simmons recommends evaluating local solutions rigorously; he also acknowledges that state and federal, top-down solutions may have a role to play—but only after these programs have been proven effective. In his conclusion, he moves to a compromise position that "blends" top-down and ground-up, local solutions.

Given the structure of his argument, Simmons held off making his concession until the end of his paper. Here is an outline for a more typical concession argument:

I. Introduction and claim

II. Important opposing argument

III. Concession that this argument has some validity

IV. Positive argument(s) that acknowledge the counterargument and (possibly) incorporate some elements of it

Sometimes, when you are developing a counterargument or concession argument, you may become convinced of the validity of the opposing point of view and change your own views. Don't be afraid of this happening. Writing is a tool for learning. To change your mind because of new evidence is a sign of flexibility and maturity, and your writing can only be the better for it.

Developing and Organizing Support for Your Arguments

- *Summarize, paraphrase, and quote supporting evidence.* Draw on the facts, ideas, and language in your sources.

- *Provide various types of evidence and motivational appeal.*

- *Use climactic order.* Save the most important evidence in support of your argument for the *end*, where it will have the most impact. Use the next most important evidence *first*.

- *Use logical or conventional order.* Use a form of organization appropriate to the topic, such as problem/solution; sides of a controversy;

(continues)

> comparison/contrast; or a form of organization appropriate to the academic or professional discipline, such as a report of an experiment or a business plan.
>
> - *Present and respond to counterarguments.* Anticipate and evaluate arguments against your position.
>
> - *Use concession.* Concede that one or more arguments against your position have some validity; reassert, nonetheless, that your argument is the stronger one.

Avoid Common Fallacies in Developing and Using Support

In Chapter 2, in the section on critical reading, we considered criteria that, as a reader, you may use for evaluating informative and persuasive writing (see pp. 54, 56–65). We discussed how you can assess the accuracy, the significance, and the author's interpretation of the information presented. We also considered the importance in good argument of clearly defined key terms and the pitfalls of emotionally loaded language. Finally, we saw how to recognize such logical fallacies as either/or reasoning, faulty cause-and-effect reasoning, hasty generalization, and false analogy. As a writer, no less than as a critical reader, you need to be aware of these common problems and how to avoid them.

Be aware, also, of your responsibility to cite source materials appropriately. When you quote a source, double- and triple-check that you have done so accurately. When you summarize or paraphrase, take care to use your own language and sentence structures (though you can, of course, also quote within these forms). When you refer to someone else's idea—even if you are not quoting, summarizing, or paraphrasing it—give the source credit. By being ethical about the use of sources, you uphold the highest standards of the academic community.

■ THE COMPARISON-AND-CONTRAST SYNTHESIS

A particularly important type of argument synthesis is built on patterns of comparison and contrast. Techniques of comparison and contrast enable you to examine two subjects (or sources) in terms of one another. When you compare, you consider *similarities.* When you contrast, you consider *differences.* By comparing and contrasting, you perform a multifaceted analysis that often suggests subtleties that otherwise might not have come to your (or your reader's) attention.

To organize a comparison-and-contrast argument, you must carefully read sources in order to discover *significant criteria for analysis.* A *criterion* is a specific point to which both of your authors refer and about which they may agree or disagree. (For example, in a comparative report on compact cars, criteria for *comparison and contrast* might be road handling, fuel economy, and comfort of ride.) The best criteria are those that allow you not only to account for obvious similarities and differences—those concerning the main aspects of your sources or subjects—but also to plumb deeper, exploring subtle yet significant comparisons and contrasts among details or subcomponents, which you can then relate to your overall thesis.

Note that comparison-and-contrast is frequently not an end in itself but serves some larger purpose. Thus, a comparison-and-contrast synthesis may be a component of a paper that is essentially a critique, an explanatory synthesis, an argument synthesis, or an analysis.

Organizing Comparison-and-Contrast Syntheses

Two basic approaches to organizing a comparison-and-contrast synthesis are organization by *source* and organization by *criteria*.

Organizing by Source or Subject

You can organize a comparative synthesis by first summarizing each of your sources or subjects and then discussing the significant similarities and differences between them. Having read the summaries and become familiar with the distinguishing features of each source, your readers will most likely be able to appreciate the more obvious similarities and differences. In the discussion, your task is to consider both the obvious and the subtle comparisons and contrasts, focusing on the most significant—that is, on those that most clearly support your thesis.

Organization by source or subject works best with passages that can be briefly summarized. If the summary of your source or subject becomes too long, your readers might have forgotten the points you made in the first summary when they are reading the second. A comparison-and-contrast synthesis organized by source or subject might proceed like this:

I.   Introduce the paper; lead to thesis.

II. Summarize source/subject A by discussing its significant features.

III. Summarize source/subject B by discussing its significant features.

IV. Discuss in a paragraph (or two) the significant points of comparison and contrast between sources or subjects A and B. Alternatively, begin the comparison-and-contrast in Section III as you introduce source/subject B.

V.   Conclude with a paragraph in which you summarize your points and, perhaps, raise and respond to pertinent questions.

Organizing by Criteria

Instead of summarizing entire sources one at a time with the intention of comparing them later, you could discuss two sources simultaneously, examining the views of each author point by point (criterion by criterion), comparing and contrasting these views in the process. The criterion approach is best used when you have a number of points to discuss or when passages or subjects are long and/or complex. A comparison-and-contrast synthesis organized by criteria might look like this:

I. Introduce the paper; lead to thesis.

II. Criterion 1

    A. Discuss what author #1 says about this point. Or present situation #1 in light of this point.

    B. Discuss what author #2 says about this point, comparing and contrasting #2's treatment of the point with #1's. Or present situation #2 in light of this point and explain its differences from situation #1.

III. Criterion 2

    A. Discuss what author #1 says about this point. Or present situation #1 in light of this point.

    B. Discuss what author #2 says about this point, comparing and contrasting #2's treatment of the point with #1's. Or present situation #2 in light of this point and explain its differences from situation #1.

And so on, proceeding criterion by criterion until you have completed your discussion. Be sure to arrange criteria with a clear method. Knowing how the discussion of one criterion leads to the next will ensure smooth transitions throughout your paper. End by summarizing your key points and perhaps raising and responding to pertinent questions.

However you organize your comparison-and-contrast synthesis, keep in mind that comparing and contrasting are not ends in themselves. Your discussion should point to a conclusion, an answer to the question "So what— why bother to compare and contrast in the first place?" If your discussion is part of a larger synthesis, point to and support the larger claim. If you write a stand-alone comparison-and-contrast synthesis, though, you must by the final paragraph answer the "Why bother?" question. The model comparison-and-contrast synthesis that follows does exactly this.

Exercise 4.6

Comparing and Contrasting

Over the course of two days, go online to the Web sites of three daily news outlets and follow how each, in its news pages, treats a particular story of national or international significance. One news outlet should be a local city outlet—perhaps the Web site of your hometown newspaper. (Note: The reporting should originate not with a syndicated newswire, like the Associated Press, but with the outlet's own staff writer.) One news outlet should have a national readership, like the *Wall Street Journal* or the *New*

York Times. The third outlet should be any news source of your choice (and it needn't exist in print).

Develop a comparison-and-contrast synthesis that leads to an argument about the news coverage. In making notes toward such a synthesis, you'll want to do the following:

- Define the news story: the who, what, when, where of the issue.
- Develop at least three criteria with which to compare and contrast news coverage. Possible criteria: Do the outlets report the same facts? Do the outlets color these facts with an editorial slant? Do the outlets agree on the significance of the issue?
- As you take notes, point to specific passages.
- Review your notes. What patterns emerge? Can you draw any conclusions? Write a thesis that reflects your assessment.
- Using your notes and guided by your thesis, write a comparison-and-contrast-paper.
- Be sure that your paper answers the "So what?" question. What is the point of your synthesis?

A Case for Comparison-and-Contrast: World War I and World War II

Let's see how the principles of comparison-and-contrast can be applied to a response to a final examination question in a course on modern history. Imagine that, having attended classes involving lecture and discussion and having read excerpts from John Keegan's *The First World War* and Tony Judt's *Postwar: A History of Europe Since 1945,* you were presented with this examination question:

> Based on your reading to date, compare and contrast the two world wars in light of any four or five criteria you think significant. Once you have called careful attention to both similarities and differences, conclude with an observation. What have you learned? What can your comparative analysis teach us?

Comparison-and-Contrast Organized by Criteria

Here is a plan for a response, essentially a comparison-and-contrast synthesis, organized by *criteria* and beginning with the thesis—and the *claim.*

> *Thesis:* In terms of the impact on cities and civilian populations, the military aspects of the two wars in Europe, and their aftermaths, the differences between World War I and World War II considerably outweigh the similarities.
>
> I. Introduction. World Wars I and II were the most devastating conflicts in history. *Thesis*
> II. Summary of main similarities: causes, countries involved, battle-grounds, global scope

III. First major difference: Physical impact of war
   A. WWI was fought mainly in rural battlegrounds.
   B. In WWII cities were destroyed.
IV. Second major difference: Effect on civilians
   A. WWI fighting primarily involved soldiers.
   B. WWII involved not only military but also massive noncombatant casualties: Civilian populations were displaced, forced into slave labor, and exterminated.
V. Third major difference: Combat operations
   A. WWI, in its long middle phase, was characterized by trench warfare.
   B. During the middle phase of WWII, there was no major military action in Nazi-occupied Western Europe.
VI. Fourth major difference: Aftermath
   A. Harsh war terms imposed on defeated Germany contributed significantly to the rise of Hitler and WWII.
   B. Victorious allies helped rebuild West Germany after WWII but allowed Soviets to take over Eastern Europe.
VII. Conclusion. Since the end of World War II, wars have been far smaller in scope and destructiveness, and warfare has expanded to involve stateless combatants committed to acts of terror.

The following model exam response, a comparison-and-contrast synthesis organized by criteria, is written according to the preceding plan. (Thesis and topic sentences are highlighted.)

MODEL EXAM RESPONSE

(1) World War I (1914–18) and World War II (1939–45) were the most catastrophic and destructive conflicts in human history. For those who believed in the steady but inevitable progress of civilization, it was impossible to imagine that two wars in the first half of the twentieth century could reach levels of barbarity and horror that would outstrip those of any previous era. Historians estimate that more than 22 million people, soldiers and civilians, died in World War I; they estimate that between 40 and 50 million died in World War II. In many ways, these two conflicts were similar: They were fought on many of the same European and Russian battlegrounds, with more or less the same countries on opposing sides. Even many of the same people

were involved: Winston Churchill and Adolf Hitler figured in both wars. And the main outcome in each case was the same: total defeat for Germany. However, in terms of the impact on cities and civilian populations, the military aspects of the two wars in Europe, and their aftermaths, the differences between World Wars I and II considerably outweigh the similarities.

2   The similarities are clear enough. In fact, many historians regard World War II as a continuation—after an intermission of about twenty years—of World War I. One of the main causes of each war was Germany's dissatisfaction and frustration with what it perceived as its diminished place in the world. Hitler launched World War II partly out of revenge for Germany's humiliating defeat in World War I. In each conflict Germany and its allies (the Central Powers in WWI, the Axis in WWII) went to war against France, Great Britain, Russia (the Soviet Union in WWII), and, eventually, the United States. Though neither conflict included literally the entire world, the participation of countries not only in Europe but also in the Middle East, the Far East, and the Western hemisphere made both conflicts global in scope. And, as indicated earlier, the number of casualties in each war was unprecedented in history, partly because modern technology had enabled the creation of deadlier weapons—including tanks, heavy artillery, and aircraft—than had ever been used in warfare.

3   Despite these similarities, the differences between the two world wars are considerably more significant. One of the most noticeable differences was the physical impact of each war in Europe and in Russia—the western and eastern fronts. The physical destruction of World War I was confined largely to the battlefield. The combat took place almost entirely in the rural areas of Europe and Russia. No major cities were destroyed in the first war; cathedrals, museums, government buildings, urban houses, and apartments were left untouched. During the second war, in contrast, almost no city or town of any size emerged unscathed. Rotterdam, Warsaw, London, Minsk, and—when the Allies began their counterattack—almost every major city in Germany and Japan, including Berlin and Tokyo, were flattened.

Of course, the physical devastation of the cities created millions of refugees, a phenomenon never experienced in World War I.

(4) The fact that World War II was fought in the cities as well as on the battlefields meant that the second war had a much greater impact on civilians than did the first war. With few exceptions, the civilians in Europe during WWI were not driven from their homes, forced into slave labor, starved, tortured, or systematically exterminated. But all of these crimes happened routinely during WWII. The Nazi occupation of Europe meant that the civilian populations of France, Belgium, Norway, the Netherlands, and other conquered lands, along with the industries, railroads, and farms of these countries, were put into the service of the Third Reich. Millions of people from conquered Europe—those who were not sent directly to the death camps—were forcibly transported to Germany and put to work in support of the war effort.

(5) During both wars, the Germans were fighting on two fronts—the western front in Europe and the eastern front in Russia. But while both wars were characterized by intense military activity during their initial and final phases, the middle and longest phases—at least in Europe—differed considerably. The middle phase of the First World War was characterized by trench warfare, a relatively static form of military activity in which fronts seldom moved, or moved only a few hundred yards at a time, even after major battles. By contrast, in the years between the German conquest of most of Europe by early 1941 and the Allied invasion of Normandy in mid-1944, there was no major fighting in Nazi-occupied Western Europe. (The land battles then shifted to North Africa and the Soviet Union.)

(6) And of course, the two world wars differed in their aftermaths. The most significant consequence of World War I was that the humiliating and costly war reparations imposed on the defeated Germany by the terms of the 1919 Treaty of Versailles made possible the rise of Hitler and thus led directly to World War II. In contrast, after the end of the Second World War in 1945, the Allies helped rebuild West Germany (the portion of a divided Germany that it controlled), transformed the new country into a

democracy, and helped make it one of the most thriving economies of the world. But perhaps the most significant difference in the aftermath of each war involved Russia. That country, in a considerably weakened state, pulled out of World War I a year before hostilities ended so that it could consolidate its 1917 Revolution. Russia then withdrew into itself and took no significant part in European affairs until the Nazi invasion of the Soviet Union in 1941. In contrast, it was the Red Army in World War II that was most responsible for the crushing defeat of Germany. In recognition of its efforts and of its enormous sacrifices, the Allies allowed the Soviet Union to take control of the countries of Eastern Europe after the war, leading to fifty years of totalitarian rule—and the Cold War.

(7)   While the two world wars that devastated much of Europe were similar in that, at least according to some historians, they were the same war interrupted by two decades and similar in that combatants killed more efficiently than armies throughout history ever had, the differences between the wars were significant. In terms of the physical impact of the fighting, the impact on civilians, the action on the battlefield at mid-war, and the aftermaths, World Wars I and II differed in ways that matter to us decades later. The wars in Iraq, Afghanistan, and Bosnia have involved an alliance of nations pitted against single nations, but we have not seen, since the two world wars, grand alliances moving vast armies across continents. The destruction implied by such action is almost unthinkable today. Warfare is changing, and "stateless" combatants like Hamas and Al Qaeda wreak destruction of their own. But we may never again see, one hopes, the devastation that follows when multiple nations on opposing sides of a conflict throw millions of soldiers—and civilians—into harm's way.

The Strategy of the Exam Response

The general strategy of this argument is an organization by *criteria*. The writer argues that although the two world wars exhibited some similarities, the differences between the two conflicts were more significant. Note that the writer's thesis doesn't merely state these significant differences; it also presents them in a way that anticipates both the content and the structure of the response to follow.

In argument terms, the *claim* the writer makes is the conclusion that the two global conflicts were significantly different, if superficially similar. The *assumption* is that key differences and similarities are clarified by employing specific criteria: the impact of the wars upon cities and civilian populations and the consequences of the Allied victories. The *support* comes in the form of historical facts regarding the levels of casualties, the scope of destruction, the theaters of conflict, the events following the conclusions of the wars, and so on.

- **Paragraph 1:** The writer begins by commenting on the unprecedented level of destruction of World Wars I and II and concludes with the thesis summarizing the key similarities and differences.

- **Paragraph 2:** The writer summarizes the key similarities in the two wars: the wars' causes, their combatants, their global scope, and the level of destructiveness made possible by modern weaponry.

- **Paragraph 3:** The writer discusses the first of the key differences: the battlegrounds of World War I were largely rural; the battlegrounds of World War II included cities that were targeted and destroyed.

- **Paragraph 4:** The writer discusses the second of the key differences: the impact on civilians. In World War I, civilians were generally spared from the direct effects of combat; in World War II, civilians were targeted by the Nazis for systematic displacement and destruction.

- **Paragraph 5:** The writer discusses the third key difference: Combat operations during the middle phase of World War I were characterized by static trench warfare. During World War II, in contrast, there were no major combat operations in Nazi-occupied Western Europe during the middle phase of the conflict.

- **Paragraph 6:** The writer focuses on the fourth key difference: the aftermath of the two wars. After World War I, the victors imposed harsh conditions on a defeated Germany, leading to the rise of Hitler and the Second World War. After World War II, the Allies helped Germany rebuild and thrive. However, the Soviet victory in 1945 led to its postwar domination of Eastern Europe.

- **Paragraph 7:** In the conclusion, the writer sums up the key similarities and differences just covered and makes additional comments about the course of more recent wars since World War II. In this way, the writer responds to the questions posed at the end of the assignment: "What have you learned? What can your comparative analysis teach us?"

■ SUMMARY OF SYNTHESIS CHAPTERS

In this chapter and in Chapter 3, we've considered three main types of synthesis: the *explanatory synthesis,* the *argument synthesis,* and the *comparison-and-contrast synthesis.* Although for ease of comprehension we've placed these in separate categories, the types are not mutually exclusive. Argument syntheses often include extended sections of explanation and/or comparison and contrast. Explanations commonly include sections of comparison-and-contrast. Which type of synthesis you choose will depend on your *purpose* and the method that you decide is best suited to achieve this purpose.

If your main purpose is to help your audience understand a particular subject, and in particular to help them understand the essential elements or significance of this subject, then you will be composing an explanatory synthesis. If your main purpose, on the other hand, is to persuade your audience to agree with your viewpoint on a subject, or to change their minds, or to decide on a particular course of action, then you will be composing an argument synthesis. If your purpose is to clarify similarities or differences, you will compose a comparison-and-contrast synthesis—which may be a paper in itself (either an argument or an explanation) or part of a larger paper (again, either an argument or explanation).

In planning and drafting these syntheses, you can draw on a variety of strategies: supporting your claims by summarizing, paraphrasing, and quoting from your sources; using appeals to *logos, pathos,* and *ethos;* and choosing from among strategies such as climactic or conventional order, counterargument, and concession the approach that will best help you to achieve your purpose.

The strategies of synthesis you've practiced in these two chapters will be dealt with again in Chapter 7, where we'll consider a category of synthesis commonly known as the research paper. The research paper involves all of the skills in preparing summary, critique, and synthesis that we've discussed thus far, the main difference being that you won't find the sources needed to write the paper in this particular text. We'll discuss approaches to locating and critically evaluating sources, selecting material from among them to provide support for your claims, and, finally, documenting your sources in standard professional formats.

We turn, now, to analysis, which is another important strategy for academic thinking and writing. Chapter 5, "Analysis," will introduce you to a strategy that, like synthesis, draws upon all the strategies you've been practicing as you move through *A Sequence for Academic Writing.*

WRITING ASSIGNMENT: ETHICAL DILEMMAS IN EVERYDAY LIFE

Now we'll give you an opportunity to practice your skills in planning and writing an argument. See Chapter 8, pages 285–312, where we provide a variety of sources on the ways "thought experiments" in ethics— scenarios that ask you to decide on courses of right action (and to justify your decisions)—can serve as a guide for facing everyday ethical dilemmas. When there is no clear right and wrong choice, how do you decide? To what principles can you turn for guidance? Your task in the synthesis will be to wrestle with ethical dilemmas and to argue for a clear course of action based on principles you make plain to your readers.

Note that your instructor may want you to complete related assignments in Chapter 8, which ask you to write summaries, explanations, and critiques in preparation for writing a larger argument.

5 ∎ Analysis

∎ WHAT IS AN ANALYSIS?

An *analysis* is a type of argument in which you study the parts of something—a physical object, a work of art, a person or group of people, an event, a scientific, economic, or sociological phenomenon—to understand how it works, what it means, or why it might be significant. The writer of an analysis uses an analytic tool: a *principle* or *definition* on the basis of which the subject of study can be divided into parts and examined.

Here are excerpts from two analyses of the movie version of L. Frank Baum's *The Wizard of Oz:*

> At the dawn of adolescence, the very time she should start to distance herself from Aunt Em and Uncle Henry, the surrogate parents who raised her on their Kansas farm, Dorothy Gale experiences a hurtful reawakening of her fear that these loved ones will be rudely ripped from her, especially her Aunt (Em—M for Mother!).[1]

> [*The Wizard of Oz*] was originally written as a political allegory about grass-roots protest. It may seem harder to believe than Emerald City, but the Tin Woodsman is the industrial worker, the Scarecrow [is] the struggling farmer, and the Wizard is the president, who is powerful only as long as he succeeds in deceiving the people.[2]

As these paragraphs suggest, what you discover through analysis depends entirely on the principle or definition you use to make your insights. Is *The Wizard of Oz* the story of a girl's psychological development, or is it a story about politics? The answer is *both.* In the first example, the psychiatrist Harvey Greenberg applies the principles of his profession and, not surprisingly, sees *The Wizard of Oz* in psychological terms. In the second example, a newspaper reporter applies the political theories of Karl Marx and, again not surprisingly, discovers a story about politics.

Different as they are, these analyses share an important quality: Each is the result of a specific principle or definition used as a tool to divide an

---

[1] Harvey Greenberg, *The Movies on Your Mind* (New York: Dutton, 1975).
[2] Peter Dreier, "Oz Was Almost Reality." *Cleveland Plain Dealer* 3 Sept. 1989.

object into parts in order to see what it means and how it works. The writer's choice of analytic tool simultaneously creates and limits the possibilities for analysis. Thus, working with the principles of Freud, Harvey Greenberg sees *The Wizard of Oz* in psychological, not political, terms; working with the theories of Karl Marx, Peter Dreier understands the movie in terms of the economic relationships among the characters. It's as if the writer of an analysis who adopts one analytic tool puts on a pair of glasses and sees an object in a specific way. Another writer, using a different tool (and a different pair of glasses), sees the object differently.

Where Do We Find Written Analyses?

Here are just a few of the types of writing that involve analysis:

ACADEMIC WRITING

- **Experimental and lab reports** analyze the meaning or implications of the study results in the Discussion section.
- **Research papers** analyze information in sources or apply theories to material being reported.
- **Process analyses** break down the steps or stages involved in completing a process.
- **Literary analyses** examine characterization, plot, imagery, or other elements in works of literature.
- **Essay exams** demonstrate understanding of course material by analyzing data using course concepts.

WORKPLACE WRITING

- **Grant proposals** analyze the issues you seek funding for in order to address them.
- **Reviews of the arts** employ dramatic or literary analysis to assess artistic works.
- **Business plans** break down and analyze capital outlays, expenditures, profits, materials, and the like.
- **Medical charts** record analytic thinking and writing in relation to patient symptoms and possible options.
- **Legal briefs** break down and analyze facts of cases and elements of legal precedents and apply legal rulings and precedents to new situations.
- **Case studies** describe and analyze the particulars of a specific medical, social service, advertising, or business case.

You might protest: Are there as many analyses of *The Wizard of Oz* as there are people to read the book or to see the movie? Yes, or at least as many analyses as there are analytic tools. This does not mean that all analyses are equally valid or useful. Each writer must convince the reader using the power of her or his argument. In creating an analytic discussion, the writer must organize a series of related insights using the analytic tool to examine first one part and then another part of the object being studied. To read Harvey Greenberg's essay on *The Wizard of Oz* is to find paragraph after paragraph of related insights—first about Aunt Em, then the Wicked Witch, then Toto, and then the Wizard. All these insights point to Greenberg's single conclusion: that "Dorothy's 'trip' is a marvelous metaphor for the psychological journey every adolescent must make." Without Greenberg's analysis, we would probably not have thought about the movie as a psychological journey. This is precisely the power of an analysis: its ability to reveal objects or events in ways we would not otherwise have considered.

The writer's challenge is to convince readers that (1) the analytic tool being applied is legitimate and well matched to the object being studied; and (2) the analytic tool is being used systematically and insightfully to divide the object into parts and to make a coherent, meaningful statement about these parts and the object as a whole.

■ HOW TO WRITE ANALYSES

Let's consider a more extended example of analysis, one that approaches excessive TV watching as a type of addiction. This analytic passage illustrates the two defining features of the analysis: a statement of an analytic principle or definition and the use of that principle or definition in closely examining an object, behavior, or event. As you read, try to identify these features. An exercise with questions for discussion follows the passage.

THE PLUG-IN DRUG

Marie Winn

This analysis of television viewing as an addictive behavior appeared originally in Marie Winn's book The Plug-In Drug: Television, Computers, and Family Life *(2002). A writer and media critic, Winn has been interested in the effects of television on both individuals and the larger culture. In this passage, she carefully defines the term* addiction *and then applies it systematically to the behavior under study.*

The word "addiction" is often used loosely and wryly in conversation. People will refer to themselves as "mystery-book addicts" or "cookie addicts." E. B. White wrote of his annual surge of interest in gardening: "We are hooked and are making an attempt to kick the habit." Yet nobody really believes that reading mysteries or ordering seeds by catalogue is serious enough to be compared with addictions to heroin or alcohol. In these cases the word "addiction" is used jokingly to denote a tendency to overindulge in some pleasurable activity.

People often refer to being "hooked on TV." Does this, too, fall into the light-hearted category of cookie eating and other pleasures that people pursue with unusual intensity? Or is there a kind of television viewing that falls into the more serious category of destructive addiction?

Not unlike drugs or alcohol, the television experience allows the participant to blot out the real world and enter into a pleasurable and passive mental state. To be sure, other experiences, notably reading, also provide a temporary respite from reality. But it's much easier to stop reading and return to reality than to stop watching television. The entry into another world offered by reading includes an easily accessible return ticket. The entry via television does not. In this way television viewing, for those vulnerable to addiction, is more like drinking or taking drugs—once you start it's hard to stop.

Just as alcoholics are only vaguely aware of their addiction, feeling that they control their drinking more than they really do ("I can cut it out any time I want—I just like to have three or four drinks before dinner"), many people overestimate their control over television watching. Even as they put off other activities to spend hour after hour watching television, they feel they could easily resume living in a different, less passive style. But somehow or other while the television set is present in their homes, it just stays on. With television's easy gratifications available, those other activities seem to take too much effort.

5   A heavy viewer (a college English instructor) observes:

> I find television almost irresistible. When the set is on, I cannot ignore it. I can't turn it off. I feel sapped, will-less, enervated. As I reach out to turn off the set, the strength goes out of my arms. So I sit there for hours and hours.

Self-confessed television addicts often feel they "ought" to do other things—but the fact that they don't read and don't plant their garden or sew or crochet or play games or have conversations means that those activities are no longer as desirable as television viewing. In a way, the lives of heavy viewers are as unbalanced by their television "habit" as drug addicts' or alcoholics' lives. They are living in a holding pattern, as it were, passing up the activities that lead to growth or development or a sense of accomplishment. This is one reason people talk about their television viewing so ruefully, so apologetically. They are aware that it is an unproductive experience, that by any human measure almost any other endeavor is more worthwhile.

It is the adverse effect of television viewing on the lives of so many people that makes it feel like a serious addiction. The television habit distorts the sense of time. It renders other experiences vague and curiously unreal while taking on a greater reality for itself. It weakens relationships by reducing and sometimes eliminating normal opportunities for talking, for communicating.

And yet television does not satisfy, else why would the viewer continue to watch hour after hour, day after day? "The measure of health," wrote the psychiatrist Lawrence Kubie, "is flexibility...and especially the freedom to cease when sated." But heavy television viewers can never be sated with their television experiences. These do not provide the true nourishment that satiation requires, and thus they find that they cannot stop watching.

Reading Critically: Winn

In an analysis, an author first presents the analytic principle in full and then systematically applies parts of the principle to the object or phenomenon under study. In her brief analysis of television viewing, Marie Winn pursues an alternative, though equally effective, strategy by *distributing* parts of her analytic principle across the essay. Locate where Winn defines key elements of addiction. Locate where she uses each element as an analytic lens to examine television viewing as a form of addiction.

What function does paragraph 4 play in the analysis?

In the first two paragraphs, how does Winn create a funnel-like effect that draws readers into the heart of her analysis?

Recall a few television programs that genuinely moved you, educated you, humored you, or stirred you to worthwhile reflection or action. To what extent does Winn's analysis describe your positive experiences as a television viewer? (Consider how Winn might argue that from within an addicted state, a person may feel "humored, moved, or educated" but is in fact—from a sober outsider's point of view—deluded.) If Winn's analysis of television viewing as an addiction does *not* account for your experience, does it follow that her analysis is flawed? Explain.

Locate and Apply an Analytic Tool

The general purpose of all analysis is to enhance one's understanding of the subject under consideration. A good analysis provides a valuable—if sometimes unusual or unexpected—point of view, a way of *seeing*, a way of *interpreting* some phenomenon, person, event, policy, or pattern of behavior that otherwise may appear random or unexplainable. How well the analysis achieves its purpose depends upon the suitability to the subject and the precision of the analytic tools selected and upon the skill with which the writer (or speaker) applies these tools. Each reader must determine for her- or himself whether the analysis enhances understanding or—in the opposite case—is merely confusing or irrelevant. To what extent does it enhance your understanding of *The Wizard of Oz* to view the story in psychological terms? In political terms? To what extent does it enhance your understanding of excessive TV watching to view such behavior as an addiction?

When you are faced with writing an analysis, consider these two general strategies:

- Locate an analytic tool—a principle or definition that makes a general statement about the way something works.

- Systematically apply this principle or definition to the subject under consideration.

Let's more fully consider each of these strategies.

Locate an Analytic Tool

In approaching her subject, Marie Winn finds in the definition of "addiction" a useful principle for making sense of the way some people watch TV. The word "addiction," she notes, "is used jokingly to denote a tendency to overindulge in some pleasurable activity." The question she decides to tackle is whether, in the case of watching TV, such overindulgence is harmless or whether it is destructive and thus constitutes an addiction.

Make yourself aware, as both writer and reader, of a tool's strengths and limitations. Pose these questions of the analytic principle and definitions you use:

- Are they accurate?
- Are they well accepted?
- Do you accept them?
- How successfully do they account for or throw light upon the phenomenon under consideration?
- What are the arguments against them?
- What are their limitations?

Since every principle of definition used in an analysis is the end product of an argument, you are entitled—even obligated—to challenge it. If the analytic tool is flawed, the analysis that follows from it will necessarily be flawed.

Some, for example, would question whether addiction is a useful concept to apply to television viewing. First, we usually think of addiction as applying only to substances such as alcohol, nicotine, or drugs (whether legal or illegal). Second, many people think that the word "addiction" carries inappropriate moral connotations: we disapprove of addicts and think that they have only themselves to blame for their condition. For a time, the American Psychiatric Association dropped the word "addiction" from its definitive guide to psychological disorders, the *Diagnostic and Statistical Manual of Mental Disorders* (DSM), in favor of the more neutral term "dependence." (The latest edition of the DSM has returned to the term "addiction.")

On the other hand, "addiction"—also known as "impulse control disorder"—has long been applied to behavior as well as to substances. People are said to be addicted to gambling, to shopping, to eating, to sex, even to hoarding newspapers. The editors of the new DSM are likely to add Internet addiction to the list of impulse control disorders. The term even has national implications: Many argue that this country must break its "addiction" to oil. Thus, there is considerable precedent for Winn to argue that excessive TV watching constitutes an addiction.

Apply the Analytic Tool

Having suggested that TV watching may be an addiction, Winn uses established psychological criteria[3] to identify the chief components of addictive behavior. She then applies each one of them to the behavior under consideration. In doing so, she presents her case that TV is a "plug-in drug," and her readers are free to evaluate the success and persuasiveness of her analysis.

In the body of her analysis, Winn systematically applies the component elements of addiction to TV watching. Winn does this by identifying the major components of addiction and applying them to television watching. Users:

1. Turn away from the real world.
2. Overestimate how much control they have over their addiction.
3. Lead unbalanced lives and turn away from social activities.
4. Develop a distorted sense of time.
5. Are never satisfied with their use.

Analysis Across the Curriculum

The principle that you select can be a theory as encompassing as the statement that *myths are the enemy of truth.* It can be as modest as the definition of a term such as *addiction* or *comfort.* As you move from one subject area to another, the principles and definitions you use for analysis will change, as these assignments illustrate:

Sociology: Write a paper in which you place yourself in American society by locating both your absolute position and relative rank on each single criterion of social stratification used by Lenski and Lenski. For each criterion, state whether you have attained your social position by yourself or have "inherited" that status from your parents.

Literature: Apply principles of Jungian psychology to Hawthorne's "Young Goodman Brown." In your reading of the story, apply Jung's principles of the *shadow, persona,* and *anima.*

Physics: Use Newton's second law ($F = ma$) to analyze the acceleration of a fixed pulley from which two weights hang: m_1 (.45 kg) and m_2 (.90 kg). Explain in

---

[3]For example, the Web site AddictionsandRecovery.org., drawing upon the *Diagnostic and Statistical Manual of Mental Disorders* (DSM) criteria, identifies seven components of substance addiction. A person who answers *yes* to three of the following questions meets the medical definition of addiction: **Tolerance** (use of drugs or alcohol increased over time); **Withdrawal** (adverse physical or emotional reactions to not using); **Difficulty controlling your use** (using more than you would like); **Negative consequences** (using even though use negatively affects mood, self-esteem, health, job, or family); **Neglecting or postponing activities** (putting off or reducing social, recreational, work in order to use); **Spending significant time or emotional energy** (spending significant time obtaining, using, concealing, planning, recovering from, or thinking about use); **Desire to cut down.**

a paragraph the principle of Newton's law and your method of applying it to solve the problem. Assume your reader is not comfortable with mathematical explanations: Do not use equations in your paragraph.

Finance: Using Guidford C. Babcock's "Concept of Sustainable Growth" [*Financial Analysis* 26 (May–June 1970): 108–14], analyze the stock price appreciation of the XYZ Corporation, figures for which are attached.

The analytic tools to be applied in these assignments must be appropriate to the discipline. Writing in response to the sociology assignment, you would use sociological principles developed by Lenski and Lenski. In your literature class, you would use principles of Jungian psychology; in physics, Newton's second law; and in finance, a particular writer's concept of "sustainable growth." But whatever discipline you are working in, the first part of your analysis will clearly state which (and whose) principles and definitions you are applying. For audiences unfamiliar with these principles, you will need to explain them; if you anticipate objections to their use, you will need to argue that they are legitimate principles capable of helping you conduct the analysis.

Guidelines for Writing Analyses

Unless you are asked to follow a specialized format, especially in the sciences or the social sciences, you can present your analysis as a paper by following the guidelines below. As you move from one class to another, from discipline to discipline, the principles and definitions you use as the basis for your analyses will change, but the following basic components of analysis will remain the same.

- *Create a context for your analysis.* Introduce and summarize for readers the object, event, or behavior to be analyzed. Present a strong case for why an analysis is needed: Give yourself a motivation to write, and give readers a motivation to read. Consider setting out a problem, puzzle, or question to be investigated.

- *Locate an analytic tool: a principle or definition that will form the basis of your analysis.* Plan to devote an early part of your analysis to arguing for the validity of this principle or definition if your audience is not likely to understand it or if they are likely to think that the principle or definition is not valuable.

- *Analyze your topic by applying your selected analytic tool to the topic's component elements.* Systematically apply elements of the analytic tool to parts of the activity or object under study. You can do this by posing specific questions, based on your analytic principle or definition, about the object or phenomenon. Discuss what you find part by part (organized perhaps by question), in clearly defined subsections of the paper.

- *Conclude by stating clearly what is significant about your analysis.* When considering your analytic paper as a whole, what new or interesting insights have you made concerning the object under study? To what extent has your application of the definition or principle helped you to explain how the object works, what it might mean, or why it is significant?

Formulate a Thesis

Like any other thesis, the thesis of an analysis compresses into a single sentence the main idea of your presentation. Some authors omit an explicit thesis statement, preferring to leave the thesis implied. Underlying Winn's analysis, for example, is an implied thesis: "By applying my multipart definition, we can understand television viewing as an addiction." Other authors may take two or perhaps even more sentences to articulate their thesis. But stated or implied, one sentence or more, your thesis must be clearly formulated at least in your own mind if your analysis is to hold together.

The analysis itself, as we have indicated, is a two-part argument. The first part states and establishes your use of a certain principle or definition that serves as your analytic tool. The second part applies specific parts or components of the principle or definition to the topic at hand.

Develop an Organizational Plan

You will benefit enormously in the writing of a first draft if you plan out the logic of your analysis. Turn key elements of your analytic principle or definition into questions, and then develop the paragraph-by-paragraph logic of the paper.

Turning Key Elements of a Principle or a Definition into Questions

Prepare for an analysis by phrasing questions based on the definition or principle you are going to apply and then directing those questions to the activity or object to be studied. The method is straightforward:

- State as clearly as possible the principle or definition to be applied.
- Divide the principle or definition into its parts.
- Using each part, form a question.

For example, Winn develops a multipart definition of addiction, each part of which is readily turned into a question that she directs at a specific behavior: television viewing. Her analysis of television viewing can be understood as *responses* to each of her analytic questions. Note that in her brief analysis,

Winn does not first define addiction and then analyze television viewing. Rather, *as* she defines aspects of addiction, she analyzes television viewing.

Developing the Paragraph-by-Paragraph Logic of Your Paper

The following paragraph from Winn's analysis illustrates the typical logic of a paragraph in an analytic paper:

> Self-confessed television addicts often feel they "ought" to do other things—but the fact that they don't read and don't plant their garden or sew or crochet or play games or have conversations means that those activities are no longer as desirable as television viewing. In a way, the lives of heavy viewers are as unbalanced by their television "habit" as drug addicts' or alcoholics' lives. They are living in a holding pattern, as it were, passing up the activities that lead to growth or development or a sense of accomplishment. This is one reason people talk about their television viewing so ruefully, so apologetically. They are aware that it is an unproductive experience, that by any human measure almost any other endeavor is more worthwhile.

We see in this paragraph the typical logic of an analysis:

- *The writer introduces a specific analytic tool.* Winn refers to one of the established components of addiction: the addictive behavior crowds out and takes precedence over other, more fruitful activities.

- *The writer applies this analytic tool to the object being examined.* Winn points out that people who spend their time watching television "don't read and don't plant their garden or sew or crochet or play games or have conversations...."

- *The writer uses the tool to identify and then examine the significance of some aspect of the subject under discussion.* Having applied the analytic tool to the subject of television viewing, Winn generalizes about the significance of what is revealed: "This is one reason people talk about their television viewing so ruefully, so apologetically. They are aware that it is an unproductive experience, that by any human measure almost any other endeavor is worthwhile."

An analytic paper takes shape when a writer creates a series of such paragraphs, links them with an overall logic, and draws a general conclusion concerning what was learned through the analysis. Here is the logical organization of Winn's analysis:

- **Paragraph 1:** Introduces the word "addiction" and indicates how the term is generally used.

- **Paragraph 2:** Suggests that television watching might be viewed as a "destructive addiction."

- **Paragraph 3:** Discusses the first component of the definition of addiction: an experience that "allows the participant to blot out the real world and enter into a pleasurable and passive mental state." Applies this first component to television viewing.

- **Paragraphs 4 and 5:** Discuss the second component of addiction—the participant has an illusion of control—and apply this to the experience of television viewing.

- **Paragraph 6:** Discusses the third component of addiction—because it requires so much time and emotional energy, the addictive behavior crowds out other, more productive or socially desirable activities—and applies this to the experience of television viewing.

- **Paragraph 7:** Discusses the fourth component of addiction—the negative consequences arising from the behavior—and applies this to the experience of television viewing.

- **Paragraph 8:** Discusses the fifth component of addiction—the participant is never satisfied because the experience is essentially empty—and applies this to the experience of television viewing. Note that in this paragraph, Winn brings in for support a relevant quotation by the psychiatrist Lawrence Kubie.

Draft and Revise Your Analysis

You will usually need at least two drafts to produce a paper that presents your idea clearly. The biggest changes in your paper will typically come between your first and second drafts. No paper that you write, analysis or otherwise, will be complete until you revise and refine your single compelling idea—in the case of analysis, your analytic conclusion about what the object, event, or behavior being examined means or how it is significant. You revise and refine by evaluating your first draft, bringing to it many of the same questions you pose when evaluating any piece of writing:

- Are the facts accurate?
- Are my opinions supported by evidence?
- Are the opinions of others authoritative?
- Are my assumptions clearly stated?
- Are key terms clearly defined?
- Is the presentation logical?
- Are all parts of the presentation well developed?
- Are significant opposing points of view presented?

Address these same questions to the first draft of your analysis, and you will have solid information to guide your revision.

Write an Analysis, Not a Summary

The most common error made in writing analyses—an error that is *fatal* to the form—is to present readers with a summary only. For analyses to succeed, you must *apply* a principle or definition and reach a conclusion about the object, event, or behavior you are examining. By definition, a summary (see Chapter 1) includes none of your own conclusions. Summary is naturally a part of analysis; you will need to summarize the object or activity being examined and, depending on the audience's needs, summarize the principle or definition being applied. But in an analysis, you must take the next step and share insights that suggest the meaning or significance of some object, event, or behavior.

Make Your Analysis Systematic

Analyses should give the reader the sense of a systematic, purposeful examination. Marie Winn's analysis illustrates the point: She sets out specific elements of addictive behavior in separate paragraphs and then uses each, within its paragraph, to analyze television viewing. Winn is systematic in her method, and we are never in doubt about her purpose.

Imagine another analysis in which a writer lays out four elements of a definition and then applies only two, without explaining the logic for omitting the others. Or imagine an analysis in which the writer offers a principle for analysis but directs it to only a half or a third of the object being discussed, without providing a rationale for doing so. In both cases the writer fails to deliver on a promise basic to analyses: Once a principle or definition is presented, it should be thoroughly and systematically applied.

Answer the "So What?" Question

An analysis should make readers *want* to read it. It should give readers a sense of getting to the heart of the matter, that what is important in the object or activity under analysis is being laid bare and discussed in revealing ways. If when rereading the first draft of your analysis, you cannot imagine readers saying, "I never thought of _____ this way," then something may be seriously wrong. Reread closely to determine why the paper might leave readers flat and exhausted, as opposed to feeling that they have gained new and important insights. Closely reexamine your own motivations for writing. Have *you* learned anything significant through the analysis? If not, neither will readers, and they will turn away. If you have gained important insights through your analysis, communicate them clearly. At some point, pull together your related insights and say, in effect, "Here's how it all adds up."

Attribute Sources Appropriately

In an analysis, you often work with just a few sources and apply insights from them to some object or phenomenon you want to understand more thoroughly. Because you are not synthesizing large quantities of data and because the strength of an analysis derives mostly from *your* application of a principle or definition, the opportunities for not appropriately citing sources are diminished. However, take special care to cite and quote, as necessary, those sources that you draw upon throughout the analysis.

■
Critical Reading for Analysis

- *Read to get a sense of the whole in relation to its parts.* Whether you are clarifying for yourself a principle or a definition to be used in an analysis or you are reading a text that you will analyze, understand how parts function to create the whole. If a definition or principle consists of parts, use them to organize sections of your analysis. If your goal is to analyze a text, be aware of its structure: Note the title and subtitle; identify the main point and subordinate points and where they are located; break the material into sections.

- *Read to discover relationships within the object being analyzed.* Watch for patterns. When you find them, be alert—for they create an occasion to analyze, to use a principle or definition as a guide in discussing what the patterns may mean.

  In fiction, a pattern might involve responses of characters to events or to each other, the recurrence of certain words or phrasings, images, themes, or turns of plot (to name a few).

  In poetry, a pattern might involve rhyme schemes, rhythm, imagery, figurative or literal language, and more.

The challenge to you as a reader is first to see a pattern (perhaps using a guiding principle or definition to do so) and then to locate other instances of that pattern. Reading carefully in this way prepares you to conduct an analysis.

When *Your* Perspective Guides the Analysis

In some cases a writer's analysis of a phenomenon or a work of art may not result from anything as structured as a principle or a definition. It may instead follow from the writer's cultural or personal outlook, perspective, or interests. Imagine reading a story or observing the lines of a new building and being asked to analyze it—based not on someone else's definition or principle, but on your own. Your analysis of the story might largely be determined by your preference for fast pacing; intrepid, resourceful heroes; and pitiless, black-hearted villains. Among the principles you might use in analyzing the building are your admiration for curved exterior surfaces and the imaginative use of glass.

Analyses in this case continue to probe the parts of things to understand how they work and what they mean. And they continue to be carefully structured, examining one part of a phenomenon at a time. The essential purpose of the analysis, to *reveal,* remains unchanged. This goal distinguishes the analysis from the critique, whose main purpose is to *evaluate* and *assess validity.*

An intriguing example of how shifts in personal perspective over time may affect one's analysis of a particular phenomenon is offered by Terri Martin Hekker. In 1977 Hekker wrote an op-ed for the *New York Times* viewing traditional marriage from a perspective very different from that of contemporary feminists, who, she felt, valued self-fulfillment through work more than their roles as traditional housewives:

> I come from a long line of women...who never knew they were unfulfilled. I can't testify that they were happy, but they *were* cheerful....They took pride in a clean, comfortable home and satisfaction in serving a good meal because no one had explained to them that the only work worth doing is that for which you get paid.

Hekker's view of the importance of what she calls "housewifery"—the role of the traditional American wife and mother—derived from her own personal standards and ideals, which themselves derived from a cultural perspective that she admitted were no longer in fashion in the late 1970s.

Almost thirty years later (2006), Hekker's perspective had dramatically shifted. Her shattering experiences in the wake of her unexpected divorce had changed her view—and as a result, her analysis—of the status, value, and prospects of the traditional wife:

> Like most loyal wives of our generation, we'd contemplated eventual widowhood but never thought we'd end up divorced....If I had it to do over again, I'd still marry the man I married and have my children....But I would have used the years after my youngest started school to further my education. I could have amassed two doctorates using the time and energy I gave myself to charitable and community causes and been better able to support myself.

Hekker's new analysis of the role of the traditional wife derives from her changed perspective, based on her own experience and the similar experiences of a number of her divorced friends.

If you find yourself writing an analysis guided by your own insights, not by someone else's, then you owe your reader a clear explanation of your guiding principles and the definitions by which you will probe the subject under study. Continue using the Guidelines for Writing Analyses (see pp. 177–178), modifying this advice as you think fit to accommodate your own personal outlook, perspective, or interests. Above all, remember to structure your analysis with care. Proceed systematically and emerge with a clear statement about what the subject means, how it works, or why it might be significant.

■ DEMONSTRATION: ANALYSIS

Linda Shanker wrote the following paper as a first-semester sophomore in response to this assignment from her sociology professor:

> Read Robert H. Knapp's "A Psychology of Rumor" in your course anthology. Use some of Knapp's observations about rumor to examine

a particular rumor that you have read about in your reading during the first few weeks of this course. Write for readers much like yourself: freshmen or sophomores who have taken one course in sociology. Your object in this paper is to draw upon Knapp to shed light on how the particular rumor you select spread so widely and so rapidly.

MODEL ANALYSIS

Shanker 1

Linda Shanker

Social Psychology 1

UCLA

17 November 2014

The Case of the Missing Kidney: An Analysis of Rumor

Rumor! What evil can surpass her speed?

In movement she grows mighty, and achieves

strength and dominion as she swifter flies...

[F]oul, whispering lips, and ears, that catch at all...

She can cling

to vile invention and malignant wrong,

or mingle with her word some tidings true.

—Virgil, *The Aeneid* (Book IV, Ch. 8)

(1)   The phenomenon of rumor has been an object of fascination since ancient times. In his epic poem *The Aeneid,* Virgil noted some insidious truths about rumors: they spread quickly—especially in our own day, by means of phones, TV, e-mail, and Twitter; they can grow in strength and come to dominate conversation with vicious lies; and they are often mixed with a small portion of truth, a toxic combination that provides the rumor with some degree of credibility. In more recent years, sociologists and psychologists have studied various aspects of rumors: why they are such a common feature of any society, how they tie in to our individual and group views of the world, how and why they spread, why people believe them, and finally, how they can be prevented and contained.

Shanker 2

(2)   One of the most important studies is Robert H. Knapp's "A Psychology of Rumor," published in 1944. Knapp's article appeared during World War II (during which he was in charge of rumor control for the Massachusetts Committee of Public Safety), and many of his examples are drawn from rumors that sprang up during that conflict; but his analysis of why rumors form and how they work remains just as relevant today. First, Knapp defines rumor as an unverified statement offered about some topic in the hope that others will believe it (22). He proceeds to classify rumors into three basic types: the *pipe-dream or wish rumor,* based on what we would like to happen; the *bogie rumor,* based on our fears and anxieties; and the *wedge-driving or aggression rumor,* based on "dividing groups and destroying loyalties" (23–24). He notes that rumors do not spread randomly through the population, but rather through certain "sub-groups and factions" who are most susceptible to believing them. Rumors spread particularly fast, he notes, when these groups do not trust officials to tell them the truth. Most important, he maintains, "rumors express the underlying hopes, fears, and hostilities of the group" (27).

(3)   Not all rumors gain traction, of course, and Knapp goes on to outline the qualities that make for successful rumors. For example, a good rumor must be "short, simple, and salient." It must be a good story. Qualities that make for a good story include "a humorous twist...striking and aesthetic detail...simplification of plot and circumstances...[and] exaggeration" (29). Knapp explains how the same rumor can take various forms, each individually suited to the groups among which it is circulating: "[n]ames, numbers, and places are typically the most unstable components of any rumor." Successful rumors adapt themselves to the particular circumstances, anxieties, prejudices of the group, and the details change according to the "tide of current swings in public opinion and interest" (30).

(4)   Knapp's insights are valuable in helping us to understand why some contemporary rumors have been so frightening and yet so effective. One version of the rumor of the missing kidney, current in 1992, is recounted

by Robert Dingwall, a sociologist at the University of Nottingham
in England:

> A woman friend of another customer had a 17-year-old
> son who went to a night club in Nottingham, called the
> Black Orchid, one Friday evening. He did not come home,
> so she called the police, who were not very interested
> because they thought that he had probably picked up a
> girl and gone home with her. He did not come back all
> weekend, but rang his mother from a call box on Monday,
> saying he was unwell. She drove out to pick him up and
> found him slumped on the floor of the call box. He said
> that he had passed out after a drink in the club and
> remembered nothing of the weekend. There was a neat,
> fresh scar on his abdomen. She took him to the Queen's
> Medical Centre, the main emergency hospital in the
> city, where the doctors found that he had had a kidney
> removed. The police were called again and showed much
> more interest. A senior officer spoke to the mother and
> said that there was a secret surveillance operation going
> on in this club and others in the same regional chain in
> other East Midlands cities because they had had several
> cases of the same kind and they thought that the organs
> were being removed for sale by an Asian surgeon. (181)

5   It is not clear where this rumor originated, though at around this time
the missing kidney story had served as the basis of a *Law and Order* episode
in 1992 and a Hollywood movie, *The Harvest*, released in 1992. In any event,
within a few months the rumor had spread throughout Britain, with the name
of the night club and other details varying according to the city where it was
circulating. The following year, the story was transplanted to Mexico; a year
later it was set in India. In the Indian version, the operation was performed

Shanker 4

on an English woman traveling alone who went to a New Delhi hospital to have an appendectomy. Upon returning to England, she still felt ill, and after she was hospitalized, it was discovered that her appendix was still there but that her kidney had been removed. In subsequent years the rumor spread to the United States, with versions of the story set in Philadelphia, New Orleans, Houston, and Las Vegas. In 1997, the following message, addressed "Dear Friends," was posted on an Internet message board:

> I wish to warn you about a new crime ring that is targeting business travelers. This ring is well organized, well funded, has very skilled personnel, and is currently in most major cities and recently very active in New Orleans. The crime begins when a business traveler goes to a lounge for a drink at the end of the work day. A person in the bar walks up as they sit alone and offers to buy them a drink. The last thing the traveler remembers until they wake up in a hotel room bath tub, their body submerged to their neck in ice, is sipping that drink. There is a note taped to the wall instructing them not to move and to call 911. A phone is on a small table next to the bathtub for them to call. The business traveler calls 911 who have become quite familiar with this crime. The business traveler is instructed by the 911 operator to very slowly and carefully reach behind them and feel if there is a tube protruding from their lower back. The business traveler finds the tube and answers, "Yes." The 911 operator tells them to remain still, having already sent paramedics to help. The operator knows that both of the business traveler's kidneys have been harvested. This is not a scam or out of a science fiction novel, it is real. It is doc-umented and confirmable. If you travel or someone close to you travels, please be careful. ("You've Got to Be")

Shanker 5

Subsequent posts on this message board supposedly confirmed this story ("Sadly, this is very true"), adding different details.

(6)   Is there any truth to this rumor? None, whatsoever—not in any of its forms. Police and other authorities in various cities have posted strenuous denials of the story in the newspapers, on official Web sites, and in internal correspondence, as have The National Business Travel Association, the American Gem Trade Association, and the Sherwin Williams Co. ("'Stolen' Kidney Myth Circulating"). As reported in the rumor-reporting website Snopes.com, "the National Kidney Foundation has asked any individual who claims to have had his or her kidneys illegally removed to step forward and contact them. So far no one's showed up." The persistence and power of the missing kidney rumor can be more fully understood if we apply four of Knapp's principles of rumor formation and circulation to this particular urban legend: his notion of the "bogie"; the "striking" details that help authenticate a "good story" and that change as the rumor migrates to different populations; the ways a rumor can ride swings of public opinion; and the mingling of falsehood with truth.

(7)   The kidney rumor is first and foremost the perfect example of Knapp's bogie rumor, the rumor that draws its power from our fears and anxieties. One source of anxiety is being alone in a strange place. (Recall the scary folk tales about children lost in the forest, soon to encounter a witch.) These dreaded kidney removals almost always occur when the victim is away from home, out of town or even out of the country. Most of us enjoy traveling, but we may also feel somewhat uneasy in unfamiliar cities. We're not comfortably on our own turf, so we don't quite know our way around; we don't know what to expect of the local population; we don't feel entirely safe, or at least, we feel that some of the locals may resent us and take advantage of us. We can relate to the 17-year-old in the Nottingham nightclub, to the young English woman alone in New Delhi, to the business traveler having a drink in a New Orleans lounge.

(8)   Of course, our worry about being alone in an unfamiliar city is nothing compared to our anxiety about being cut open. Even under the best of

Shanker 6

circumstances (such as to save our lives), no one looks forward to surgery. The prospect of being drugged, taken to an unknown facility, and having members of a crime ring remove one of our organs without our knowledge or consent—as apparently happened to the various subjects of this rumor—would be our worst nightmare. It's little wonder that this particular "bogie" man has such a powerful grip on our hearts.

(9)   Our anxiety about the terrible things that may happen to us in a strange place may be heightened because of the fear that our fate is just punishment for the bad things that we have done. In the Nottingham version of the rumor, the victim "had probably picked up a girl and gone home with her" (Dingwall 181). Another version of the story features "an older man picked up by an attractive woman" (Dingwall 182). Still another version of the story is set in Las Vegas, "Sin City, the place where Bad Things Happen to the Unwary (especially the 'unwary' who were seen as deservedly having brought it upon themselves, married men intent upon getting up to some play-for-pay hanky panky)" ("You've Got to Be"). As Dingwall notes of this anxiety about a deserved fate, "[t]he moral is obvious: young people ought to be careful about night clubs, or more generally, about any activity which takes them out of a circle of family and friends" (183).

(10)   In addition to its being a classic bogie rumor, Knapp would suggest that the missing kidney rumor persists because its "striking and aesthetic detail[s]," while false, have the ring of truth and vary from one version to another, making for a "good story" wherever the rumor spreads. Notice that the story includes the particular names of the bar or nightclub, the medical facility, and the hotel; it describes the size and shape of the scar; and it summarizes the instructions of the 911 operator to see if there is a tube protruding from the victim's back. (The detail about the bathtub full of ice and the advice to "call 911" was added to the story around 1995.) As Knapp observes, "[n]ames, numbers, and places are typically the most unstable components of any rumor" (30), and so the particular cities in

which the kidney operations are alleged to have been performed, as well as the particular locations within those cities, changed as the rumor spread. Another changing detail concerns the chief villains of this story. Knapp notes that rumors adapt themselves to the particular anxieties and prejudices of the group. Many groups hate or distrust foreigners and so we find different ethnic or racial "villains" named in different cities. In the Nottingham version of the story, the operation is performed by an "Asian surgeon." The English woman's kidney was removed by an Indian doctor. In another version of the story, a Kurdish victim of the kidney operation was lured to Britain "with the promise of a job by a Turkish businessman" ("You've Got to Be").

(11)   Third, Knapp observes that successful rumors "ride the tide of current swings in public opinion and interest" (30). From news reports as well as medical and police TV dramas, many people are aware that there is a great demand for organ transplants and that such demand, combined with a short supply, has given rise to a black market for illegally obtained organs. When we combine this awareness with stories that appear to provide convincing detail about the medical procedure involved (the "neat fresh scar," the tube, the name of the hospital), it is not surprising that many people accept this rumor as truth without question. One Internet correspondent, who affirmed that "Yes, this does happen" (her sister-in-law supposedly worked with a woman whose son's neighbor was a victim of the operation), noted that the only "good" thing about this situation was that those who performed the procedure were medically trained, used sterile equipment, made "exact and clean" incisions ("You've Got to Be"), and in general took measures to avoid complications that might lead to the death of the patient.

(12)   Finally, this rumor gains credibility because, as Virgil noted, rumor "mingle[s] with her word some tidings true." Although no documented case has turned up of a kidney being removed without the victim's knowledge and consent, there have been cases of people lured into selling their kidneys

and later filing charges because they came to regret their decisions or were unhappy with the size of their payment ("You Got to Be").

(13)   Rumors can destroy reputations, foster distrust of government and other social institutions, and create fear and anxiety about perceived threats from particular groups of outsiders. Writing in the 1940s about rumors hatched during the war years, Knapp developed a powerful theory that helps us understand the persistence of rumors sixty years later. The rumor of the missing kidney, like any rumor, functions much like a mirror held up to society: it reveals anxiety and susceptibility to made-up but seemingly plausible "facts" related to contemporary social concerns. By helping us to understand the deeper structure of rumors, Knapp's theories can help free us from the "domination" and the "Foul, whispering lips" that Virgil observed so accurately 2,000 years ago.

Works Cited

Dingwall, Robert. "Contemporary Legends, Rumors, and Collective Behavior: Some Neglected Resources for Medical Technology." *Sociology of Health and Illness* 23.2 (2001): 180–202. Print.

Knapp, Robert H. "A Psychology of Rumor." *Public Opinion Quarterly* 8.1 (1944): 22–37. Print.

"'Stolen' Kidney Myth Circulating: Organ Donation Hurt by Story of Kidney Heist." *UNOS*. United Network for Organ Sharing Newsroom Archive, 20 Aug. 1999. Web. 13 Oct. 2014.

Virgil. *The Aeneid*. Trans. Theodore C. Williams. Perseus 4.0. *Perseus Digital Library*. Web. 17 Oct. 2014.

"You've Got to Be Kidneying." *Snopes.com*. Snopes, 12 Mar. 2008. Web. 4 Nov. 2014.

Informal Analysis of the Model Analysis

Before reading our analysis of this model analysis, write your own informal response to the analysis. What are its strengths and weaknesses? To what extent does it follow the general Guidelines for Writing Analyses that we outlined on pages 177–178? What function does each paragraph serve in the analysis as a whole?

The Strategy of the Analysis

- **Paragraph 1** creates a context for the analysis by introducing the phenomenon of rumor, indicating that it has been an object of fascination and study from ancient times (the poet Virgil is quoted) to the present.

- **Paragraphs 2 and 3** introduce the key principle that will be used to analyze the selected rumor, as explained by Robert H. Knapp in his article "A Psychology of Rumor." The principle includes Knapp's definition of rumor, his classification of rumors into three types, and the qualities that make for a successful rumor.

- **Paragraph 4** begins by indicating how Knapp's principles can be used to help us understand how rumor works and then presents one particular manifestation of the rumor to be analyzed, the rumor of the missing kidney. Much of the paragraph consists of an extended quotation describing one of the original versions of the rumor, set in Nottingham, England.

- **Paragraph 5** describes how the missing kidney rumor metamorphosed and spread, first throughout England and then to other countries, including Mexico, India, and the United States. A second extended quotation describes a version of the rumor set in New Orleans.

- **Paragraph 6** explains that the missing kidney rumor has no factual basis, but that its persistence and power can be accounted for by applying Knapp's principles. The final sentence of this paragraph is the thesis of the analysis.

- **Paragraph 7** applies the first of Knapp's principles to the missing kidney rumor: It is a bogie rumor that "draws its power from our fears and anxieties." One such fear is that of being alone in an unfamiliar environment.

- **Paragraph 8** continues to apply Knapp's principle of the bogie rumor, this time focusing on our fears about being unwillingly operated upon.

- **Paragraph 9** discusses another aspect of the bogie rumor, the fear that what happens to us is a form of punishment for our own poor choices or immoral actions.

- **Paragraph 10** deals with a second of Knapp's principles, that the "facts" in rumors are constantly changing: Names, places, and other details change as the rumor spreads from one city to another, but the reference to specific details lends the rumor a veneer of authenticity.

- **Paragraph 11** deals with a third of Knapp's principles: that successful rumors are often based on topics of current public interest—in this case, organ transplants—and that, once again, a surface aura of facts makes the rumor appear credible.

- **Paragraph 12** returns to Virgil (cited in Paragraph 1), who notes that successful rumors also appear credible because they often mix truth with fiction.

- **Paragraph 13**, concluding the analysis, indicates why it is important to analyze rumor: Shedding light on how and why rumors like this one spread may help us to counteract rumors' destructive effects.

WRITING ASSIGNMENT: ANALYSIS

Select *one* of the following two assignments in analysis.

Assignment 1

Use Marie Winn's definition of addiction (pp. 172–173) and the subsequent discussion (pp. 172–174) to analyze some behavior—other than TV viewing—that you know well. Do not write on behaviors associated with chemical dependence (nicotine, alcohol, or legal or illegal drugs). The purpose of your analysis is to determine the extent to which the behavior you're examining is an addiction, according to Winn's definition. Your analysis should be structured like Winn's essay, as outlined on page 174.

Assignment 2

Every day, in thousands of courtrooms across the nation, jurors are asked to engage in analysis. After sitting through one or more days of testimony concerning an alleged crime or a lawsuit, they are instructed on the applicable law by the judge and then asked to apply this law to the facts of the case in the process of arriving at a reasoned verdict. Here's your chance to engage in a similar process.

1. Read the following two cases, "For Fallen Stop Sign, Vandals Face Life," by Mike Clary, and *State of Utah v. Hallett and Felsch*.

2. Read the law governing criminal homicide, a category that includes murder, manslaughter, and negligent homicide. The law also includes definitions of these terms.

3. Then write an analytic paper in which you apply the law and determine whether or not the defendants in one or both of these cases are guilty of murder, manslaughter, or negligent homicide.

In making your determination, systematically apply the components of the law (and the definitions of key terms) to the facts of each case. You may decide that there are differences in the two cases that are significant enough to justify different verdicts. Or you may decide that the cases are essentially the same in their key facts, and so the verdicts in each case should be the same. However you decide your verdicts, be sure to justify your conclusions by referring to the applicable law.

FOR FALLEN STOP SIGN, VANDALS FACE LIFE

Mike Clary[4]

Tampa, Fla.—It was a clear, dark February night when the fates collided in front of Tim's Cafe at a rural intersection where a stop sign lay face-down by the side of the road.

One of the vehicles involved was an eight-ton Mack truck loaded with phosphate. The other was a white Camaro carrying three 18-year-old friends on a one-way ride to eternity. Chances are, police said, they never knew what hit them.

Tow trucks and sheriff's deputies were still on the scene a few hours later when a fourth young man named Thomas Miller pulled up. He and a friend had just finished working the graveyard shift at a welding shop and were heading to Tim's for breakfast.

Miller got out of his car to see the wreckage better and, he recalled later, he stood right next to the fallen stop sign.

5   Now, 16 months after that fatal crash, Miller and two friends stand convicted on three counts of manslaughter, guilty of causing three deaths by pulling that stop sign out of the ground days earlier.

Although Miller, 20, and his housemates, Nissa Baillie, 21, and her boyfriend, Christopher Cole, 20, admitted taking about 20 road signs during a late-night spree sometime before the fatal crash, they denied tampering with the stop sign in front of Tim's Cafe.

But a jury did not believe them.

On June 19 Miller, Baillie, and Cole could be sentenced to life in prison in what is believed to be the first case in the United States in which the vandalism of a traffic sign has led to a multiple manslaughter conviction.

What has become known as the "stop sign case" has had a wrenching effect on the families of the six young people involved, while sparking a passionate community debate on the nexus of crime and punishment.

10   On one side is Assistant State Atty. Leland Baldwin, who prosecuted the three young people. "I have heard people ask: 'How dare you charge them with

---

[4] Mike Clary, "For Fallen Stop Sign, Vandals Face Life." *Los Angeles Times* 11 June 1997.

manslaughter? This was a prank. It was an unintentional crime,'" she said. "But this was not a prank. These were not young kids. These were young adults. So give me a break."

On the other side is Joseph Registrato, chief assistant to the Hillsborough County public defender, which represented Cole and Baillie.

"It's one thing to take a car when you're drunk and recklessly kill somebody," Registrato said. "That law is well-understood. But in this case, they may have committed criminal mischief and then later three people died. But others had gone through that intersection and didn't die. So there is a serious question about whether the [fallen] stop sign caused the deaths.

"From that they could get life in prison? It's hard to follow the ball here."

Road Sign Theft Called a Commonplace Prank

About this there is no debate: The chain of events that led up to that horrific crash in front of Tim's Cafe makes up a cautionary tale of sobering complexity.

15   Joe Episcopo figures at least half the population of America at one time or another has stolen a road sign to hang on a bedroom wall, to win a scavenger hunt or just for kicks.

In fact, says Episcopo, a lawyer who represents Miller, road sign theft is so common that, when potential jurors in the case against his client were asked if they had ever taken a sign, half the pool raised a hand and three of those who answered yes ended up being seated on the six-member panel. "Everybody has somebody in their family who takes signs," he said.

Indeed, vandalism and theft of road signs is a problem all across the country. After the trial here in the Hillsborough County courthouse was broadcast by Court TV, public officials from as far away as Washington state have been speaking out about the expense and danger resulting from defaced or stolen road signs.

In Iowa, a county engineer has announced plans to use the Tampa case as a springboard for a national education campaign on the issue.

Dave Krug, Hillsborough County public works department engineer, estimated that 25% of all road signs ever put up in the Tampa area are damaged by vandals, knocked down or stolen. Most road sign vandalism, however, does not result in triple fatalities, attract media attention and provoke heart-wrenching community anguish over wasted lives.

20   Moreover, most sign vandalism does not give rise to the sea of regrets among thousands of people—including at least 11 people who testified in the trial here— who noticed the downed stop sign during the 24 hours preceding the crash and failed to report it.

"Well, what did you do?" Baldwin asked of one witness who noticed that the stop sign was down.

"We just went back to work, got busy," the witness replied.

Three Target Signs "for a Rush"

Miller, Baillie, and Cole lived together in a rented $300-a-month mobile home on a country road less than three miles from the intersection of Keysville and

Lithia-Pinecrest roads in eastern Hillsborough County where the fatal crash occurred just before midnight on Feb. 7, 1996.

According to interviews they gave to a local television station and Cole's testimony at trial, the three had been shopping at a nearby Wal-Mart, had drunk a couple of beers and were headed home when one of the three suggested that they take a few railroad signs. Cole told a television reporter that they began taking signs "for a rush."

25   Over a period of a couple of hours and a distance of about five miles, they unbolted and pulled up railroad signs, street name signs, a "Dead End" sign, a "Do Not Enter" sign and—from neighboring Polk County—at least one stop sign, tossing all of them in the back of their pickup truck.

Was it fun? Cole was asked. "I suppose so, yeah," he replied. "Yeah, it was fun at the time."

Night of Bowling Ends in Collision

Kevin Farr, who worked in his family's data processing business, had been bowling with his father, Les, and his two older brothers on the evening of his death. He rolled a 218 in his final league game and, as he left the bowling alley, he shouted at one of his brothers: "Tell Mom I'll be home between 11 o'clock and 12. I don't want her to worry."

From the bowling alley Farr drove to the house of Brian Hernandez, his best and oldest friend, and the pair then picked up Randall White. No one seems to know where they were going.

June Farr said that the death of the youngest of her four children has condemned her to live day by day. "And day by day takes on a whole new meaning after something like this," she said. "Sometimes it's more like a few minutes at a time."

30   The case against Miller, Cole and Baillie was circumstantial. There were no fingerprints on the stop sign and no eyewitnesses who put them at the scene. But the fallen stop sign was well within the general area of the thefts to which the three had confessed and prosecutors presented expert testimony that the stop sign appeared to have been pulled from the ground, not run over by a vehicle.

The defense also had its own expert witness, a mechanical engineer who testified that the stop sign had been struck by a "lateral force."

Defendants Say They Panicked Next Day

Perhaps the most damning evidence against Cole, Miller, and Baillie came from their own statements to police. Ron Bradish, a Sheriff's Department traffic homicide investigator, testified that Cole and Miller admitted that—during their stealing spree—they sometimes would pull signs from the ground and, if a car came by, leave them to pick up later.

The day after the fatal crash, the three defendants admitted to police, they panicked. They gathered up most of the stolen signs from inside and outside their mobile home and tossed them off a bridge into nearby Alafia Creek. According to

Bradish, Cole said that they got rid of the signs "so no one would think they took the stop sign down at the crash."

Held without bail, Cole, Miller, and Baillie are to be sentenced next week after the judge hears from lawyers on both sides, as well as from relatives of the convicted and those who died.

35   While she will not lobby for life sentences, Baldwin says, she will insist on long terms. "I hope this case will be a deterrent, or, at least, somewhat thought-provoking," she said. "Perhaps this is one of the types of cases that have to be tried every generation to remind high school kids and others that vandalism has consequences. And this does have an effect. Just days ago some kids in Leon County [Tallahassee] had a stop sign in a scavenger hunt and the media [publicly] stopped them."

Again, Registrato demurs. "This case is useless as a deterrent," he said. "Send these three children to prison for life and the kids in Hillsborough County where it happened won't have a clue about it the next day."

Episcopo and Registrato said they have prepared their clients for the worst. Sentencing guidelines call for 28 years to life and Judge Bob Anderson Mitcham has been known to use the suggested maximum as a starting point. Last year he put a man convicted of wounding two Tampa police officers in prison for seven consecutive life terms, ignoring guidelines that called for 14 to 24 years.

For June Farr, the sentencing decision seems straightforward. "My child got the maximum penalty and he had no choice in the matter," she said. "They knew exactly what was going to happen. They just didn't know who the victims would be. This was not a prank. Pranks don't kill."

To those who would find life in prison too harsh a price to pay for yanking out a stop sign, Farr responds: "They didn't have to go pick out a coffin."

40   Registrato said he would argue that Miller, Cole and Baillie could better atone for their sins and better service society by doing "a couple of years hard time in Florida State Prison and then be required for the next 18 years to go to high schools twice a month and tell about the consequences of criminal mischief."

But Miller, Thomas Miller's father, clings to hope that his son will win a retrial and be found not guilty. He acknowledged that his son, who has a juvenile record for theft, has lied to him before. But this time, Miller said, "Tommy says he didn't take that sign and I believe it with all my heart. We know when he's lying."

Whatever the outcome, said Miller, 69, a retired postal worker, he knows that the lives of his family, as well as the other five families involved, are forever changed.

"I was in court every day," he said, "sitting in the front row on one side, across from the families of the dead boys. We didn't speak but I felt for them.... They lost their children. I understand.

"Now they have to understand that I've lost mine. Win or lose, this is a tragedy for both sides."

State of Utah v. Kelly K. Hallett and Richard James Felsch

Supreme Court of Utah Oct. 20, 1980[5]

Facts of the Case

On the evening of September 24, 1977, a number of young people gathered at the defendant's home in Kearns. During the evening, some of them engaged in drinking alcoholic beverages. At about 10:30 P.M., they left the home, apparently bent on revelry and mischief. When they got to the intersection of 5215 South and 4620 West, defendant and the codefendant Richard Felsch...bent over a stop sign, which faced northbound traffic on 4620 West, until it was in a position parallel to the ground. The group then proceeded north from the intersection, uprooted another stop sign and placed it in the backyard of a Mr. Arlund Pope, one of the state's witnesses. Traveling further on, defendant and his friends bent a bus stop sign over in a similar manner.

The following morning, Sunday, September 25, 1977, at approximately 9:00 A.M., one Krista Limacher was driving east on 5215 South with her husband and children, en route to church. As she reached the intersection of 4620 West, the deceased, Betty Jean Carley, drove to the intersection from the south. The stop sign was not visible, since the defendant had bent it over, and Ms. Carley continued into the intersection. The result was that Mrs. Limacher's vehicle struck the deceased's car broadside causing her massive injuries which resulted in her death in the hospital a few hours later.

Statements on the Law

Utah Criminal Code[6] (statutory law)

Criminal Homicide
Criminal homicide — elements — designations of offenses

1. a. A person commits criminal homicide if he intentionally, knowingly, recklessly, with criminal negligence, or acting with a mental state otherwise specified in the statute defining the offense, causes the death of another human being, including an unborn child.

Murder

1. Criminal homicide constitutes murder if the actor:
   a. intentionally or knowingly causes the death of another;
   b. intending to cause serious bodily injury to another commits an act clearly dangerous to human life that causes the death of another;
   c. acting under circumstances evidencing a depraved indifference to human life engages in conduct which creates a grave risk of death to another and thereby causes the death of another....

2. Murder is a first degree felony.

---

[5] *State of Utah v. Hallett.* 619 P.2d 337 (1980).
[6] *Utah Code Unannotated,* 1996. Vol. 4. Charlottesville, VA: Michie Law Publishers, 1988–96.

Manslaughter

1. Criminal homicide constitutes manslaughter if the actor:
   a. recklessly causes the death of another; or
   b. causes the death of another under the influence of extreme emotional disturbance for which there is a reasonable explanation or excuse; or
   c. causes the death of another under circumstances where the actor reasonably believes the circumstances provide a legal justification or excuse for his conduct although the conduct is not legally justifiable or excusable under the existing circumstances.

2. Under Subsection (1)(b), emotional disturbance does not include a condition resulting from mental illness.

3. The reasonableness of an explanation or excuse under Subsection (1)(b), or the reasonable belief of the actor under Subsection (1)(c), shall be determined from the viewpoint of a reasonable person under the then existing circumstances.

4. Manslaughter is a felony of the second degree.

Negligent homicide

1. Criminal homicide constitutes negligent homicide if the actor, acting with criminal negligence, causes the death of another.

2. Negligent homicide is a class A misdemeanor.

Definitions

Requirements of criminal conduct and criminal responsibility

No person is guilty of an offense unless his conduct is prohibited by law and:

1. He acts intentionally, knowingly, recklessly, with criminal negligence, or with a mental state otherwise specified in the statute defining the offense, as the definition of the offense requires...

Definitions of "intentionally, or with intent or willfully"; "knowingly, or with knowledge"; "recklessly, or maliciously"; and "criminal negligence or criminally negligent"

A person engages in conduct:

1. Intentionally, or with intent or willfully with respect to the nature of his conduct or to a result of his conduct, when it is his conscious objective or desire to engage in the conduct or cause the result.

2. Knowingly, or with knowledge, with respect to his conduct or to circumstances surrounding his conduct when he is aware of the nature of his conduct or the existing circumstances. A person acts knowingly, or with knowledge, with respect to a result of his conduct when he is aware that his conduct is reasonably certain to cause the result.

3. Recklessly, or maliciously, with respect to circumstances surrounding his conduct or the result of his conduct when he is aware of but consciously disregards a substantial and unjustifiable risk that the circumstances exist or the result will occur. The risk must be of such a nature and degree that

its disregard constitutes a gross deviation from the standard of care that an ordinary person would exercise under all the circumstances as viewed from the actor's standpoint.

4. With criminal negligence or is criminally negligent with respect to circumstances surrounding his conduct or the result of his conduct when he ought to be aware of a substantial and unjustifiable risk that the circumstances exist or the result will occur. The risk must be of such a nature and degree that the failure to perceive it constitutes a gross deviation from the standard of care that an ordinary person would exercise in all the circumstances as viewed from the actor's standpoint.

State v. Fisher[7] (caselaw)

Negligent homicide and manslaughter. The general rule is that negligent homicide is a lesser included offense of manslaughter. . . . the only difference between manslaughter and negligent homicide is an accused's mental state at the time of the incident. . . . Manslaughter is established where a person, aware of a substantial and unjustifiable risk that his or her conduct will cause the death of another, consciously disregards that risk. Negligent homicide is established where a person fails to perceive the substantial and unjustifiable risk that his or her conduct will cause the death of another. The element of the greater not found in the lesser is awareness of the risk.

Epilogue

All three defendants, Miller, Baillie, and Cole, were convicted of manslaughter and each was sentenced to 15 years in prison. The following year, however, an appeals court overturned the convictions, saying that the jury had been tainted by prosecutorial remarks. After the state attorney's office decided not to proceed with a second trial, the charges against the defendants were dropped.

---

[7] *State v. Fisher.* 686 P.2nd 750 (1984).

Part Two ▪ *Strategies*

6. Writing as a Process

■ WRITING AS THINKING

Most of us regard writing as an activity that culminates in a finished product: a paper, an application letter, study notes, and the like. We focus on the result rather than on the process of getting there. But how *do* we produce that paper or letter? Does the thought you write down not exist until it appears on the page? Does thought precede writing? If so, is writing merely a translation of prior thought? The relationship between thinking and writing is complex and not entirely understood. But it is worth reflecting on, especially as you embark on your writing-intensive career as a college student. Every time you pick up a pen or sit down at a computer to write, you engage in a thinking process—and what and how and when you think both affects and is affected by your writing in a variety of ways. Consider the possibilities as you complete the following brief exercises:

> **A:** You find yourself enrolled in a composition class at a particular school. Why are you attending this school and not another? Write for five minutes on this question.

> **B:** What single moment in your freshman experience thus far has been most (a) humorous, (b) promising, (c) vexing, (d) exasperating? Choose *one* and write for five minutes on this topic.

> **C:** Select one page of notes from the presumably many you have taken in any of your classes. Reread the page and rewrite it, converting your first-pass notes into a well-organized study guide that would help you prepare for an exam. Devote five minutes to the effort.

Reflect on these exercises. Specifically, locate in your response to each one the point at which you believe your thinking took place. (Admittedly, this may be difficult, but give it a try.) Before completing Exercise A, you probably gave considerable thought to *where* you are or would like to be attending college. Examine your writing and reflect on your thinking: Were you in any way rethinking your choice of school as you wrote? Or were you explaining a decision you've already made—that is, reporting on *prior* thinking? Perhaps some combination of these?

Now turn to your work for Exercise B, for which you wrote (most likely) on a new topic. Where did thinking occur here? As you wrote? Moments prior to your writing, as you selected the topic and focused your ideas?

Last, consider Exercise C. Where did your thinking take place? How did revision change your first-draft notes? What makes your second draft a better study guide than your first draft?

Finally, consider the differences in the relationship between writing and thinking *across* Exercises A, B, and C as you wrote on a topic you'd previously thought (but not written) about, on a new topic, and on a topic you've written about and are revising. Note the changing relationship between writing and thinking. Note especially how rewriting is related to rethinking.

In completing and reflecting on these exercises, you have glimpsed something of the marvelous complexity of writing. The job of this chapter is to help you develop some familiarity and comfort with this mysterious but crucial process.

■ STAGES OF THE WRITING PROCESS

By breaking the process into stages, writers turn the sometimes overwhelming task of writing a paper into manageable chunks, each requiring different activities that, collectively, build to a final draft. Generally, the stages involve *understanding the task, gathering data, invention, drafting, revision,* and *editing.*

Broadly speaking, the six stages of the writing process occur in the order we've listed. But writing is *recursive;* the process tends to loop back on itself. You generally move forward as you write, toward a finished product. But moving forward is seldom a straight-line process.

The Writing Process

- *Understanding the task:* Read—or create—the assignment. Understand its purpose, scope, and audience.

- *Gathering data:* Locate and review information—from sources and from your own experience—and formulate an approach.

- *Invention:* Use various techniques (e.g., listing, outlining, freewriting) to generate promising ideas and a particular approach to the assignment. Gather more data if needed. Aim for a working thesis, a tentative (but well-reasoned and well-informed) statement of the direction you intend to pursue.

- *Drafting:* Sketch the paper you intend to compose and then write all sections necessary to support the working thesis. Stop if necessary to gather more data. Typically, you will both follow your plan and

(continues)

revise and invent a new (or slightly new) plan as you write. Expect to discover key parts of your paper as you write.

- *Revision:* Rewrite in order to make the draft coherent and unified.

  Revise at the *global* level, reshaping your thesis and adding to, rearranging, or deleting paragraphs in order to support the thesis. Gather more data as needed to flesh out paragraphs in support of the thesis.

  Revise at the *local* level of paragraphs, ensuring that each is well reasoned and supports the thesis.

- *Editing:* Revise at the *sentence* level for style and brevity. Revise for correctness: grammar, punctuation, usage, and spelling.

■ STAGE 1: UNDERSTANDING THE TASK

Papers in the Academic Disciplines

Although most of your experience with academic papers in high school may have been in English classes, you should be prepared for instructors in other academic disciplines to assign papers with significant research components. Here is a sampling of topics that have been assigned recently in a broad range of undergraduate courses:

Art History: Discuss the main differences between Romanesque and Gothic sculpture, using the sculptures of Jeremiah (St. Pierre Cathedral) and St. Theodore (Chartres Cathedral) as major examples.

Physics: Research and write a paper on solar cell technology, covering the following areas: basic physical theory, history and development, structure and materials, types and characteristics, practical uses, state of the art, and future prospects.

Political Science: Explain the contours of California's referendum process in recent years and then, by focusing on one specific controversial referendum, explain and analyze the origins of this proposed measure, the campaign for and against it, its fate at the polls, and the political effects and legacy of this measure (whether it passed or failed).

Religious Studies: Select a particular religious group or movement present in the nation for at least twenty years and show how its belief or practice has changed since members of the group have been in America or, if the group began in America, since its first generation.

Some of these assignments allow students a considerable range of choice (within the general subject); others are highly specific in requiring students to address a particular issue. Most call for some library or online research; a few call for a combination of online, library, and field research; others may be based entirely on field research. As with all academic writing, your first task is to make sure you understand the assignment. Remember to critically read and analyze the specific task(s) required of you in a paper assignment. One useful technique for doing this is to locate the assignment's key verb(s), which will stipulate exactly what is expected of you.

Exercise 6.1

Analyze an Assignment

Reread the instructions for a recent assignment from another course.

1. Identify the key verb(s).
2. List the type of print, interview, or graphical data you were to gather to complete the assignment.
3. Reflect on your own experience to find some anecdote that might be appropriately included in a paper (or, absent that, a related experience that would provide a personal motivation for writing the paper).

■ STAGE 2: GATHERING DATA

When you begin a writing assignment, consider three questions:

1. What is the assignment?
2. What do I know about the subject?[1]
3. What do I need to know in order to begin writing?

These questions prompt you to reflect on the assignment and define what is expected. Taking stock of class notes, readings, and whatever resources are available, you survey what you already know. Having identified the gaps between what you know and what you need to know in order to write, you can begin to gather data—most likely in stages. You may gather enough, at first, to formulate initial ideas. You may begin to write, see new gaps, and realize you need more data.

Types of Data

Data is a term used most often to refer to quantitative information such as the frequencies or percentages of natural phenomena in the sciences (e.g., the rate at which glaciers melt) or of social phenomena in the social sciences (e.g., the average age of Americans when they first marry). But not all data

---

[1] *Note:* The terms *subject* and *topic* are often used interchangeably. In this chapter, we use *subject* to mean a broad area of interest that, once narrowed to a *topic*, becomes the focus of a paper. Within a thesis (the major organizing sentence of the paper), we speak of *topic*, not *subject*.

is quantifiable. For example, interviews recorded by a social scientist are also considered to be *data*. In the humanities, *data* can refer to the qualitative observations one makes of a particular art object that one is interpreting or evaluating. Generally, quantitative data encompasses issues of "how many?" or "how often?," whereas qualitative research accounts for such issues as "what kind?" and "why?"

Primary and Secondary Sources

Whether quantitative or qualitative, the kind of information that a researcher gathers directly by using the research methods appropriate to that particular field of study—experiments or observations in the sciences, surveys or interviews in the social sciences, close reading and interpretation of unpublished documents and literary texts or works of art in the humanities—is considered *primary* data. As an undergraduate, you will more commonly collect *secondary* data: information and ideas collected or generated by others who have performed their own primary and/or secondary research. The data gathering for most undergraduate academic writing involves library research and, increasingly, research conducted online via Internet databases and other resources.

Chapter 7 provides an in-depth discussion of locating and using secondary sources. Refer also to the material in Chapters 1 and 2 on summary, critical reading, and critique; the techniques of critical reading and assessment of sources will help you make the best use of your sources. And the material in Chapter 1 on avoiding plagiarism will help you conform to the highest ethical standards in your research and writing.

■ STAGE 3: INVENTION

Your preliminary data gathering completed, you can now frame your writing project: give it scope, develop your main idea, and create conditions for productive writing. You must define what you are writing about, after all, and you do this in the *invention* stage. This stage might also be termed "brainstorming" or "predrafting." Regardless of the name, invention is an important part of the process that typically overlaps with data gathering. The preliminary data you gather on a topic will inform the choices you make in defining (that is, in "inventing" ideas for) your project. As you invent, you will often return to gather more data.

Writers sometimes skip the invention stage, preferring to save time by launching directly from gathering data into writing a draft. This is a serious mistake. Time spent narrowing your ideas to a manageable scope at the beginning of a project will pay dividends all through the writing process. Papers head down the wrong track when writers choose topics that are too broad (resulting in the superficial treatment of subtopics) or too narrow (resulting in writers "padding" their work to meet a length requirement).

The Myth of Inspiration

Some people believe that good writing comes primarily from a kind of magical—and unpredictable—formation of ideas that occurs as one sits down in front of a blank page or computer screen. According to this myth, a writer must be inspired in order to write, as if receiving his or her ideas from some muse. While some element of inspiration may inform your writing, most of the time it is hard work—especially in the invention stage—that gets the job done. The old adage attributed to Thomas Edison—"Invention is one part inspiration and ninety-nine parts perspiration"—applies here.

Choosing and Narrowing Your Subject

Suppose you have been assigned a ten-page paper in an introductory course on environmental science. The assignment is open ended, so not only do you need to choose a subject, you also need to narrow it sufficiently and formulate your thesis.

Where will you begin?

First, you need to select broad subject matter from the course and become knowledgeable about its general features. But what if no broad area of interest occurs to you?

- Work through the syllabus or your textbook(s). Identify topics that sparked your interest.

- Review course notes and pay especially close attention to lectures that held your interest.

- Scan recent newspapers and newsmagazines that bear on your coursework.

Assume for your course in environmental science that you've settled on the broad subject of energy conservation. At this point, the goal of your research is to limit this subject to a manageable scope. A subject can be limited in at least two ways. First, you can seek out a general article (perhaps an encyclopedia entry, though it would not typically be accepted as a source in a college-level paper). A general article may do the work for you by breaking the larger topic down into smaller subtopics that you can explore and, perhaps, limit even further. Second, you can limit a subject by asking questions about it:

Who?

Which aspects?

Where?

(continues)

When?

How?

Why?

These questions will occur to you as you conduct your research and notice the ways in which various authors have focused their discussions. Having read several sources on energy conservation and having decided that you'd like to use them, you might limit the subject by asking *which aspects* and deciding to focus on energy conservation as it relates to motor vehicles.

The Myth of Talent

Many inexperienced writers believe that you either have writing talent or you don't, and that if you don't, you are fated to go through life as a "bad writer." But again, hard work, rather than talent, is what leads to competent writing. Yes, some people have more natural verbal ability than others—we all have our areas of strength and weakness. But in any endeavor, talent alone can't ensure success, and with hard work, writers who don't yet have much confidence can achieve impressive results. Not everyone can be a brilliant writer, but everyone *can* be a competent writer.

Certainly, "energy-efficient vehicles" offers a more specific focus than does "energy conservation." Still, the revised focus is too broad for a ten-page paper. (One can easily imagine several book-length works on the subject.) So again, you try to limit your subject by posing other questions from the same list. You might ask which types of energy-efficient vehicles are possible and feasible and how auto manufacturers can be encouraged to develop them. In response to these questions, you may jot down preliminary notes:

- Types of energy-efficient vehicles

    All-electric vehicles

    Hybrid (combination of gasoline and electric) vehicles

    Fuel-cell vehicles

- Government action to encourage development of energy-efficient vehicles

    Mandates to automakers to build minimum quantities of energy-efficient vehicles by certain deadlines

    Additional taxes imposed on high-mileage vehicles

    Subsidies to developers of energy-efficient vehicles

Focusing on any *one* of these aspects as an approach to encouraging the use of energy-efficient vehicles could provide the focus of a ten-page paper.

Practice Narrowing Subjects

In groups of three or four classmates, choose one of the following subjects and collaborate on a paragraph or two that explores the questions we listed for narrowing subjects: Who? Which aspects? Where? When? How? Why? See if you can narrow the subject.

- Downloading music off the Internet
- Internet chat rooms
- College sports
- School violence or bullying
- America's public school system

Invention Strategies

You may already be familiar with a variety of strategies for thinking through your ideas. Here are four of these strategies:

Directed Freewriting

To freewrite is to let your mind go and write spontaneously, often for a set amount of time or a set number of pages. The process of "just writing" can often free up thoughts and ideas about which we aren't even fully conscious or that we haven't articulated to ourselves. In *directed freewriting,* you focus on a subject and let what you think and know about the subject flow out of you in a focused stream of ideas. As a first step in the invention stage, you might sit down with an assignment and write continuously for fifteen minutes. If even one solid idea comes through, you've succeeded in using freewriting to help "free up" your thinking. As a second step, you might take that one idea and freewrite about it, shift to a different invention strategy to explore that one idea, or even begin to draft a thesis and then a rough draft, depending on how well formed your idea is at this stage.

Listing

Some writers find it helpful to make *lists* of their ideas, breaking significant ideas into sublists and seeing where they lead. Approach this strategy as a form of freewriting; let your mind go, and jot down words and phrases that are related. Create lists by pulling related ideas out of your notes or your course readings. *A caution:* The linear nature of lists can lead you to jump prematurely into planning your paper's structure before working out your ideas. Instead, list ideas as a way of brainstorming, and then generate another list that works out the best structure for your points in a draft.

Outlining

A more structured version of a list, an *outline* groups ideas in hierarchical order, with main points broken into subordinate points, sometimes indicating evidence in support of these points. Use outlines as a first stage in generating ideas during your invention process or as a second step in invention. After freewriting and/or listing, refine and build on your ideas by inserting them into an outline for a workable structure in which you can discuss the ideas you've brainstormed. (See the example of an outline on pp. 138–139.)

Clustering and Branching

These two methods of invention are more graphic, nonlinear versions of listing and outlining. With both clustering and branching, you start with an assignment's main topic or with an idea generated by freewriting or listing, and you brainstorm related ideas that flow from that main idea. *Clustering* involves writing an idea in the middle of a page and circling it; you then draw lines leading from that circle, or "bubble," to new bubbles containing subtopics of the central idea. Picking the subtopics that interest you most, draw lines leading to more bubbles in which you note important aspects of the subtopics. (See illustration below.)

Branching follows the same principle, but instead of placing ideas in bubbles, you write them on lines that branch off to other lines that, in turn, contain the related subtopics of your larger topic.

Clustering and branching are useful first steps in invention, for each helps isolate the topics about which you are most knowledgeable. As you branch off into the subtopics of a main paper topic, the number of ideas you generate in relation to these topics will help show where you have the most knowledge and/or interest.

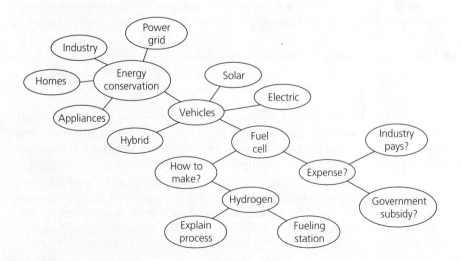

You can modify and combine invention techniques in a number of ways. There is no one right way to generate ideas—or to write a paper—and every writer will want to try different methods to find those that work best. What's important to remember is that regardless of the method, the time spent on invention creates the conditions for writing a solid first draft.

Exercise 6.3

Practice Invention Strategies

After completing the group exercise (Exercise 6.2, p. 209) in which you narrowed a subject, work individually to brainstorm ideas about the subject your group chose. Use one of the invention strategies listed above—preferably one that you haven't used before. After brainstorming on your own, meet with your group again to compare the ideas you each generated.

■ STAGE 4: DRAFTING

It's usually best to begin drafting a paper after you've settled on at least a working or preliminary thesis. While consulting the fruits of your efforts during invention (notes, lists, outlines, and so on), you'll face a number of choices about how to proceed with drafting your paper. Let's consider some of those choices, including the crucial step of drafting the thesis.

Strategies for Writing the Paper

Some people can sit down very early in the process and put their ideas into an orderly form as they write. This drafting method results in a completed *rough draft*. But even professional writers rarely produce an adequate piece of writing the first time around. Most need to plan the structure of a paper before they can sit down to write a first draft. Even if this initial structure proves to be little more than a sketch that changes markedly as the paper develops, some sort of scaffolding usually helps in taking the step from planning to writing a first draft.

Ultimately, *you* will decide how best to proceed. And don't be surprised if you begin different writing projects differently. Whether you jump in without a plan, plan rigorously, or commit yourself to the briefest preliminary sketch, ask yourself:

- What's the main point of my paper?
- What subpoints do I need to address in order to develop and support my main point?
- In what order should my points be arranged? (Do certain subpoints lead naturally to others?)

At Stage 3, as you clarify the direction in which you believe your paper is heading, you ought to be able to formulate at least a *preliminary thesis* (see below). Your thesis can be quite rough, but if you don't have some sense of your main point, writing the first draft won't be possible. In this case, you would have to consider what you've written a preliminary or *discovery draft* (more of an invention strategy than an actual draft)—which is a perfectly sensible way to proceed if you're having difficulty clarifying your thoughts. Even if you begin with what you regard as a clearly stated point, don't be surprised if by the end of the draft—just at the point where you are summing up—you discover that the paper you have in fact written differs from the paper you intended to write. However firm your ideas may be when you begin, the act of writing a draft will usually clarify matters for you.

As we've suggested, the drafting and invention stages overlap. How much planning you do after working out your ideas and before drafting your paper is a matter of personal preference. Try different methods to see which work best for you, and keep in mind that different assignments may require different methods for invention and drafting.

Writing a Thesis

A thesis, as we have seen, is a one- or two-sentence summary of a paper's content. Whether explanatory, mildly argumentative, or strongly argumentative, the thesis is an assertion about that content—for instance, what the content is, how it works, what it means, if it is valuable, if action should be taken, and so on. A paper's thesis is similar to its conclusion, but it lacks the conclusion's concern for broad implications and significance. The thesis is the product of your thinking; it therefore represents *your* conclusion about the topic on which you're writing. So you have to have spent some time thinking about this conclusion (that is, during the invention stage) in order to arrive at the thesis that will govern your paper.

For a writer in the drafting stages, the thesis establishes a focus, a basis on which to include or exclude information. For the reader of a finished product, the thesis forecasts the author's discussion. A thesis, therefore, is an essential tool for both writers and readers of academic papers.

The Components of a Thesis

Like any other sentence, a thesis includes a subject and a predicate that makes an assertion about the subject. In the sentence "Lee and Grant were different kinds of generals," "Lee and Grant" is the subject and "were different kinds of generals" is the predicate. What distinguishes a thesis from any other sentence with a subject and a predicate is that *the thesis presents the controlling idea of the paper.* The subject of a thesis, and the assertion about it, must present the right balance between the general and the specific to allow for a thorough discussion within the allotted length of the paper. The discussion might include definitions, details, comparisons, contrasts—whatever is needed to illuminate a subject and support the assertion. (If the sentence about Lee and Grant were a thesis, the reader would assume that the rest of the paper contained comparisons and contrasts between the two generals.)

Bear in mind when writing theses that the more general your subject and the more complex your assertion, the longer your discussion must be to cover the subject adequately. The broadest theses require book-length treatments, as in this case:

> Meaningful energy conservation requires a shrewd application of political, financial, and scientific will.

You couldn't write an effective ten-page paper based on this thesis. The topic alone would require pages just to define what you mean by "energy conservation" and "meaningful." Energy can be conserved in homes, vehicles, industries, appliances, and power plants, and each of these areas would need consideration. Having accomplished this first task of definition, you would then turn your attention to the claim, which entails a discussion of how politics, finance, and science individually and collectively influence energy conservation. Moreover, the thesis requires you to argue that "shrewd application" of politics, finance, and science is required. The thesis may very well be accurate and compelling. Yet it promises entirely too much for a ten-page paper.

So to write an effective thesis and therefore a controlled, effective paper, you need to limit your subject and your claims about it. We discussed narrowing your subject during the invention stage (pp. 206–211); this narrowing process should help you arrive at a manageable topic for your paper. You will convert that topic to a thesis when you make an assertion about it—a *claim* that you will explain and support in the paper.

Making an Assertion

Thesis statements make an assertion or claim *about* your paper's topic. If you have spent enough time reading and gathering information and brainstorming ideas about the assignment, you'll be knowledgeable enough to have something to say based on a combination of your own thinking and the thinking of your sources.

If you have trouble coming up with such an assertion, devote more time to invention strategies: Try writing your subject at the top of a page and then listing everything you now know and feel about it. Often from such a list you'll venture an assertion you can then use to fashion a working thesis. One good way to gauge the reasonableness of your claim is to see what other authors have asserted about the same topic. Keeping good notes on the views of others will provide you with a useful counterpoint to your own views as you write and think about your claim, and you may want to use those notes in your paper.

Next, make several assertions about your topic, in order of increasing complexity, as in the following:

1. Fuel-cell technology has emerged as a promising approach to developing energy-efficient vehicles.

2. To reduce our dependence on nonrenewable fossil fuel, the federal government should encourage the development of fuel-cell vehicles.

3. The federal government should subsidize the development of fuel-cell vehicles as well as the hydrogen infrastructure needed to support them; otherwise, the United States will be increasingly vulnerable to recession and other economic dislocations resulting from our dependence on the continued flow of foreign oil.

Keep in mind that these are *working theses*. Because you haven't begun a paper based on any of them, they remain *hypotheses* to be tested. You might choose one and use it to focus your initial draft. After completing a first draft, you would revise it by comparing the contents of the paper to the thesis and making adjustments as necessary for unity. The working thesis is an excellent tool for planning broad sections of the paper, but—again—don't let it prevent you from pursuing related discussions as they occur to you.

Starting with a Working Thesis

As a student, you are not yet an expert on the subjects of your papers and therefore don't usually have the luxury of beginning writing tasks with a definite thesis in mind. But let's assume that you *do* have an area of expertise, that you are in your own right a professional (albeit not in academic matters). We'll assume that you understand some nonacademic subject—say, backpacking—and have been given a clear purpose for writing: to discuss the relative merits of backpack designs. Your job is to write a recommendation for the owner of a sporting-goods chain, suggesting which line of backpacks the chain should carry. Because you already know a good deal about backpacks, you may have some well-developed ideas on the subject before you start doing additional research.

Yet even as an expert in your field, you will find that crafting a thesis is challenging. After all, a thesis is a summary, and it is difficult to summarize a presentation yet to be written—especially if you plan to discover what you want to say during the process of writing. Even if you know your material well, the best you can do at first is to formulate a working thesis—a hypothesis of sorts, a well-informed hunch about your topic and the claim you intend to make about it. After completing a draft, you can evaluate the degree to which your working thesis accurately summarizes the content of your paper. If the match is a good one, the working thesis becomes the final thesis. But if sections of the paper drift from the focus of the working thesis, you'll need to revise the thesis and the paper itself to ensure that the presentation is unified. (You'll know that the match between content and thesis is good when every paragraph directly refers to and develops some element of the thesis.) Later in this chapter we'll discuss useful revision techniques for establishing unity in your work.

This model works whether dealing with a subject in your area of expertise—backpacking, for example—or one that is more in your instructor's territory, such as government policy or medieval poetry. The difference is that when approaching subjects that are less familiar to you, you'll likely spend more time gathering data and brainstorming in order to make assertions about your subject.

Using the Thesis to Plan a Structure

A working thesis will help you sketch the structure of your paper because an effective structure flows directly from the thesis. Consider, for example, the third thesis (see p. 214) on fuel-cell technology:

> The federal government should subsidize the development of fuel-cell vehicles as well as the hydrogen infrastructure needed to support them; otherwise, the United States will be increasingly vulnerable to recession and other economic dislocations resulting from our dependence on the continued flow of foreign oil.

This thesis is *strongly argumentative,* or *persuasive.* The economic crises mentioned suggest urgency in the need for the solution recommended: the federal subsidy of a national hydrogen infrastructure to support fuel-cell vehicles. A well-developed paper based on this thesis would require you to commit yourself to explaining (1) why fuel-cell vehicles are a preferred alternative to gasoline-powered vehicles; (2) why fuel-cell vehicles require a hydrogen infrastructure (i.e., you must explain that fuel cells produce power by mixing hydrogen and oxygen, generating both electricity and water in the process); (3) why the government needs to subsidize industry in developing fuel-cell vehicles; and (4) how continued reliance on fossil fuel technology could make the country vulnerable to economic dislocations.

How Ambitious Should Your Thesis Be?

Writing tasks vary according to the nature of the thesis.

- The *explanatory thesis* is often developed in response to short-answer exam questions that call for information, not analysis (e.g., "How does James Barber categorize the main types of presidential personality?").

- The *mildly argumentative thesis* is appropriate for organizing reports (even lengthy ones), as well as for essay questions that call for some analysis (e.g., "Discuss the qualities of a good speech").

(continues)

- The *strongly argumentative thesis* is used to organize papers and exam questions that call for information, analysis, *and* the writer's forcefully stated point of view (e.g., "Evaluate the proposed reforms of health maintenance organizations").

The strongly argumentative thesis, of course, is the riskiest of the three because you must state your position forcefully and make it appear reasonable—which requires that you offer evidence and defend against logical objections. But such intellectual risks pay dividends, and if you become involved enough in your work to make challenging assertions, you will provoke challenging responses that enliven classroom discussions as well as your own learning.

This thesis therefore helps you plan the paper, which should include a section on each of the four topics. Assuming that the argument follows the organizational plan we've proposed, the working thesis would become the final thesis. Based on this thesis, a reader could anticipate sections of the paper to come. A focused thesis therefore becomes an essential tool for guiding readers.

At this stage, however, your thesis is still provisional. It may turn out that as you do research or begin drafting, the paper to which this thesis commits you looks to be too long and complex. You may therefore decide to drop the second clause of the thesis (concerning the country's vulnerability to economic dislocations) and focus instead on the need for the government to subsidize the development of fuel-cell vehicles and a hydrogen infrastructure, relegating the economic concerns to your conclusion (if at all). With such a change, your final thesis might read: "The federal government should subsidize the development of fuel-cell vehicles as well as the hydrogen infrastructure needed to support them."

This revised thesis makes an assertive commitment to the subject even though the assertion is not as complex as the original. Still, it is more argumentative than the second proposed thesis:

> To reduce our dependence on nonrenewable fossil fuel energy sources, the federal government should encourage the development of fuel-cell vehicles.

Here we have a *mildly argumentative* thesis that enables the writer to express an opinion. We infer from the use of the words "should encourage" that the writer endorses the idea of the government's promoting fuel-cell development. But a government that "encourages" development is making a lesser commitment than one that "subsidizes," which means that it allocates funds for a specific policy. So the writer who argues for mere encouragement takes a milder position than the one who argues for subsidies. Note also the contrast between the second thesis and the first one, in which the writer is committed to no involvement in the debate and suggests no government involvement whatsoever:

> Fuel-cell technology has emerged as a promising approach to developing energy-efficient vehicles.

This, the first of the three thesis statements, is *explanatory*, or *informative*. In developing a paper based on this thesis, the writer is committed only to explaining how fuel-cell technology works and why it is a promising approach to energy-efficient vehicles. Given this thesis, a reader would *not* expect to find the writer strongly recommending, for instance, that fuel-cell engines replace internal combustion engines in the near future. Neither does the thesis require the writer to defend a personal opinion; he or she need only justify the use of the relatively mild term *promising*.

In sum, for any topic you might explore in a paper, you can make any number of assertions—some relatively simple, some complex. On the basis of these assertions, you set yourself an agenda for your writing—and readers set for themselves expectations for reading. The more ambitious the thesis, the more complex will be the paper and the greater the readers' expectations.

To review: A thesis (a one-sentence summary of your paper) helps you organize your discussion and helps your reader anticipate it. Theses are distinguished by their carefully worded subjects and predicates, which should be just broad and complex enough to be developed within the length limitations of the assignment. Both novices and experts typically begin the initial draft of a paper with a working thesis—a statement that provides writers with sufficient structure to get started but latitude enough to discover what they want to say as they write. Once you have completed a first draft, you test the "fit" of your thesis with what you have written. If the fit is good, every element of the thesis will be developed in the paper that follows. Discussions that drift from your thesis should be deleted or the thesis revised to accommodate the new discussions. These revision concerns will be more fully addressed when we consider the revision stage of the writing process.

Exercise 6.4

Drafting Thesis Statements

After completing the group exercise in narrowing a subject (Exercise 6.2, p. 209) and the individual invention exercise (Exercise 6.3, p. 211), work individually or in small groups to draft three theses based on your earlier ideas: one explanatory thesis, one mildly argumentative thesis, and one strongly argumentative thesis.

Writing Introductions and Conclusions

Writing introductions and conclusions is usually difficult. How to start? What's the best way to approach your topic? With a serious tone, a light touch, an anecdote? And how to end? How to leave the reader feeling satisfied, intrigued, provoked?

Often, writers avoid such decisions by putting them off—and productively so. Bypassing careful planning for the introduction and conclusion, they begin writing the body of the piece. Only after they've finished the body do they go back to write the opening and closing paragraphs. There's a lot to be said for this approach: Because you've presumably spent more time thinking and writing about the topic itself than about how you're going to introduce or conclude it, you're in a better position to set out your ideas. Often it's not until you've actually seen the text on paper or on screen and read it over once or twice that a natural or effective way of introducing or concluding it occurs to you. Also, you're generally in better psychological shape to write both the introduction and the conclusion after the major task of writing is behind you and you've already set down the main body of your discussion or argument.

Introductions

An effective introduction prepares the reader to enter the world of your paper. It makes the connection between the more familiar world inhabited by the reader and the less familiar world of the writer's topic; it places a discussion in a context that the reader can understand. If you find yourself getting stuck on an introduction at the beginning of a first draft, skip over it for the moment. State your working thesis directly and move on to the body of the paper.

Here are some of the most common strategies for opening a paper.

Quotation   Consider the two introductory paragraphs to an article titled "Blinded by the War on Terrorism," from journalist Sarah Chayes's article in the *Los Angeles Times:*

> "This is a great time to be a white-collar criminal."
> An assistant U.S. attorney I know startled me with this remark in 2002. The bulk of her FBI investigators, she explained, had been pulled off to work on terrorism, which left traditional crime investigations sorely understaffed.[2]

Chayes uses a provocative remark by a U.S. attorney to grab our attention. Our assumption, perhaps naïve, is that in a stable society governed by laws there should *never* be a good time to be a white-collar (or any other kind of) criminal. But we learn that this is apparently not the case, as Chayes pivots on the quotation to open her report on the stretched resources at the U.S. Department of Justice. Quoting the words of others offers many points of departure for your paper: You can agree with the quotation. You can agree

---

[2]Sarah Chayes. "Blinded by the War on Terrorism." *Los Angeles Times* 28 Jul. 2013.

and expand. You can sharply disagree. Or you can use the quotation to set a historical context or establish a tone.

Historical Review   Often the reader will be unprepared to follow the issue you discuss without some historical background. Consider this introduction to an article on second-term presidents:

> Second terms in the White House have, in many cases, ranged from the disappointing to the disastrous. Sick of the political infighting that intensified after his reelection, George Washington could hardly wait to retire to Mount Vernon. Ulysses S. Grant's second term was plagued by political scandal and economic panic. Woodrow Wilson left office a broken man, having suffered a massive stroke during his failed crusade to persuade America to join the League of Nations. Republican Dwight D. Eisenhower was routed in his last political battle, leaving Democrats in control of the presidency, the House, the Senate, and the Supreme Court for nearly the rest of his life. More recently, Richard Nixon resigned in disgrace; Ronald Reagan was tarred by the Iran-Contra scandal; Bill Clinton was impeached; and George W. Bush watched helplessly as his opponents surged into both houses of Congress and then the White House.
>
> Hence the legendary "second-term curse." In the early days of the republic, second-termers were by tradition discouraged from seeking another term, and nowadays, presidents are legally barred from a third term, thanks to the Twenty-Second Amendment. Popular wisdom has it that second-termers are therefore lame ducks. Unable to run again, how can a term-limited president reward his allies or restrain his adversaries? If he is seen as a fading force, won't his allies hitch themselves to the next rising star? Won't his adversaries attack relentlessly?
>
> Fortunately for Barack Obama, the situation is not that bleak.[3]

In this introduction, Akhil Reed Amar reviews how badly previous presidents have fared in their second terms to explain the "second-term curse." This review sets a context for his thesis, which begins his next paragraph: that Obama's experience may well be more positive than those of his predecessors. Setting a historical context requires familiarity with a topic, and for most student writers this will involve research. Readers will appreciate this research (they didn't have to do it, after all!). Note that the historical review lends itself to chronological development. Amar organizes his introduction as a sequence, from the presidency of George Washington to the presidency of George W. Bush.

Review of a Controversy   A particular type of historical review provides the background on a controversy or debate. Consider this introduction:

> The *American Heritage Dictionary*'s definition of civil disobedience could not be more direct: "the refusal to obey civil laws that are regarded as unjust, usually by employing methods of passive

---

[3] Akhil Reed Amar. "Second Chances." *Atlantic* Jan/Feb 2013.

resistance." However, despite such famous (and beloved) examples of civil disobedience as the movements of Mahatma Gandhi in India and the Reverend Martin Luther King, Jr., in the United States, the question of whether or not civil disobedience should be considered an asset to society is hardly clear cut. For instance, Hannah Arendt, in her article "Civil Disobedience," holds that "to think of disobedient minorities as rebels and truants is against the letter and spirit of a constitution whose framers were especially sensitive to the dangers of unbridled majority rule." On the other hand, a noted lawyer, Lewis Van Dusen, Jr., in his article "Civil Disobedience: Destroyer of Democracy," states that "civil disobedience, whatever the ethical rationalization, is still an assault on our democratic society, an affront to our legal order and an attack on our constitutional government." These two views are clearly incompatible. I believe, though, that Van Dusen's is the more convincing. On balance, civil disobedience is dangerous to society.[4]

The case against civil disobedience, rather than Van Dusen's article, is the topic of this paper. But to introduce this topic, the writer has provided quotations and references that represent opposing sides of the controversy over civil disobedience. By focusing at the outset on the particular rather than on the abstract qualities of the topic, the writer hopes to secure the attention of her readers and involve them in the controversy that forms the subject of her paper.

From the General to the Specific   Another way of providing a transition from the reader's world to the less familiar world of the paper is to work from a general subject to a specific one. The following introduction begins a paper on improving air quality by urging people to trade the use of their cars for public transportation.

> While generalizations are risky, it seems pretty safe to say that most human beings are selfish. Self-interest may be part of our nature, and probably aids the survival of our species, since self-interested pursuits increase the likelihood of individual survival and genetic reproduction. Ironically, however, our selfishness has caused us to abuse the natural environment on which we depend. We have polluted, deforested, depleted, deformed, and endangered our earth, water, and air to such an extent that now our species' survival is gravely threatened. In America, air pollution is one of our most pressing environmental problems, and it is our selfish use of the automobile that poses the greatest threat to clean air, as well as the greatest challenge to efforts to stop air pollution. Very few of us seem willing to give up our cars, let alone use them less. We are spoiled by the individual freedom afforded us when we can hop into our gas-guzzling vehicles and go where we want, when we want. Somehow, we as a nation will have to wean ourselves from this addiction to the automobile, and we can do this by designing alternative forms of transportation that serve our selfish interests.[5]

---

[4] Michele Jacques. Unpublished paper, used by permission.
[5] Travis Knight. Unpublished paper, used by permission.

Anecdote and Illustration: From the Specific to the General   The following three paragraphs offer an anecdote that moves the reader from a specific case to a more general subject:

> On April 13 of this year, a Wednesday, my wife got up later than usual and didn't check her e-mail until around 8:30 a.m. The previous night, she had put her computer to "sleep," rather than shutting it down. When she opened it that morning to the Gmail account that had been her main communications center for more than six years, it seemed to be responding very slowly and jerkily. She hadn't fully restarted the computer in several days, and thought that was the problem. So she closed all programs, rebooted the machine, and went off to make coffee and have some breakfast.
>
> When she came back to her desk, half an hour later, she couldn't log into Gmail at all. By that time, I was up and looking at e-mail, and we both quickly saw what the real problem was. In my inbox I found a message purporting to be from her, followed by a quickly proliferating stream of concerned responses from friends and acquaintances, all about the fact that she had been "mugged in Madrid." The account had seemed sluggish earlier that morning because my wife had tried to use it at just the moment a hacker was taking it over and changing its settings—including the password, so that she couldn't log in again....
>
> It was at about this time that I started thinking about the ramifications of this problem beyond our own situation....[6]

The previous introduction about the need to design alternative forms of energy-efficient transportation moved from the general (the statement that humans are "selfish") to the specific (that the alternative forms of transportation we design must meet "our selfish interests"). This introduction moves from the specific (a particular instance of computer hacking) to the general (the ramifications of trusting critical electronic information to storage in the "cloud"). The anecdote is one of the most effective means at your disposal for capturing and holding your reader's attention. It's also one of the most commonly used types of introduction in popular articles. For decades, speakers have begun their remarks with a funny, touching, or otherwise appropriate story. (In fact, plenty of books are nothing but collections of such stories, arranged by subject.)

Question   Frequently you can provoke the reader's attention by posing a question or a series of questions:

> At what point in the history of domestic service, I wonder, did lords and ladies start saying *Thank you* to their staff, instead of just kicking them into the fireplace? When did it begin, this treacherous

---

[6]James Fallows, "Hacked!" *The Atlantic* Nov. 2011.

>acquisition of personhood by the dishwashing classes? Was there perhaps a single, pivotal moment, deep in some ancestral pile, when a purple-faced baronet looked upon his vassal and experienced—wildly, disconcertingly—the first fizzings of human-to-human recognition? Blame Saint Francis of Assisi. Blame Charles Dickens. By the early 20th century, at any rate, the whole master-servant thing was plainly in ruins. *Individuals* were everywhere. The housekeeper had opinions; the chauffeur had a private life; and the gentleman found himself obliged to take an interest, however slight, in the affairs of his gentleman's gentleman. "And what will you do with your weekend off, Bassett?"[7]

Opening your paper with a question invites readers to formulate a response and then to test that response against the one you will develop in your paper. At what point did the British aristocracy begin treating servants as fellow humans? It's a question that hooks readers, who are likely to continue reading with interest.

Statement of Thesis   Perhaps the most direct method of introduction is to begin immediately with the thesis:

>Nuclear power was beginning to look like a panacea—a way to lessen our dependence on oil, make our energy supply more self-sufficient and significantly mitigate global warming, all at the same time. Now it looks more like a bargain with the devil.
> I wish this were not so....[8]

This selection begins with a two-sentence general assertion—that reliance on nuclear fission is inherently dangerous (as any "bargain with the devil" is bound to be). This is Eugene Robinson's thesis for an article titled "Japan's Nuclear Crisis Might Not Be the Last," in which he addresses what he thinks is a naïve enthusiasm for nuclear power as a route to energy independence. Beginning with a thesis statement (as opposed to a quotation, question, or anecdote) works well when, as in this case, a debate is well understood (there's no need to provide context for readers) and you want to settle immediately into making your argument. Opening with your thesis also works well when you want to develop an unexpected, or controversial, argument. If, for example, you open with the provocative assertion that "Reading is dead" in a paper examining the problem of declining literacy in the digital age, the reader is bound to sit up and take notice, perhaps even protest: "No, it's not—I read all the time!" This strategy "hooks" a reader, who is likely to want to find out how you will support such an emphatic thesis.

---

[7]James Parker, "Brideshead Regurgitated: The Ludicrous Charms of *Downton Abbey*, TV's Reigning Aristo-soap." *The Atlantic* Jan./Feb. 2013, p. 36.
[8]Eugene Robinson. "Japan's Nuclear Crisis Might Not Be the Last." *Washington Post* 14 Mar. 2011.

One final note about our model introductions: They may be longer than introductions you have been accustomed to writing. Many writers (and readers) prefer shorter, snappier introductions. The ideal length of an introduction depends on the length of the paper it introduces, and it may also be a matter of personal or corporate style. There is no rule concerning the correct length of an introduction. If you feel that a short introduction is appropriate, use one. Conversely, you may wish to break up what seems like a long introduction into two paragraphs.

Exercise 6.5

Drafting Introductions

Imagine that you are writing a paper using the topic, ideas, and thesis you developed in the exercises in this chapter. Conduct some preliminary research on the topic, using an Internet search engine such as Google or Bing or an article database available at your college. Choose one of the seven types of introductions we've discussed—preferably one you have never used before—and draft an introduction that would work to open a paper on your topic. Use our examples as models to help you draft your introduction.

Conclusions

You might view your conclusion as an introduction in reverse: a bridge from the world of your paper back to the world of your reader. The simplest conclusion is a summary of the paper, but at this point you should go beyond mere summary. You might begin with a summary, for example, and then extend it with a discussion of the paper's significance or its implications for future study, for choices that individuals might make, for policy, and so on. You could urge readers to change an attitude or modify behavior. Certainly, you're under no obligation to discuss the broader significance of your work (and a summary, alone, will satisfy the formal requirement that your paper have an ending); but the conclusions of effective papers often reveal that their authors are "thinking large" by placing their limited subject into a larger social, cultural, or historical context.

Two words of advice: First, no matter how clever or beautifully executed, a conclusion cannot salvage a poorly written paper. Second, by virtue of its placement, the conclusion carries rhetorical weight: It is the last statement a reader will encounter before turning from your work. Realizing this, writers who expand on the basic summary conclusion often wish to give their final words a dramatic flourish, a heightened level of diction. Soaring rhetoric and drama in a conclusion are fine as long as they do not unbalance the paper and call attention to themselves. Having labored long hours over your paper, you may be inclined at this point to wax eloquent. But keep a sense of proportion and timing. Make your points quickly and end crisply.

Summary (Plus)   Concluding paragraphs that summarize the article as a whole are useful if the article is lengthy or if the writer simply wants to reemphasize the main point. In his article "Wind Power Puffery," H. Sterling Burnett argues that the benefits of wind power have been considerably exaggerated and the drawbacks considerably downplayed. He explains why wind is an unreliable source of steady power and how conventional power plants must, at considerable expense, supplement the electrical energy derived from wind farms. Wind power also creates its own environmental problems, Barnett argues, and wind towers pose deadly hazards to birds and other flying creatures. He concludes with a summary of his main points—and an opinion that follows from these points:

> Wind power is expensive, doesn't deliver the environmental benefits it promises and has substantial environmental costs. In short, wind power is no bargain. Accordingly, it doesn't merit continued government promotion or funding.[9]

The final sentence goes beyond summary to articulate the main conclusion Barnett draws from the arguments he has made.

Statement of the Subject's Significance   One of the more effective ways to conclude a paper is to discuss the larger significance of your subject. Here you move from the specific concern of your paper to the broader concerns of the reader's world. A paper on the Wright brothers might end with a discussion of air travel as it affects economies, politics, or families; a paper on contraception might end with a discussion of its effect on sexual mores, population, or the church. But don't overwhelm your reader with the importance of your remarks. Keep your discussion focused.

In this paragraph, folklorist Maria Tatar concludes the introduction to her book *The Annotated Classic Fairy Tales* (2002):

> Disseminated across a wide variety of media, ranging from opera and drama to cinema and advertising, fairy tales have become a vital part of our cultural capital. What keeps them alive and pulsing with vitality and variety is exactly what keeps life pulsing: anxieties, fears, desires, romance, passion, and love. Like our ancestors, who listened to these stories at the fireside, in taverns, and in spinning rooms, we remained transfixed by stories about wicked stepmothers, bloodthirsty ogres, sibling rivals, and fairy godmothers. For us, too, the stories are irresistible, for they offer endless opportunities to talk, to negotiate, to deliberate, to charter, and to prattle on endlessly as did the old wives from whom the stories are thought to derive. And

---

[9] H. Sterling Barnett, "Wind Power Puffery." *Washington Times* 4 Feb. 2004.

from the tangle of that talk and chitchat, we begin to define our own values, desires, appetites, and aspirations, creating identities that will allow us to produce happily-ever-after endings for ourselves and our children.[10]

After a lengthy discussion of what fairy tales are about and how they work, Tatar concludes with a theory about why these ancient stories are still important: they are "a vital part of our cultural capital." They deal with "what keeps life pulsing," and in the way that they encourage opportunities to talk about these classic motifs, they serve to connect our ancestors' "values, desires, appetites, and aspirations" with our own and our children's. Ending the paper with a statement of the subject's significance is another way of saying, "The conclusions of this paper matter." If you have taken the trouble to write a good paper, the conclusions *do* matter. Don't be bashful: State the larger significance of the point(s) you have made. (But avoid claiming too great a significance for your work, lest by overreaching you pop the balloon and your reader thinks, "No, the subject's not *that* important.")

Call for Further Research Scientists and social scientists often end their papers with a review of what has been presented (as, for instance, in an experiment) and the ways in which the subject under consideration needs to be further explored. *A word of caution:* If you raise questions that you call on others to answer, make sure you know that the research you are calling for hasn't already been conducted.

The following conclusion ends an article titled "Toward an AIDS Vaccine" by Bruce D. Walker and Dennis R. Burton:

> With few exceptions, even the most critical and skeptical of scientists, who have stressed the difficulties of developing an HIV vaccine, feel that this is no time to give up. However, far more selectivity than hereto in advancing immunogens to large-scale clinical trials is required. The mantra of "the only way we will know if it is likely to be effective is to try it in humans" is not appropriate given the current state of knowledge. Trust in science, making full use of the tool kit that is provided by modern molecular biology, immunology, virology, structural biology, chemistry, and genomics is crucial. There is a critical need to understand how other vaccines work with a level of detail that has never been necessary for pathogens less adapted to immune evasion. The way forward is without question very difficult and the possibility of failure high, but the global need is absolutely desperate, and this is an endeavor that must be pursued, now with greater passion than ever.[11]

---

[10] Maria Tatar, "An Introduction to Fairy Tales." *The Annotated Classic Fairy Tales* (2002), ed. and trans. by Maria Tatar. W. W. Norton & Company, Inc.

[11] Bruce D. Walker and Dennis R. Burton. "Toward an AIDS Vaccine." *Science* 9 May 2008, p. 764. DOI: 10.1126/science.1152622.

Notice how this call for further research emphasizes both the difficulty of the task ahead and the critical nature of pursuing that task. The authors point to some of the pitfalls ahead and, in their plea to "[t]rust in science," point to a way forward.

Solution/Recommendation   The purpose of your paper might be to review a problem or controversy and to discuss contributing factors. In such a case, after summarizing your discussion, you could offer a solution based on the knowledge you've gained while conducting research, as in the following conclusion. Of course, if your solution is to be taken seriously, your knowledge must be amply demonstrated in the body of the paper. Here's the concluding paragraph from a student paper called "Don't Ban Junk-food Commercials!"

> With progress, albeit low progress, being made, now is not the time to ban television advertisements for high-calorie junk foods targeted at children. Parents and schools can take direct action in combating childhood obesity by encouraging exercise and teaching portion control. The best way to address the problem is to combine education, at home and in the schools, with improved self-regulation by a food industry that is continually prodded by the government and advocacy groups to improve the nutritional quality of its products and to air responsible advertisements. A ban is always possible and one day may prove necessary. But it is the most severe policy that Congress and the Federal Trade Commission could implement, and it should be used only as a last resort.[12]

In this conclusion, the author recommends dealing with the junk-food problem not by banning commercials, but rather by a combination of education at home and in school with self-regulation by the food industry. Her recommendation is a classically conservative one: to fix the problem, favor private initiative and local action over government regulation.

Anecdote   As we've seen in our discussion of introductions, an anecdote is a briefly told story or joke, the point of which is to shed light on your subject. The anecdote is more direct than an allusion. With an allusion, you merely refer to a story ("We would all love to go floating down the river like Huck..."); with the anecdote, you retell the story. The anecdote allows readers to discover for themselves the significance of a reference to another source—an effort most readers enjoy because they get to exercise their creativity.

The following anecdote concludes an article by Newton Minow, former chairman of the Federal Communications Commission who, more than fifty years ago, gained instant celebrity by declaring that television was a "vast wasteland." In his article, "A Vaster Wasteland," Minow discusses "critical choices about the values we want to build into our 21st-century

---

[12] Rhoda Beall. Unpublished student paper, used by permission.

communications system—and the public policies to support them." He explains how we should commit to six major goals and concludes:

> As we think about the next 50 years, I remember a story President Kennedy told a week before he was killed. The story was about French Marshall Louis-Hubert-Gonzalve Lyautey, who walked one morning through his garden with his gardener. He stopped at a certain point and asked the gardener to plant a tree the next morning. The gardener said, "But the tree will not bloom for 100 years." The marshall replied, "In that case, you had better plant it this afternoon."[13]

Minow doesn't bother to explain the significance of the anecdote, which he assumes should be clear: The task ahead will not see fruit for a long time, but unless we get to work immediately, it will take even longer.

Quotation   A favorite concluding device is the quotation—the words of a famous person, an authority in the field on which you are writing, or simply someone in a position to know a great deal about the subject. By quoting another, you link your work to that person's, thereby gaining authority and credibility. The first criterion for selecting a quotation is its suitability to your thesis. But consider carefully what your choice of sources says about you. Suppose you are writing a paper on the American work ethic. If you could use a line either by the comedian Jon Stewart or by the current secretary of labor to make the final point of your conclusion, which would you choose and why? One source may not be inherently more effective than the other, but the choice would affect the tone of your paper.

The following paragraph concludes an article called "Tiger Mom vs. Tiger Mailroom." The author, Patrick Goldstein, who writes about the film industry for the *Los Angeles Times*, joined the "Tiger Mom" debate, sparked by Amy Chua. In an earlier article titled "Chinese Mothers Are Superior," Chau explained why she forbade her children to engage in normal childhood recreational and after-school activities (except for learning the piano or violin), insisting that they work as hard as possible to earn grades no lower than A. Goldstein argues that in most professions, drive and initiative are more important than grade point averages: "charm, hustle, and guile are the aces in the deck." He concludes:

> In Hollywood, whether you were a C student or a *summa cum laude*, it's a level playing field. "When you're working on a movie set, you've got 50 film professors to learn from, from the sound man to the cinematographer," says producer David Permut, who dropped out of UCLA to work for [independent filmmaker] Roger Corman. "I've never needed a resume in my whole career. All you need is a 110-page script that someone is dying to make and you're in business."[14]

---

[13] Newton S. Minow, "A Vaster Wasteland." *The Atlantic* Apr. 2011, p. 52.
[14] Patrick Goldstein, "Tiger Mom vs. Tiger Mailroom." *Los Angeles Times* 6 Feb. 2011.

Goldstein's quotation from Permut drives home his point that, in the real world, it's not grades but talent, connections, and old-fashioned "hustle" that are the crucial elements in professional success.

Question   Just as questions are useful for opening papers, they are useful for closing them. Opening and closing questions function in different ways, however. The introductory question promises to be addressed in the paper that follows. But the concluding question leaves issues unresolved, calling on the readers to assume an active role by offering their own answers. Consider the following two paragraphs, written to conclude an article on artificial intelligence, as represented by the IBM computer named Watson that in 2011 defeated a group of humans on the television game show *Jeopardy!*:

> As these computers make their way into law offices, pharmaceutical labs and hospitals, people who currently make a living by answering questions must adjust. They'll have to add value in ways that machines cannot. This raises questions not just for individuals but for entire societies. How do we educate students for a labor market in which machines answer a growing percentage of the questions? How do we create curricula for uniquely human skills, such as generating original ideas, cracking jokes, carrying on meaningful dialogue? How can such lessons be scored and standardized?
>
> These are the challenges before us. They're similar, in a sense, to what we've been facing with globalization. Again we will find ourselves grappling with a new colleague and competitor. This time around, it's a machine. We should scrutinize that tool, focusing on the questions it fails to answer. Its struggles represent a road map for our own cognitive migration. We must go where computers like Watson cannot.[15]

The questions Stephen Baker raises in the penultimate paragraph of his article are meant to stimulate the reader to consider possible answers. In his final paragraph, Baker makes no attempt to provide his own answers to these questions, preferring to leave them hanging. Instead, he continues to ponder the nature of the problem.

Speculation   When you speculate, you consider what might happen as well as what has happened. Speculation involves a spinning out of possibilities. It stimulates readers by immersing them in your discussion of the unknown, implicitly challenging them to agree or disagree. The following paragraphs conclude a student paper on the effects of rising sea levels.

> The fate of low-lying coastal cities like Tacloban in the Philippines or Pacific island nations like Tuvalu can now be plotted, and the news is not good either for them or for coastal dwellers in more developed areas of the world. We have seen numerous examples of how rising sea

---

[15] Stephen Baker, "Watson Is Far From Elementary." *Wall Street Journal* 14 Mar. 2011.

levels have resulted in storm surges responsible for destroying dwellings and farms and for killing thousands. According to a recent United Nations report, sixty million people now live in low-lying coastal areas "within one meter of sea level," and by the end of the century that number is likely to double (United Nations Radio). We know enough to understand the risks of concentrating populations by the oceans. Yet even after devastating storms, governments continue to rebuild communities, indeed whole villages and towns, in the same vulnerable areas.

Over time, Nature generally doesn't lose contests like these, and sooner or later we will find ourselves contemplating the unthinkable: abandoning great coastal cities like New York, Calcutta, and Tokyo for higher ground. If the potential human destruction isn't enough to force policy makers to relocate whole populations away from the coasts, in time the loss of money will. Insurance companies, the ones who pay out on billion-dollar losses from major storms, may simply stop insuring cities and businesses that insist on living and working by the sea. When people can no longer insure themselves against heavy losses from climate-related events, the inevitable course of action will be clear: to build on higher ground, further from danger. In two hundred years, the coastal maps of the world will look very different than they do today.[16]

The prospect of nations abandoning great coastal cities like New York and Tokyo might seem extreme, but that is exactly the author's intent: to suggest a scenario that challenges readers to agree or not. If you have provided the necessary information prior to your concluding speculation, you will send readers back into their lives (and away from your paper) with an implicit challenge: Do they regard the future as you do? Whether they do or not, you have set an agenda. You have got them thinking.

Exercise 6.6

Drafting Conclusions

Imagine that you have written a paper using the topic, ideas, and thesis you developed in the earlier exercises in this chapter. Conduct some preliminary research on the topic, using an Internet search engine such as Google or Bing or an article database available at your college library. Choose one of the eight types of conclusions we've discussed—preferably one you have never used before—and draft a conclusion that would work to end your paper. Use our examples as models to help you draft your conclusion.

■ STAGE 5: REVISION

Perhaps it's stating the obvious to say that rough drafts need revision, yet too often students skimp on this phase of the writing process. The word *revision* can be used to describe all modifications one makes to a

---
[16] Allen Hawkins. Unpublished student paper, used by permission.

written document. But it's useful to distinguish among three kinds of revision:

Global revisions focus on the thesis, the type and pattern of evidence employed, the overall organization, the match between thesis and content, and the tone. A global revision may also emerge from a change in purpose.

Local revisions focus on paragraphs: topic and transitional sentences; the type of evidence presented within a paragraph; evidence added, modified, or dropped within a paragraph; and logical connections from one sentence (or set of sentences) within a paragraph to another.

Surface revisions deal with sentence style and construction as well as word choice. Sentence editing involves correcting errors of grammar, mechanics, spelling, and citation form.

Global and local revisions fall within Stage 5 of the writing process; surface revisions are covered in Stage 6, editing.

We advise separating large-scale (global and local) revision from later (sentence-editing) revision as a way of keeping priorities in order. If you take care of larger, global problems, you may find that, in the process, you have fixed or simply dropped awkward sentences. Get the large components in place first: *content* (your ideas), *structure* (the arrangement of your paragraphs), and *paragraph structure* (the arrangement of ideas within your paragraphs). Then tend to the smaller elements, much as you would in building a house. You wouldn't lay the carpet before setting the floor joists.

Think of revision as re-vision, or "seeing anew." In order to re-see, it's often useful to set your paper aside for a time and come back later to view your rough draft with a fresh eye. Doing so will better allow you to determine whether your paper effectively deals with its subject—whether it comes across as unified, coherent, and fully developed.

Characteristics of Good Papers

Apply these principles of *unity, coherence,* and *development* to the whole revision process. Let's start with unity, which we've already discussed in the context of the thesis.

Unity

A paper is unified when it is focused on a main point. As we've noted, the chief tool for achieving paper unity is the thesis: It's hard to achieve unity in a paper when its central point remains unstated. But unity doesn't stop at the thesis; the body paragraphs that follow must clearly support and explain that thesis. To determine unity, therefore:

1. examine your introduction and make sure you have a clear, identifiable thesis;

2. check your paper's interior paragraphs to make sure that all your points relate to that thesis; and

3. ask yourself how your conclusion provides closure to the discussion.

Coherence

Coherence means "logical interconnectedness." When things cohere, elements come together and make a whole. Coherence is closely related to unity: Good papers cohere. They hold together logically and stay focused on a main point. All subordinate points in the body of the paper clearly relate to the main point expressed in the thesis. Moreover, all those subpoints, examples, and supporting quotations are presented in a logical order so that connections between them are clear. You could write a highly unified paper, but the reader will have a hard time following your argument or staying focused on your point if your points are discussed in haphazard order. Guide readers along with your writing. Show them not only how subpoints relate to the main point, but also how they relate to one another.

Development

Good papers are also well developed, meaning that their points are fully explained and supported. Readers do not live inside your head. They will not fully understand your points unless you adequately explain them. A reader may also not be persuaded that your paper's main point is valid unless you provide support for your arguments by using examples, the opinions of authorities on the subject, and your own sound logic to hold it all together.

Use the three principles of unity, coherence, and development to analyze what you have written and make necessary revisions. Does your paper stay focused on the main point? Do your paper's points clearly relate to each other? Do you need better transitions between some paragraphs to help the ideas flow more logically and smoothly? Have you fully explained and given adequate support for all your points?

These three principles for good papers also apply to the composition of good paragraphs. Paragraphs are "minipapers": they should stick to a main point (the topic sentence) and fully develop that point in an orderly fashion. Transitional words or phrases such as *however, thus, on the other hand,* and *for example* help clarify for a reader how the sentences within individual paragraphs are related.

The Reverse Outline

The *reverse outline* is a useful technique for refining a working thesis and for establishing unity between your thesis statement and the body of your paper. When you outline a paper you intend to write, you do so *prospectively*—that is, before the fact of writing. In a reverse outline you outline the paper *retrospectively*—after the fact. The reverse outline is useful for spotting gaps in logic or development as well as problems with unity or coherence. Follow these steps to generate a reverse outline:

1. On a fresh sheet of paper (or electronic document), restate your thesis, making certain that the thesis you began with is the thesis that in fact governs the logic of the paper. (Look for a competing thesis in your conclusion. In summing up, you may have clarified for yourself your *actual* governing idea, as opposed to the idea you thought would organize the paper.)

2. In the margin of your draft, summarize *each* paragraph in a phrase. If you have trouble writing a summary, place an asterisk by the paragraph as a reminder to summarize it later.

3. Beneath your thesis, write your paragraph-summary phrases, one to a line, in outline format.

4. Review the outline you have just created. Is the paper divided into readily identifiable major points in support of the thesis? Have you sufficiently supported each major point? Do the sections of the outline lead logically from one to the next? Do all sections develop the thesis?

5. Be alert for uneven development. Add or delete material as needed to ensure a balanced presentation.

■ STAGE 6: EDITING

Only after revising a paper's large-scale elements—its unity, coherence, and content development; its overall structure; and its paragraph structure—are you ready to polish your paper by editing its sentences for style and correctness. At this stage you may be tired and strongly tempted to merely correct the obvious mistake here and there. Resist that impulse! Don't risk ruining a thoughtful, well-developed paper with sentence-level errors like incorrect word choice and faulty parallelism. After all your work, you don't want readers distracted by easily correctible mistakes in grammar, punctuation, and spelling.

Editing for Style

Developing an engaging writing style takes long practice. It's beyond the scope of this book to teach you the nuances of writing style, but you can consult many other fine books for help. (See, for example, William Zinsser's *On Writing Well.*) Here we'll focus on just one common stylistic problem: short, choppy sentences.

Perhaps out of fear of making common sentence errors like run-ons or comma splices, some writers avoid varying their sentence types, preferring strings of simple sentences. The result is usually unsatisfying. Compare, for instance, two versions of the same paragraph on a study of the human genome:

> Scientists have finally succeeded in decoding the human genome. This accomplishment opens up a whole new field of study. Researchers now have new ways to understand human biological functioning. We may also be able to learn new perspectives on human behavior. For centuries people have wondered about how much we are shaped by genetics. They have also wondered how much environment shapes us. The age-old questions about nature vs. nurture may now be answered. Each individual's genetic heritage as well as his or her genetic future will be visible to geneticists. All of these discoveries may help us to improve and extend human life. Many diseases will be detectable. New treatments will be developed. These new discoveries open up a new area of ethical debate. Scientists and the public are going to have to decide how far to take this new genetic technology.

This paragraph illustrates the problems with choppy, repetitive sentences. First, the writer hasn't connected ideas, and sentences don't flow smoothly from one to the next. Second, the same sentence structure (the simple sentence) appears monotonously, each following the simple subject-predicate form. The result, while grammatically correct, taxes the reader's patience. Compare the preceding version to this revision (which represents just one way the paragraph could be rewritten):

> Scientists have opened a whole new field of study following their recent decoding of the human genome. Armed with new ways of understanding human biological and behavioral functioning, researchers may someday sort out the extent to which we are shaped by our genes and by our environment. When geneticists can examine an individual's genetic past and future, they may also be able to alter these things, with the goal of improving and extending human life through early disease detection and the development of new treatments. However, such promise is not without its pitfalls: genetic research must be scrutinized from an ethical standpoint, and scientists and the public will have to decide the uses and the limits of this new technology.

Not only is the revised version of this paragraph easier to read, it's also more concise, clear, and coherent. Sentences with related content have been combined. Brief sentences have been converted to clauses or phrases and incorporated into the structure of other sentences to form more complex units of meaning.

Guard against strings of short, choppy sentences in your own writing. Learn strategies for sentence-level revision by learning how different sentence structures work. You can link related ideas with subordinating conjunctions (*because, since, while, although,* etc.), commas and coordinating conjunctions (*for, and, nor, but, or, yet, so*), and semicolons and coordinating adverbs (*however, thus, therefore,* etc.).

Editing for Correctness

On matters of sentence style, there is no "correct" approach. Often, personal style and taste influence sentence construction, paragraph and sentence length, and word choice. Grammar and punctuation, on the other hand, follow more widely accepted, objective standards. Of these, we (and your instructors) can speak in terms of "correctness"—of agreed-upon conventions, or rules, that people working in academic, professional, and business environments adopt as a standard of communication. You will find the rules (for comma placement, say, or the use of *amount* versus *number* and *affect* versus *effect*) in up-to-date writing handbooks. Review the list in the Common Sentence-Level Errors box, and eliminate such errors from your papers before submitting them.

The Final Draft

When you have worked on a paper for days (or weeks), writing and revising several drafts, you may have trouble knowing when you're finished. Referring to the writing of poetry, the Pulitzer Prize–winning poet Henry Taylor once remarked that a writer is done when revisions begin to move the project sideways instead of forward. We think the same distinction applies to academic writing. Assuming you have revised at the sentence level for grammar and punctuation, when you get the impression that your changes *do not actively advance* the main point with new facts, arguments, illustrations, or supporting quotations, you are probably done. Stop writing and prepare a clean draft. Set it aside for a day or two (if you have that luxury), and read it one last time to catch remaining sentence-level errors.

Common Sentence-Level Errors

ERRORS IN GRAMMAR

Sentence fragments—word groups lacking a subject or a predicate

Run-on sentences—two independent clauses joined without the proper conjunction (connecting word) or punctuation

Comma splices—two independent clauses joined by a comma alone when they need stronger linkage such as a coordinating conjunction, a conjunctive adverb, a semicolon, or a period

Subject-verb agreement errors—the verb form doesn't match the plural or singular nature of the subject

Pronoun usage—pronoun reference errors, lack of clarity in pronoun reference, or errors of pronoun-antecedent agreement

(continues)

ERRORS IN PUNCTUATION

Misplaced commas, missing commas, improper use of semicolons or colons, missing apostrophes, and the like

ERRORS IN SPELLING

Misspelled words

Most difficult will be deciding when the paper is done stylistically, especially for the papers you care most deeply about. With respect to style, one could revise endlessly—and many writers do because there is no one correct way (stylistically speaking) to write a sentence. As long as a sentence is grammatical, you can write it numerous ways. Still, if a given sentence is dull, you will want to improve it, for an excessively dull style will bore the reader and defeat the paper as surely as a flawed argument or a host of grammatical errors. But having devoted time to polishing your sentences, you will at some point need to pronounce yourself finished. When your changes make your work merely different, not better, stop.

Your instructor will (likely) return the paper with comments and suggestions. Read them carefully. If you or the instructor feels that a revision is appropriate, think through the options for recasting the paper. Instructors generally respond well when you go into a conference with an action plan.

At some point, instructor's comments or no, the paper will be done and graded. Read it through one last time, and learn from it. Once you have determined what you did well and what you could improve on for the next effort, it is time to move on.

WRITING ASSIGNMENT: PROCESS

Choose either of the following writing assignments.

1. Write a paper following the process outlined in this chapter. As a guide, you may want to complete Exercises 6.1–6.6, which will serve as prompts. As you write, keep a log in which you record brief observations about each stage of the writing process. Share the log with your classmates and discuss the writing process with them.

2. In this chapter you have learned to approach writing as a task divided into stages that blend together and loop back on one another: data gathering, invention, drafting, revision, and editing. Write a one- or two-page statement in which you compare your writing process *prior* to taking a composition course to the process you've learned from this text and from your instructor. What are the main differences? similarities? At the end of your statement, speculate on the ways you might alter this process to better suit you.

■ Locating, Mining, and Citing Sources

■ **SOURCE-BASED PAPERS**

Research extends the boundaries of your knowledge and enables you to share your findings with others. The process of locating and working with multiple sources draws on many of the skills we have discussed in this book:

1. taking notes;

2. organizing your findings;

3. summarizing, paraphrasing, and quoting sources accurately and ethically;

4. critically evaluating sources for their value and relevance to your topic;

5. synthesizing information and ideas from several sources that best support your own critical viewpoint; and

6. analyzing topics for meaning and significance.

The model argument synthesis in Chapter 4, "Responding to Bullies" (pp. 140–151), is an example of a research paper that fulfills these requirements. The quality of your research and the success of any paper on which it is based are directly related to your success in locating relevant, significant, reliable, and current sources. This chapter will help you in that process.

Where Do We Find Written Research?

Here are just a few of the types of writing that involve research:

ACADEMIC WRITING

• **Research papers** investigate an issue and incorporate results in a written or oral presentation.

• **Literature reviews** research and review relevant studies and approaches to a particular science, social science, or humanities topic.

(continues)

- **Experimental reports** describe primary research and may draw on previous studies.
- **Case studies** draw upon primary and sometimes secondary research to report on or analyze an individual, a group, or a set of events.
- **Position papers** research approaches to an issue or solutions to a problem in order to formulate and advocate a new approach.

WORKPLACE WRITING

- **Reports** in business, science, engineering, social services, medicine
- **Market analyses**
- **Business plans**
- **Environmental impact reports**
- **Legal research:** memoranda of points and authorities

Writing the Research Paper

Here is an overview of the main steps involved in writing research papers. Keep in mind that, as with other writing projects, writing such papers is a recursive process. For instance, you will gather data at various stages of your writing, as the list below illustrates.

DEVELOPING THE RESEARCH QUESTION

- *Find a subject.*
- *Develop a research question.* Formulate an important question that you propose to answer through your research.

LOCATING SOURCES

- *Conduct preliminary research.* Consult knowledgeable people, including academic librarians, general and specialized encyclopedias, general databases (such as *Academic Search Complete* and *JSTOR*) and discipline-specific databases (such as *EconLit* and *Sociological Abstracts*), and overviews and bibliographies/references in recent books and articles. Begin your search with well-chosen keywords and pay attention to *subject tags* (key words and phrases) assigned to the results of your search. Some of these subject tags—along with key words and phrases in the titles, abstracts, tables of contents, and subject headings of your search results—may give you new leads in expanding or refining your search.

(continues)

- *Refine your research question.* Based on your preliminary research, brainstorm about your topic and ways to answer your research question. Sharpen your focus, refining your question and planning the sources you'll need to consult.
- *Conduct focused research.* Consult books and online general and discipline-specific databases for articles in periodicals. Also consult biographical indexes, general and specialized dictionaries, government publications, and other appropriate sources. Conduct interviews and surveys, as necessary.

MINING SOURCES

- *Develop a working thesis.* Based on your initial research, formulate a working thesis that responds to your research question.
- *Develop a working bibliography.* Keep track of your sources, either on paper or digitally, including both bibliographic information and key points about each source. Make this bibliography easy to sort and rearrange.
- *Evaluate sources.* Determine the veracity and reliability of your sources; use your critical reading skills; check book reviews in databases like *Academic Search Complete* (or its associated databases such as *Academic Search Elite* and *Academic Search Premier*), *Alternative Press Index* (1969–present), *Periodicals Index Online* (1965–99), *Reader's Guide Retrospective* (1890–1982), *JSTOR,* and *Project Muse.* Book reviews may also be found in *Book Review Digest, Publishers Weekly,* and Amazon.com. Look up biographies of authors, and read the "About the author" statements that often accompany scholarly articles.
- *Take notes from sources.* Paraphrase and summarize important information and ideas from your sources. Copy down important quotations. Note page numbers from sources of this quoted and summarized material.
- *Develop a working outline and arrange your notes according to your outline.*

DRAFTING; CITING SOURCES

- *Write your draft.* Write the preliminary draft of your paper, working from your notes and according to your outline.
- *Avoid plagiarism.* Take care to cite all quoted, paraphrased, and summarized source material, making sure that your own wording and sentence structure differ from those of your sources.

(continues)

> • *Cite sources.* Use in-text citations and a Works Cited or References list, according to the conventions of the discipline (e.g., MLA, APA, CSE).
>
> REVISING (GLOBAL AND LOCAL CHANGES)
>
> • *Revise your draft.* Consider global, local, and surface revisions. Check that your thesis still reflects your paper's focus. Review topic sentences and paragraph development and logic. Use transitional words and phrases to ensure coherence. Make sure that the paper reads smoothly and clearly from beginning to end.
>
> EDITING (SURFACE CHANGES)
>
> • *Edit your draft.* Check for style, combining short, choppy sentences and ensuring variety in your sentence structures. Check for grammatical correctness, punctuation, and spelling.

■ THE RESEARCH QUESTION

Pose a question to guide your research, one that interests you and allows you to fulfill the requirements of an assignment. In time, the short answer to this research question will become the thesis of your paper. By working with a question (as opposed to a thesis) early in the research process, you acknowledge that you still have ideas and information to discover before reaching your conclusions and beginning to write.

Research questions can be more or less effective in directing you to sources. Here are three suggestions for devising successful questions.

1. Pose neutral questions that open you to a variety of ideas and information. Avoid biased questions that suggest their own answers.

    EFFECTIVE How do musicians use computers to help them create songs?

    LESS EFFECTIVE Are musicians who rely on computers to compose and produce music cheating the creative process? [The use of "cheating" suggests that the researcher has already answered the question.]

2. Emphasize *how/why/what* questions that open discussion. Avoid yes-or-no questions that end discussion.

    EFFECTIVE How do software engineers create algorithms that map patterns in music?

    LESS EFFECTIVE Does music lend itself to mathematical analysis? [The yes-or-no question yields less information and leads to less understanding than the *how* question.]

3. Match the scope of your question to the scope of your paper. Avoid too-broad topics for brief papers; avoid too-narrow topics for longer papers.

> EFFECTIVE How has the use of computers affected both the production and the consumption of popular music in America?
>
> LESS EFFECTIVE How has the use of computers affected American popular culture? [Assuming a brief paper, the topic is too broad.]

Narrowing the Topic via Research

If you need help narrowing a broad subject, try one or both of the following:

- Try searching for the subject heading in your library's online catalog. The catalog will show you items that match your search terms and will probably show you other subject tags on the same topic (see Fig. 7.2b, on page 243). This will give you a better idea of how to narrow down your search.
- Search by subject in an online database such as *Academic Search Premier* or *Academic OneFile*. The database may suggest different ways to break down the search into smaller or similar subjects or topics. Note subject tags (key words and phrases) in your search results to see how the subject breaks down into components. Then narrow your search by following up on promising subject tags.

Exercise 7.1

Constructing Research Questions

Moving from a broad topic or idea to the formulation of precise research questions can be challenging. Practice this skill by working with a small group of your classmates to construct research questions about the following topics (or come up with topics of your own). Write at least one research question that narrows each topic listed; then discuss these topics and questions with the other groups in class.

Racial or gender stereotypes in television shows

Drug addiction in the U.S. adult population

Global environmental policies

Employment trends in high-technology industries

U.S. energy policy

■ LOCATING SOURCES ■

Once you have a research question, find out what references are available. In your preliminary research, familiarize yourself quickly with basic issues and generate a preliminary list of sources. This will help narrow your investigations before moving to focused research.

Types of Research Data (see also Chapter 6, pp. 205–206)

PRIMARY SOURCES

• Data gathered using research methods appropriate to a particular field

  sciences: experiments, observations

  social sciences: experiments, observations, surveys, interviews

  humanities: diaries, letters, and other unpublished documents; close reading, observation, and interpretation

SECONDARY SOURCES

• Information and ideas collected or generated by others who have conducted their own primary and/or secondary research

  library research: books, periodicals, etc.

  online research

■ PRELIMINARY RESEARCH

Effective search strategies often begin with the most general reference sources: encyclopedias, biographical works, and dictionaries. Such sources are designed for people who need to familiarize themselves relatively quickly with the basic information about a particular topic. Authors of general sources assume that their readers have little or no prior knowledge of the subjects covered and of the specialized terminology of the field. By design, they cover a subject in less depth than do specialized sources. So review such comprehensive sources relatively early in your search even though you probably won't refer to them or cite them in your paper because they are so general.

Consulting Knowledgeable People

When you think of research, you may immediately think of libraries and print and online sources. But don't neglect a key reference: other people.

Your *instructor* can probably suggest fruitful areas of research and some useful sources. Try to see your instructor during office hours, however, rather than immediately before or after class, so that you'll have enough time for a productive discussion.

Beyond your instructor, *academic librarians* are among the most helpful people you can find in guiding you through the research process. Your librarian can suggest which reference sources (e.g., databases, specialized encyclopedias, dictionaries, and directories) might be fruitful for your particular area of research. They can also work with you to develop search strategies; to help you choose the best keywords to describe the various facets of your topic; to use Boolean operators, truncation, and string (or phrase) searching (see Using Keywords and Boolean Logic to Refine Online Searches, pp. 255–256); to examine database results and bibliographies to find ways to extend your search; and to evaluate sources you identify through searches using the library's databases. In short, academic librarians play a significant teaching role in the process of providing access to the library's resources. Draw upon their expertise!

Familiarizing Yourself with Your Library's Resources

Knowing how to use the resources of your library is half the battle in conducting research. Among the most helpful guides to these resources are research guides, subject guides, or LibGuides. These are topically focused lists of your library's resources. LibGuides are used to note resources held or subscribed to by your library—in print and online—as well as resources freely available on the Web. Many guides also offer tips on how to search effectively within a particular field of study. Figure 7.1 (p. 243) shows an example of a library subject guide to world history.

Note the double row of tabs near the top of the page that offers different approaches to historical material and the "how to" guides to research (top row of tabs). The main part of the page, the large section on the right, describes key features of some of the most useful sources for research in world history.

Look for subject guides, research guides, or LibGuides on your own academic library home page. Alternatively, Google "library AND guide AND (subject word, e.g., psychology) site:edu" to see lists of resources at other libraries—as some of these resources may be held by your home library.

Locating Preliminary Sources

- Ask your instructor to recommend sources on the subject.
- Scan the "Suggestions for Further Reading" sections of your textbooks. Ask your college librarian for useful reference tools in your subject area.

- Read an encyclopedia article on the subject and use the bibliography following the article to identify other sources.

- Read the introduction to a recent book on the subject and review that book's bibliography to identify more sources.

- Use an online database or search engine to explore your topic. Type in different keyword or search term combinations and browse the sites you find for ideas and references to sources you can look up later (see the box on pp. 255–256 for details).

Figure 7.1   A LibGuide Screen

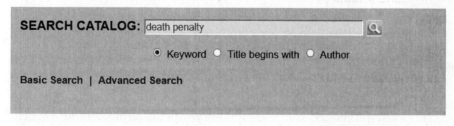

Figure 7.2a   Subject Headings or Subject Tags

Full View of Record Add to "Saved Items"   E-Mail

Choose format   Full View   Citation   Short View   MARC tags

Record 1 out of 1

Material type	<Book>
Author	Steelwater, Eliza.
Title	The hangman's knot : lynching, legal execution, and America's struggle with the death penalty / Eliza Steelwater.
Published	Boulder, Colo. : Westview Press, c2003.
Description	ix, 280 p. : ill. ; 24 cm.
Call Number	Main Library HV8699.U5 S72 2003 [Regular Loan]
Bibliography	Includes bibliographical references (p. 243-272) and index.
Subject	Capital punishment -- United States -- History.
	Executions and executioners -- United States -- History.
ISBN	081334042X (alk. paper)
Sys. no.	002485711

▉ Figure 7.2b

Searching for sources on the death penalty, the student finds a relevant book. By clicking on the assigned subject headings ("Capital punishment" or "Executions and Executioners") in the "Search Results" box, the student can find other sources that have been "tagged" with the same subject headings.

Encyclopedias

Reading an encyclopedia entry about your subject will give you a basic understanding of the most significant facts and issues. Whether the subject is American politics or the mechanics of genetic engineering, the encyclopedia article—written by a specialist in the field—offers a broad overview that may serve as a launching point to more specialized research in a particular area. The article may illuminate areas or raise questions that motivate you to pursue further. Equally important, the encyclopedia article frequently concludes with an *annotated bibliography* describing important books and articles on the subject. Encyclopedias have limitations, however.

1. Most professors don't accept encyclopedia articles—and particularly *Wikipedia* articles (see below)—as legitimate sources for academic papers. You should use encyclopedias primarily to familiarize

yourself with (and to select a particular aspect of) the subject area and as a springboard for further research.

2. Because new editions of the diminishing numbers of print encyclopedias appear only once every five or ten years, the information they contain—including bibliographies—may not be current. A number of former print encyclopedias are now available online—*Britannica Online,* for example—and this may mean, but not guarantee, that their information is up to date.

Among the well-known general encyclopedias (mostly available only online) are:

Academic American Encyclopedia

Encyclopedia.com (a compendium of more than 100 encyclopedias and dictionaries)

Encyclopedia Americana

Funk and Wagnalls New World Encyclopedia

New Encyclopaedia Britannica (or *Britannica Online*)

Wikipedia (online) [But see "Let the Buyer Beware" note below.]

But you will likely find it more helpful to consult *specialized* encyclopedias, such as the *Grove* encyclopedias of art and architecture, the *McGraw-Hill Encyclopedia of Science and Technology, Digital World Biology,* and Corsini's *Encyclopedia of Psychology.* Specialized encyclopedias restrict themselves to a particular disciplinary area, such as chemistry, law, or film, and are considerably more detailed in their treatment of a subject than are general encyclopedias.

Wikipedia: Let the Buyer Beware

Perhaps the Web's most widely used site for general information is *Wikipedia* (http://www.wikipedia.org). According to *Wikipedia* itself, the site contains 30 million articles in 287 languages, 4.3 million of them in the English edition. Launched in 2001 by the Internet entrepreneur Jimmy Wales and philosopher Larry Sanger, *Wikipedia* bills itself as "the free encyclopedia that anyone can edit." This site is thoroughly democratic: Not only can anyone write articles for *Wikipedia,* anyone can edit articles others have written.

At the same time and for the same reasons, these articles can be of doubtful accuracy and reliability. Authors of *Wikipedia* articles need no qualifications to write on their chosen subject, and their entries are subject to no peer review or fact-checking. (On numerous occasions, vandals have written or rewritten defamatory articles.)

(continues)

The bottom line on *Wikipedia?* It can be a source of useful information not readily available elsewhere, but *caveat emptor*: let the buyer beware. Even if researchers can't always be sure of the reliability of *Wikipedia* entries, however, many articles conclude with a section of footnote references and "External Links." These references and links often provide access to sources of established reliability, such as government agencies or academic sites.

Exercise 7.2

Exploring Specialized Encyclopedias

Go to the reference section of your campus library and locate several specialized encyclopedias within your major or area of interest. Conduct an "advanced search" in the library's catalog, using a word that describes the broader discipline encompassing the topic (e.g., "film," "chemistry," or "law," along with the word "encyclopedia*" OR "dictionary*". (See pp. 254–256 in Searching Databases Effectively on the use of truncation symbols like asterisks.) Look through the encyclopedias, noting their organization, and read entries on topics that interest you. Jot down notes describing the kinds of information you find. You might look for important concepts or terms related to your topic or for the names of important people associated with the topic or for events, dates, or definitions. These can make up the sets of words (keywords) that you subsequently take to the library catalog or article databases.

In addition, browse the reference section, especially right around the area where you found a particularly useful encyclopedia or book. Because of the way that books are arranged in the library (whether according to the Library of Congress system or the Dewey Decimal System), you'll be able to find books on similar topics near each other. For example, the books on drug abuse should be clustered near each other. Browsing can be a powerful tool for finding unexpectedly useful material.

Biographical Sources

Your preliminary research may prompt you to look up information on particular people. In these cases, consult biographical sources, which can be classified in several ways: by person (living or dead), geography, subject area, gender, race, or historical period.

Here are examples of biographical sources:

Biography in Context (a general biographical reference, incorporating numerous previously separate specialized biographical guides)

Black Americans in Congress, 1870–2007, 3rd ed.

Contemporary Authors

Current Biography (magazine) and *Current Biography Yearbook*

Notable American Women: A Biographical Dictionmary (5 vols.)

Who's Who in America

Who's Who in the Arab World

These online biographical sources are included in the database collections of many academic libraries:

American National Biography Online

Biography and Genealogy Master Index

Biography Reference Bank Contemporary Authors

Dictionary of Literary Biography

Oxford Dictionary of National Biography (replaces and extends *Dictionary of National Biography*)

Almanacs and Yearbooks

Once you settle on a broad topic still in need of narrowing, you may want to consult almanacs and yearbooks, which are generally issued annually and provide facts, lists of data, and chronologies of events. Titles include the following:

Almanac of American Politics (also a good source for biographical information)

CQ Almanac (formerly *Congressional Quarterly Almanac*, available both in print and online versions)

State of the World's Children (published by UNICEF)

World Almanac

World Trade Organization Annual Report

You can also find facts, lists of data, and chronologies by conducting an advanced search in the library's catalog, using a word that describes the broader discipline that encompasses the topic (e.g., "history," "sociology," or "medicine") along with the phrase "almanac* OR yearbook*". In addition, consult the online library guide accessible from your own library's home page (see LibGuide graphic on p. 243). See what you can find, for example, in the way of social science statistics available at your library.

Literature Guides and Handbooks

Guides to the literature of a certain subject area or handbooks can help you to locate useful sources. Pay particular attention to how these guides break broad topics into subtopics—a matter of particular interest to researchers in the early stages of their work. You may become interested in a particular subtopic for your research paper. Here are examples:

The Basic Business Library: Core Resources and Services

Bearing Witness: A Resource Guide to Literature and Videos by Holocaust Victims and Survivors

CRC Handbook of Chemistry and Physics

Gallup public opinion polls (there are numerous Gallup polls; search by subject matter and year)

Guide to Everyday Economic Indicators

Information Resources in the Humanities and the Arts

Voice of the Shuttle (UCSB-based online guide to resources in the humanities, the social sciences, the sciences, and law): vos.ucsb.edu

Overviews and Bibliographies

If your professor or a bibliographic source directs you to an important recent book on your topic, skim the introductory (and possibly concluding) material, along with the table of contents, for an overview of key issues. Check also for a bibliography, Works Cited, and/or References list. These lists are extremely valuable resources for locating material for research. For example, Robert Dallek's 2003 book *An Unfinished Life: John Fitzgerald Kennedy, 1917–1963,* includes a seven-page bibliography of reference sources on President Kennedy's life and times.

Subject-Heading Guides

Seeing how a general subject (e.g., education) is broken down (e.g., into math instruction/public schools/Massachusetts/K8) in other sources also could stimulate research in a particular area. In subject-heading guides, general subjects are divided into secondary subject headings. The most well-known subject-heading guide is the *Library of Congress Subject Headings* catalog. You might also consult the *Propaedia* volume of the *Encyclopaedia Britannica* (2007) and the "Syntopicon" volumes of the *Great Books of the Western World* set. Online look for these subject directories:

IPL2 (Internet Public Library (http://ipl.sils.umich.edu/index.text.html)

Librarians' Index to the Internet (http://lii.org)

WWW Virtual Library (http://www.vlib.org for general subject directory)

Having used such tools to narrow the scope of your research to a particular topic and having devised an interesting research question, you're ready to undertake more focused investigations.

■ FOCUSED RESEARCH

Once you have completed preliminary research, your objective becomes learning as much as you can about your topic. By the end of your inquiries, you'll have read enough to become something of an expert on your topic—or, if that's not possible given time constraints, you will at least have become someone whose critical viewpoint is based solidly on the available evidence. The following pages will suggest how to find sources for this kind of focused research.

In most cases, your research will be *secondary* in nature, based on (1) books; (2) print and online articles found through online databases; and (3) specialized reference sources. In certain cases, you may gather your own *primary* research, using (perhaps) interviews, surveys, structured observations, diaries, letters, and other unpublished sources.

Databases

Much of the information that is available in print—and a good deal that is not—is also available in digital form. Today, researchers typically access magazine, newspaper, and journal articles and reports, abstracts, and other forms of information through *online databases*, some of them freely available on the Web (e.g., Google Scholar) and some of them available to subscribers or subscriber institutions only. In rare instances, databases are accessed via *CD-ROM*. One great advantage of using databases (as opposed to print indexes) is that you can search several years' worth of different periodicals at the same time. In addition, many databases allow you to download and/or print the full text of articles.

Your library may offer access to hundreds of general and subject-specific databases, including the following:

General Databases:

> *Academic Search Complete* (and *Academic Search Elite, Academic Search OneFile,* or *Academic Search Premiere*) (multi-disciplinary range of academic journals)
>
> *Alternative Press Index*
>
> *EBSCOhost* (EBSCO is a vendor offering hundreds of individual databases of articles, e-books, and e-journals)
>
> *InfoTrac* (database of more than 5000 journals, magazines, and newspapers)
>
> *JSTOR* (digital library of academic journals, books, and primary sources)
>
> *LexisNexis* (general and legal databases)
>
> *Periodicals Index Online*
>
> *Project Muse* (humanities and social science articles from nonprofit publishers)
>
> *ProQuest* (newspapers and periodicals)
>
> *Reader's Guide Retrospective* (covers 1890–1982)

Subject-Specific Databases:

> **Anthropology:** *Anthropology Plus*
>
> **Art:** *Art Full Text* (fine, decorative, and commercial art; photography; folk art; film; architecture; etc.)
>
> *Art Index Retrospective*

Biology: *Biosis* (biology and life sciences)
   Biological Science Database
Business: *ABI/Inform*
   Business Source Complete
   EconLit
Classics: *Le Année Philologique*
Education: *ERIC*
English and Other Literatures: *MLA International Bibliography*
History: *America: History and Life* (history)
   Historical Abstracts (history)
Law: *LexisNexis*
Medicine: *MEDLINE*
   PubMed
Music: *Music Index Online*
   RILM Abstracts of Music Literature
Political Science: *PAIS International* (political science, administration of justice, education, environment, labor conditions, military policy, etc.)
   Worldwide Political Science Abstracts (political science, international relations, law, public administration/policy)
   ProQuest Congressional (public policy, law, social, economic issues)
Psychology: *PsycINFO* and *PsycARTICLES* (psychology, behavioral sciences, and mental health)
Religion: *ATLA*
Sociology: *Sociological Abstracts*

News Databases:

Access World News
Historical New York Times
New York Times
The Times (London)
Wall Street Journal

Smartphones and Database Searching

Not everyone accesses online databases using desktops, laptops, or tablets; some use their smartphones, which have smaller screens. Fortunately, some database vendors offer interfaces that are viewable and usable on smartphones. Others, such as JSTOR and EBSCO, have apps that can be

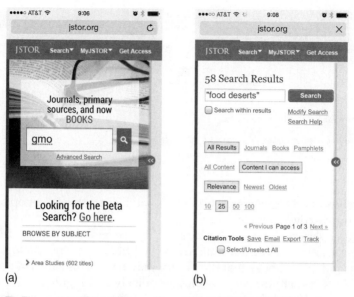

(a)   (b)

Figure 7.3   Smart Phone Search Results (MyJSTOR App)

downloaded to smartphones to allow for direct access. Fig. 7.3 shows a search screen for the database JSTOR, as seen on a smartphone.

As you can see, the format of the search screen is simplified so to be easily viewed on a small screen. Yet many of the same features of the Web version of the database are still available, such as the Advanced Search function and the ability to browse by subject. The results screen is similarly resized to fit on a smartphone screen.

The JSTOR app not only allows users to access the full text of the articles, but also allows them to restrict the search to articles, books, pamphlets, or only those articles that are accessible full-text.

Smartphone technology has also changed how to access the library Web sites through which you search these databases. Many Web sites are now scalable for smartphone screens, and some college and university library Web sites have their own apps, through which you may use the library catalog and find library information. Some specific groups of journals, such as those published by the American Psychological Association, have their own apps. See if your favorite database has a smartphone app. Such apps change constantly, so it's a good idea to check regularly for updates as well as for new offerings.

Discovery Services

Your library's Web site may be using a *discovery service*. This service may have a name like Primo (as it is called at the University of Idaho, which uses Ex Libris' Primo product). Or it may have a catchy name, such as Smart Search (which the University of Iowa gives its discovery service). Or, as at Seton Hall University, the service may not be a name at all: You may see just

| SHUsearch | Search Books | Search e-Books | E-Journals | Databases | Google Scholar |

Search multiple databases, journals and books and e-books at SHU Libraries.

Advanced Search *Give us feedback*

| Keyword ▾ | | Search |

☐ Full-Text (online)   ☐ Scholarly Journals

This search tool is made available through the support of SHU Information Technology.

■ Figure 7.4   A Discovery Service Search Box

a search box and be given the option to "search everything," an option that utilizes the discovery service.

The discovery service operates by searching several databases at the same time. The search also includes hits from the library's online catalog, online journals, and any e-books that the library may have. This can be a powerful tool, locating a vast number of resources quickly and highlighting the variety of tools at your fingertips. In addition, it offers a friendly interface that you are probably used to seeing in other contexts.

When using a discovery service, however, keep certain things in mind:

- Each individual database is unique and has its own strengths. For example, PsycARTICLES allows users to restrict searches to articles that have quantitative research. But discovery services cannot access these unique elements; they are generally restricted to limiting searches by subject headings, dates, call number ranges, or other more general elements. If you know your specific needs, you may get better results in a specific database.

- The number of results you get from a search in a discovery service can be overwhelming. You must develop good search strategies (see below, under Searching Databases Effectively) in order to retrieve a reasonable number of hits.

In some cases, you may find exactly what you are looking for via a discovery service. In other instances, the discovery tool may serve as a gateway, giving you ideas for terms to use for effective searching and steering you toward databases where you can do more targeted searches.

Web Searches

The *World Wide Web* offers print, graphic, and video content that can be enormously helpful to your research. Keep in mind, however, that search engines like Google and Bing are only tools and that your own judgment in devising a precise search query will determine how useful these tools will be to your inquiries. Good queries yield good results; poor queries, poor results—or as the early programmers termed it, GIGO (garbage in/garbage out).

Up to now most of your online searches have likely been through such search engines as Google or Bing. While the World Wide Web has vast quantities of information, a good deal of it (apart from information on federal and state government sites) is of questionable reliability and usefulness for academic research. The Web itself has far fewer good resources than your academic library. Why? Your library subscribes to resources that aren't publicly available. Someone has to pay to see them. As a student, you have already paid for access to this greater pool of good resources. So why search the smaller, poorer Web pool?

One good general Web source is Google Scholar, which offers free, full-text access to articles in the scholarly literature (and references to books) in a broad range of disciplines. You may also find it useful to explore scholarly Web portals, such as the *Voice of the Shuttle* and *INFOMINE* (both, multi-disciplinary) as well as the *Internet Public Library* and *Librarians' Index to the Internet*. Sources referenced in Web sites like these have a better-than-average likelihood of being reliable.

Effective database searches are built on well-chosen keywords or phrases that you enter into a search engine's query box before clicking the Search button. A well-constructed query will return a list of useful Web sites. Use the following tips.

1. **Focus on a noun: a person, place, or thing.** The most important terms in your query should be *objects*—that is, tangible "things." The thing (or person or place) you want to learn more about is the center of your search, your subject.

2. **Narrow the search with another noun or a modifier.** Some search engines, such as Google, assume that all of the terms that you are searching for are joined together by the word AND. That means you are searching for *all* of the terms you typed in. When you qualify your search terms by combining them in meaningful ways, database searches become more pointed and useful. You could create a more productive search by narrowing the keyword "computers" to "computers music" or "computers music culture." See the section below on Boolean logic (pp. 255–256) for more information on this topic.

3. **Try substituting words if the search is not working.** When a search does not yield useful information, change your search terms. Think of synonyms for keywords in your query. For nonacademic topics, you might use a thesaurus to locate synonyms. For example, you might substitute "cardiac" for "heart" and "aircraft" for "plane."

(continues)

4. *Re*-search. Librarians sometimes describe the process of library research as one of *re*-searching. A student will search with one set of words, get some good results, along with ideas of other words to use when searching, then vary the set of search words, get some more good results, and so on.

5. **Use "advanced" features to refine your search.** Search engines typically provide a "refine" function—sometimes called an "advanced" or "power" search tool—that allows you to narrow a search by date, type of publication, and type of Web site. You might instruct the engine to search only the sites of organizations, the government, or the military. You can also search in fields such as title, author, industry code, reviews, and so on. Refining your searches is easy: Locate the advanced feature option and fill in (or, in some cases, click to check) a box.

Searching Databases Effectively

Database systems in use today are still pretty dumb—that is, they are literal. They will return only the specific information requested and nothing more, however closely related. If we search for sources on AIDS, we will get lots on AIDS, but we will miss those items in the database that specify, instead, HIV or "acquired immune deficiency syndrome" or other ways of saying, basically, AIDS.

So we need to start the research process by thinking of the variety of ways an experienced researcher writing on our topic might refer to the different facets of our topic. We may be looking for articles on *college* students, but a scholar might write about *university* students. We may be looking for articles on *children*, but a scholar might write about *boys* OR *girls* OR *adolescents*.

Effective database searches are conducted according to the rules of Boolean logic. Fig. 7.5 illustrates such logic.

Substitute for "cats" and "dogs" terms appropriate to your search and you will find yourself with an effective search strategy, one that yields a high number of relevant results while eliminating a high number of irrelevant results.

In addition to Boolean operators, researchers use truncation—often an asterisk (*), sometimes a question mark (?)—immediately following the search term (no space) as a "wild card." A search for the word "children" will identify items in which the title or abstract or subject tags include the word *children*, but we will not see items that instead refer to *childhood* or to the *child*. A truncated search for "child*" will yield results in which any variation of *child-* appears: *child, childhood, childish, childlike, children*, and so on.

Researchers also do string or phrase searching. If, for instance, we search in many databases using the words "United" and "States," we will (as one would expect) identify items on the United States of America. But since

Boolean Operators help define the relationship between search terms. When searching in a database, Boolean operators help you narrow or broaden your set of search results. The three Boolean operators are **AND, OR** and **NOT**.

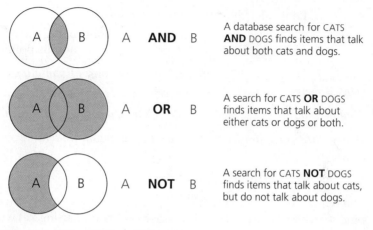

A   **AND**   B   A database search for CATS **AND** DOGS finds items that talk about both cats and dogs.

A   **OR**   B   A search for CATS **OR** DOGS finds items that talk about either cats or dogs or both.

A   **NOT**   B   A search for CATS **NOT** DOGS finds items that talk about cats, but do not talk about dogs.

Figure 7.5   Boolean Operators

most database search engines merely search for the occurrence of each word we specify, we might also turn up things on altered *states* of consciousness in the *United* Kingdom (Brits under the influence). To help the database know specifically what we want, we can use quotation marks around the search phrase "United States."

Using Keywords and Boolean Logic to Refine Online Searches

You'll find more—and more relevant—sources on Internet search engines and library databases if you carefully plan your search strategies.

Note: Some online databases have their own systems for searching, so review the "Help" section of each database or search engine and use "Advanced Search" options where available. The following tips are general guidelines, and their applicability in different search engines may vary somewhat.

1. *Identify multiple keywords:*

   Write down your topic and/or your research question, and then brainstorm synonyms and related terms for the words in that topic/ question.

(continues)

Sample topic: Political activism on college campuses

Sample research question: What kinds of political activism are college students involved in today?

Keywords: Political activism; college students

Synonyms and related terms: politics; voting; political organizations; protests; political issues; universities; colleges; campus politics

2. **Conduct searches using different combinations of synonyms and related terms.**

3. **Find new terms in the sources you locate and search with them.**

4. **Use quotation marks around words you want linked:** "political activism"

5. **Use "Boolean operators" to link keywords:**

The words AND, OR, and NOT are used in "Boolean logic" to combine search terms and get more precise results than using keywords alone.

AND: Connecting keywords with AND narrows a search by retrieving only those sources that contain *both* keywords:

> political activism AND college students

OR: Connecting keywords with OR broadens a search by retrieving all sources that contain at least one of the search terms. This operator is useful when you have a topic/keyword for which there are a number of synonyms. Linking synonyms with OR will lead you to the widest array of sources:

> political activism OR protests OR political organizing OR voting OR campus politics college OR university OR campus OR students

AND and **OR:** You can use these terms in combination, by putting the OR phrase in parentheses:

> (political activism OR protests) AND (college OR university)

NOT: Connecting keywords with NOT (or, in some cases, AND NOT) narrows a search by excluding certain terms. If you want to focus on a very specific topic, NOT can be used to limit what the search engine retrieves; however, this operator should be used carefully as it can cause you to miss sources that may actually be relevant:

> college students NOT high school

> political activism NOT voting

Evaluating Web Sources

The Web makes it possible for people at home, work, or school to gain access to corporate, government, and personal Web pages. Academic researchers are obligated to read Web-based material just as critically as they read print-based material. Chapter 2, Critical Reading and Critique, offers criteria for evaluating the quality and reliability of information and ideas in *any* source (pp. 54–65). Web sources are no exception, particularly self-published Web pages that are not subject to editorial review.

Reference librarians Jan Alexander and Marsha Tate have offered useful guidelines for helping researchers assess Web sources. First, they point out, it's important to determine what *type* of Web page you are dealing with. Web pages generally fall into one of five types, each with a different purpose:

1. business/marketing
2. reference/information
3. news
4. advocacy of a particular point of view or program
5. personal page

The purpose of a Web site—to sell, persuade, entertain—has a direct bearing on the objectivity and reliability of the information presented. When evaluating a site and determining its reliability for use in a research project, apply the same general criteria that you apply to print sources: (1) accuracy, (2) authority, (3) objectivity, (4) currency, (5) coverage. You might pose these questions in an effort to assess reliability:

- What's the likelihood that the information has been checked by anyone other than the author?
- What are the author's qualifications to write on the subject?
- What is the reputation of the publisher?
- Who is the author?
- What are the biases—stated or unstated—of the Web site?
- How current is the site?
- Which topics are included (and not included) in the site? To what extent are the topics covered in depth?

Pose these questions and determine, as you would for any non-Web source, reliability and suitability for your research project.

Other Pitfalls of Web Sites

Because reliable sites may include links to other sites that are inaccurate or outdated, users cannot rely on the link as a substitute for evaluating the five criteria just outlined. Web pages are also notoriously unstable, frequently changing and even disappearing without notice.

Remember: As a researcher working in an academic setting, you should apply the same critical reading skills to all your sources—no matter what types they are or where you found them, including on the Web.

Exercise 7.3

Exploring Online Sources

Go online and access one of the search engines or academic/professional databases discussed in this chapter. Select a topic/research question that interests you. Review the box on pages 255–256 and try different combinations of keywords and Boolean operators to see what sources you can find for your topic. Jot down notes describing the kinds of sources you find and which terms seem to yield the best results.

Exercise 7.4

Practice Evaluating Web Sources

To practice applying the evaluation criteria discussed in the section on Web sources, go to an Internet search engine and look for sources addressing a topic of interest to you (perhaps after completing Exercise 7.3). Try to locate one source representing each of the five types of Web pages (business/marketing, reference/information, news, advocacy, and personal). Print the home page of each source and bring the copies to class. In small groups of classmates, look over the sites each student found and make notes on each example's (1) accuracy, (2) authority, (3) objectivity, (4) currency, and (5) coverage.

Periodicals: General

Because many more periodical articles than books are published every year, you are likely (depending on the subject) to find more information in periodicals than in books. General periodicals are the magazines and newspapers that are usually found on newsstands or in bookstores, such as the *New York Times*, *Time*, and *The New Yorker*. Periodicals often have Web sites where many of their current articles are available online; you can also subscribe to these periodicals via e-readers. By their nature, recent general periodical articles are more current than books. For example, the best way to find out about a political party's position on Social Security reform is to look for current articles in periodicals and newspapers. But periodical articles may have less critical distance than books, and like books, they may become dated, to be superseded by more recent articles.

Magazines

General periodicals such as *The Atlantic*, the *New Republic*, and the *Nation* are intended for nonspecialists. Their articles, which tend to be highly readable, may be written by staff writers, freelancers, or specialists. But they usually don't provide citations or other indications of sources, so they're of limited usefulness for scholarly research. Increasingly, texts and abstracts of articles in general sources are available in online databases.

Newspapers

News stories, feature stories, and editorials (even letters to the editor) may be important sources of information. Your college library may have indexes to the *New York Times* and other important newspapers such as the *Washington Post*, the *Los Angeles Times*, the *Chicago Tribune*, the *Wall Street Journal*, and the *Christian Science Monitor*. It is also entirely possible that your library opts to forego print indexes in favor of online databases such as *EBSCO Newspaper Source Plus* or ProQuest's *New York Times* interface.

Periodicals: Specialized

Some professors will expect at least some of your research to be based on articles in specialized periodicals or scholarly journals. So instead of (or in addition to) relying on an article from *Psychology Today* (considered a general periodical even though its subject is somewhat specialized) for an account of the effects of crack cocaine on mental functioning, you might also rely on an article from the *Journal of Abnormal Psychology*. If you are writing a paper on the satirist Jonathan Swift, in addition to a recent reference to him that may have appeared in *The New Yorker*, you may need to locate a relevant article in *Eighteenth-Century Studies*.

Articles in such journals are normally written by specialists and professionals in the field rather than by staff writers or freelancers, and the authors will assume that their readers already understand the basic facts and issues concerning the subject. Other characteristics of scholarly journals:

- They tend to be heavily researched, as indicated by their numerous notes and references.

- They are generally published by university presses.

- Most of the authors represented are university professors.

- The articles, which have a serious, formal, and scholarly tone (and so are less reader-friendly than those in general magazines), are generally peer reviewed by other scholars in the field.

To find articles in specialized periodicals, you'll use specialized databases (see pp. 249–250)—that is, databases for particular disciplines, such as *ProQuest Education Plus* and *Business Source Complete*. You may also find it helpful to refer to *abstracts*, such as *Sociological Abstracts*. Like specialized databases, abstracts list articles published in a particular discipline over a given period, but they also provide summaries of the articles listed. They can save you a lot of time in determining which articles you should read and which ones you can safely skip. Don't treat abstracts alone as sources for research, however; when you find useful material in an abstract, locate the article to which it applies and use that as the source you reference. You will also find a lot of information on periodicals of all types via online databases. These databases run the gamut from those that provide bibliographic indexing or abstracting information, such as *Alternative Press Index* and *Sociological Abstracts,* to full-text databases such as *Academic Search Premier* that provide access to the full-length article.

One caution: Students too often think that they can simply browse their way to enough sources to write their papers. But this would be a hit-or-miss approach. To be a successful (more purposeful and systematic) browser, try instead to use the article databases in your discipline to identify one or two or twelve potentially interesting sources; then browse within those issues of journals to see if anything else seems interesting.

Exercise 7.5

Exploring Specialized Periodicals

Visit your campus library and locate online or print specialized periodical indexes for your major or area of interest (ask a reference librarian for help). Use your online catalog or ask a librarian for assistance in finding your library's print periodicals, if they are available. Note the call numbers for specialized periodicals (also called academic journals) in your field, and visit the section of the library where recent editions of academic journals are usually housed. If your library keeps its journals in call number order, browse the area where the journals are located, and look at journals around it. If periodicals are listed alphabetically, do a keyword search in the catalog for journal names, and find where those journals are located in the library. If your library does not keep its journals accessible in print form, do a search in a database on your topic. Look at the titles of the journals that come up in your search results. Look through the specialized periodicals in your field. The articles you find in these journals represent some of the most recent scholarship in the field—the kind of scholarship many of your professors are busy conducting. Write half a page or so describing the articles you find interesting and why.

Books

Books are useful for providing both breadth and depth of coverage of a subject. Because they are generally published at least a year or two after the events treated, they also tend to provide the critical distance that is sometimes missing from articles. Conversely, this delay in coverage means that the information in books won't be as current as the information you find in periodicals. Any piece of writing, books included, may be inaccurate, outdated, or biased.

Book Reviews

One way to determine the reliability and credibility of a book you may want to use is to look up the reviews published in resources such as *Publishers Weekly*, *Library Journal*, or the *New York Times Book Review*. You can also look at book reviews either in the online *Book Review Digest* or on Amazon.com. Reviews may often be searched for by:

- author
- title
- subject
- keyword

The online *Book Review Digest* offers brief descriptions of thousands of books and, more importantly, provides excerpts from (and references to) reviews. Another useful list of print and online resources for book reviews in the humanities is available at the UCSB library guide site (search: "guides library ucsb book reviews"). If a book receives bad reviews, you don't necessarily have to avoid it (the book may still have something useful to offer, and the review itself may be unreliable). But you should take any negative reaction into account when using that book as a source.

Government Publications and Other Statistical Sources

The collection, organization, and analysis of data take us into the realm of statistics, where researchers typically focus on changing patterns of numbers and percentages. How much money did consumers spend on entertainment last year—as opposed to the year before? How has the makeup of immigrant population changed over the past twenty years? Is the divorce rate rising or falling? How much money was spent on Head Start during the past five years? Since 1878, researchers looking for statistical information about the United States have relied heavily upon the *Statistical Abstracts of the United States*, produced by the Statistical Compendia program of the U.S. Census Bureau. For budgetary reasons, the *Statistical Abstracts* and related resources were terminated in 2011. As an alternative, the Census Bureau recommended that researchers looking for this kind of statistical information refer to the organizations cited in the source notes of the most recent (2012) *Statistical Abstracts* (http://www.census.gov/compendia/statab/). In addition, ProQuest, the publisher of a general database, announced that it will take over publication for updating and releasing its own version of *Statistical Abstracts* in print and online formats (http://cisupa.proquest.com).

Beyond the *Statistical Abstracts*, a huge quantity of reference information (both statistical and nonstatistical) is available on government Web sites. A valuable tool for finding online government information is USA.gov (http://www.usa.gov). This site is an online portal for the U.S. government and allows users to search the Web sites of all the federal government's Web sites; in addition, users can find information on state and federal Web sites.

A useful (and free) Web site for medical information is MedlinePlus, produced by the National Institutes of Health (NIH) (http://www.nlm.nih .gov/medlineplus). This Web site is not only a source of reliable medical information, but it also provides access to medical studies, dictionaries, publications from the National Library of Medicine, and health news.

Among other databases of government publications:

American Statistics Index (a guide and index to U.S. government statistical publications)

Congressional Information Service (legislative and statistical works recently acquired by ProQuest)

A good list of social sciences data and statistics sources may be found by searching: "guides and library and ucsb and socialsci stats." Statistical data on politics may be found by searching "guides and library and ucsb and politics."

Historical statistics may be found in the following sources:

Historical Statistics of the United States (online and print)

International Historical Statistics: Africa, Asia and Oceania, 1750–2000 (print)

International Historical Statistics: The Americas, 1750–2000 (print)

International Historical Statistics: Europe, 1750–2000 (print)

U.S. Census Bureau—Historical Census Browser (University of Virginia)
(http://mapserver.lib.virginia.edu)

U.S. Census Bureau—Census of Population and Housing
(http://www.census.gov/prod/www/decennial.html) [digitized copies of print volumes, 1790–2010]

For current information on a subject as of a given year, consult an *almanac* (such as *World Almanac*). For annual updates of information, consult a *yearbook* (such as *The Statesman's Yearbook*). For maps and other geographic information, consult an *atlas* (such as *New York Times Atlas of the World*). Often, simply browsing through the reference shelves for data on your general subject—such as biography, public affairs, psychology—will reveal valuable sources of information.

Interviews and Surveys

Depending on the subject of your paper, you may want to *interview* your professors, your fellow students, or other individuals knowledgeable about your subject. Additionally, or alternatively, you may wish to conduct *surveys* via *questionnaires* (see the related box). When well prepared and insightfully interpreted, such tools can produce valuable information about the ideas or preferences of a group of people.

Guidelines for Conducting Interviews

- Become knowledgeable about the subject before the interview so that you can ask intelligent questions. Prepare most of your questions beforehand.
- Ask "open-ended" questions designed to elicit meaningful responses, rather than "forced-choice" questions that can be answered with a word or two or "leading questions" that presume a particular answer. For example, instead of asking, "Do you think that male managers should be more sensitive to women's concerns for equal pay in the workplace?," ask, "To what extent do you see evidence that male managers are insufficiently sensitive to women's concerns for equal pay in the workplace?"
- Ask follow-up questions to elicit additional insights or details.
- If you record the interview (in addition to or instead of taking notes), get your subject's permission, preferably in writing.

Guidelines for Conducting Surveys and Designing Questionnaires

- Determine your *purpose* in conducting the survey: what kind of *information* you seek and *whom* (i.e., what subgroup of the population) you intend to survey.
- Decide whether you want to collect information on the spot or have people send their responses back to you. (You will get fewer responses if they are sent back to you, but those you do get will likely be more complete than surveys conducted on the spot.)
- Devise and word questions carefully so that they (1) are understandable and (2) don't reflect your own biases. For example, for a survey on attitudes toward capital punishment, if you ask, "Do you believe that the state should endorse legalized murder?," you've loaded the question to influence people to answer in the negative.
- Devise short-answer or multiple-choice questions; open-ended questions encourage responses that are difficult to quantify. (You may want to leave space, however, for "additional comments.") Conversely, yes-or-no responses or rankings on a five-point scale are easy to quantify.
- It may be useful to break out the responses by as many meaningful categories as possible—for example, gender, age, ethnicity, religion, education, geographic locality, profession, and income.

■ MINING SOURCES ■

Having located your sources (or at least having begun the process), you'll proceed to "mining" them—that is, extracting from them information and ideas that you can use in your paper. Mining sources involves three important tasks:

- Compiling a working bibliography to keep track of what information you have and how it relates to your research question.
- Taking notes on your sources and evaluating them for reliability and relevance.
- Developing some kind of *outline*—formal or informal—that allows you to see how you might subdivide and organize your discussion and at which points you might draw on relevant sources.

Critical Reading for Research

- *Use all the critical reading tips we've suggested thus far.* The tips contained in the boxes Critical Reading for Summary on page 5, Critical Reading for Critique on pages 79–80, Critical Reading for Synthesis on pages 120–121, and Critical Reading for Analysis on page 182 are all useful for the kinds of reading engaged in when conducting research.
- *Read for relationships to your research question.* How does the source help you formulate and clarify your research question?
- *Read for relationships among sources.* How does each source illustrate, support, expand upon, contradict, or offer an alternative perspective to those of your other sources?
- *Consider the relationship between your source's form and content.* How does the form of the source—specialized encyclopedia, book, article in a popular magazine, article in a professional journal—affect its content, the manner in which that content is presented, and its relationship to other sources?
- *Pay special attention to the legitimacy of Internet sources.* Consider how the content and validity of the information on the Web page may be affected by the purpose of the site. Assess Web-based information for its (1) accuracy, (2) authority, (3) objectivity, (4) currency, and (5) coverage (see p. 259).

■ THE WORKING BIBLIOGRAPHY

As you conduct your research, keep a *working bibliography*, a record of bibliographic information on all the sources you're likely to use in preparing the paper. If you are careful to record *full* bibliographic information—author(s), title, publisher, and so on—you'll spare yourself the frustration of hunting for it during the composition of your paper.

In addition to a working bibliography, it's a good idea to keep a *research log*. As you search, keep note of which database you are searching and which words you use in each search. Note significant sources that you find (your "working bibliography"), but also note new words or phrases or concepts that you might use on subsequent searches. By keeping a running research log, you can go back to previously searched databases with new search strategies—without risking running the same search over and over again.

Online catalogs and databases make it easy to copy and paste your sources' (or potential sources') bibliographic information into a document or to e-mail citations to yourself for cutting and pasting later. A more traditional but still very efficient way to compile bibliographic information is on 3" × 5" cards. (Note, also, that certain software programs allow you to create sortable digital records.) Using any of these methods, you can easily add, delete, and rearrange individual bibliographic records as your research progresses. Whether you keep bibliographic information on 3" × 5" cards or in a digital document, be sure to record the following:

- The author or editor (last name first) and, if relevant, the translator
- The title (and subtitle) of the book or article
- The publisher and place of publication (if a book) or the title of the periodical
- The date and/or year of publication; if a periodical, volume and issue number
- The date you accessed the source (if you are working with a Web site)
- The edition number (of a book beyond its first edition)
- The inclusive page numbers (if an article)
- The specific page number of a quotation or other special material you might paraphrase

You'll also find it helpful to include this additional information:

- A brief description of the source (to help you recall it later in the research process)
- The library call number or the URL, so that you can readily return to the source
- A code number, which you can use as a shorthand reference to the source in your notes (see the sample note records below)

Here's an example of a working bibliography record:

> Gorham, Eric B. *National Service, Political Socialization, and Political Education*. Albany: SUNY P, 1992.
>
> Argues that the language government uses to promote national service programs betrays an effort to "reproduce a postindustrial, capitalist economy in the name of good citizenship." Chap. 1 provides a historical survey of national service.

Here's an example of a working bibliography record for an article:

> Gergen, David. "A Time to Heed the Call." *U.S. News & World Report* 24 Dec. 2001: 60–61.
>
> Argues that in the wake of the surge of patriotism that followed the September 11 terrorist attacks, the government should encourage citizens to participate in community and national service. Supports the McCain-Bayh bill.

Here's an example of a working bibliography record for an online source:

> Bureau of Labor Statistics. "Table 1: Volunteers by Selected Characteristics, September 2009." 27 Jan. 2010. Web. 17 Feb. 2011. <http://www.bls.gov/news.release/ volun.t01.htm>.
>
> Provides statistical data on volunteerism in the U.S.

Some instructors may ask you to prepare—either in addition to or instead of a research paper—an *annotated bibliography*. This is a list of relevant works on a subject, with the contents of each work briefly described or assessed. The sample bibliography records above could become the basis for three entries in an annotated bibliography on national service. Annotations differ from abstracts in that annotations aren't comprehensive summaries; rather, they indicate how the items may be useful to the researcher.

Note-Taking

People have their favorite ways of note-taking. Some use legal pads or spiral notebooks; others type notes into a laptop or tablet computer, perhaps using a database program. Some prefer 4" × 6" cards for note-taking. Such cards have some of the same advantages that 3" × 5" cards have for working bibliographies: They can easily be added to, subtracted from, and rearranged to accommodate changing organizational plans. Also, discrete pieces of information from the same source can easily be arranged (and rearranged) into subtopics. Whatever your preferred approach, consider including the following along with the note:

- a topic or subtopic label corresponding to your outline (see below)

- a code number, corresponding to the number assigned the source in the working bibliography
- a page reference at the end of the note

Here's a sample note record for the table "Volunteers by Selected Characteristics, September 2009" from the Bureau of Labor Statistics (bibliographic record above):

Pervasiveness of Volunteerism (I)   7

Shows that 26.8 percent of Americans age 16 and older, 63.3 million in all, devote time to community service.

Here's a note record for the periodical article by Gergen (see bibliography note on the previous page):

Beneficial Paid Volunteer Programs (II)   12

Says that both the community and the individual benefit from voluntary service programs. Cites Teach for America, Alumni of City Year, Peace Corps as programs in which participants receive small stipends and important benefits (60). "Voluntary service when young often changes people for life. They learn to give their fair share." (60)

Both note records are headed by a topic label followed by the tentative location (indicated by a Roman numeral) in the paper outline where the information may be used. The number in the upper right corner corresponds to the number you assigned to the source in your bibliography note. The note in the first record uses *summary*. The note in the second record uses *summary* (sentence 1), *paraphrase* (sentence 2), and *quotation* (sentence 3). Notice the inclusion of page references, which the writer will reference in the paper itself (if the note is used). For hints on when to choose summary, paraphrase, and quotation, see Chapter 1, page 48.

Remember: Use quotation marks to distinguish between your language and the source author's language. Cite page references when you note an author's exact language *or* ideas. If you're careful to keep the distinctions between your language and that of authors clear, you'll avoid plagiarizing your sources. See the discussion of plagiarism on pages 50–52 and later in this chapter for more details.

Getting the Most from Your Reading

Fig. 7.6 presents some tips to help you determine how useful particular books will be in answering your research question.

In evaluating your sources, whether print or online, whether in book, article, or statistical form, try using the mnemonic "A-CRAB" to remember to pose a series of questions (see Fig. 7.7).

HOW TO READ A BOOK (OR ANY OTHER SOURCE)

First, don't read it word-for-word. Not yet,

Flip through the book to see how it is organized. Look for a TABLE OF CONTENTS and an INDEX. Do these seem to indicate that your topic is covered in enough depth to be useful?

Skim through the book's PREFACE or INTRODUCTION. For a journal article, read the ABSTRACT if there is one. What does the author say the accomplishes in this work? Do her claims appear to be grounded is fact? Or is this opinion or propaganda? Skim the first and last paragraphs of each chapter; these will reveal major points the author makes along the way. For an article, skim the introductory and concluding paragraphs. Note HEADINGS and SUBHEADINGS within chapters that can guide your progress in reading. Look for tables, charts, graphs, diagrams, maps, photographs, and any other VISUAL RESOURCES that can help you understand the author's train of thought.

Sample the author's writing as you skim the work. Does the level of information she presents appear to be appropriate for your needs? Is the author either too general or too technical in covering your topic? Do the author's claims appear to be backed by sound reasoning? Is there enough evidence presented to back up the author's point of view? Check the author's FOOTNOTES and CITATIONS to see if they appear relevant to your topic. Does the author cite solid, scholarly sources to support her points of view?

If, after this quick review, it appears to be a useful source **... Read the Book!**

Figure 7.6   How to Read a Book

Credibility of Sources

WHILE YOU READ ...		
	Authority	Ask yourself, who wrote this? Do the author's credentials, education, past writings and experience impress you? Does the author cite credible, authoritative sources?
	Currency	When was it written? Is the source current and up-to-date for your topic?
	Relevance	Is the information useful to you? Is the source extensive or marginal in its coverage of your topic?
	Audience	Who is the intended reader? Is this source written for a popular audience? Or a scholarly audience?
THINK LIKE **A-CRAB**	**B**ias	Does the author have a specific bias? Is the author trying to persuade the reader to accept a particular point of view?

Figure 7.7   Credibility of Sources

Guidelines for Evaluating Sources

- *Skim the source.* With a book, look over the table of contents, the introduction and conclusion, and the index; zero in on passages that your initial survey suggests are important. With an article, skim the introduction and the headings.
- *Be alert for references* in your sources to other important sources, particularly to sources that several authors treat as important.
- Other things being equal, the *more recent* the source, the better. Recent work usually incorporates or refers to important earlier work.
- If you're considering making multiple references to a book, look up the reviews in the *Book Review Digest* or via articles found using on-line databases. Also, check the author's credentials in a source such as *Contemporary Authors* or *Current Biography Illustrated.* If an author is not listed in either of these sources, you may choose to do a Web search for the author and look for online résumés, online portfolios, or references to the author's work.

■ ARRANGING YOUR NOTES: THE OUTLINE

You won't use all the notes you take during the research process. Instead, you'll need to do some selecting, which requires you to distinguish more important from less important (and unimportant) material. Using your original working thesis (see Chapter 6 on theses)—or a new thesis that you have developed during the course of data gathering and invention—you can begin constructing a *preliminary outline* of your paper. This outline will indicate which elements of the topic you intend to discuss and in what order. You can then arrange relevant note cards (or digital files) accordingly and remove, to a separate location, notes that will not likely find their way into the paper.

Some people prefer not to develop an outline until they have more or less completed their research. At that point they look over their notes, consider the relationships among the various pieces of evidence, possibly arrange notes or cards into separate piles, and then develop an outline based on their perceptions and insights about the material. Subsequently, they rearrange and code the notes to conform to their outline—an informal outline indicating just the main sections of the paper and possibly one level below that.

The model paper on bullying (see Chapter 4) could be informally outlined as follows

> **Introduction:** Examples of bullying (physical and cyber), who is bullied, anti-bullying laws
> **Thesis:** A blend of local, ground-up strategies and state-mandated programs and laws promises to be the best approach to dealing with bullying in American schools.

Problems with anti-bullying laws: Rushed, some elements unconstitutional, some laws ignore standard definitions, often ineffective
Alternate solution needed: Think local
Limits of local solutions: Flaws, difficulty evaluating
Conclusion

Such an outline will help you organize your research and should not be an unduly restrictive guide to writing.

The *formal outline* is a multilevel plan with Roman and Arabic numerals and uppercase and lowercase lettered subheadings that can provide a useful blueprint for composition as well as a guide to revision. See pages 138–139 in Chapter 4 for a formal outline of the paper on bullying. Here is one section of that outline. Compare its level of detail with the level of detail in the informal outline immediately above:

> III. An alternate solution to the problem of bullying
>   A. Rationale and blueprint for alternate approach
>   B. A local "ground-up" solution
>   1. Emily Bazelon
>   2. Lee Hirsch and Cynthia Lowen
>   3. Philip Rodkin

Outlining your draft after you have written it may help you discern structural problems: illogical sequences of material, confusing relationships between ideas, poor unity or coherence, or unevenly developed content. (See the discussion of *reverse outlines* in Chapter 6, pp. 231–232.)

Instructors may require that a formal outline accompany the finished research paper. Formal outlines are generally of two types: *topic outlines* and *sentence outlines*. In the topic outline, headings and subheadings are words or phrases. In the sentence outline, each heading and subheading is a complete sentence. Both topic and sentence outlines are typically preceded by the thesis.

■ RESEARCH AND PLAGIARISM

All too easily, research can lead to plagiarism. See Chapter 1, pages 50–52, for a definition and examples of plagiarism. The discussion here will suggest ways of avoiding plagiarism.

None of the situations that lead to plagiarism discussed below assumes the plagiarist is a bad person. All kinds of pressures can cause someone to plagiarize. By understanding those pressures, you may come to recognize them and take corrective action before plagiarism seems like a reasonable option.

Time Management and Plagiarism

The problem: You do not allocate time well and face crushing deadlines. Work, sports, and family responsibilities are the kinds of commitments that can squeeze the time needed to conduct research and write.

A solution: Learn time management. If you do not manage time well, admit that and seek help (it will be a further asset when you graduate). Consider taking three steps:

1. Begin the paper on the day it is assigned. Work on the paper for a set amount of time each day.

2. Visit the on-campus learning-skills center and enroll in a time management class. (Most schools offer this on a noncredit basis. If your school has no such class, you can readily find one online.)

3. When (despite your best efforts) you discover that you will not make a deadline, explain the situation to your instructor and seek an extension *before* the paper is due. State that you are seeking help and do not expect the problem to recur. Do not ask for a second extension.

Confidence and Plagiarism

The problem: You lack the confidence to put forward your ideas.

A solution: Understand that knowledge about your topic, and your confidence to present it in your own words, will increase in direct proportion to your research. Suggestions:

1. Stop worrying and begin. The longer you wait, the greater will be the pressure to plagiarize.

2. Seek out the on-campus writing center and let a trained tutor help you to break the assignment into manageable parts. Then you can sit down to research or write one part of your paper at a time. Complete enough parts, and you will have finished the assignment.

Note-Taking and Plagiarism

The problem: Inaccurate note-taking results in plagiarism: You neglect to place quotation marks around quoted language and later copy the note into the paper without using quotation marks.

A solution: Develop careful note-taking skills. Some useful approaches and techniques:

1. Enroll in a study skills class on working with sources, in which you will learn techniques for improving the accuracy and efficiency of note-taking.

2. Make certain to gather bibliographic information for every source and to link every note with a source.

3. Photocopy sources when possible, making sure to include publication information. When you use a source in a paper, check your language against the original language. Make corrections and add quotation marks as needed.

4. Learn the difference between quotation, summary, and paraphrase (see Chapter 1).

Digital Life and Plagiarism

The problem: Plagiarism has never been easier, given the volume of information on the Internet and the ease of digital copying and pasting.

A solution: Recall some of the reasons you are in college:

1. to improve your ability to think critically
2. to learn how to think independently
3. to discover your own voice as a thinker and writer

Borrowing the work of others without giving due credit robs you of an opportunity to pursue these goals. Don't allow the ease of plagiarism in the digital age to compromise your ethics. Easily managed or not, plagiarism is cheating.

■ DETERMINING COMMON KNOWLEDGE

Note one exception to the rule that you must credit sources: when ideas and information are considered common knowledge. You can best understand common knowledge through examples:

General Lee commanded the Confederate forces during the Civil War.

Mars is the fourth planet from the sun.

Ernest Hemingway wrote *The Sun Also Rises.*

These statements represent shared, collective information. When an idea or item of information is thus shared, or commonly known, you do not need to cite it even though you may have learned of that information in a source. What is considered common knowledge changes from subject area to subject area. When in doubt, ask your instructor.

The key issue underlying the question of common knowledge is the likelihood of readers' mistakenly thinking that a certain idea or item of information originated with you when, in fact, it did not. If there is *any* chance of such a mistake occurring, cite the source.

A Guideline for Determining Common Knowledge

If the idea or information you intend to use can be found unattributed (that is, *not* credited to a specific author) in three or more sources, then you can consider that material common knowledge. But remember: If you quote a source (even if the material could be considered common knowledge), you must use quotation marks and give credit.

Here is an example of a paragraph in which the writer summarizes one source, quotes another, and draws on common knowledge twice. Only the summary and the quotation need to be cited.

Very soon, half of America will communicate via e-mail, according to analysts (Singh 283). We can only assume that figure will grow— rapidly—as children who have matured in the Internet era move to college and into careers. With e-mail becoming an increasingly common form of communication, people are discovering and conversing with one another in a variety of ways that bring a new twist to old, familiar patterns. Using e-mail, people meet "to exchange pleasantries and argue, engage in intellectual discourse, conduct commerce, exchange knowledge, share emotional support, make plans, brainstorm, gossip, feud, [and] fall in love" (Chenault). That is, through e-mail, people do what they have always done: communicate. But the medium of that communication has changed, which excites some people and concerns others.

In both places where the writer draws on common knowledge, sources that could have been cited were not because evidence for the statements appeared in at least three sources.

■ PLAGIARISM, THE INTERNET, AND FAIR USE

The Internet is a medium like paper, television, or radio. Intellectual property (stories, articles, pictures) is transmitted through the medium. *The same rules that apply to not plagiarizing print sources also apply to not plagiarizing Internet sources.* Any content posted on the Internet that is not your original work is the intellectual property of others. Doing either of the following constitutes plagiarism:

- Copying and pasting digital content from the Internet into your document without citing the source.
- Buying a prewritten or custom-written paper from the Internet.[1]

Internet Paper Mills

Online "paper mills" merit special attention, for they make available prewritten papers on almost any topic. Remember that instructors know how to use Internet search engines to find the same papers and identify cases of plagiarism.

---

[1] Buying or using any part(s) of a paper written by another person is considered plagiarism regardless of its source.

Fair Use and Digital Media

U.S. copyright law permits "fair use" of copyrighted materials—including print (paper- and digital-based), images, video, and sound—for academic purposes. As long as you fully credit your sources, you may quote "excerpts in a review or criticism for purposes of illustration or comment; [and]...short passages in a scholarly or technical work."[2] The key to fair use of any material relies on the extent to which you have "transformed" the original work for your purposes. Thus:

- It is illegal for a student to copy a song from a CD and place it on a peer-to-peer file sharing network.

- It would be legal to "transform" that same song by including it as the background track to a digital movie or podcast, which includes other media elements created by the student, so long as it is created for educational purposes and cited on a bibliography page.

■ CITING SOURCES ■

When you refer to or quote the work of another, you are obligated to credit or cite your source properly. There are two types of citations—*in-text citations* in the body of a paper and *full citations* (Works Cited or References) at the end of the paper—and they work in tandem.

Many academic libraries (and writing centers) maintain brief guides to APA, MLA, and other format styles. Students can find these easily by Googling "MLA AND guide site:.edu."

The Purdue Online Writing Lab (OWL) maintains an excellent online guide to APA, Chicago, and MLA (http://owl.english.purdue.edu/owl/).

Types of Citations

- In-text citations indicate the source of quotations, paraphrases, and summarized information and ideas. These citations, generally limited to author's last name, relevant page number, and publication date of source, appear *in the text,* within parentheses.

- Full citations appear in an alphabetical list of "Works Cited" (MLA) or "References" (APA) *at the end of the paper,* always starting on a new page. These citations provide full bibliographical information on the source.

---

[2] "Fair Use." U.S. Copyright Office. May 2009. Web. 23 Mar. 2010.

If you are writing a paper in the humanities, you will probably be expected to use the Modern Language Association (MLA) format for citation. This format is fully described in the *MLA Handbook for Writers of Research Papers*, 7th ed. (New York: Modern Language Association of America, 2009). A paper in the social sciences will probably use the American Psychological Association (APA) format. This format is fully described in the *Publication Manual of the American Psychological Association*, 6th ed. (Washington, D.C.: American Psychological Association, 2010).

In the following section, we provide a brief guide to the major MLA and APA citation types you will use when researching and writing a paper. Look online for format guidance when citing sources not listed here. And bear in mind that instructors often have their own preferences. Check with your instructor for the preferred documentation format if this is not specified in the assignment.[3]

■ APA DOCUMENTATION BASICS

APA In-Text Citations in Brief

When quoting or paraphrasing, place a parenthetical citation in your sentence that includes the author, publication year, and page or paragraph number.

Direct quotation, author and publication year not mentioned in sentence

> Research suggests that punishing a child "promotes only momentary compliance" (Berk & Ellis, 2002, p. 383).

Paraphrase, author and year mentioned in the sentence

> Berk and Ellis (2002) suggest that punishment may be ineffective (p. 383).

Direct quotation from Internet source

> Others have noted a rise in "problems that mimic dysfunctional behaviors" (Spivek, Jones, & Connelly, 2006, Introduction section, para. 3).

APA References List in Brief

On a separate, concluding page titled "References," alphabetize sources by author, providing full bibliographic information for each.

---

[3]Some instructors require the documentation style specified in the *Chicago Manual of Style*, 16th ed. (Chicago: University of Chicago Press, 2010). This style is similar to the American Psychological Association style, except that publication dates are not placed within parentheses. Instructors in the sciences often follow the Council of Science Editors (CSE) formats, one of which is a number format: Each source listed on the bibliography page is assigned a number, and all text references to the source are followed by the appropriate number within parentheses. Some instructors prefer the old MLA style, which called for footnotes and endnotes.

Article from a Journal   Conclude your entry with the digital object identifier—the article's unique reference number. When a DOI is not available and you have located the article on the Web, conclude with *Retrieved from* and the URL of the home page. For articles located through a database such as *LexisNexis,* do not list the database in your entry.

ARTICLE (WITH VOLUME AND ISSUE NUMBERS) LOCATED VIA PRINT OR DATABASE

Ivanenko, A., & Massie, C. (2006). Assessment and management of

sleep disorders in children. *Psychiatric Times, 23*(11), 90–95.

ARTICLE (WITH DOI AND VOLUME NUMBER) LOCATED VIA PRINT OR DATABASE

Jones, K. L. (1986). Fetal alcohol syndrome. *Pediatrics in Review,* 8,

122–126. doi:10.1542/10.1542/pir.8-4-122

ARTICLE LOCATED VIA WEB

Ivanenko, A., & Massie, C. (2006). Assessment and management of

sleep disorders in children. *Psychiatric Times, 23*(11), 90–95.

Retrieved from http://www.psychiatrictimes.com

Article from a Magazine

ARTICLE (WITH VOLUME AND ISSUE NUMBERS) LOCATED VIA PRINT OR DATABASE

Landi, A. (2010, January). Is beauty in the brain of the beholder?

ARTnews, 109(1), 19–21.

ARTICLE LOCATED VIA WEB

Landi, A. (2010, January). Is beauty in the brain of the beholder?

ARTnews, 109(1). Retrieved from http://www.artnews.com

Article from a Newspaper

ARTICLE LOCATED VIA PRINT OR DATABASE

Wakabayashi, D. (2010, January 7). Sony pins future on a 3-D revival.

The Wall Street Journal, pp. A1, A14.

ARTICLE LOCATED VIA WEB

Wakabayashi, D. (2010, January 7). Sony pins future on a 3-D revival.

The Wall Street Journal. Retrieved from http://www.wsj.com

Book

Book located via print

Mansfield, R. S., & Busse, T. V. (1981). *The psychology of creativity and discovery: Scientists and their work. Chicago*, IL: Nelson-Hall.

Book located via Web

Freud, S. (1920). *Dream psychology: Psychoanalysis for beginners* (M. D. Elder, Trans.). Retrieved from http://www.gutenberg.org

Selection from an edited book

Halberstam, D. (2002). Who we are. In S. J. Gould (Ed.), *The best American essays 2002* (pp. 124–136). New York, NY: Houghton Mifflin.

Later edition

Samuelson, P., & Nordhaus, W. D. (2005). *Economics* (18th ed.). Boston, MA: McGraw-Hill Irwin.

■ MLA DOCUMENTATION BASICS

MLA In-Text Citations in Brief

When referring to a source, use parentheses to enclose a page number reference. Include the author's name if you do not mention it in your sentence.

From the beginning, the AIDS test has been "mired in controversy" (Bayer 101). Or if you name the author in the sentence:

Bayer claims the AIDS test has been "mired in controversy" (101).

MLA Works Cited List in Brief

At the end of the paper, on a separate page titled "Works Cited," alphabetize each cited source by author's last name. Provide full bibliographic information, as shown. State how you accessed the source, via print, Web, or downloaded digital file. As appropriate, precede "Web" with a database name (e.g., *LexisNexis*) or the title of a Web site and a publisher. Follow "Web" with your date of access. Note the use of punctuation and italics.

In MLA style, the medium by which you access a source (print, Web, database, download) determines its Works Cited format.

Magazine or Newspaper Article

Article accessed via print magazine or newspaper

Packer, George. "The Choice." *New Yorker* 28 Jan. 2008: 28–35. Print.

Warner, Judith. "Goodbye to All This." *New York Times* 18 Dec. 2009,
late ed.: A27. Print.

ARTICLE (VERSION EXISTS IN PRINT) ACCESSED VIA DOWNLOADED FILE

Packer, George. "The Choice." *New Yorker* 28 Jan. 2008: 28–35. AZW file.

Warner, Judith. "Goodbye to All This." *New York Times* 18 Dec. 2009,
late ed.: A27. PDF file.

ARTICLE (VERSION EXISTS IN PRINT) ACCESSED VIA DATABASE

Packer, George. "The Choice." *New Yorker* 28 Jan. 2008: 28–35.
Academic Search Premier. Web. 12 Mar. 2010.

Warner, Judith. "Goodbye to All This." *New York Times* 18 Dec. 2009,
late ed.: A27. *LexisNexis*. Web. 14 Jan. 2010.

ARTICLE (VERSION EXISTS IN PRINT) ACCESSED VIA WEB

Packer, George. "The Choice." *NewYorker.com*. CondéNet, 28 Jan. 2008.
Web. 12 Mar. 2010.

Warner, Judith. "Goodbye to All This." *New York Times*. New York
Times, 18 Dec. 2009. Web. 14 Jan. 2010.

Scholarly Article

SCHOLARLY ARTICLE ACCESSED VIA PRINT JOURNAL

Ivanenko, Anna, and Clifford Massie. "Assessment and Management
of Sleep Disorders in Children." *Psychiatric Times* 23.11 (2006):
90–95. Print.

SCHOLARLY ARTICLE (VERSION EXISTS IN PRINT) ACCESSED VIA DOWNLOADED FILE

Ivanenko, Anna, and Clifford Massie. "Assessment and Management
of Sleep Disorders in Children." *Psychiatric Times* 23.11 (2006):
90–95. PDF file.

SCHOLARLY ARTICLE (VERSION EXISTS IN PRINT) ACCESSED VIA DATABASE

Ivanenko, Anna, and Clifford Massie. "Assessment and Management
of Sleep Disorders in Children." *Psychiatric Times* 23.11 (2006):
90–95. *Academic OneFile*. Web. 3 Nov. 2010.

SCHOLARLY ARTICLE (VERSION EXISTS IN PRINT) ACCESSED VIA WEB

> Ivanenko, Anna, and Clifford Massie. "Assessment and Management of Sleep Disorders in Children." *Psychiatric Times.* United Business Media, 1 Oct. 2006. Web. 3 Nov. 2010.

SCHOLARLY ARTICLE FROM AN E-JOURNAL THAT HAS NO PRINT EQUIVALENT

> Blackwood, Jothany. "Coaching Educational Leaders." *Academic Leadership: The Online Journal* 7.3 (2009): n. pag. Web. 2 Feb. 2010.

Book

BOOK ACCESSED VIA PRINT

> James, William. *The Varieties of Religious Experience: A Study in Human Nature; Being the Gifford Lectures on Natural Religion Delivered at Edinburgh in 1901–1902.* New York: Longmans, 1902. Print.

BOOK (VERSION EXISTS IN PRINT) ACCESSED VIA DOWNLOADED FILE

> James, William. *The Varieties of Religious Experience: A Study in Human Nature; Being the Gifford Lectures on Natural Religion Delivered at Edinburgh in 1901–1902.* New York: Longmans, 1902. MOBI file.

BOOK (VERSION EXISTS IN PRINT) ACCESSED VIA WEB OR DATABASE

> James, William. *The Varieties of Religious Experience: A Study in Human Nature; Being the Gifford Lectures on Natural Religion Delivered at Edinburgh in 1901–1902.* New York: Longmans, 1902. *U. of Virginia Etext Center.* Web. 12 Jan. 2010.

> James, William. *The Varieties of Religious Experience: A Study in Human Nature; Being the Gifford Lectures on Natural Religion Delivered at Edinburgh in 1901–1902.* New York: Longmans, 1902. *ACLS Humanities E-Book.* Web. 12 Mar. 2010.

ONLINE BOOK THAT HAS NO PRINT EQUIVALENT

> Langer, Maria. *Mastering Microsoft Word. Designprovideo.com.* Nonlinear Educating, 2009. Web. 23 Jan. 2010.

Web-Only Publication (Content Created for and Published on the Web)

HOME PAGE

> Boucher, Marc, ed. Home page. *The Space Elevator Reference.*
>
> *Spaceelevator.com.* SpaceRef Interactive, 2009. Web. 17 Dec.
>
> 2009.

WEB-BASED ARTICLE ON A LARGER SITE

> Landau, Elizabeth. "Stem Cell Therapies for Hearts Inching Closer to
>
> Wide Use." *CNN.com.* Cable News Network, 18 Dec. 2009. Web. 14
>
> Jan. 2010.
>
> White, Veronica. "Gian Lorenzo Bernini." *Heilbrunn Timeline of Art*
>
> *History.* Metropolitan Museum of Art, New York, 2009. Web. 18
>
> Mar. 2010.

BLOG

> Lubber, Mindy. "The Climate Treaty Announcement." *Climate Experts'*
>
> *Forum—Copenhagen.* Financial Times, 19 Dec. 2009. Web. 22 Dec.
>
> 2009.

WRITING ASSIGNMENT: SOURCE-BASED PAPER

Using the methods we have outlined in this chapter—and incorporating the skills covered in this textbook as a whole—conduct your own research on a topic and research question that fall within your major or your area of interest. Your research process should culminate in a 1500- to 1700-word paper that draws upon your sources to present an answer to your research question.

Practicing Academic Writing ∎ 8

∎ ETHICAL DILEMMAS IN EVERYDAY LIFE

The word "ethics" is connected intrinsically with questions of correct conduct within society. Etymologically, "ethics" comes from the Greek "ethos" meaning "character" which indicates a concern for virtuous people, reliable character and proper conduct. "Morality" is derived from "mores" or custom—the rules of conduct of a group or society. An initial definition of ethics, then, is *the analysis, evaluation, and promotion of correct conduct and/or good character, according to the best available standards.*

Ethics asks what we should do in some circumstance, or what we should do as participants in some form of activity or profession. Ethics is not limited to the acts of a single person. Ethics is also interested in the correct practices of governments, corporations, professionals and many other groups. To these issues, ethics seeks a reasoned, principled, position. An appeal to existing practice or the command of a powerful leader is not sufficient.... Some ethical questions will require reflection on our basic values and the purpose of human society.

Ethics is best conceived of as something we "do," a form of on-going inquiry into practical problems. Ethics is the difficult practical task of applying norms and standards to ever new and changing circumstances.

—Stephen J. A. Ward, "Ethics in a Nutshell"

In the spring of 2013, Edward Snowden, a former employee of the CIA and former technical contractor for the National Security Agency, leaked to the press thousands of documents detailing top-secret U.S. mass-surveillance programs. Snowden's actions rocked the national security establishment and divided the country. Some saw him as a hero performing a great public service in tearing the veil of secrecy from such programs and making them known to the American public. Others viewed him as a traitor who had violated his oath and endangered the security of his country. Snowden saw himself as following in the footsteps of others who believed that they were acting honorably in what they regarded as the public interest, such as Private Bradley Manning, who in 2010 passed classified national defense information to the Web site *Wikileaks*, and

Daniel Ellsberg, who in 1971 released to the *New York Times* the "Pentagon Papers," a secret Department of Defense history of the Vietnam War, which was raging at the time.

Honorable men or traitors? How we view such people depends upon the ethical standards we bring to bear upon their actions. Are the social benefits of releasing classified information in the interest of transparency outweighed by the harm that may result from these releases? Is it so inherently wrong to violate laws covering official secrecy that there can be no justification for such acts?

To answer such questions, we rely upon ethical frameworks, belief systems forged by our culture, our religion, our parents, our teachers, and our life experience. Sometimes we respond to weighty questions like "Is abortion acceptable under any circumstances?" or "Was the United States justified in dropping the atomic bomb on Japan in 1945 to end World War II?" Generally, though, the ethical dilemmas we face are more mundane: What do we do about a friend we see shoplifting? A family member who makes a racist, sexist, or simply inconsiderate remark? A co-worker who habitually arrives late and leaves early and ignores your protests on the subject? How are we to act—and what do our actions say about us?

Large or small, the ethical dilemmas we face can be vexing. In this practice chapter, you'll get to work through a series of (mostly hypothetical) dilemmas, guided by distinct ethical principles that will help you to clarify what, in your view, is a proper course of action. You'll learn about classic theories of ethics: the utilitarian approach, the rights approach, the fairness approach, and the virtues approach. You'll also learn how stages of moral development affect the way we judge behavior, our own and that of others. You'll draw upon all these approaches, alone and in combination, to help resolve the ethical dilemmas inherent in the example cases.

Your main assignment in this chapter is to write an argument that synthesizes your own insights on one or more ethical dilemmas along with what various authors have written. In preparation, you will complete several briefer exercises that require you to draw on your sources. During this progression of assignments, you will write a combination of summaries, paraphrases, critiques, and explanations that will prepare you for—and that will produce sections of—your more ambitious argument synthesis. In this respect, the assignments here are typical of other writing you will do in college: While at times you will be called on to write a stand-alone critique or a purely explanatory paper, you will also write papers that blend the basic forms of college writing that you have studied in this text. Both your critiques and your explanations will rely in part on summaries—or partial summaries—of specific articles. Your arguments may rely on summaries, critiques, and explanations. The assignments in this chapter will therefore help prepare you for future academic research tasks while broadening your understanding of the world of ethical analysis.

Read; Prepare to Write

As you read these selections, prepare for the assignments by marking up the texts: Write notes to yourself in the margins, and comment on what the authors have said.

To prepare for the more ambitious of the assignments that follow—the explanatory and argument syntheses—consider drawing up a topic list of your sources as you read. For each topic about which two or more authors have something to say, jot down notes and page (or paragraph) references. Here's an example entry concerning one type of ethical dilemma you will read about in this chapter:

To speak up—or not—when you see something wrong

- The director of safety in the "Collapsed Mine"—DeGeorge, par.1, p. 288
  He sees a safety problem, reports it to his boss, boss ignores it, safety director is told to say nothing more—and mine collapses.
- The bank teller case—par. 1, p. 308
  One bank teller "borrows" $10k from a dormant account to pay for kid's operation and is paying back the money. Should a second teller, a friend, speak up?
- Should a doctor violate doctor/patient confidentiality? par. 1, p. 308
  A doctor promises he will keep a patient's confession in confidence. This confession reveals that an innocent man has gone to jail. Should the doctor violate his promise and speak up to save the falsely imprisoned man?

Such a topic list, keyed to your sources, will spare you the frustration of reading these three sources and flipping through them later, saying, "Now where did I read that?" At this early point, you don't need to know how you might write a paper based on this or any other topic. But a robust list with multiple topics and accurate notes for each lays the groundwork for your own discussion later and puts you in a good position to write a synthesis.

The sample entry above should be useful for responding to one of the explanatory synthesis assignments that follows the readings: to explain what an ethical dilemma is. In your reading of the various theories of ethics and the casebook of dilemmas that follow, you may decide to explain ethical dilemmas in part by explaining *types* of dilemmas—one of which would be "speaking up or not." There would be others, for instance killing (or letting another die) for the greater good and choosing to protect life over enforcing a law. Creating a topic list with multiple entries like the example above will add to your reading time, but it will save time as you prepare to write.

Following an introduction to the study of ethical dilemmas as "thought experiments," you'll read a number of cases that challenge you to decide

Group Assignment #1: Make a Topic List

Working in groups of three or four, create a topic list for the selections in this chapter, jotting down notes and page (or paragraph) references. Try several of the following topics to get you started. Find and take notes on other topics common to two or more sources. When you are done, share your topic lists with fellow group members.

- Definition of ethics
- Examples of consequence-based (teleological) ethical dilemmas/ decisions
- Examples of morality-based (deontological) ethical dilemmas/decisions
- Examples of Kohlberg's stages of moral development
- Using intuition vs. formal ethics to make decisions
- When both sides are right (or wrong)
- Difference between what is legal and what is ethical
- When must rules be overridden?
- Individual conscience vs. social order

Group Assignment #2: Create a Topic Web

Before dividing the group into three subgroups, all group members should read the selection by Ronald White. That done, each subgroup should take charge of rereading a particular ethical theory in the selection: rule-based ethics (deontology), consequence-based ethics (teleology), and virtue-based ethics. Now, reconvened as a large group, choose an ethical dilemma featured in this chapter (see pages 305–312) and discuss it from the three formal ethical perspectives. Each subgroup can present its understanding of the dilemma from one of the three ethical perspectives. Then open the discussion: To what extent do these perspectives, applied to the dilemma, suggest different courses of action? Discuss as well the differences between formal and informal responses to ethical dilemmas.

Group Assignment #3: Decide for Yourself

Two cases in this chapter come with clear arguments about ethical action(s) to be taken: "No Edit" and "Should I Protect a Patient?" Read these cases and discuss each as a group. Do you agree with the positions these authors take? Develop a logic for your responses. Provide reasons for suggesting a particular course of action.

upon a fair and reasonable course of action. What counts as "fair" and "reasonable," of course, depends on your standard of fairness and the logic you use to apply that standard. Change the standard and you may well change your decision. So we also provide in this chapter a review of formal ethical theories, or standards, that you can draw on to guide your decision making about each case. Look as well for search engine keywords that will point you to YouTube presentations of ethical dilemmas. Whether written, acted out in an episode of *Grey's Anatomy,* or reduced to a provocative animation, the ethical dilemmas that you encounter in the pages to follow will call on you to decide, if only in your mind's eye, and to defend your decision.

■ THE READINGS AND VIDEOS

WHAT IF...

Daniel Sokol

"Is there a difference between killing someone and letting them die? Are consequences all that matter, or are there some things we should never do, whatever the outcome?" Such questions lie at the heart of "thought experiments" like the four famous ones posed by Daniel Sokol in the following article (and indeed in the rest of this chapter). How we respond to such scenarios, some admittedly far-fetched, provides some insight into the moral perspectives from which we make choices every day. This piece first appeared on the BBC News Web site on May 2, 2006. Dr. Daniel K. Sokol is a medical ethicist at Imperial College in London and a barrister at Kings Bench Walk Chambers. A regular contributor to the BBC, he is also a columnist (the "Ethics Man") for the *British Medical Journal* and the author of the book *Doing Clinical Ethics,* published in 2012.

Suppose you could save five lives by taking one—what would be the correct thing to do? Such ethical dilemmas provide classic "experiments" for philosophers. Here [*BBC News* presents] four such quandaries and asks readers to vote on what they think is right....

Like scientists, philosophers use experiments to test their theories. Unlike scientists, their experiments do not require sophisticated laboratories, white-robed technicians or even rodents. They occur in the mind, and start with 'What if....'

These "thought experiments" help philosophers clarify their understanding of certain concepts and intuitions. In the field of ethics, thought experimenters typically present a dilemma, examine the most popular "intuitive" response and then show the implications for real-world issues.

But such experiments are rarely tested on large numbers of people. So to reach a larger group, here are four typical experiments. Readers are invited to vote on how they think they would act in each case.

5   Here is a well-known example:

1. Thomson's Violinist

One day, you wake up in hospital. In the nearby bed lies a world famous violinist who is connected to you with various tubes and machines.

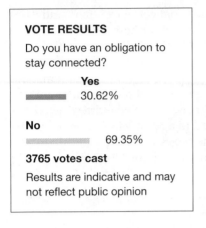

VOTE RESULTS

Do you have an obligation to stay connected?

Yes
30.62%

No
69.35%

3765 votes cast

Results are indicative and may not reflect public opinion

To your horror, you discover that you have been kidnapped by the Music Appreciation Society. Aware of the maestro's impending death, they hooked you up to the violinist.

If you stay in the hospital bed, connected to the violinist, he will be totally cured In nine months. You are unlikely to suffer harm. No one else can save him. Do you have an obligation to stay connected?

The creator of the experiment, Judith Thomson, thinks the answer is "no." It would be generous if you did, she claims, but there is no obligation to stay, even if that means the violinist will die.

So how is this bizarre scenario related to the real world? Thomson used the experiment to show that a pregnant woman need not go to full term with her baby, as long as she had taken reasonable steps to avoid getting pregnant. It is thus a "pro-choice" argument.

The violinist represents the baby, and you—in the hospital bed—play the role of the mother. If you think unhooking yourself from the violinist is acceptable, but aborting an unwanted foetus is not, what are the moral differences between the two cases? In both situations, you could save a person by bearing a great burden for nine months.

One major flaw with thought experiments, especially in ethics, is that they are rarely tested on people. The sample size is minuscule. The philosopher will simply assume that most people think that one option is right (or wrong).

10   Philippa Foot, a renowned British philosopher, believed that if a doctor, about to save a patient's life with a large dose of a scarce drug, was suddenly interrupted by the arrival of five patients each in need of one fifth of the drug (without which death would be certain), then the doctor should give it to the five. It is, after all, better to let one person die than five.

Elizabeth Anscombe, another prominent philosopher, disagreed: "There seems to me nothing wrong with giving the single patient the massive dose and letting the others die." As these assumptions about people's intuition are central to the arguments of many philosophers, and as these assumptions can be tested, why not do so?

2. The Runaway Trolley Car

One of the most famous thought experiments in ethics is "the runaway trolley." It aims to clarify how we should distinguish right from wrong.

Here is the scenario with two well-known variations.

VOTE RESULTS

Should you flip the switch?

Yes
76.85%

No
23.15%

3814 Votes Cast

Results are indicative and may not reflect public opinion

A runaway trolley car is hurtling down a track. In its path are five people who will definitely be killed unless you, a bystander, flip a switch which will divert it on to another track, where it will kill one person. Should you flip the switch?

3. The Fat Man and the Trolley Car

The runaway trolley car is hurtling down a track where it will kill five people. You are standing on a bridge above the track and, aware of the imminent disaster, you decide to jump on the track to block the trolley car. Although you will die, the five people will be saved.

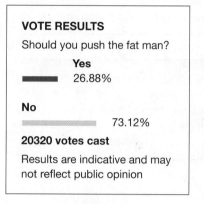

VOTE RESULTS

Should you push the fat man?

Yes

26.88%

No

73.12%

20320 votes cast

Results are indicative and may not reflect public opinion

Just before your leap, you realise that you are too light to stop the trolley. Next to you, a fat man is standing on the very edge of the bridge. He would certainly block the trolley, although he would undoubtedly die from the impact. A small nudge and he would fall right onto the track below. No one would ever know. Should you push him?

Philippa Foot would say that everyone ("without hesitation") would choose to flip the switch in the first trolley case, but that most of us would be appalled at the idea of pushing the fat man.

15

The philosophical puzzle is this: Why is it acceptable to sacrifice the one person in The Runaway Trolley Car but not in The Fat Man case? Can it ever be morally acceptable to kill an innocent person if that is the only way to save many? Should some actions—such as deliberately killing innocent people against their wishes—never be done? The last thought experiment explores this idea:

4. The Cave Explorers

An enormous rock falls and blocks the exit of a cave you and five other tourists have been exploring. Fortunately, you spot a hole elsewhere and decide to let "Big Jack" out first. But Big Jack, a man of generous proportions, gets stuck in the hole. He cannot be moved and there is no other way out.

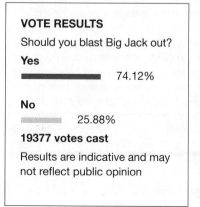

VOTE RESULTS

Should you blast Big Jack out?

Yes

74.12%

No

25.88%

19377 votes cast

Results are indicative and may not reflect public opinion

The high tide is rising and, unless you get out soon, everyone but Big Jack (whose head is sticking out of the cave) will inevitably drown. Searching through your backpack, you find a stick of dynamite. It will not move the rock, but will certainly blast Big Jack out of the hole. Big Jack, anticipating your thoughts, pleads for his life. He does not want to die, but neither do you and your four companions. Should you blast Big Jack out?

If the roles were reversed, what would you advise your trapped companions to do?

Thought experiments, although abstract, possibly implausible and open to different interpretations, can have important repercussions on the way we think and act as individuals. They raise thorny questions about morality in medicine, war, politics and indeed in everyday life.

Is there a difference between killing someone and letting them die? Are consequences all that matter, or are there some things we should never do, whatever the outcome?

By pointing out inconsistencies in our thinking, or simply encouraging us to reflect on issues we usually ignore, they can sharpen our intellect and enrich our moral lives. They also make for great conversation topics at the dinner table or at the pub. But be warned: you may lose friends as a result. And stay away from caves and bridges.

Video Link: The Trolley Car

The trolley problem discussed by Sokol and referenced in numerous books and articles on ethics has also been treated in several YouTube videos. Here's one of the best. You may want to look at others, as well, to get an idea of the various perspectives from which this particular scenario can be viewed.

Go to: YouTube

Search terms: *"presentation part 1 trolley problem"*

THE CASE OF THE COLLAPSED MINE*
Richard T. De George

Business ethics is an important subcomponent of the broader study of ethics, with many business schools requiring students to take at least one course on the subject. Studying business ethics can make one sensitive to issues and questions that might otherwise have escaped notice. A business situation fraught with dilemmas for one person might for another be simply business as usual. And this is the problem: One person sees a conflict of values; another sees none. So here is a selection that demonstrates how someone who is sensitive to ethical dilemmas would approach a particular incident. In "The Case of the Collapsed Mine," Richard T. De George presents a case study and then raises a series of questions that, in effect, provides an overview of business ethics. For instance, De George takes up questions on the value of human life as measured against the cost of designing very safe, or relatively safe, products and on the need to restructure systems that reward loyalty at the expense of morality. You may be surprised by the number of questions De George can draw from this case. As you begin to think like an ethicist, you, too, will recognize and pose such questions.

Richard T. De George is University Distinguished Professor of Philosophy and Courtesy Professor of Management at the University of Kansas. He is the author or editor of more than fifteen books and more than one hundred scholarly articles on business ethics.

The following case illustrates the sorts of questions that might arise in business ethics and various ways to approach them. Consider the case of the collapsed mine shaft. In a coal mining town of West Virginia, some miners were digging coal in a tunnel thousands of feet below the surface. Some gas buildup had been detected during the two preceding days. This had been reported by the director of safety to the mine manager. The buildup was sufficiently serious to have closed down operations until it was cleared. The owner of the mine decided that the buildup was only marginally dangerous, that he had coal orders to fill, that he could not afford to close down the mine, and that he would take the chance that the gas would dissipate before it exploded. He told the director of safety not to say anything about the danger. On May 2nd, the gas exploded. One section of the tunnel collapsed, killing three miners and trapping eight others in a pocket. The rest managed to escape.

The explosion was one of great force and the extent of the tunnel's collapse was considerable. The cost of reaching the men in time to save their lives would amount to several million dollars. The problem facing the manager was whether the expenditure of such a large sum of money was worth it. What, after all, was a human life worth? Whose decision was it and how should it be made? Did the manager owe more to the stockholders of the corporation or to the trapped workers? Should he use the slower, safer, and cheaper way of reaching them and save a large sum of money or the faster, more dangerous, and more expensive way and possibly save their lives?

He decided on the latter and asked for volunteers. Two dozen men volunteered. After three days, the operation proved to be more difficult than anyone had anticipated. There had been two more explosions and three of those involved in the rescue operation had already been killed. In the meantime, telephone contact had been made with the trapped men who had been fortunate enough to find a telephone line that was still functioning. They were starving. Having previously read about a similar case, they decided that the only way for any of them to survive long enough was to draw lots, and then kill and eat the one who drew the shortest straw. They felt that it was their duty that at least some of them should be found alive; otherwise, the three volunteers who had died rescuing them would have died in vain.

After twenty days the seven men were finally rescued alive; they had cannibalized their fellow miner. The director of safety who had detected the gas before the explosion informed the newspapers of his report. The manager was charged with criminal negligence; but before giving up his position, he fired the director of safety. The mine eventually resumed operation.

5   There are a large number of issues in the above account....

The director of safety is in some sense the hero of the story. But did he fulfill his moral obligation before the accident in obeying the manager and in not making known either to the miners, the manager's superior, or to the public the fact that the mine was unsafe? Did he have a moral obligation after the explosion and rescue to make known the fact that the manager knew the mine was unsafe? Should he have gone to the board of directors of the company with the story or to someone else within the company rather than to the newspapers? All these questions are part of the phenomenon of worker responsibility. To whom is a worker responsible and for what? Does his moral obligation end when he does what he is told? Going public with inside information such as the director of safety had is commonly known as "blowing the whistle" on the company. Frequently those who blow the whistle are fired, just as the director of safety was. The whole phenomenon of whistle blowing raises serious questions about the structure of companies in which employees find it necessary to take such drastic action and possibly suffer the loss of their jobs. Was the manager justified in firing the director of safety?

The manager is, of course, the villain of the story. He sent the miners into a situation which he knew was dangerous. But, he might argue, he did it for the good of the company. He had contracts to fulfill and obligations to the owners of the company to show a profit. He had made a bad decision. Every manager has to take risks. It just turned out that he was unlucky. Does such a defense sound plausible? Does a manager have an obligation to his workers as well as to the owners of a company? Who should take precedence and under what conditions does one group or the other become more important? Who is to decide and how?

The manager decided to try to save the trapped miners even though it would cost the company more than taking the slower route. Did he have the right to spend more of the company's money in this way? How does one evaluate human life in comparison with expenditure of money? It sounds moral to say that human life is beyond all monetary value. In a sense it is. However, there are limits which society and people in it can place on the amount they will, can, and should spend to save lives. The way to decide, however, does not seem to be to equate the value of a person's life with the amount of income he would produce in his remaining years, if he lives to a statistically average age, minus the resources he would use up in that period. How does one decide? How do and should people weigh human lives against monetary expenditure? In designing automobiles, in building roads, in making many products, there is a trade-off between the maximum safety that one can build into the product and the cost of the product. Extremely safe cars cost more to build than relatively safe cars. We can express the difference in terms of the number of people likely to die driving the relatively safe ones as opposed to the extremely safe ones. Should such decisions be made by manufacturers, consumers, government, or in some other way?

The manager asked for volunteers for the rescue work. Three of these volunteers died. Was the manager responsible for their deaths in the same way that he was responsible for the deaths of the three miners who had died in the first mine explosion? Was the company responsible for the deaths in either case? Do companies have obligations to their employees and the employees' families in circumstances such as these, or are the obligations only those of the managers? If the manager had warned the miners that the level of gas was dangerous, and they had decided that they wanted their pay for that day and would work anyway, would the manager have been responsible for their deaths? Is it moral for people to take dangerous jobs simply to earn money? Is a system that impels people to take such jobs for money a moral system? To what extent is a company morally obliged to protect its workers and to prevent them from taking chances?

10   The manager was charged with criminal negligence under the law. Was the company responsible for anything? Should the company have been sued by the

family of the dead workers? If the company were sued and paid damages to the families, the money would come from company profits and hence from the profits of the shareholders. Is it fair that the shareholders be penalized for an incident they had nothing to do with? How is responsibility shared and/or distributed in a company, and can companies be morally responsible for what is done in their name? Are only human beings moral agents and is it a mistake to use moral language with respect to companies, corporations, and businesses?

The decision of the trapped miners to cast lots to determine who would be killed and eaten also raises a number of moral issues. Our moral intuitions can provide in this case no ready answer as to whether their decision was morally justifiable, since the case is not an ordinary one. How to think about such an issue raises the question of how moral problems are to be resolved and underscores the need for some moral theory as guidelines by which we can decide unusual cases. A number of principles seem to conflict—the obligation not to kill, the consideration that it is better for one person to die rather than eight, the fact noted by the miners that three persons had already died trying to rescue them, and so on. The issue here is not one peculiar to business ethics, but it is rather a moral dilemma that requires some technique of moral argument to solve.

The case does not tell us what happened to either the manager or the director of safety. Frequently the sequel to such cases is surprising. The managers come off free and ultimately rewarded for their concern for the company's interest, while the whistle blower is black-balled throughout the industry. The morality of such an outcome seems obvious—justice does not always triumph. What can be done to see that it triumphs more often is a question that involves restructuring the system.

Business ethics is sometimes seen as conservative and is also used as a defense of the status quo. Sometimes it is seen as an attack on the status quo and hence viewed as radical. Ideally it should be neither. It should strive for objectivity. When there are immoral practices, structures, and actions occurring, business ethics should be able to show that these actions are immoral and why. But it should also be able to supply the techniques with which the practices and structures that are moral can be defended as such. The aim of business ethics is neither defense of the status quo nor its radical change. Rather it should serve to remedy those aspects or structures that need change and protect those that are moral. It is not a panacea. It can secure change only if those in power take the appropriate action. But unless some attention is paid to business ethics, the moral debate about practices and principles central to our society will be more poorly and probably more immorally handled than otherwise.

A FRAMEWORK FOR THINKING ETHICALLY
Manual Velasquez, Dennis Moberg, Michael J. Meyer et al.

Some people confronted with an ethical dilemma might find no dilemma at all: They seem to instinctively know which is the right choice (for them) and to act upon it. Others find themselves in the archetypal predicament of having a devil perched on one shoulder and an angel on the other, with devil and angel offering conflicting advice. In some situations, there may be a devil on *each* side, with the choice being between two terrible alternatives—the worst of these being known as a "Sophie's Choice" dilemma, a reference to the main character of William Styron's novel, forced to choose which of her two children will be executed at a Nazi concentration camp.

Although ethics can offer little useful guidance in such worst-case scenarios, it can, in most everyday situations, offer a framework that will help people to make choices they can feel good about. One such framework is offered in the following selection, produced by the Markkula Center for Applied Ethics. After explaining what ethics is *not*, the authors provide an overview of the main approaches to ethical decision making: the utilitarian approach, the rights approach, the fairness or justice approach, and so on. The authors conclude with a series of questions that, when answered, will help people make ethical choices based on which approach they find most useful.

The Markkula Center for Applied Ethics, based at Santa Clara University, a Jesuit institution south of San Francisco, "seeks to encourage dialogue on the ethical dimensions of current issues." This piece appears on the center's Web site. Throughout the chapter, we will refer to this selection as the "Markkula framework."

This document is designed as an introduction to thinking ethically. We all have an image of our better selves—of how we are when we act ethically or are "at our best." We probably also have an image of what an ethical community, an ethical business, an ethical government, or an ethical society should be. Ethics really has to do with all these levels—acting ethically as individuals, creating ethical organizations and governments, and making our society as a whole ethical in the way it treats everyone.

What Is Ethics?

Simply stated, ethics refers to standards of behavior that tell us how human beings ought to act in the many situations in which they find themselves—as friends, parents, children, citizens, businesspeople, teachers, professionals, and so on.

It is helpful to identify what ethics is NOT:

• Ethics is not the same as feelings. Feelings provide important information for our ethical choices. Some people have highly developed habits that make them feel bad when they do something wrong, but many people feel good even though they are doing something wrong. And often our feelings will tell us it is uncomfortable to do the right thing if it is hard.

• Ethics is not religion. Many people are not religious, but ethics applies to everyone. Most religions do advocate high ethical standards but sometimes do not address all the types of problems we face.

• Ethics is not following the law. A good system of law does incorporate many ethical standards, but law can deviate from what is ethical. Law can become ethically corrupt, as some totalitarian regimes have made it. Law can be a function of power alone and designed to serve the interests of narrow groups. Law may have a difficult time designing or enforcing standards in some important areas, and may be slow to address new problems.

• Ethics is not following culturally accepted norms. Some cultures are quite ethical, but others become corrupt or blind to certain ethical concerns (as the United States was to slavery before the Civil War). "When in Rome, do as the Romans do" is not a satisfactory ethical standard.

- Ethics is not science. Social and natural science can provide important data to help us make better ethical choices. But science alone does not tell us what we ought to do. Science may provide an explanation for what humans are like. But ethics provides reasons for how humans ought to act. And just because something is scientifically or technologically possible, it may not be ethical to do it.

Why Identifying Ethical Standards Is Hard

There are two fundamental problems in identifying the ethical standards we are to follow:

1. On what do we base our ethical standards?
2. How do those standards get applied to specific situations we face?

5 If our ethics are not based on feelings, religion, law, accepted social practice, or science, what are they based on? Many philosophers and ethicists have helped us answer this critical question. They have suggested at least five different sources of ethical standards we should use.

Five Sources of Ethical Standards

The Utilitarian Approach

Some ethicists emphasize that the ethical action is the one that provides the most good or does the least harm, or, to put it another way, produces the greatest balance of good over harm. The ethical corporate action, then, is the one that produces the greatest good and does the least harm for all who are affected—customers, employees, shareholders, the community, and the environment. Ethical warfare balances the good achieved in ending terrorism with the harm done to all parties through death, injuries, and destruction. The utilitarian approach deals with consequences; it tries both to increase the good done and to reduce the harm done.

The Rights Approach

Other philosophers and ethicists suggest that the ethical action is the one that best protects and respects the moral rights of those affected. This approach starts from the belief that humans have a dignity based on their human nature per se or on their ability to choose freely what they do with their lives. On the basis of such dignity, they have a right to be treated as ends and not merely as means to other ends. The list of moral rights—including the rights to make one's own choices about what kind of life to lead, to be told the truth, not to be injured, to a degree of privacy, and so on—is widely debated; some now argue that non-humans have rights, too. Also, it is often said that rights imply duties—in particular, the duty to respect others' rights.

The Fairness or Justice Approach

Aristotle and other Greek philosophers have contributed the idea that all equals should be treated equally. Today we use this idea to say that ethical actions treat all human beings equally—or if unequally, then fairly based on some standard that is defensible. We pay people more based on their harder work or the greater amount that they contribute to an organization, and say that is fair. But there is a debate over CEO salaries that are hundreds of times larger than the pay of others; many ask whether the huge disparity is based on a defensible standard or whether it is the result of an imbalance of power and hence is unfair.

The Common Good Approach

The Greek philosophers have also contributed the notion that life in community is a good in itself and our actions should contribute to that life. This approach suggests that the interlocking relationships of society are the basis of ethical reasoning and that respect and compassion for all others—especially the vulnerable—are requirements of such reasoning. This approach also calls attention to the common conditions that are important to the welfare of everyone. This may be a system of laws, effective police and fire departments, health care, a public educational system, or even public recreational areas.

The Virtue Approach

10   A very ancient approach to ethics is that ethical actions ought to be consistent with certain ideal virtues that provide for the full development of our humanity. These virtues are dispositions and habits that enable us to act according to the highest potential of our character and on behalf of values like truth and beauty. Honesty, courage, compassion, generosity, tolerance, love, fidelity, integrity, fairness, self-control, and prudence are all examples of virtues. Virtue ethics asks of any action, "What kind of person will I become if I do this?" or "Is this action consistent with my acting at my best?"

Putting the Approaches Together

Each of the approaches helps us determine what standards of behavior can be considered ethical. There are still problems to be solved, however.

The first problem is that we may not agree on the content of some of these specific approaches.

We may not all agree to the same set of human and civil rights.

We may not agree on what constitutes the common good. We may not even agree on what is a good and what is a harm.

15   The second problem is that the different approaches may not all answer the question "What is ethical?" in the same way. Nonetheless, each approach gives us important information with which to determine what is ethical in a particular circumstance. And much more often than not, the different approaches do lead to similar answers.

Making Decisions

Making good ethical decisions requires a trained sensitivity to ethical issues and a practiced method for exploring the ethical aspects of a decision and weighing the considerations that should impact our choice of a course of action. Having a method for ethical decision making is absolutely essential. When practiced regularly, the method becomes so familiar that we work through it automatically without consulting the specific steps.

The more novel and difficult the ethical choice we face, the more we need to rely on discussion and dialogue with others about the dilemma. Only by careful exploration of the problem, aided by the insights and different perspectives of others, can we make good ethical choices in such situations.

We have found the following framework for ethical decision making a useful method for exploring ethical dilemmas and identifying ethical courses of action.

A Framework for Ethical Decision Making

Recognize an Ethical Issue

1. Could this decision or situation be damaging to someone or to some group? Does this decision involve a choice between a good and bad alternative, or perhaps between two "goods" or between two "bads"?

2. Is this issue about more than what is legal or what is most efficient? If so, how?

Get the Facts

3. What are the relevant facts of the case? What facts are not known? Can I learn more about the situation? Do I know enough to make a decision?

4. What individuals and groups have an important stake in the outcome? Are some concerns more important? Why?

5. What are the options for acting? Have all the relevant persons and groups been consulted? Have I identified creative options?

Evaluate Alternative Actions

6. Evaluate the options by asking the following questions:
   - Which option will produce the most good and do the least harm? (The Utilitarian Approach)
   - Which option best respects the rights of all who have a stake? (The Rights Approach)
   - Which option treats people equally or proportionately? (The Justice Approach)
   - Which option best serves the community as a whole, not just some members? (The Common Good Approach)
   - Which option leads me to act as the sort of person I want to be? (The Virtue Approach)

Make a Decision and Test It

7. Considering all these approaches, which option best addresses the situation?

8. If I told someone I respect—or told a television audience—which option I have chosen, what would they say?

Act and Reflect on the Outcome

9. How can my decision be implemented with the greatest care and attention to the concerns of all stakeholders?

10. How did my decision turn out and what have I learned from this specific situation?

This framework for thinking ethically is the product of dialogue and debate at the Markkula Center for Applied Ethics at Santa Clara University. Primary contributors include Manuel Velasquez, Dennis Moberg, Michael J. Meyer, Thomas Shanks, Margaret R. McLean, David DeCosse, Claire André, and Kirk O. Hanson. It was last revised in May 2009.

MORAL INQUIRY

Ronald F. White

In the following selection, Ronald F. White provides a closer examination of some of the major approaches to ethical decision making that are discussed in the Markkula framework. Don't be intimidated by White's terminology: what he calls "teleological approaches" is essentially the same as what the authors of "A Framework for Thinking Ethically" call "the utilitarian approach." And when White contrasts teleological theories with "deonotological theories," he's actually making the same distinction as Daniel Sokol ("What If..."), who asks: "Are consequences all that matter, or are there some things we should never do, whatever the outcome?" The first question is a teleological one; the second is deontological. White fleshes out these distinct approaches with his discussions of particular examples.

White is a professor of philosophy at the College of St. Joseph in Cincinnati. With specialties in health care ethics, business ethics, and societal and political philosophy, he has written numerous essays and book reviews for professional journals. This selection is an excerpt from his unpublished book *Moral Inquiry* (available online).

Whatever Truth is, we do know that our beliefs about it have a tendency to change over time. I used to believe in Santa Claus, the Easter Bunny, and governmental efficiency. Scientists used to believe that the earth is the center of the universe, and that bloodletting cures insanity. Based on the flow of history, it is safe to assume that most of what we believe to be true today will eventually be regarded as either imprecise or false. We also know that human beliefs concerning Truth vary between individuals, groups of individuals, and between cultures. Generally speaking, we deal with this *cognitive dissonance* by summarily dismissing beliefs that conflict with our own. Our beliefs are true, theirs are false.

Human beings also believe that some human behavior is good and praiseworthy, and that other behavior is bad and blameworthy. It is true that human beings murder each other, steal from each other, drive too fast, and fart in elevators. Under most circumstances, none of these behaviors are considered to be good or praiseworthy, although there may be particular circumstances when they might be. Farting is a perfectly natural phenomenon open to descriptive inquiry. It can be explained in terms of the laws of human physiology, (the production of nitrogenous waste) and the laws of physics: our knowledge of both sets of laws change over time. Killing and stealing can also be explained in biological terms. But many philosophers argue that there is a difference between inquiring into whether something is true and/or whether it is good.

• • •

All moral theories address the questions of what is Good, why it's Good, and where the Good is located? If there is anything "easy" about moral inquiry it's the fact that there are only three basic kinds of prescriptive moral theories: *teleological theories*, *deontological theories, and virtue-based theories.* Unfortunately, they often (but not always) provide different and mostly conflicting answers to these basic questions.

Teleological Ethical Theories

Teleological moral theories locate moral goodness in the consequences of our behavior and not the behavior itself. According to teleological (or *consequentialist*) moral theory, all rational human actions are teleological in the sense that we reason about the *means* of achieving certain *ends*. Moral behavior, therefore, is goal-directed. I have ice in my gutters right now. I am deliberating about when and how to get that ice out in order to prevent water damage inside the house. There are many strategies (means) that I might employ to remove that ice (end). Should I send my oldest son, Eli, up on the icy roof today? After careful deliberation I finally decided not send him on the roof because it is slippery and he might fall. How did I decide? Well, I took into account the possible consequences. There is nothing inherently wrong with climbing on the roof. What made roof climbing the morally wrong thing to do at this particular time and place were the possible consequences. The issue has moral significance in so far as it affects persons. So from the teleological point of view, human behavior is neither right nor wrong in and of itself. What matters is what might happen as a consequence of those actions in any given context. Thus, it is the contextualized consequences that make our behavior, good or bad, right or wrong. In the case of roof climbing in the winter, I decided to climb up on the roof myself, because it's dangerous. Eli might fall off and get hurt. If that happened, my wife would blame me and so would the community. But if I fell off the roof, I would be judged to be imprudent, but not necessarily immoral.

5   From a teleological standpoint, stealing, for example, could not be judged to be inherently right or wrong independent of the context and the foreseeable consequences. Suppose I am contemplating stealing a loaf of bread from the neighborhood grocery store. Many moral theorists would argue that morality requires an analysis of my motives (or intent) that brought about that behavior. However, from a teleological perspective, motives really have nothing to do with the rightness or wrongness of the act. What really matters lies in the potential pains and pleasures associated with the short-term and long-term consequences. If my children were starving, and if stealing a loaf of bread would immediately prevent them from starving, then I might seriously consider stealing. But I'd have to know if the consequences would significantly harm the grocery store. What would be the odds of getting caught? If I got caught, what would happen to me? Would I go to jail? Get fined? If I went to jail, who would take care of my children? Therefore, even if my motive (preventing my children from starving) was praiseworthy, the act of stealing might still be wrong because other actions might be more cost-effective in bringing about the desired consequences. Perhaps I'd be better off signing up for food stamps or asking the storeowner to give me day-old bread. On the other hand, suppose that there were no other options and that

I invented a foolproof system for stealing bread. Would I be wrong for doing it? If you think about the consequences of your actions when you make moral decisions, you are applying teleological moral theory.

• • •

Deontological Theories

There are many philosophers who reject the entire teleological agenda by arguing that moral goodness has nothing to do with...consequences. *Deontological theories* are by definition *duty-based.* That is to say, that morality, according to deontologists, consists in the fulfillment of moral *obligations*, or *duties.* Duties, in the deontological tradition, are most often associated with obeying *absolute moral rules.* Hence, human beings are morally required to do (or not to do) certain acts in order to uphold a rule or law. The rightness or wrongness of a moral rule is determined independent of its consequences or how happiness or pleasure is distributed as a result of abiding by that rule, or not abiding by it.

It's not difficult to see why philosophers would be drawn to this position.... In early nineteenth-century America, many members of the anti-slavery movement argued that slavery was wrong, even though slaveholders and southern society in general, economically benefited from it. Suppose, also that the slaveholders were also able to condition the slaves to the point where they actually enjoyed living under slavery. From a teleological perspective, slavery might appear to be an ideal economic institution. Everybody is happy!

A deontologist, however, would argue that even if the American government conducted a detailed cost/benefit analysis of slavery and decided that it created more pleasure in society than pain, it would still be wrong. Therefore, deontologists believe that right and wrong have nothing to do with pleasure, pain, or consequences. Morality is based on whether acts conflict with moral rules or not, and the motivation behind those acts. An act is therefore good if and only if it was performed out of a desire to do one's duty and obey a rule. In other words, act out of a good will. Hence, slavery is wrong, not because of its negative consequences, but because it violates an absolute moral rule. The problem here is: "How does one distinguish absolute moral rules from mere convention, prudence, or legality...?"

• • •

Virtue-Based Moral Theories

In the Western world (and the Eastern World) there is a venerable system of moral reasoning based on the idea of virtue. Let's call those various systems *virtue-based moral systems.* In the history of Western moral theory, there are two different types of virtue-based systems. The nonsecular line of inquiry relies on divine command theory in order to discern moral virtues from vices, as illustrated by the Judeo-Christian moral tradition. The secular line of inquiry relies primarily on reason and experience, and not divine command theory. It goes back to the ancient Greeks, via the writings of Homer, Hesiod, Plato, and Aristotle....

10   All virtue-based moral systems focus on big questions such as: "What is the 'Good Life?'" And "How do I go about living the 'Good Life?'" Therefore, they tend to focus on how to live one's life over the long run, rather than how to address

particular issues that pop up at any given time. In short, virtue-based systems focus on character development within harmonious communities. These systems also tend to rely on moral exemplars, or role models. Once a person has internalized the virtue of kindness, then that person will exemplify that virtue in his/her actions.

All virtue-based moral systems differentiate between virtues (good behavior) and vices (bad behavior). Ultimately, non-secular virtue-based theories differentiate between virtues and vices based on religions authorities, usually traced back to the authority of the Bible and/or its official interpreters. The Christian authorities have identified *faith, hope*, and *charity* as its primary virtues. If you pursue these ideals over the course of your lifetime, you'll lead a "good life."

Aristotle believed moral virtue consists in choosing the mean between the extremes of excess and deficiency within any given sphere of action. The vice of excess consists in choosing too much of a good thing and the vice of deficiency consists of not enough. Excellence is found midway between the two. For example, the virtue of bravery can be found midway between the vices of cowardice and foolhardiness.

■ Video Link: Grey's Anatomy (a medical dilemma)

Go to: YouTube

Search terms: *"greys anatomy presentation"* (length: 9:32)

HEINZ'S DILEMMA: KOHLBERG'S SIX STAGES OF MORAL DEVELOPMENT*

William Crain

A distinctly different take on ethical decision making is provided by William Crain in the following selection, which discusses the theory of Lawrence Kohlberg (1927–87), a psychologist at the Department of Psychology at the University of Chicago and the Graduate School of Education at Harvard University. Kohlberg was much influenced by the work of Swiss psychologist Jean Piaget (1896–1980), who studied the cognitive and moral development of children. Kohlberg studied both children and adolescents in developing his own approach to moral development. It was in his 1958 doctoral dissertation, based upon his interviews with boys and girls from the United States and around the world, that he first expounded his six stages of moral development, each showing a different and progressively more complex approach to moral reasoning and decision making.

In the following selection, Crain discusses Kohlberg's six stages of moral development, focusing on how they apply to his famous example of the Heinz dilemma ("Heinz steals the drug"). You should be able to draw upon Crain's discussion of Kohlberg's stages and Heinz's dilemma when you later attempt to analyze the choices represented in other cases in this chapter.

This selection is drawn from Crain's *Theories of Development: Concepts and Applications*.

---

*Crain, William, *Theories of Development: Concepts and Applications*, 6th Ed., © 2011, pp. 159–165. Reprinted and Electronically reproduced by permission of Pearson Education, Inc., Upper Saddle River, New Jersey.

Kohlberg's Method

Kohlberg's (1958a) core sample was comprised of 72 boys, from both middle- and lower-class families in Chicago. They were ages 10, 13, and 16. He later added to his sample younger children, delinquents, and boys and girls from other American cities and from other countries (1963, 1970).

The basic interview consists of a series of dilemmas such as the following:

Heinz Steals the Drug

> In Europe, a woman was near death from a special kind of cancer. There was one drug that the doctors thought might save her. It was a form of radium that a druggist in the same town had recently discovered. The drug was expensive to make, but the druggist was charging ten times what the drug cost him to make. He paid $200 for the radium and charged $2,000 for a small dose of the drug. The sick woman's husband, Heinz, went to everyone he knew to borrow the money, but he could only get together about $1,000 which is half of what it cost. He told the druggist that his wife was dying and asked him to sell it cheaper or let him pay later. But the druggist said: "No, I discovered the drug and I'm going to make money from it." So Heinz got desperate and broke into the man's store to steal the drug for his wife. Should the husband have done that? (Kohlberg, 1963, p. 19)

Kohlberg is not really interested in whether the subject says "yes" or "no" to this dilemma but in the reasoning behind the answer. The interviewer wants to know why the subject thinks Heinz should or should not have stolen the drug. The interview schedule then asks new questions which help one understand the child's reasoning. For example, children are asked if Heinz had a right to steal the drug, if he was violating the druggist's rights, and what sentence the judge should give him once he was caught. Once again, the main concern is with the reasoning behind the answers. The interview then goes on to give more dilemmas in order to get a good sampling of a subject's moral thinking. [See the Video Link following this reading (p. 305) for two videos dealing with the Heinz dilemma.]

Once Kohlberg had classified the various responses into stages, he wanted to know whether his classification was *reliable*. In particular, he wanted to know if others would score the protocols in the same way. Other judges independently scored a sample of responses, and he calculated the degree to which all raters agreed. This procedure is called *interrater reliability*. Kohlberg found these agreements to be high, as he has in his subsequent work, but whenever investigators use Kohlberg's interview, they also should check for interrater reliability before scoring the entire sample.

Kohlberg's Six Stages

Level 1. Preconventional Morality

5 **Stage 1. Obedience and Punishment Orientation.** Kohlberg's stage 1 is similar to Piaget's first stage of moral thought. The child assumes that powerful authorities hand down a fixed set of rules which he or she must unquestioningly obey. To the Heinz dilemma, the child typically says that Heinz was wrong to steal the drug because "It's against the law," or "It's bad to steal," as if this were all there were

to it. When asked to elaborate, the child usually responds in terms of the consequences involved, explaining that stealing is bad "because you'll get punished" (Kohlberg, 1958b).

Although the vast majority of children at stage 1 oppose Heinz's theft, it is still possible for a child to support the action and still employ stage 1 reasoning. For example, a child might say, "Heinz can steal it because he asked first and it's not like he stole something big; he won't get punished" (see Rest, 1973). Even though the child agrees with Heinz's action, the reasoning is still stage 1; the concern is with what authorities permit and punish.

Kohlberg calls stage 1 thinking "preconventional" because children do not yet speak as members of society. Instead, they see morality as something external to themselves, as that which the big people say they must do.

Stage 2. Individualism and Exchange. At this stage children recognize that there is not just one right view that is handed down by the authorities. Different individuals have different viewpoints. "Heinz," they might point out, "might think it's right to take the drug, the druggist would not." Since everything is *relative,* each person is free to pursue his or her *individual* interests. One boy said that Heinz might steal the drug if he wanted his wife to live, but that he doesn't have to if he wants to marry someone younger and better-looking (Kohlberg, 1963, p. 24). Another boy said Heinz might steal it because maybe they had children and he might need someone at home to look after them. But maybe he shouldn't steal it because they might put him in prison for more years than he could stand. (Colby and Kauffman. 1983, p. 300)

What is right for Heinz, then, is what meets his own self-interests.

10   You might have noticed that children at both stages 1 and 2 talk about punishment. However, they perceive it differently. At stage 1 punishment is tied up in the child's mind with wrongness; punishment "proves" that disobedience is wrong. At stage 2, in contrast, punishment is simply a risk that one naturally wants to avoid.

Although stage 2 respondents sometimes sound amoral, they do have some sense of right action. This is a notion of *fair exchange* or fair deals. The philosophy is one of returning favors—"If you scratch my back, I'll scratch yours." To the Heinz story, subjects often say that Heinz was right to steal the drug because the druggist was unwilling to make a fair deal; he was "trying to rip Heinz off." Or they might say that he should steal for his wife "because she might return the favor some day" (Gibbs et al., 1983, p. 19).

Respondents at stage 2 are still said to reason at the preconventional level because they speak as isolated individuals rather than as members of society. They see individuals exchanging favors, but there is still no identification with the values of the family or community.

Level II. Conventional Morality

Stage 3. Good Interpersonal Relationships. At this stage children—who are by now usually entering their teens—see morality as more than simple deals. They believe that people should live up to the expectations of the family and community and behave in "good" ways. Good behavior means having good motives and interpersonal feelings such as love, empathy, trust, and concern for others. Heinz, they typically argue, was right to steal the drug because "He was a good man for wanting to save her," and "His intentions were good, that of saving the life of someone he loves." Even if Heinz doesn't love his wife, these subjects often say, he should steal the drug because "I don't think any husband should sit back and watch his wife die" (Gibbs et al., 1983, pp. 36–42; Kohlberg, 1958b).

If Heinz's motives were good, the druggist's were bad. The druggist, stage 3 subjects emphasize, was "selfish," "greedy," and "only interested in himself, not another life." Sometimes the respondents become so angry with the druggist that they say that he ought to be put in jail (Gibbs et al., 1983, pp. 26–29, 40–42). A typical stage 3 response is that of Don, age 13:

> It was really the druggist's fault, he was unfair, trying to overcharge and letting someone die. Heinz loved his wife and wanted to save her. I think anyone would. I don't think they would put him in jail. The judge would look at all sides, and see that the druggist was charging too much. (Kohlberg, 1963, p. 25)

15   We see that Don defines the issue in terms of the actors' character traits and motives. He talks about the loving husband, the unfair druggist, and the understanding judge. His answer deserves the label "conventional morality" because it assumes that the attitude expressed would be shared by the entire community— "anyone" would be right to do what Heinz did (Kohlberg, 1963, p. 25).

As mentioned earlier, there are similarities between Kohlberg's first three stages and Piaget's two stages. In both sequences there is a shift from unquestioning obedience to a relativistic outlook and to a concern for good motives. For Kohlberg, however, these shifts occur in three stages rather than two.

Stage 4. Maintaining the Social Order. Stage 3 reasoning works best in two-person relationships with family members or close friends, where one can make a real effort to get to know the other's feelings and needs and try to help. At stage 4, in contrast, the respondent becomes more broadly concerned with *society as a whole*. Now the emphasis is on obeying laws, respecting authority, and performing one's duties so that the social order is maintained. In response to the Heinz story, many subjects say they understand that Heinz's motives were good, but they cannot condone the theft. What would happen if we all started breaking the laws whenever we felt we had a good reason? The result would be chaos; society couldn't function. As one subject explained,

> I don't want to sound like Spiro Agnew[1], law and order and wave the flag, but if everybody did as he wanted to do, set up his own beliefs as to right and wrong, then I think you would have chaos. The only thing I think we have in civilization nowadays is some sort of legal structure which people are sort of bound to follow. [Society needs] a centralizing framework. (Gibbs et al., 1983, pp. 140–41)

---

[1]Spiro Agnew, Vice President of the United States (1969–73) under President Richard M. Nixon, was famous (or notorious) for his blistering attacks on anti-government protestors and counter-culture types. He characterized one group of opponents as "an effete corps of impudent snobs who characterize themselves as intellectuals" and was given to alliterative insults like "pusillanimous pussyfooters" and "nattering nabobs of negativism." Agnew resigned the vice presidency in 1973 just before pleading no contest to criminal charges of tax evasion for accepting bribes while serving as governor of Maryland.

Because stage 4, subjects make moral decisions from the perspective of society as a whole, they think from a full-fledged member-of-society perspective (Colby and Kohlberg, 1983, p. 27).

You will recall that stage 1 children also generally oppose stealing because it breaks the law. Superficially, stage 1 and stage 4 subjects are giving the same response, so we see here why Kohlberg insists that we must probe into the reasoning behind the overt response. Stage 1 children say, "It's wrong to steal" and "It's against the law," but they cannot elaborate any further, except to say that stealing can get a person jailed. Stage 4 respondents, in contrast, have a conception of the function of laws for society as a whole—a conception which far exceeds the grasp of the younger child.

Level III. Postconventional Morality

20 **Stage 5. Social Contract and Individual Rights.** At stage 4, people want to keep society functioning. However, a smoothly functioning society is not necessarily a good one. A totalitarian society might be well-organized, but it is hardly the moral ideal. At stage 5, people begin to ask, "What makes for a good society?" They begin to think about society in a very theoretical way, stepping back from their own society and considering the rights and values that a society ought to uphold. They then evaluate existing societies in terms of these prior considerations. They are said to take a "prior-to-society" perspective (Colby and Kohlberg, 1983, p. 22).

Stage 5 respondents basically believe that a good society is best conceived as a social contract into which people freely enter to work toward the benefit of all. They recognize that different social groups within a society will have different values, but they believe that all rational people would agree on two points. First they would all want certain basic *rights,* such as liberty and life, to be protected. Second, they would want some *democratic* procedures for changing unfair law and for improving society.

In response to the Heinz dilemma, stage 5 respondents make it clear that they do not generally favor breaking laws; laws are social contracts that we agree to uphold until we can change them by democratic means. Nevertheless, the wife's right to live is a moral right that must be protected. Thus, stage 5 respondents sometimes defend Heinz's theft in strong language:

> It is the husband's duty to save his wife. The fact that her life is in danger transcends every other standard you might use to judge his action. Life is more important than property.

This young man went on to say that "from a moral standpoint" Heinz should save the life of even a stranger, since to be consistent, the value of a life means any life. When asked if the judge should punish Heinz, he replied:

> Usually the moral and legal standpoints coincide. Here they conflict. The judge should weight the moral standpoint more heavily but preserve the legal law in punishing Heinz lightly. (Kohlberg, 1976, p. 38)

Stage 5 subjects, then, talk about "morality" and "rights" that take some priority over particular laws. Kohlberg insists, however, that we do not judge people to be at stage 5 merely from their verbal labels. We need to look at their social perspective and mode of reasoning. At stage 4, too, subjects frequently talk about the "right to life," but for them this right is legitimized by the authority of their social or religious group (e.g., by the Bible). Presumably, if their group valued property over life, they would too. At stage 5, in contrast, people are making more of an independent effort to think out what any society ought to value. They often reason, for example, that property has little meaning without life. They are trying to determine logically what a society ought to be like (Kohlberg, 1981, pp. 21–22; Gibbs et al., 1983, p. 83).

25   **Stage 6: Universal Principles.** Stage 5 respondents are working toward a conception of the good society. They suggest that we need to (a) protect certain individual rights and (b) settle disputes through democratic processes. However, democratic processes alone do not always result in outcomes that we intuitively sense are just. A majority, for example, may vote for a law that hinders a minority. Thus, Kohlberg believes that there must be a higher stage—stage 6—which defines the principles by which we achieve justice.

Kohlberg's conception of justice follows that of the philosophers Kant and Rawls, as well as great moral leaders such as Gandhi and Martin Luther King. According to these people, the principles of justice require us to treat the claims of all parties in an impartial manner, respecting the basic dignity of all people as individuals. The principles of justice are therefore universal; they apply to all. Thus, for example, we would not vote for a law that aids some people but hurts others. The principles of justice guide us toward decisions based on an equal respect for all.

In actual practice, Kohlberg says, we can reach just decisions by looking at a situation through one another's eyes. In the Heinz dilemma, this would mean that all parties—the druggist, Heinz, and his wife—take the roles of the others. To do this in an impartial manner, people can assume a "veil of ignorance" (Rawls, 1971), acting as if they do not know which role they will eventually occupy. If the druggist did this, even he would recognize that life must take priority over property; for he wouldn't want to risk finding himself in the wife's shoes with property valued over life. Thus, they would all agree that the wife must be saved—this would be the fair solution. Such a solution, we must note, requires not only impartiality, but the principle that everyone is given full and equal respect. If the wife were considered of less value than the others, a just solution could not be reached.

Until recently, Kohlberg had been scoring some of his subjects at stage 6, but he has temporarily stopped doing so, For one thing, he and other researchers had not been finding subjects who consistently reasoned at this stage. Also, Kohlberg has concluded that his interview dilemmas are not useful for distinguishing between stage 5 and stage 6 thinking. He believes that stage 6 has a clearer and broader conception of universal principles (which include justice as well as individual rights), but feels that his interview fails to draw out this broader understanding. Consequently, he has temporarily dropped stage 6 from his scoring manual, calling it a "theoretical stage" and scoring all postconventional responses as stage 5 (Colby and Kohlberg, 1983, p. 28).

Theoretically, one issue that distinguishes stage 5 from stage 6 is civil disobedience. Stage 5 would be more hesitant to endorse civil disobedience because of its commitment to the social contract and to changing laws through democratic agreements. Only when an individual right is clearly at stake does violating the law seem justified. At stage 6, in contrast, a commitment to justice makes the rationale for civil disobedience stronger and broader. Martin Luther King, for example, argued that laws are only valid insofar as they are grounded in justice, and that a commitment to justice carries with it an obligation to disobey unjust laws. King also recognized, of course, the general need for laws and democratic processes (stages 4 and 5), and he was therefore willing to accept the penalties for his actions. Nevertheless, he believed that the higher principle of justice required civil disobedience (Kohlberg, 1981, p. 43).

Summary

30 At stage 1 children think of what is right as that which authority says is right. Doing the right thing is obeying authority and avoiding punishment. At stage 2, children are no longer so impressed by any single authority; they see that there are different sides to any issue. Since everything is relative, one is free to pursue one's own interests, although it is often useful to make deals and exchange favors with others.

At stages 3 and 4, young people think as members of the conventional society with its values, norms, and expectations. At stage 3, they emphasize being a good person, which basically means having helpful motives toward people close to one. At stage 4, the concern shifts toward obeying laws to maintain society as a whole.

At stages 5 and 6 people are less concerned with maintaining society for its own sake, and more concerned with the principles and values that make for a good society. At stage 5 they emphasize basic rights and the democratic processes that give everyone a say, and at stage 6 they define the principles by which agreement will be most just.

Video Link: The Heinz Dilemma

There are many treatments on the Heinz Dilemma on YouTube. Among the best:

Go to: YouTube

Search terms: *"heinz dilemma kohlbergs theory moral development"* (select video with length: 3:00)

"kohlbergs moral development theory" (select video with length: 4:17)

■ A CASEBOOK OF ETHICAL DILEMMAS

This section presents an array of cases, both real and hypothetical, that invite you to decide on an ethical course of action. In making your decision, you should be guided not only by your innate sense of what is the right thing to do, but also by the kind of ethical frameworks discussed in Velasquez et al.,

White, and Crain's treatment of Kohlberg's stages of moral development. Consider, for example, the "lifeboat" case, in which ten people want to climb into a lifeboat that can only hold six. In choosing, for example, whether to allow either a lifeguard or an elementary school teacher into the lifeboat, should utilitarian considerations prevail? Considerations of justice or of rights? And in the Klosterman scenario, is it better for a doctor to respect the right of a patient to have his doctor maintain confidentiality or the right of an innocent man not to have to rot in jail?

THE LIFEBOAT
Rosetta Lee

This case, a version of the familiar lifeboat scenario, was developed by Rosetta Lee as an assignment for The Seattle Girls' School. Note that while this scenario is quite specific, it has applications in a variety of other contexts. For example, which of several candidates should be first in line for an organ transplant? How do we decide who gets the vaccine when only limited supplies are available?

Note: You can see an intriguing dramatization of the issues posed in "The Lifeboat" (and at least one of the other scenarios in this chapter, such as "The Runaway Trolley") in the 2014 film *After the Dark*, which poses the question: Which 10 of 21 individuals should be allowed to enter a survival bunker after a nuclear apocalypse has destroyed most human life on earth?

The ship is sinking and the seas are rough. All but one lifeboat has been destroyed. The lifeboat holds a maximum of six people. There are ten people (listed below) that want to board the lifeboat. The four individuals who do not board the boat will certainly die.

Woman who thinks she is six months pregnant

Lifeguard

Two young adults who recently married

Senior citizen who has fifteen grandchildren

Elementary school teacher

Thirteen year old twins

Veteran nurse

Captain of the ship

LIFEBOAT ETHICS: THE CASE AGAINST HELPING THE POOR
Garrett Hardin

The following selection is excerpted from the first part of Garrett Hardin's essay of the same name, which first appeared in *Psychology Today* in September 1974. Hardin (1915–2003) was an often controversial ecologist who taught at the University of California, Santa Barbara, from 1963 to 1978. His most well-known paper was "The Tragedy of the Commons" (1963), which drew attention to "the damage that innocent actions by individuals can inflict on the environment." In particular, he warned against the dangers of human overpopulation in a world of limited resources. Hardin is the author of numerous articles and several books, including *The Limits of Altruism: An Ecologist's View of Survival* (1977), *Filters Against Folly: How to Survive Despite Economists, Ecologists, and the Merely Eloquent* (1985), and *The Ostrich Factor: Our Population Myopia* (1999).

Note: This passage is not a case, per se, but takes the "lifeboat" scenario and extrapolates the situation onto a global scale to argue against helping the poor—that is, against bringing people onto the "lifeboat."

If we divide the world crudely into rich nations and poor nations, two thirds of them are desperately poor, and only one third comparatively rich, with the United States the wealthiest of all. Metaphorically each rich nation can be seen as a lifeboat full of comparatively rich people. In the ocean outside each lifeboat swim the poor of the world, who would like to get in, or at least to share some of the wealth. What should the lifeboat passengers do?

First, we must recognize the limited capacity of any lifeboat. For example, a nation's land has a limited capacity to support a population and as the current energy crisis has shown us, in some ways we have already exceeded the carrying capacity of our land.

Adrift in a Moral Sea

So here we sit, say 50 people in our lifeboat. To be generous, let us assume it has room for 10 more, making a total capacity of 60. Suppose the 50 of us in the lifeboat see 100 others swimming in the water outside, begging for admission to our boat or for handouts. We have several options: we may be tempted to try to live by the Christian ideal of being "our brother's keeper," or by the Marxist ideal of "to each according to his needs." Since the needs of all in the water are the same, and since they can all be seen as "our brothers," we could take them all into our boat, making a total of 150 in a boat designed for 60. The boat swamps, everyone drowns. Complete justice, complete catastrophe.

Since the boat has an unused excess capacity of 10 more passengers, we could admit just 10 more to it. But which 10 do we let in? How do we choose? Do we pick the best 10, "first come, first served"? And what do we say to the 90 we exclude? If we do let an extra 10 into our lifeboat, we will have lost our "safety factor," an engineering principle of critical importance. For example, if we don't leave room for excess capacity as a safety factor in our country's agriculture, a new plant disease or a bad change in the weather could have disastrous consequences.

5   Suppose we decide to preserve our small safety factor and admit no more to the lifeboat. Our survival is then possible although we shall have to be constantly on guard against boarding parties.

While this last solution clearly offers the only means of our survival, it is morally abhorrent to many people. Some say they feel guilty about their good luck. My reply is simple: "Get out and yield your place to others." This may solve the problem of the guilt-ridden person's conscience, but it does not change the ethics of the lifeboat. The needy person to whom the guilt-ridden person yields his place will not himself feel guilty about his good luck. If he did, he would not climb aboard. The net result of conscience-stricken people giving up their unjustly held seats is the elimination of that sort of conscience from the lifeboat.

This is the basic metaphor within which we must work out our solutions....The harsh ethics of the lifeboat become even harsher when we consider the reproductive differences between the rich nations and the poor nations. The people inside the lifeboats are doubling in numbers every 87 years; those swimming around outside are doubling, on the average, every 35 years, more than twice as fast as the rich. And since the world's resources are dwindling, the difference in prosperity between the rich and the poor can only increase.

THE BANK TELLER

You have worked as a bank teller for several months when one of the other tellers who has become a good friend tells you that her daughter is extremely ill and must have an operation to survive. She also tells you that she has no insurance and the operation will cost $10,000. Sometime later you ask her about her daughter and she tells you she is just fine now. She then confides in you that she took $10,000 from a dormant account at the bank to pay for the operation. She assures you that she has already started paying it back and will continue to do so until it is all returned.

What do you do?

Video Link: An Ethical Dilemma Concerning Theft of Military Supplies

Go to: YouTube

Search terms: *"zoom military interview tell me time ethical dilemma"*

SHOULD I PROTECT A PATIENT AT THE EXPENSE OF AN INNOCENT STRANGER? *

Chuck Klosterman

The following selection originally appeared in "The Ethicist" column of the *New York Times Magazine* on May 10, 2013. In addition to regularly writing this column for the *Times*, Klosterman has also been a columnist for *Esquire*. He has also published several essay collections (including *Sex Drugs and Cocoa Puffs: A Low Culture Manifesto* [2004]), two novels, and eight books on American popular culture, including *I Wear the Black Hat: Grappling with Villains (Real and Imagined)* (2013).

I am a physician. Years ago, I saw a young patient with headaches, who disclosed—reluctantly—that he had committed a serious crime and that somebody else took the fall for it. I believe he was telling me the truth (his headaches soon resolved after the confession). Before his admission, I assured him that whatever he told me would not leave the room. Later, without giving specifics,

I consulted our hospital lawyer, who told me that we were under no obligation to report the incident, because the patient wasn't in danger of hurting himself or others. But the future of an innocent man hinges on two people's consciences, my patient's and my own. I feel like a coward, hiding behind the Hippocratic oath, doing nothing. —NAME WITHHELD

I'm (obviously) not a doctor, and I assume some doctors will vehemently disagree with what I'm about to write. But I feel that the first thing we need to recognize is that the Hippocratic oath represents the ideals of a person who died in the historical vicinity of 370 B.C. Now, this doesn't make it valueless or inherently flawed. It's a good oath. But we're dealing with a modern problem, so I would separate the conditions of that concept from this discussion. And even if you refuse to do that—even if you feel your commitment to this symbolic oath supersedes all other things keep in mind that one of its cornerstones is to "do no harm." Are you latently doing harm by allowing someone to be penalized for a crime he did not commit? This is not exactly a medical issue, but your relationship to the problem is still an extension of your position as a physician.

Here is the root of the problem: You promised a man that you would keep his secret in confidence, only to have him tell you something you now view as too important to remain unspoken. The stakes are pretty high; the possibility of someone's being convicted of a crime that he did not commit is awful. But you've painted yourself into a comer. You should not tell someone "Whatever you tell me will never leave this room" if that promise only applies to anecdotes you deem as tolerable. It doesn't matter if you're a physician or anyone else. The deeper question, of course, is whether breaking this commitment is ethically worse than allowing someone to go to jail for no valid reason. On balance, I have to say it is not.

I would advise the following: Call the patient back into your office. Urge him to confess what happened to the authorities and tell him you will assist him in any way possible (helping him find a lawyer before going to the police, etc.). If he balks, you will have to go a step further; you will have to tell him that you were wrong to promise him confidentiality and that your desire for social justice is greater than your personal integrity as a professional confidant. There is, certainly, danger in doing this. I don't know what the real impact will be (considering the circumstances, it seems as if it would be easy for him to claim his confession came under mental distress and that you coerced or misinterpreted his admission but the information still might help the innocent man's case).

This is a situation in which I'm personally uncomfortable with my own advice. If I told someone "Whatever you tell me will never leave this room," it would be almost impossible for me to contradict that guarantee, regardless of whatever insane thing the person proceeded to tell me. That is my own human weakness. But given the advantage of detached objectivity, it's very difficult to argue that the significance of your promise to a guilty stranger is greater than an innocent stranger's freedom from wrongful prosecution. You should not have made the original promise, and you should not allow that bad promise to stand. But keep in mind I'm only looking at this from a civilian perspective. The conditions of doctor-patient privilege might make this untenable. I'm merely weighing the two evils and deeming one to be greater, at least in this specific case.

No Edit

Randy Cohen

A writer and humorist, Randy Cohen preceded Chuck Klosterman as the writer of the *New York Times'* "Ethicist" column. He has written articles for the *Village Voice* and the online magazine *Slate*. He has also written for several TV shows, including *TV Nation, The Rosie O'Donnell Show*, and (for 950 episodes) *The David Letterman Show*. Among his books are *Diary of a Flying Man* (1989), a collection of humor pieces; *The Good, The Bad, & The Difference: How to Tell Right from Wrong in Everyday Situations* (2002); and *Be Good: How to Navigate the Ethics of Everything* (2012). He currently hosts the public radio show *Person Place Thing.*

> As a high-school English teacher, I am frequently asked to proofread and make rewriting suggestions for students' college-application essays. I decline on the grounds that admissions officers assume that these essays accurately represent the students' work. Other teachers argue that our students lose the editing advantage many students receive. Is it ethical for me to read student essays?
> —NAME WITHHELD

The all-the-kids-are-doing-it defense? Unpersuasive. A teacher may read student essays but not write them. You should eschew anything as hands-on as editing or proofreading and instead find ways to guide students toward producing first-rate work that is their own.

This is a more conservative stance than that of at least one person who will judge the finished product. Jeffrey Brenzel, dean of undergraduate admissions at Yale, says, "I would think it foolish of a student not to have an essay proofed for spelling, grammar and syntax by someone competent to do so."

As to your concern—and mine—that such direct involvement by the teacher can mislead a college about a student's language skills and undermine the student's integrity and sense of accomplishment, Brenzel replies: "We are not looking to take the measure of writing ability, genius or cleverness. We simply want to know something about personal outlook and perspective—how a student sees things or what a student has learned from his or her experiences."

Admissions offices are wise to use these essays as a way to learn more about applicants but disingenuous to suggest that they are uninfluenced by the quality of the writing. How could they not be?

5   Your challenge is to help your students without distorting their voices or misrepresenting their abilities. One technique recommended by College Summit, a nonprofit organization that helps public-school systems increase college enrollment, is to ask students probing questions about their essays—why did you spend your summer vacation in that shark tank? Is there a word in standard English that is clearer than "aieeee"?—but not proffer answers. That is, help a student identify a problem, but let the student solve it.

THE TORTURED CHILD
Kelley L. Ross

"The Tortured Child" was developed by Kelley L. Ross for his Web site *Some Moral Dilemmas*. Ross is retired from the Department of Philosophy at Los Angeles Valley College in Van Nuys, California. The moral dilemmas he discusses are adapted from those provided in Victor Grassian's *Moral Reasoning: Ethical Theory and Some Contemporary Moral Problems* (1981).

Dostoyevsky... imagines a classic right vs. good dilemma:

> "Tell me yourself—I challenge you: let's assume that you were called upon to build the edifice of human destiny so that men would finally be happy and would find peace and tranquility. If you knew that, in order to attain this, you would have to torture just one single creature, let's say the little girl who beat her chest so desperately in the outhouse, and that on her unavenged tears you could build that edifice, would you agree to do it? Tell me and don't lie!"
>
> "No I would not," Alyosha said softly. [Fyodor Dostoevsky, *The Brothers Karamazov*, 1880, translated by Andrew H. MacAndrew, Bantam Books, 1970, p. 296]

This could stand as a *reductio ad absurdum* of Utilitarianism; but Dostoyevsky himself cites one innocent person who is indeed sacrificed to build an "edifice" of "peace and tranquility," namely Jesus Christ. Jesus went to his fate willingly, unlike the little girl of the example here; but those who sent him there had something else in mind. Dostoyevsky's thought experiment was developed into a science fiction short story, "The Ones Who Walk Away from Omelas" [1973], by Ursula K. Le Guin. Le Guin, however, originally credited the device to William James, having read it in James and forgotten that it was in Dostoyevsky.

THE ONES WHO WALK AWAY FROM OMELAS
Ursula Le Guin

In "The Tortured Child" (previous selection), Kelley L. Ross indicates that Ursula Le Guin's 1973 short story "The Ones Who Walk Away from Omelas" was derived from Dostoyevsky's "classic right vs. good dilemma" from *The Brothers Karamazov*. Le Guin's beautifully written and yet disturbing story is available online. It evokes in the most vivid manner possible the ethical dilemma that is briefly suggested by Dostoyevsky. After you read it, you may find yourself turning to the ethical approaches discussed by authors like White, Velasquez et al., and Crain to make moral sense of the choices made by both those who remain in Omelas and those who walk away.

Ursula Le Guin (1929–) is a prolific author of children's books, novels, and short stories focusing on science fiction and fantasy. Among her books are *Planet of Exile* (1966), *A Wizard of Earthsea* (1968), *The Dispossessed: An Ambiguous Utopia* (1974), *The Compass Rose* (1982), *Always Coming Home* (1985), *The Other Wind* (2001), and *Lavinia* (2008).

Online you'll discover many analyses of Le Guin's story. You may or may not want to read them—but either way, the fun and the benefit of this "case" derive from thinking through the ethical dilemmas yourself and discussing them with your classmates.

Go to: Google or Bing

Search terms: *"pdf the ones who walk away from omelas"*

■ Video Link: *The Drowning Child* by Peter Singer

Australian Philosopher and ethicist Peter Singer (1946–), author of *Animal Liberation* (1975) and now a professor of bioethics at Princeton University and Laureate Professor of Philosophy at the University of Melbourne, poses an ethical question that appears to point to an obvious choice—until he adds a twist.

Go to: YouTube

Search terms: *"drowning child singer"* (1:58 or 3:18 version; shorter version includes visuals)

A CALLOUS PASSERBY

Roger Smith, a quite competent swimmer, is out for a leisurely stroll. During the course of his walk he passes by a deserted pier from which a teenage boy who apparently cannot swim has fallen into the water. The boy is screaming for help. Smith recognizes that there is absolutely no danger to himself if he jumps in to save the boy; he could easily succeed if he tried. Nevertheless, he chooses to ignore the boy's cries. The water is cold and he is afraid of catching a cold—he doesn't want to get his good clothes wet, either. "Why should I inconvenience myself for this kid?" Smith says to himself and passes on. Does Smith have a moral obligation to save the boy? If so, should he have a legal obligation ["Good Samaritan" laws] as well?

■ THE ASSIGNMENTS

Summary

Summarize "What If..." by Sokol. In preparing your summary, consult the Guidelines for Writing Summaries on pages 6–7.

Alternate Summary Assignment

In preparation for writing an argument about Ursula Le Guin's "The Ones Who Walk Away from Omelas," summarize this short story.

A work of fiction is based on narrative logic, not the expository logic of facts and opinions you find in most writing—in Sokol, for instance. For this reason, summarizing a work of fiction differs from summarizing a selection that explains and argues. So for this assignment, you won't be relying on the Guidelines for Writing Summaries.

Instead, briefly relate the main events of the story, providing an account of both the characters and action. Make notes as you read and prepare to summarize "Omelas." A useful strategy is to respond to a journalist's questions: *who* (is the story about), *what* (happens), *where* (does it happen), *when* (does it happen), and *why* (does it happen).

Try using this typical common opening in summarizing a narrative: "'X' tells the story of a _____ who _____." Consult your notes (who, what, etc.) and follow with your account of the broad action of the story and the motivations of its main actors. Write the summary of a narrative using present-tense verbs, as in these examples:

> The happiness of Omelas is conditional on the imprisonment and torture of a single person.
> Periodically, some citizens decide to leave Omelas.

When used in summarizing works of fiction, the present tense is referred to as the "historical" present tense. This tense suggests that the action of a story is always present to readers each time they return to the story. However often we read *The Great Gatsby*, we find Jay Gatsby staring across the water at a green light at the end of a dock. The actors in that and any other fiction are continually present to us, no matter how often we visit with them—as if they are frozen in an eternal *now*.

If you choose to develop the first alternate assignment for Argument Synthesis you'll put this summary to use in the larger paper. Note that, on occasion, you may occasionally need to vary your use of the present tense to clarify sequences of events.

Critique

> Critique Garrett Hardin's use of the lifeboat metaphor to argue against helping the poor.

In writing this critique, develop both an introduction and a conclusion as well as the main body of the critique. See Chapter 2 for advice on critical reading. See particularly the Guidelines for Writing Critiques box on pages 71–72, along with the hints on incorporating quoted material into your own writing on pages 44–50. In general, follow the advice above for developing a critique. Organize and develop the body of your evaluation around specific points:

- State the point of evaluation as a clear topic sentence.
- Cite specific examples in the article that illustrate this observation.

- Discuss these examples in two or three follow-on sentences in one paragraph or at greater length in two or more paragraphs.

In preparing to write, consider the following questions. Your responses may help you to formulate elements of your critique:

- Classify Hardin's thinking as primarily *teleological* (consequence-based ethics) or *deontological* (morality-based ethics). To help you make this classification, see the selection by Ronald White.
- What assumptions does Hardin make about the ability of progress in technology to make the lifeboat bigger and able to accommodate more people?
- What assumptions does Hardin make about the possibilities of human cooperation to accommodate more people in the lifeboat?
- What assumptions does Hardin make about the worthiness of people who already find themselves *in* the lifeboat? By what right do they find themselves in the boat? Do they deserve to be there? Why?
- To what extent do you agree that the lifeboat metaphor is an appropriate one on which to base policies dealing with the poor? Explain.
- What other metaphors can you think of to describe the obligations of a nation to its citizens and those who wish to become citizens? Does this alternate metaphor suggest policies different than the ones Hardin recommends?
- In what ways can a metaphor (such as Hardin's lifeboat) both open and limit a conversation?
- What evidence do you see of "lifeboat" thinking in Congressional debates today?

Explanatory Synthesis

> Explain—in no more than two pages—an ethical dilemma that you've faced in your life and the choice you eventually made.

This assignment requires you to answer a key question: *What* is an ethical dilemma? Start by defining both parts of that term. Several sources in the chapter define ethics, including the introduction to this chapter. Consider developing explanations for *types* of ethical dilemmas. For a definition of *dilemma*, review the many examples in the chapter and infer a definition; review also what the Velasquez et al. (of the Markkula Center) and White write on the matter.

In relating your experience, be sure to identify all participants in the dilemma and their stakes in the outcome; the issues or values in conflict; the course of action you chose; and the ramifications of that choice. This explanation will form the first part of a later analysis (should you choose the alternate assignment for Analysis). Try to bring real richness to your explanation. Help your readers *feel* the tension of a difficult decision.

In developing your explanation, consult to the Guidelines for Writing Syntheses on pages 90–91. More specifically, consider the following:

Suggestions for Developing the Assignment

Develop your explanation systematically, remembering throughout that you're a *storyteller*. Be true to your experience, but at the same time think of your readers. Dilemmas involve conflict; conflict creates tension. How do you plan to create tension for readers so that they'll want to keep reading and learn what you did (or did not do)? How vividly can you describe the participants?

- Provide the who, when, and where of the situation.
- What was the dilemma? *Why* was it a dilemma? To answer this question, provide a definition of *dilemma*.
- How did this dilemma involve ethics? To answer this question, start with a clear definition of *ethics*—and you can draw on sources in the chapter, including the chapter introduction, to do so.
- *What choices* did you have?
- Devote a paragraph or two to discussing the choice you made when faced with the dilemma. There's no need to analyze that decision—assessing whether or not you did the right thing. (You may choose to do that later as a part of an analysis assignment.) Instead, focus on your choice. Since this was a dilemma, which means there were (at least) two courses of action open to you, discuss the tension involved in making that choice. What forces were in play—for instance, religious or parental training/rules, the advice of friends or teachers, the expectations of coaches?

Keep in mind that this brief paper is an explanation—not, at this point, an analysis of your decision or a consideration of whether or not you did the right thing. The success of this paper is based on how carefully you can present your experience in a way that enables readers to appreciate an ethical dilemma. In defining this dilemma, draw on the sources in this chapter. Be sure to set up your references to those sources (which can be summaries, paraphrases, or quotations) using an appropriate citation format, most likely MLA (see pp. 274–280).

Analysis

Choose an ethical dilemma from this chapter (from either the casebook or Sokol's article—The Runaway Trolley, The Cave Explorers, Thomson's Violinist). Analyze this dilemma using two (or more) ethical principles as discussed in White's "Moral Inquiry" or the Markkula framework (Velasquez et al.).

This is a *comparative* analysis. That is, you will be applying at least two principles to a particular case in order to reveal insights that will suggest (possibly) different courses of action. As a conclusion, recommend one course of action over another and justify this recommendation. In organizing your thoughts and then writing the analysis, follow either the Guidelines for Writing Analyses on pages 177–178 in Chapter 5 or the Markkula framework (Velasquez et al.) on pages 291–296.

Suggestions for Developing the Assignment

This assignment requires two parallel analyses of a single case—and a follow-on comparison-and-contrast. Before beginning, you may find it useful to review the discussion of comparison-and-contrast on pages 159–167. We recommend the following structure for organizing your paper:

- Paragraph 1: Summarize the case, and provide a context, indicating its significance.

- Paragraph 2: Define the first analytic tool or principle—for instance, teleological (consequence-based) ethics or deontological (morality-based) ethics. Recall that there are other analytic tools, or principles, discussed in the readings.

- Paragraphs 3–4: Apply the first principle to the case, concluding with a course of action consistent with that principle.

- Paragraph 5: Define the second analytic tool or principle.

- Paragraphs 6–7: Apply the second principle to the case, concluding with a course of action consistent with that principle.

- Paragraphs 8–10: Compare and contrast your applications of the ethical principles. Use the "criteria" approach for comparison-and-contrast. (See pp. 160–166.) Choose three criteria, or key points, for comparison and contrast and discuss the two ethical principles and their applications to the case.

- Paragraph 11+: Argue that one ethical principle and the decision following from it makes for the better outcome.

Alternate Analysis Assignment

Explain an ethical dilemma that you've faced in your life and the choice you made. (See the assignment for Explanatory Synthesis.) Analyze that choice based on at least two ethical principles discussed in this chapter, using the Markkula framework (Velasquez et al.) to conduct the analysis. Conclude by assessing whether or not you "did the right thing." Would you change your decision today, had you to decide all over again?

Argument

Suppose a friend in another class looked over the cases you've been studying in this chapter and asserted that many of the dilemmas they presented—the runaway trolley, for example—were so far-fetched and unrealistic that they were useless as a guide to ethical decision making. Your classmate also raised questions about the ethical frameworks themselves, contending that they were too complicated for most people to apply in everyday situations. Develop an argument responding to these assertions—one expressing agreement, disagreement, or something in between.

Suggestions for Developing the Assignment

- A paragraph or so laying out in somewhat greater detail the situation outlined in the assignment above.

- A paragraph or two briefly describing some of (1) the cases presented in this chapter and (2) the ethical frameworks. Cite examples that appear, at least on the surface, to support your friend's assertions.

- **Thesis**: A paragraph detailing your own response to your friend's assertions. Conclude this paragraph with a clearly worded statement, your thesis, explaining the extent to which you agree and disagree.

- Several paragraphs in which you systematically respond to your friend's assertions. Discuss some of the representative cases presented in the chapter in light of the argument that they are (or are not) useful as guides to ethical decision making. Explain why the particularly "far-fetched" examples may (or may not) be useful for this purpose. Note, for example, Sokol's explanation of the significance of the Thomson's violinist scenario. Do you find this explanation plausible? Discuss also some of the ethical frameworks presented in the chapter in light of how easy (or how difficult) they might be in helping to resolve ethical dilemmas in everyday life.

- A paragraph of counterargument, in which you concede that others might justifiably find fault with your central argument. Explain your concession.

- A "nevertheless" section, in which you respond to the counterargument(s) and reaffirm your own position.

- A paragraph or two of conclusion. See Chapter 6 (pp. 223–229) for advice on concluding your argument.

It's up to you to decide *where* you place the individual elements of this argument synthesis. It's also up to you to decide which sources to use and what logic to present in defense of your claim. See pages 136–140 and pages 155–162 for help in thinking about structuring and supporting your argument.

Alternate Argument Assignment #1

Read Ursula Le Guin's "The Ones Who Walk Away from Omelas" and decide whether or not you would be one of the people who walked away. Draw on other selections in this chapter to argue for your choice. Use your summary of Le Guin from the earlier alternate summary assignment if you chose that assignment. As you put that summary to use in your argument, you'll have to change its form a bit, presenting the summary in parts:

- a main section, early in the paper, which relates the overall arc of the story, its actors, and its main themes.

- *brief* summaries of individual parts of the story, which call your reader's attention to particular scenes that you will discuss, each in its turn.

Alternate Argument Assignment #2

Three cases in this chapter turn on the rightness of a person's decision to speak up or remain silent when confronted with what he or she thinks is an ethical lapse: the bank teller (p. 308), the director of safety in the "Collapsed Mine" (p. 288), and the doctor (p. 308).

Building on the ethical principles you've learned about in this chapter, develop guidelines to help *you* decide when to speak or remain silent when confronted with dilemmas. That is, choose among ethical principles or combine them as you see fit; then shape them into a personal approach. Argue in support of this approach, showing its strengths—and acknowledging its weaknesses—as you apply it to some or all of the cases just mentioned. If you're feeling ambitious, apply your approach to the case of Edward Snowden, alluded to briefly in the introduction to this chapter (page 281). You'll find detailed accounts of Snowden's leaks in online news sources.

A Note on Incorporating Quotations and Paraphrases Identify those sources that you intend to use in your synthesis. Working with a phrase, sentence, or brief passage from each, use a variety of the techniques discussed in the Incorporating Quotations into Your Sentences section (pp. 44–50) to advance your argument. Some of these sentences should demonstrate the use of ellipses and brackets. (See pp. 46–49 in Chapter 1.) Paraphrase passages as needed, incorporating the paraphrases into your paragraphs.

CREDITS ■

TEXT CREDITS

CHAPTER 1

pp. 8–14: *Sticks and Stones* (Random House), Emily Bazelon.

pp. 25–26: Steven A. Camarota. *Immigration Studies (CIS), Immigrants in the United States: A Profile of America's Foreign-Born Population.* Reprinted by permission of the Center for Immigration Studies.

p. 26, Figure 1.1: Figure 2. Top Sending Countries (Comprising at Least Half of All L[egal] P[ermanent] R[esidents]. Selected Periods." Ruth Ellen Wasem [Specialist in Immigration Policy], *U.S. Immigration Policy: Chart Book of Key Trends, C[ongressional] R[esearch] S[ervice]: Report for Congress.* p. 3. Source: *CRS Analysis of Table 2, Statistical Yearbook of Immigration,* U.S. Department of Homeland Security, Office of Immigration Statistics, FY2010. www.crs.gov http://www.fas.org/sgp/crs/homesec/R42988.pdf

p. 28, Figure 1.2: Source: Pew Research Center. "Immigration: Key Data Points from Pew Research." 26 June 2013. 3rd chart. http://www.pewresearch.org/key-data-points/immigration-tip-sheet-on-u-s-public-opinion/. Used by permission.

p. 28, Figure 1.3: "Figure 6. Nonimmigrant Visas Issued by the U.S. Department of State." Source: CRS presentation of data from Table XVIII of the annual reports of the U.S. Department of State Office of Visa Statistics. Ruth Ellen Wasem [Specialist in Immigration Policy], "U.S. Immigration Policy: Chart Book of Key Trends, C[ongressional] R[esearch] S[ervice]: Report for Congress. p. 7 www.crs.gov http://www.fas.org/sgp/crs/homesec/R42988.pdf

p. 29, Figure 1.4: "Growth of Total U.S. Immigrant Population Compared to Decline in Unauthorized Immigration." *Pew Research Hispanic Center tabulations of 2011 American Community Survey (1% IPUMS,* Chart 5. http://www.pewhispanic.org/2013/02/15/u-s-immigration-trends/ph_13-01-23_ss_immigration_01_title/. Used with permission.

p. 30, Figure 1.5: "Percentages of Immigrant Adults with and Without High School Diplomas." *Pew Research Hispanic Center tabulations of 2011 American Community Survey (1% IPUMS).* http://www.pewhispanic.org/2013/02/15/u-s-immigration-trends/ph_13-01-23_ss_immigration_01_title/. Chart 14. Used by permission.

p. 31, Figure 1.6: Ruth Ellen Wasem [Specialist in Immigration Policy], "U.S. Immigration Policy: Chart Book of Key Trends," *C[ongressional] R[esearch] S[ervice]: Report for Congress.* www.crs.gov, http://www.fas.org/sgp/crs/homesec/R42988.pdf, p. 5 (second chart—pie). Used by permission.

p. 32, Figure 1.7: Pew Research Hispanic Center. "The U.S. is the World's Leader as a Destination for Immigrants." *Tabulations of 2011 American Community Survey (1% IPUMS),* Chart 3. http://www.pewhispanic.org/2013/02/15/u-s-immigration-trends/ph_13-01-23_ss_immigration_01_title/. Used by permission.

p. 33, Figure 1.8 "Visas Issued in 2012." Jill H. Wilson, Brookings Institute, "Immigration Facts: Temporary Foreign Workers" 18 June 2013. pictogram under paragraph 2. http://www.brookings.edu/research/reports/2013/06/18-temporary-workers-wilson. Used by permission.

pp. 35–36, Figure 1.9: "Legal Permanent Resident Flow by Region and Country of Birth, Fiscal Years 2010 to 2012." Source: *U.S. Department of Homeland Security, Computer Linked Application Information Management System (CLAIMS), Legal Immigrant Data, Fiscal Years 2010 to 2012.* Dept. of Homeland Security, "U.S. Legal Permanent Residents 2012." p. 4. http://www.dhs.gov/sites/default/files/publications/ois_lpr_fr_2012_2.pdf

pp. 38–39: Dietmar Mieth, "In Vitro Fertilization: From Medical Reproduction to Genetic Diagnosis," *Biomedical Ethics: Newsletter of the European Network for Biomedical Ethics 1.1* (1996): 45. Used by permission of Dietmar Mieth.

p. 40: Sigmund Freud. *General Introduction to Psychoanalysis.*

p. 41: Franklin D. Roosevelt.

p. 42: John Keegan.

p. 42: From *Biology, 2/e,* by Helena Curtis. Copyright © 1975 by Worth Publishers. Used with permission of the publisher.

p. 43: David Chandler.

p. 44: "Gates Receipts and Glory" article © SEPS licensed by Curtis Licensing, Indianapolis, IN. All rights reserved.

pp. 44–45: Robert Hutchins, "Gate Receipts and Glory," *Saturday Evening Post*, 3 Dec. 1983: 38.

p. 46: Henry David Thoreau, *Walden* (New York: Signet Classic, 1960): 72.

p. 47: Jane Yolen, "America's 'Cinderella,'" *Children's Literature in Education* 8 (1977): 22. Used by permission of Springer.

pp 48–49: Walter Isaacson's biography of Albert Einstein, *Einstein: His Life and Universe.*

p. 51: Richard Rovere, "The Most Gifted and Successful Demagogue This Country Has Ever Known," *New York Times Magazine,* 30 Apr. 1967.

pp. 52–53: "Breakfast Helps Kids Handle, Basic Math, Study Suggests," by Terry Pivik. *Agricultural Research,* November/December 2013. This research is part of Human Nutrition, an ARS national program (#107) described at www.nps.ars.usda.gov

CHAPTER 2

p. 60: Charles Murray, "The Coming White Underclass," *Wall Street Journal,* October 20, 1993.

p. 69: Alan Greenspan.

p. 69: United States. Cong. House Committee on Oversight and Government Reform. *The Financial Crisis and the Role of Federal Regulators.* 110th Cong., 2nd sess. Washington: GPO, 2008.

p. 74: John F. Kennedy.

pp. 74–79: Andrew Harlan.

82–83: Ethan Gilsdorf, "Why We Need Violent Video Games." WBUR 90.9, Boston's NPR News Station. 13 Jan. 2013. Radio. Used with permission.

CHAPTER 3

pp. 87–88, What Are Genetically Modified (Gm) Foods?: *Genetically Modified Foods And Organisms,* The United States Department of Energy, November 5, 2008.

p. 88, Why a GM Freeze?: *The GM Freeze Campaign,* November 11, 2010. Used with permission.

pp. 93–94, The History Of The Space Elevator: Reprinted with permission from "The Physics of the Space Elevator" by P.K. Aravind in *American Journal of Physics* 75.2 (2007): 125. Copyright © 2007 American Association of Physics Teachers.

pp. 93–94, The History Of The Space Elevator: Reprinted with permission by the author from "The Physics of the Space Elevator" by P.K. Aravind in American Journal of Physics 75.2 (2007): 125.

pp. 94–96, Applications Of The Space Elevator: Edwards, Bradley C.The Space Elevator: National Institute for Advanced Concepts Phase II Report. N.p.: 2003. PDF file.

pp 99–100: Leonard Rosen.

pp. 106–109, Explanatory Synthesis: First Draft: Sheldon Kearney.

pp. 112–119, Model Explanatory Synthesis: Sheldon Kearney, Professor Leslie Davis, Technology and Culture, October 12, 2014.

113: Kent, Jason R. *Getting into Space on a Thread: Space Elevator as Alternative Access to Space.* Maxwell AFB: Air War College, 2007. PDF file.

CHAPTER 4

p. 125: John F. Kennedy, Address to the Nation, June 1963.

p. 125: Senator Robert C. Byrd.

p. 125: Edward M. Kennedy.

pp. 126–127: California Voter's Guide.

p. 127: L. A. Kauffman, "Socialism: No," Progressive, 1 Apr. 1993.

pp. 127–128: Ronald Reagan.

p. 128: Bill Clinton.

p. 129: Susan Jacoby, "Talking to Ourselves: Americans Are Increasingly Close-Minded and Unwilling to Listen to Op-posing Views," *Los Angeles Times* 20 Apr. 2008: M10.

pp. 132–133: Kosciw, Joseph G., Emily A. Greytak, Mark J. Bartkiewicz, Madelyn J. Boesen, and Neal A. Palmer. *The 2011 National School Climate Survey: The Experiences of Lesbian, Gay, Bisexual and Transgender Youth in Our Nation's Schools.* New York: Gay, Lesbian and Straight Education Network, 2012.

p. 133: Hazelden Foundation. "Olweus Bullying Prevention Program: Scope and Sequence." Hazelden.org. Hazelden, 2007. PDF file. Used by permission.

p. 133: Olweus, Dan. *Bullying At School: What We Know and What We Can Do.* Oxford, England: Blackwell, 1993. Print.

pp. 134–135: Rodkin, Philip C. Personal Interview. 15 Oct. 2014. "White House Report/ Bullying—And the Power of Peers." *Educational Leadership: Promoting Respectful Schools* 69.1 (2011): 10–16. ASCD.Web. 16 Oct. 2014. Used by permission.

pp. 140–148: Peter Simmons, Professor Lettelier, Composition 201, 8 November 2014.

p. 142: Eva Porter. *Bully Nation.*

p. 142: Smith, J., David, Barry H. Schneider, Peter K. Smith, and Katerina Ananiadou. "The Effectiveness of Whole-School Antibullying Programs: A Synthesis of Evaluation Re-search." *School Psychology Review* 33.4 (2004): 547–560. PDF file.

p. 142: Villarreal, Daniel. "Jamey Rodemeyer's Bullies Are Happy He's Dead, But Is It a Bad Idea to Prosecute Them?" *Queerty.* Queerty, Inc., 27 Sept. 2011. Web. 16 Oct. 2014. Used by permission.

p. 142: Gay-Straight Alliance Project. "Make It Better." Gay-Straight Alliance Project. GSANetwork, 26 Sept. 2011. Web. 15 Oct. 2014.

p. 143: Olweus, Dan. *Bullying At School: What We Know and What We Can Do.* Oxford, England: Blackwell, 1993. Print.

p. 143: Emily Bazelon. *Sticks and Stones: Defeating the Culture of Bullying and Rediscovering the Power of Character and Empathy.* New York: Random, 2013. Print.

pp. 143–144: Rodkin, Philip C. Personal Interview. 15 Oct. 2014. "White House Report/ Bullying—And the Power of Peers." *Educational Leadership: Promoting Respectful Schools 69.1* (2011): 10–16. ASCD. Web. 16 Oct. 2014.

p. 144: Hu, Winnie. "Bullying Law Puts New Jersey Schools on Spot." *New York Times.* New York Times, 20 Aug. 2011. Web. 12 Oct. 2014.

p. 144: Ferguson, Christopher J., Claudia San Miguel, John C. Kilburn, JR, and Patricia Sanchez. "The Effectiveness of School-Based Anti-Bullying Programs: A Meta-Analytic Review." *Criminal Justice Review* 32.4 (2007): 401-414. Sage Publications. Web. 15 Oct. 2014.

p. 144: Merrell, Kenneth W, Barbara A. Gueldner, Scott W. Ross, and Duane M. Isava. "How Effective are School Bullying Intervention Programs? A Meta-analysis of Intervention Research." *School Psychology Quarterly* 23.1 (2008): 26-42. PDF file.

p. 144: Hazelden Foundation. "Olweus Bullying Prevention Program: Scope and Sequence." Hazelden.org. Hazelden, 2007. PDF file.

p. 145: Fox, James Alan, Delbert S. Elliott, R. Gil Kerlikowske, Sanford A. Newman, and William Christenson. *Bullying Prevention is Crime Prevention.* Fightcrime.org. Fight Crime/Invest in Kids, 2003. PDF file.

p. 145: Rodkin, Philip C. Personal Interview. 15 Oct. 2014. "White House Report/Bullying— And the Power of Peers." *Educational Leadership: Promoting Respectful Schools* 69.1 (2011): 10–16. ASCD. Web. 16 Oct. 2014.

pp. 145–146: Flannery, Mary Ellen. "Bullying: Does It Get Better?" National Education Association. *National Education Association,* Jan./Feb. 2011. Web. 16 Oct. 2014.

p. 146: Sacco, Dena, Katharine Silbaugh, Felipe Corredor, June Casey, and Davis Doherty. *An Overview of State Anti-Bullying Legislation and Other Related Laws.* Cambridge: Berk-man Center for Internet and Society, 2012. PDF file.

CHAPTER 5

pp. 172–173: From *The Plug-In Drug, Revised and Updated-25th Anniversary Edition* by Marie Winn, copyright © 1977, 1985, 2002 by Marie Winn Miller. Used by permission of Viking Penguin, a division of Penguin Group (USA) LLC.

pp. 172, 175: Marie Winn.

p. 179: From *The Plug-In Drug, Revised and Updated-25th Anniversary Edition* by Marie Winn, copyright © 1977, 1985, 2002 by Marie Winn Miller. Used by permission of Viking Penguin, a division of Penguin Group (USA) LLC.

p. 170: Harvey Greenberg, The Movies on Your Mind (New York: Dutton, 1975).

p. 170: Peter Dreier, "Oz Was Almost Reality," Cleveland Plain Dealer 3 Sept. 1989.

p. 170: Harvey Greenberg, The Movies on Your Mind (New York: Dutton, 1975).

p. 183: The New York Times, Op-Ed Page.

p. 183: (2006), Hekker.

p. 184: Virgil. *The Aeneid.* Trans. Theodore C. Williams. Perseus 4.0. Perseus Digital Library. Web. 17 Oct. 2014.

pp. 184–191: Linda Shanker, *Social Psychology 1,* UCLA, 17 November 2014.

p. 185: Knapp, Robert H. "A Psychology of Rumor." *Public Opinion Quarterly* 8.1 (1944): 22–37. Print.

p. 186: Dingwall, Robert. "Contemporary Legends, Rumors, and Collective Behavior: Some Neglected Resources for Medical Technology." *Sociology of Health and Illness* 23.2 (2001): 180–202. Print.

pp. 187–188: "You've Got to Be Kidneying." Snopes.com. *Snopes,* 12 Mar. 2008. Web. 4 Nov. 2014. Used by permission.

p. 189: Dingwall, Robert. "Contemporary Legends, Rumors, and Collective Behavior: Some Neglected Resources for Medical Technology." *Sociology of Health and Illness* 23.2 (2001): 180–202. Print.

pp. 189–190: Knapp, Robert H. "A Psychology of Rumor." *Public Opinion Quarterly* 8.1 (1944): 22–37. Print.

pp. 194–197: Mike Clary, "For Fallen Stop Sign, Vandals Face Life." *Los Angeles Times,* 11 June 1997. Used by permission.

pp. 198–200: *State of Utah v. Hallett.* 619 P.2d 337 (1980).

pp. 198–200: *Utah Code Unannotated,* 1996. Vol. 4. Charlottesville, VA: Michie Law Publishers, 1988–96.

p. 200: *State v. Fisher.* 686 P.2nd 750 (1984).

CHAPTER 6

p. 207: Thomas Edison.

p. 218: Sarah Chayes. "Blinded by the War on Terrorism." *Los Angeles Times,* 28 Jul. 2013.

p. 219: © 2013 The Atlantic Media Co., as first published in *The Atlantic Magazine.* All rights reserved. Distributed by Tribune Content Agency, LLC.

pp. 219–220: Michele Jacques, "Civil Disobedience: Van Dusen vs. Arendt," unpublished paper, 1993. Used by permission.

p. 220: Travis Knight, "Reducing Air Pollution with Alternative Transportation", unpublished paper, 1998. Used by permission.

p. 221: James Fallows. "Hacked!" *The Atlantic.* November 2011.

pp. 221–222: James Parker, "Brideshead Regurgitated: The Ludicrous Charms of Downton Abbey, TV's Reigning Aristo-soap." *The Atlantic*, Jan./Feb. 2013, p. 36.

p. 222: Eugene Robinson, "Japan's Nuclear Crisis Might Not Be the Last." *The Washington Post*. March 15, 2011.

p. 224: H. Sterling Barnett, "Wind Power Puffery." *Washington Times*, 4 Feb. 2004.

pp. 224–225: Maria Tatar, "An Introduction to Fairy Tales." *The Annotated Classic Fairy Tales* (2002), ed. and trans. By Maria Tatar. W.W. Norton & Company, Inc. Used by permission.

p. 225: Bruce D. Walker and Dennis R. Burton. "Towards an AIDS Vaccine." *Science* 9 May 2008: 760-764, p. 764. DOI: 10.1126/science.1152622. Used by permission of the American Association for the Advancement of Science.

p. 226: Rhoda Beall. Unpublished student paper, used by permission.

p. 226–227: Newton S. Minow. "A Vaster Wasteland." *The Atlantic*, Apr 2011, p. 52.

p. 227: Patrick Goldstein. "Tiger Mom vs. Tiger Mailroom." *Los Angeles Times*, 6 Feb. 2011.

p. 228: Stephen Baker. "Watson is Far From Elementary." *Wall Street Journal*, 14 Mar. 2011. Reproduced with permission of Dow Jones, Inc. in the format Republish in a book via Copyright Clearance Center.

pp. 228–229: Allen Hawkins.

CHAPTER 7

p. 243, Figure 7.1: Used by permission of Springshare LLC and UCSB Library.

p. 243, Figure 7.2: UCSB Library.

p. 245: Wikipedia.

p. 251, Figure 7.3a, b: Used by permission of JSTOR.

p. 252, Figure 7.4: SHU information technology. Used by permission.

p. 266: Gorham, Eric B. National Service, Political Socialization, and Political Education. Albany: SUNY P, 1992.

p. 266: Bureau of Labor Statistics. 27 Jan. 2010. Web. 17 Feb. 2011. http://www.bls.gov/news.release/volun.t01.htm

p. 267: Gergen, David. "A Time to Heed the Call." *U.S. News & World Report*, 24 Dec. 2001: 60-61

p. 273: Chenault.

p. 274: "Fair Use." U.S. Copyright Office. May 2009. Web. 23 Mar. 2010.

CHAPTER 8

p. 281: Stephen J. A. Ward, "Ethics in a Nutshell" from Center for Journalism Ethics at the University of Wisconsin: http://ethics.journalism.wisc.edu/resources/ethics-in-a-nutshell

pp. 285–288: Daniel Sokol, "What if…" *BBC News*. 2 May 2006. Web. http://news.bbc.co.uk/2/hi/uk_news/magazine/4954856.stm. Used by permission of BBC Worldwide America, Inc.

pp. 291–296, A Framework for Thinking Ethically: Manuel Velasquez et al. "A Framework for Thinking Ethically." Reprinted with permission of the Markkula Center For Applied Ethics at Santa Clara University (www.scu.edu/ethics).

pp. 296–299: Ronald F. White. "Moral Inquiry." Excerpts from pp. 3–4, 11–12, 15–16, 23–24. Web. http://inside.msj.edu/academics/faculty/whiter/ETHICSBOOK.pdf

p. 306: Rosetta Lee. Seattle Girls' School. [2706 S. Jackson Street, Seattle, WA 98144; 206-709-2228] From teaching packet titled: "The Lifeboat." Web. n.d. Page 58. http://nwabr.org/sites/default/files/Lifeboat.pdf. Used by permission of Rosetta Lee.

pp. 306–308: Garrett Hardin, "Lifeboat Ethics." Sept. 1974. *Psychology Today* © Copyright 1974 www.Psychologytoday.com. Used by permission.

p. 310: "No Edit," by Randy Cohen, originally published in *The NY Times Magazine*. Used by permission.

PHOTO CREDITS

CHAPTER 3

INDEX

"Responding to Bullies" (student author), 140–151
Reverse outlines, 231–232, 270
Revision. *See also* Drafts/drafting
  of analysis, 180–181
  of argument, 140–151
  for coherence, 231
  for development, 231
  explanation of, 229–230
  global, 110, 230
  local, 110, 111, 230
  of research papers, 239
  reverse outline technique for, 231–232
  as stage in writing process, 204, 229–232
  of summaries, 7
  surface, 110, 111, 230
  of synthesis, 91, 110–111
  for unity, 230–231
RILM Abstracts of Music Literature, 250
Rodkin, Philip, 134–135
Ross, Kelley L., 311

Secondary data, 206, 241, 248
Sentences
  editing of, 233, 234
  grammatical errors in, 234
  punctuation errors in, 235
  topic, 90, 104
"Should I Protect a Patient at the Expense of an Innocent Stranger?" (Klosterman), 308–309
Signal phrases, 49, 51
Smartphones, 250–251
Sociological Abstracts, 250, 259, 260
Sokol, Daniel, 285–288
Solutions, in conclusions, 226
Source documentation
  APA style of, 274–277
  for argument, 159
  for exploratory synthesis, 91
  MLA style of, 140–151, 274, 275, 277–280
  types and styles of, 274–275
Source material. *See also* Research sources
  for analysis, 181
  for argument, 130–131, 137–138
  critical evaluation of, 54

for explanatory synthesis, 85–87, 90, 91, 101
"So What?" question, 181
Speculation, 228–229
Spelling, errors in, 235
"State of Utah v. Kelly K. Hallett and Richard James Felsch" (Felsch), 198–200
Statesman's Yearbook, 262
Statistical Abstracts of the United States, 261
Style, editing for, 232–233
Subject-heading guides, 248
Subjects. *See* Topics
Subordinate point, 5
Subtitles, 5
Summaries
  in academic writing, 3, 312–313
  in analysis, 180–181
  of charts, 25–26, 30–34
  in conclusions, 224
  critical reading for, 5–6
  in critiques, 71
  demonstration for writing, 7–14
  drafts of, 7, 20
  of each stage of thought, 15–17
  examples of, 42
  exercises involving, 24, 27, 40, 52–53
  explanation of, 2, 54, 70
  for explanatory synthesis, 102–103
  of graphs, 25–30
  guidelines to write, 6–7, 14–15
  objectivity of, 2–3
  optimal length for, 24
  paraphrases vs., 37–40
  quotations vs., 41–43
  reading process and, 4–5
  revision of, 7
  strategy for longer, 23–24
  strategy for shorter, 21–23
  of tables, 25–26, 34–37
  thesis statement in, 6–7, 18–19
  types of writing that involve, 3
  use of, 3–4, 48, 70
  in workplace writing, 3
  writing assignment for, 52–53
Support, for argument, 123, 155–159
Surface revision, 110, 111, 230
Surveys
  guidelines to conduct, 263
  as research source, 262, 263